TH**I**NK

INTERPERSONAL COMMUNICATION

Canadian Edition

ISA N. ENGLEBERG
Prince George's Community College

DIANNA R. WYNN
Nash Community College

MARIA ROBERTS
Centennial College

PEARSON

Toronto

Editor-in-Chief: Michelle Sartor
Senior Acquisitions Editor: David S. Le Gallais
Senior Marketing Manager: Loula March
Project Manager: Marissa Lok
Supervising Developmental Editor: John Polanszky
Freelance Developmental Editor: Katherine Goodes
Production Services: Cenveo® Publisher Services
Permissions Project Manager: Daniela Celebre-Glass
Photo Permissions Research: Abdul Khader, PreMediaGlobal
Text Permissions Research: Samantha Bingenheimer, Electronic Publishing Services
Art Director: Zena Denchik
Cover Designer: Suzanne Behnke, Central Design
Interior Designer: Cenveo® Publisher Services
Cover Image: SoleilC/Shutterstock

Credits and acknowledgments for material borrowed from other sources and reproduced, with permission, in this textbook appear on the appropriate page within the text or on page 313.

Library and Archives Canada Cataloguing in Publication

Engleberg, Isa N., author
    Think interpersonal communication / Isa N. Engleberg, Prince George's Community College, Dianna R. Wynn, Nash Community College, Maria Roberts, Centennial College.

Includes bibliographical references and index.
ISBN 978-0-205-20897-5 (pbk.)

    1. Interpersonal communication—Textbooks. I. Wynn, Dianna, author II. Roberts, Maria (Professor), author III. Title. IV. Title: Interpersonal communication.

HM1166.E55 2014   302   C2014-900039-1

ISBN 13: 978-0-205-20897-5

THINK
INTERPERSONAL COMMUNICATION
Canadian Edition

brief CONTENTS

on the cover:
▼

THINK
Canadian Edition
INTERPERSONAL COMMUNICATION
ENGLEBERG • WYNN • ROBERTS

Are You a Connected Communicator?
Canada is a world leader!

Social Media... Online Etiquette
Do you know how others view you online?

Presenting... More than just Words
Do you know how to be unforgettable?

Culture, Diversity, Values, and Acceptance
Communication Can Lead the Way

ISBN 978-0-205-20897-4
www.thethinkspot.ca

Chapter 14
Language and Delivery

Chapter 3
Adapting to Canada's Changing Faces

Chapter 12
Communicating in a Digital World

CONTENTS

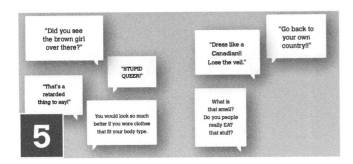

PART FOUR: **THINK**
Presentational
Communication

contents

acknowledgments

I appreciate the sound text provided by the original authors, Isa Engleberg and Dianna Wynn. It made a solid base for the adaption of the Canadian edition. Thanks also goes to David S. Le Gallais, acquisitions editor, and to Pearson Canada for this opportunity to adapt *Think Communication* for the Canadian college student.

I appreciate the confidence shown to me as I worked through the process of adapting an already important communication text. Throughout this process, Katherine Goodes has supported me, answered my questions, and most significantly guided me as a first-time author. I am truly grateful for her expertise and kindness. The manuscript benefited greatly from the help of the developmental editor, Katherine Goodes; project manager, Susan McIntyre; and copy editor, Tara Tovell.

My husband, Tom, has always encouraged me to reach beyond my comfort zone to accomplish my dreams, and for this I thank him. My daughters, strong remarkable women, Christine and Alison, continue to inspire me to keep learning and growing. My colleagues at Centennial College energize me every day with their commitment to providing excellent learning opportunities for all students.

Finally, I want to thank all of the amazing college learners I have met over the many years of teaching. Their diversity, questions, and challenges have all helped me to become a better listener and communicator, and each semester they assist me in refining my own teaching practice.

ISA ENGLEBERG, Professor Emerita at Prince George's Community College in Largo, Maryland, served as president of the National Communication Association (NCA) in 2003 and chaired the NCA Research Board from 1995 to 1998. She has written six college textbooks in communication studies, published more than three dozen articles in academic journals, and made hundreds of convention and seminar presentations. Dr. Engleberg received the Outstanding Community College Educator Award from the NCA and the President's Medal from Prince George's Community College for outstanding teaching, scholarship, and service. She has focused her professional career on improving both the content and teaching of basic communication courses at all levels of higher education as well as teaching and consulting internationally.

DIANNA WYNN is a professor at Nash Community College in Rocky Mount, North Carolina. Previously she taught at Midland College in Texas and Prince George's Community College in Maryland, where she was chosen by students as the Outstanding Teacher of the Year. She has coauthored two communication textbooks and has written articles in academic journals. She served as an officer in the Community College Section and a member of the Legislative Assembly of the National Communication Association and has participated in dozens of convention programs. In addition to teaching and college service, she has many years of experience as a trial consultant, assisting attorneys in developing effective communication strategies for the courtroom.

MARIA ROBERTS has served on the faculty at Centennial College in the Early Childhood Education program for nine years. During this time she has also assisted in the development of the post diploma online courses. She has presented many workshops for early childhood education professionals on a variety of topics including team building, facilitation, motivation, and conflict resolution. She has also spent 30 years working as part of multi-disciplinary  teams in college and community settings. Her committee work includes the Centre for Students and Their Families (Centennial College) and the Scarborough Special Needs Committee for Children. Maria is a certified early childhood educator and resource teacher and has a certificate in volunteer management from Conestoga College. She is currently completing her bachelor of arts in adult education at Brock University.

Dedicated to Violet, Hannah, Wyatt, Sophia, Ella, and Lena. They will be the leaders of tomorrow and they will communicate in ways we can't even imagine today.

Maria Roberts

THINK

INTERPERSONAL COMMUNICATION

Canadian Edition

Human
COMMUNICATION

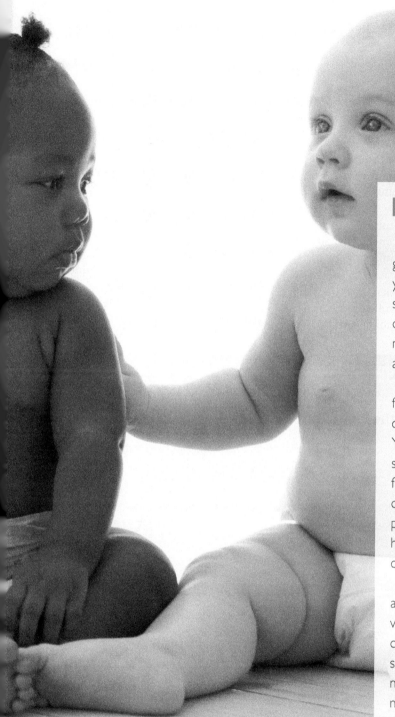

The instant you were born, you began communicating. You squirmed, cried, and even screamed when you were hungry or hurt. You smiled and gurgled when you were happy and content. And as you fussed and cooed, you also began learning how to speak and listen. From a very early age, you faced hundreds of communication challenges—and still do. Communication occupies more of your waking time than anything else you do.[1]

You communicate every day: when you greet your friends, participate in a class discussion, interact with coworkers, or shake hands with a new acquaintance. You also live in a competitive world where effective speaking allows you and your message to stand out from the rest of the crowd. Your ability to communicate, regardless of whether you're interacting with one person, a small group, or a large audience, determines how well you inform, persuade, delight, inspire, and comfort other people.

Most of the time, you communicate well, but what about when you're in the middle of a heated argument, when you can't think of what to say to a troubled friend, or when an important presentation falls short? In these situations, you need more than common sense. Like most complex processes, effective interpersonal communication requires knowledge, skills, and motivation.

Monkey Business/Fotolia

1.1

Communication in Your Life

What is communication, and how does it affect your everyday life?

Communication is the process of using verbal and nonverbal messages to generate meaning within and across various contexts, cultures, and channels.[2] The key phrase in this definition is *generate meaning*. You generate meaning when you speak, write, act, and create visual images as well as when you listen, read, and react to messages. Although you communicate all the time, you can always learn how to communicate better. And it is worth the effort. Your personal, academic, and professional success throughout your lifetime will depend on how well you communicate.[3] Personal relationships are richer and more rewarding when both parties communicate effectively. Colleagues who express respect for one another and argue/debate constructively are more likely to enjoy productive interactions. Work groups and team members who communicate effectively with one another are more likely to achieve their goals. And if you speak clearly, often, and well, you are more likely to be an effective leader.

According to the *Chronicle of Higher Education*, college faculty members identify speaking, listening, problem solving, interpersonal skills, working in groups, and leading groups as essential skills for every college graduate.[4] A national survey of 1,000 human resource managers concluded that oral communication skills are the *most* critical factor for obtaining jobs and advancing in a career.[5] Executives with Fortune 500 companies claim that the college graduates they employ need stronger communication skills as well as a demonstrated ability to work in teams and with people from diverse backgrounds.[6]

To become an effective communicator, you need to do more than learn a set of "fool-proof" rules or the "tricks of the trade." You also need to learn how to apply interpersonal communication theories, strategies, and skills to multiple communication contexts. To gauge whether you communicate effectively in a variety of interpersonal communication situations, ask yourself the following questions:

- *Personal.* Do I have meaningful personal relationships with close friends, relatives, and romantic partners?
- *Professional.* Do I communicate effectively within and on behalf of a business, organization, or work team?
- *Educational.* Do I demonstrate what I have learned in collegiate, corporate, and other training settings?
- *Intercultural.* Do I understand, respect, and adapt to people from diverse backgrounds?
- *Intellectual.* Do I analyze and evaluate the meaning of multiple and complex messages in an ever-changing world?
- *Societal.* Do I critically analyze and appropriately respond to public and mediated messages?
- *Ethical.* Do I apply ethical standards to personal and public communication in a variety of situations?

Know Thy SELF

Do You Have the Right Stuff for the Job?

The U.S. National Association of Colleges and Employers (NACE) asked employers to rate the skills they seek in the college and university graduates they hire.[7] In your opinion, which of the following skills are most important to employers? Rank them in order of preference, with 1 being the most prized skill, 2 being the next most prized skill, and so on. Then ask yourself, "Am I strong, moderate, or weak in terms of these skills"?

Now compare your rankings to the NACE study results. Numbers indicate rankings, with 1 going to the most important skill, 2 to the next most important, and so on.

Employee Skills	Rank Order	Your Skill
a. Analytical skills		____ Strong ____ Moderate ____ Weak
b. Computer skills		____ Strong ____ Moderate ____ Weak
c. Interpersonal skills		____ Strong ____ Moderate ____ Weak
d. Leadership skills		____ Strong ____ Moderate ____ Weak
e. Oral communication skills		____ Strong ____ Moderate ____ Weak
f. Proficiency in field of study		____ Strong ____ Moderate ____ Weak
g. Teamwork skills		____ Strong ____ Moderate ____ Weak
h. Written communication skills		____ Strong ____ Moderate ____ Weak

Desired skills in college and university graduates: a (4); b (8); c (2); d (5); e (1); f (7); g (3); h (6)

1.2
Communication Principles

*What do you need to know to become
a more effective communicator?*

A long time ago, in the Greek city-states of the eighth through third centuries B.C.E., educated citizens studied and practised the art of oral communication. Ancient philosophers such as Plato and Aristotle discussed the role of communication in their personal and civic lives as well as its ability to help people to achieve personal goals, govern effectively, and defend freedom. Throughout Western history—in ancient Rome, in Christian Europe during the Renaissance and Enlightenment, and in our modern world—the study of communication relied on a rich intellectual foundation.[8]

In the twenty-first century, communication studies expanded beyond public speaking to encompass interpersonal and intercultural communication, group and organizational communication, and mediated and mass communication. In this book, we introduce the innovative ideas of contemporary theorists and researchers in communication studies as well as the enduring wisdom of historically significant philosophers, speakers, and communication scholars.

The rich history of communication studies has endured and evolved in part because communication is a *process* rather than a simple *activity* or unchanging *thing*. David Berlo, a twenty-first century communication pioneer, described a *process* as something that is constantly moving and in which the elements interact with one another to bring about a result.[9] Thus, the characteristics of other communicators can affect your purpose, your choice of message content can affect your style of speaking, and your personal values can determine how you adapt to the context in which you communicate.

Consider, for example, what happens when you look at photos from a wedding or party. How do you interpret an image of a guest holding up a broken wineglass? Although the

The 7 Key Elements and Guiding Principles of Effective Communication

1 SELF — Know thy SELF
2 OTHERS — Connect with OTHERS
3 PURPOSE — Determine your PURPOSE
4 CONTEXT — Adapt to CONTEXT
5 CONTENT — Select Appropriate CONTENT
6 STRUCTURE — STRUCTURE your message
7 EXPRESSION — Practise skilful EXPRESSION

person in the photo is captured in a moment of communication, the picture tells you very little about the background, complexity, and outcome of the communication situation. Why is the glass broken? Does the context of the situation tell you more? What can you learn from examining the person's facial expression and posture?

In scientific disciplines such as physics, chemistry, or biology, you learn "laws" that explain predictable outcomes that occur under the *same* conditions. For example, you learn that if you raise the temperature of water to 100 degrees Celsius under standard conditions at sea level, it will boil.

In interpersonal communication studies, we do not have such strict "laws" because we cannot predict communication outcomes with such certainty. At best, we can explain how communication works in general under *similar* conditions. Rather than following strict laws, we apply accepted principles about the nature of human communication.

The Seven Key Elements and Guiding Principles of Effective Communication graphic on this page represent critical decision points in the communication process. When you communicate effectively, you make many strategic decisions about how to present your *self* and how to connect with *others*. You communicate for a *purpose* in a specific *context*, both of which affect the *content*, *structure*, and *expression* of your message.

Much like a set of interacting gears, the decisions you make about each key element affect the others. But unlike a linear process that follows an established pathway or a set of predictable steps, communication is a psychological, emotional and behavioural process that asks you to make multiple, interdependent decisions about how you will use verbal and nonverbal messages to generate meaning.

1 Know Thy Self

The first effective communication guideline is to *know thy self*. Communication is personal: Each of you communicates in your own unique way. Your genetic code is one of a kind among the billions of genetic codes on earth. Your communication abilities and instincts are also one of a kind. Therefore, make sure you understand how *your* characteristics and attitudes affect the way you communicate.

2 Connect with Others

Regardless of whether you are talking to one person or a large audience, always consider and *connect with others*. Communication is relational; the nature of your relationship with others affects what, when, where, why, and how you communicate. An invitation such as "Let's grab a drink after work" can mean one thing coming from your

best friend, but it can mean something entirely different coming from your manager or a colleague who would like to start dating you. The nature of your relationship with another person affects your choice of specific communication strategies and skills.

Cultural diversity plays a critical role in communication. We use the term **culture** to describe "a learned set of shared interpretations about beliefs, values, norms, and social practices which affect the behaviours of a relatively large group of people."[10] Given this definition, a rancher from

Alberta and an advertising executive from Toronto can have different cultural perspectives about how to greet an acquaintance, as can a Nigerian, an Indonesian, and an Ojibwa tribal member. Consider what happens when you share a message with or respond to someone whose race, age, gender, religious beliefs, political attitudes, or educational level differs from yours.

3 Determine Your Purpose

When you communicate with another person or a group of people,

COMMUNICATION&CULTURE

DOES EVERYONE COMMUNICATE THE SAME WAY?

Do the differences between people outweigh what they have in common? How do these differences affect the way we communicate with one another? Carefully consider the following questions and answer *yes* or *no*.

Now think about how you responded to each of these questions. Why did you respond this way? After reading Chapter 3, "Adapting to Canada's Changing Faces," return to this survey and think about whether you would change any of your answers. If so, why? If not, why not?

Yes No

☐ ☐ 1. Is the U.S. culture the most individualistic (independent, self-centred, me-first) culture in the world?

☐ ☐ 2. Are Asian Canadian students smarter than African Canadian and Caribbean Canadian students?

☐ ☐ 3. Do women talk more than men?

☐ ☐ 4. Are racial classifications based on significant genetic differences?

Ben Cooper/Alamy

"WHY ARE YOU HERE?" THE EFFECTS OF CONTEXT

In the classroom

"Why are you here?" (Meaning: I can help you achieve your goals if I know why you have enrolled in this course.)

At the doctor's office

"Why are you here?" (Meaning: Tell me how you're feeling.)

On the job

"Why are you here?" (Meaning: How will each of you contribute to this project?)

PURPOSE: What's the Point?

- What do you want others to know, think, believe, feel, or do as a result of communicating with them?
- How might others misunderstand or misinterpret your purpose?
- Can you correctly identify the purpose of other communicators?

you usually have a reason for interacting with them. That reason, or goal, can be as weighty as proposing marriage, securing a lucrative business contract, or resolving a world crisis or as simple as asking for the time. *Determining your purpose*—what you and others are trying to accomplish by communicating—is essential when deciding what, when, and how to communicate.

Even when you're not fully conscious of your intentions, your communication is purposeful. When you say, "Hi, how ya doin'?" as you pass a friend in the hallway, unconsciously nod as someone talks to you, or touch the arm of a colleague who has received bad news, you are maintaining and strengthening your friendships and working relationships. Even when you have no intention of

---

INTERRELATED **COMMUNICATION** CONTEXTS

PSYCHOSOCIAL CONTEXT	LOGISTICAL CONTEXT	INTERACTIONAL CONTEXT	MEDIATED CONTEXT
Relates to both the psychological and social contexts of a situation.	Refers to physical time, place, setting, and occasion where the interpersonal communication takes place.	How many people are involved in the communication? One, two, three, or more?	Something, usually technology of some type, is between those interacting and communicating.
CONSIDERATIONS			
Your relationship with other communicators. Their personality traits, cultural attitudes, beliefs, values, behaviours and yours. Their age, gender, race, ethnicity, religion, sexual orientation, levels of ability, and socioeconomic status and yours.	How busy or quiet a setting can affect the quality of the interpersonal communication. Awareness of the impact of space, time and the ability to attend free from distractions is important when communicating with others.	Decide whether you are speaking to only one or two other people (interpersonal communication) or if you are speaking to three or more (group communication). Knowing this will change your message and your method of communication.	Personal forms include phone calls, social media, text messages and email messages. Mass communication, between a person and a large, often unknown audience, includes radio, television, film, blogs, websites, newspapers, magazines, and books.

communication principles

communicating, someone else may perceive that you have sent a purposeful message. For example, if Fred overhears you talking about a good movie you have seen, have you communicated with Fred? If you see your professor frowning, should you assume that she wants you to know she is unhappy, worried, or angry? In a very general sense, some communication occurs whether we intend it or not.

Psychosocial Context

Dmitry Kalinovsky/Shutterstock

Logistical Context

Mario Beauregard/Fotolia

Interactional Context

Lucky Business/Shutterstock

Mediated Context

Maridav/Fotolia

4 Adapt to the Context

All communication occurs within a **context**, the circumstances and setting in which communication takes place. Although this definition may appear simple—after all, communication must occur somewhere—context is anything but simple. Effective interpersonal communicators analyze and *adapt to the context*. Consider, for example, how various contexts affect the implied meaning of the question "Why are you here?" In addition to the contexts shown in the images on the previous page, there are countless other meanings for the phrase that change as the context changes. A mother asking her teenage daughter, "Why are you here?" at home in the morning may mean, "You are late for school and need to get going." A person asking, "Why are you here?" at a funeral could be saying, "Tell me how you knew Gloria." In a workplace conference room, "Why are you here?" means, "We need to determine how your department will contribute to and benefit from this meeting."

Presentational communication occurs between speakers and their audience members.[11] Presentational communication comes in many forms, from formal wedding speeches, student campaign speeches, and conference lectures to informal class reports, staff briefings, and training sessions. You will make many presentations in your

lifetime—at school, at work, at family and social gatherings, or at community or public events.

5 Select Appropriate Content

Although both animals and humans can send and receive messages, human beings are "unique in [their] ability to communicate or convey an open-ended volume of concepts."[12] Put another way, our language is symbolic; we have the distinct ability to generate meaning by combining letters and/or sounds. We can invent new words, say sentences that have never been said before, and communicate creative ideas. Effective communicators enlist the power of good ideas and language by *selecting appropriate content*.

A symbol is something that represents something else. In language, a **symbol** is an *arbitrary* collection of sounds or letters that in certain combinations stand for a concept but do

COMMUNICATION

Exercise

In small groups choose one of the four types of interrelated communication contexts and create a scenario to illustrate that particular context. Do not identify the context your scenario is illustrating.

Exchange scenarios with another group and attempt to identify the context portrayed by the scenario.

1. Describe how your group would communicate with the people (person) in the scenario based on the contextual information provided.
2. What factors shape your method or style of communication based on the contextual information provided in the scenario?

FACTS THINK ABOUT THEORY
TEST IDEA PLAN
EXPERIMENT
METHOD
KNOWLEDGE

Media Richness Theory

Media richness theory examines how the qualities of different media affect communication. The theory also helps explain why your physical presence makes a significant difference in how well you communicate. Let's say you have a message you want to share with a group of people. You can share that message in several ways: face-to-face, on the telephone, through email or text messages, by sending a personal letter, by posting a notice or using social media.

Face-to-face communication (be it in a conversation, group meeting, or presentation) is the richest communication medium because you can (1) see and respond instantly to others, (2) use nonverbal communication (body movement, vocal tone, and facial expression) to clarify and reinforce messages, (3) use a natural speaking style, and (4) convey your personal feelings and emotions. In contrast, text-based communication

John Giustina/Stone/Getty Images

channels such as email are quite the opposite. Readers have to rely exclusively on printed words and illustrations to interpret the sender's meaning. In short, face-to-face communication engages more of our senses and sensibilities than any other form of communication.[13]

CONTENT: Will They Get What You Mean?

- What ideas, information, and opinions should you include in your message to make it clear and interesting?
- How should you support the ideas and opinions in your message?
- How well do you interpret messages from others?

not have a direct relationship to the things they represent.

Symbols are *not* the things they represent. There is absolutely nothing in the letters *C*, *A*, and *T* that looks, smells, sounds, or feels like a cat. And even though dictionaries may define *cat* as a carnivorous mammal domesticated as a catcher of rodents and as a pet, you would be hard pressed to imagine what a cat looks, smells, sounds, or feels like if you had never seen one.

Since there is no tangible relationship between a symbol, the thing it represents, and how you may feel about it, there is always the potential for misunderstanding. For example, what does it mean to you if someone says that it's cold outside? If you live in the far north, "cold" can mean more than 40 degrees Celsius below zero. If you live at sea level near the equator, "cold" can mean 5 degrees Celsius above zero.

CAT

6 Structure Your Message

Once you address the challenges of developing an appropriate and purposeful message, you face the additional challenge of *structuring your message* in a way that others will understand.

The word *structure* refers to how the components or parts of something are assembled and arranged to form a whole. You would not build a house without knowing something about who will live in it, the location and setting, and the materials needed to assemble it. House construction involves putting all of these elements together into a well-designed, durable structure. The same is true in communication. **Structure** involves organizing message content into a coherent and purposeful order.

STRUCTURE: Can They Follow You?

- What are the most effective ways to organize your message?
- How can your organizational structure generate attention and interest?
- In what order should you share your ideas and information?

communication principles

7 Practise Skilful Expressions

When two children argue on a playground, one child may yell, "Take it back!" while the other might shriek, "I will not!" Whether you say something you regret or hit the Send button on your email before you're ready, you can't undo communication. At best, you can attempt to clarify what you've said or try to repair unintended consequences. You can sincerely apologize to someone about something you've said, but you can't literally "take it back." Because communication is irreversible, you must express your message skilfully and thoughtfully. Effective communicators prepare for and *practise skilful expression*.

Interpersonal communication **channels** are the physical and electronic media through which we express messages. You can transmit messages using one or more of your sensory channels: sight, sound, touch, taste, and smell.

Although we use sight and sound most frequently when we speak and listen to others, do not dismiss the power of the other three senses. Perfumes and colognes are designed to communicate attractiveness or mask offensive odours. A carefully prepared dinner or an expensive restaurant meal to which you have been specially invited can communicate a great deal about how the other person feels about you. A warm hug or a rough shove can exhibit intense emotions.

In addition, the communication channels you use today extend well beyond a face-to-face environment into the far reaches of cyberspace. The personal computer is also an interpersonal computer. Technology enables you to enlist a variety of media: telephones, television, personal computers, tablets, smartphones, and the World Wide Web. Whether you're engaged in an online chat or participating in a videoconference, the media you choose and use affect the nature and outcome of your communication.

EXPRESSION: Talk, Touch, or Twitter?

- Which channels are most appropriate given your purpose, the other communicators, the context, and the message of your content?
- What skills and techniques will improve your ability to express your message?
- How effectively do you express and listen to verbal and nonverbal messages?

GETTING IN **GEAR**

The seven guiding principles of effective communication just described apply to all types of communication, regardless of whether you are talking to a friend, delivering a speech to a large audience, planning a business meeting, or participating in online courses. No matter how well you structure the content of your message, you won't achieve your purpose if you do not think carefully about the other factors involved in the communication process. If you offend your listeners or use words they don't understand, you won't achieve your purpose. If you dress perfectly for a job interview but fail to speak clearly and persuasively, you may lose out on a career opportunity. If you hug someone who dislikes being touched, you've chosen the wrong communication channel.

What forms of expression are represented in this photo? How many different communication channels are being used?

Mandy Godbehear/Shutterstock

The Trouble with Twitter

In the first edition of THINK *Communication*, the following headline introduced this topic: *Is Twittering the Next New Frontier?* We noted that although social network sites such as Facebook and MySpace were popular ways of communicating with others near and far, Twitter had grabbed the spotlight and was poised to be the next new communication frontier.

Twitter has its critics on other fronts as well. Probably the biggest complaint about Twitter is that many tweets are "dumb" or "empty." Who cares that you bought a new pair of shoes or that you're tired? Do we really need to know that you're tweeting during a boring biology class? A second criticism is that it wastes a lot of time. However, Darren Rowse, a popular blogger, puts this complaint in perspective. He asserts that twittering is no less a waste of time than blogging, attending conferences, social messaging, or talking on the phone. "I would argue," he concludes, "that there's never been a type of communication invented that can't be used in a way that is a waste of time."[14]

Tumblr may soon overshadow Twitter.[15] Who knows? Rather than picking on Twitter, in the next edition we may title a box "The Trouble with Tumblr."

David Paul Morris/Getty Images

Evan Williams, Twitter co-founder and former CEO

Communication Models

How do communication models help you address interpersonal communication challenges?

When we discuss the nature of communication, we sometimes use **communication models**. Communication scholars Rob Anderson and Veronica Ross write "a model of communication—or any other process, object, or event—is a way of simplifying the complex interactions of elements in order to clarify relevant relationships, and perhaps to help predict outcomes."[16] Communication models

- identify the basic components in the communication process,
- show how the various components relate to and interact with one another, and
- help explain why a communicative act succeeds or fails.

Early Communication Models

The earliest type of communication model, a **linear communication model**, functions in only one direction:

a source creates a message and sends it through a channel to reach a receiver. Linear models identify several important components but do not address the interactive nature of human communication.

Communication theorists next devised **interactive communication models**, which include the concepts of noise and feedback to show that communication is not an unobstructed or one-way street. When feedback is

Linear Communication Model

Source → Message → Channel → Receiver

Interactive Communication Model

Source · Channel · Message ⚡ · Feedback · Source · Channel · Receiver · Receiver · ⚡ Noise

Stockbyte/Getty Images; Pavel L Photo and Video/Shutterstock

---

added, each communicator becomes both the source *and* the receiver of messages. When noise is added, every component becomes vulnerable to disruption.

Feedback **Feedback** is any verbal or nonverbal response you can see or hear from others. A person giving feedback may smile or frown, ask questions or challenge your ideas, listen intently, or tune you out. If you accurately interpret feedback, you can evaluate how well your message is being received and whether it is likely to achieve your purpose.

Expert communicators are sensitive to listener reactions. They use feedback—whether positive or negative—to evaluate whether and how well they are achieving their purpose, and then they adjust their message accordingly.

Noise Interactive communication models also recognize obstacles that can prevent a message from reaching its receivers as intended; in communication studies, this is referred to as **noise**. Noise can be external or internal. **External noise** consists of physical elements in the environment that interfere with effective communication. Noise is often a noticeable problem: heavy traffic outside the window, a soft-speaking voice, or a difficult-to-understand accent. However, noise is not limited to just the sounds you hear. An uncomfortably warm room, an unpleasant odour, or even bright and distracting wall designs can

interfere with your ability to be an attentive and effective communicator.

While external noise can be any distracting element in your environment, internal noise is a mental distraction within yourself. **Internal noise** consists of thoughts, feelings, and attitudes that interfere with your ability to communicate and understand a message as it was intended. A listener preoccupied with personal thoughts can miss or misinterpret a message. As a speaker, you may be distracted and worried about how you look during a presentation instead of focusing on your message and your audience. Or you may be thinking about your upcoming vacation rather than listening to a co-worker's instructions. Such preoccupations can

inhibit your ability to speak and listen effectively.

Encoding and Decoding In most of the early models, communicators have two important functions: they serve as both the source and the receiver of messages. The communication **source** is a person or group of people who create a message intended to produce a particular response. Your message has no meaning until it arrives at a **receiver**, another person or group of people who interpret and evaluate your message. These two actions, sending and receiving, are called *encoding* and *decoding*.

When you communicate with others, you *encode* your ideas: you transform them into verbal and nonverbal messages, or "codes." **Encoding** is the decision-making process by which you create and send **messages** that generate meaning.

Decoding converts a "code" or message sent by someone else into a form you could understand and use. Decoding is the decision-making process you use to interpret, evaluate, and respond to the meaning of verbal and nonverbal messages. Your own unique characteristics and attitudes influence the decoding process.

Transactional Communication Models

Communication is more complex than the processes depicted in linear or interactive models. In reality,

Transactional Communication Model

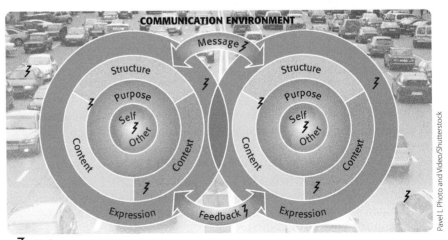

⚡ = Noise

Pavel L Photo and Video/Shutterstock

communication is a *simultaneous* trans-action in which we continuously exchange verbal and nonverbal messages, and share meanings. Transactional communication is also fluid, not a "thing" that happens. **Transactional communication models** recognize that we send and receive messages simultaneously within specific contexts. Even when we listen to someone, our nonverbal reactions send messages to the speaker.

Recall the seven key elements and guiding principles of effective communication. In an ideal communication transaction, you have a *clear purpose* in mind. You have adapted your message *to others* and the *context*.

Your message contains appropriate and *well-structured content* as it is *expressed* through one or more channels with a minimum of interfering noise.

Effective communicators accept the fact that they may never create or deliver a perfect message, but they never stop trying to reach that ideal.

Exercise

Follow this link to a YouTube video that explores the transactional communication model.

www.youtube.com/watch?v=mQSL8aqTDLg

After watching the video, create your paper airplane.

(Template: www.paperaeroplanes.com/thedart)

Create your message and explore the sender, receiver, and noise relationship in having your message understood by someone else in the class.

STOP&THINK

How Noisy Can It Get?

Noise can affect *every* aspect of the communication process, threatening or preventing you from achieving the intended outcome of your message. For each type of noise described below, add a second example.

- *Noise and Self:* Personal problems and anxieties: (1) Because Katya was worried about her grade, she had trouble concentrating during her class presentation.

  (2) _____
  _____ .

- *Noise and Others:* Failure to analyze the characteristics, culture, and opinions of others: (1) When Michelle asked Gerald to work on Saturday morning, she forgot that he goes to synagogue that day.

  (2) _____
  _____ .

- *Noise and Purpose:* Unclear thinking: (1) When no one donated $25 to buy Jill's present, Jack realized he was asking for too much money.

  (2) _____
  _____ .

- *Noise and Context:* Distraction within and outside a room: (1) When police and fire trucks came screaming down the street, everyone stopped talking and listening.

  (2) _____
  _____ .

- *Noise and Content:* Invalid research, unclear explanations, or inappropriately chosen words: (1) When Lex began swearing about the group's lack of progress, members

Alan Poulson Photography/Shutterstock

decided they would rather stop working than listen to Lex and his foul language.

  (2) _____
  _____ .

- *Noise and Structure:* A poorly organized message: (1) Caleb's stories can be entertaining except for when he rambles on and on without making a point or coming to some sort of conclusion.

  (2) _____
  _____ .

- *Noise and Expression:* A weak voice, defensive posture, or poor graphics: (1) Wanda made a poor impression when she kept twirling her hair and taking her glasses on and off during her presentation.

  (2) _____
  _____ .

1.4

Communication Theories, Strategies, and Skills

How do theories help you choose effective interpersonal communication strategies and skills?

Most of us would laugh if someone tried to become a champion tennis player, a professional airline pilot, or a gourmet chef just by reading a book. Likewise, no textbook or classroom lecture alone can teach you to become a more effective communicator. The best way to study interpersonal communication is to apply an understanding of communication theories to appropriate strategies and skills. Mastering isolated skills will not help you resolve a conflict, lead a discussion, or plan a presentation. Understanding the relationship among theories, strategies, and skills will.

Learn About Theories

Theories are statements that explain how the world works. They describe, explain, and predict events and behaviour.

Communication theories have emerged from extensive observation, empirical research, and rigorous scholarship. They help you understand *what* is happening when you communicate and *why* communication is sometimes effective and sometimes ineffective.

Learning about theories in isolation will not make you a more effective communicator. Theories do not necessarily tell you what to do or what to say. Nevertheless, without theories, we would have difficulty understanding why or how a particular strategy works or how strategies and skills interact.

Choose Appropriate Strategies

Strategies are the specific plans of action you select to help you communicate. The word *strategy* comes from the Greek word *strategia* and refers to the office of a military general. Like great generals, effective communicators

marshal their "forces" to achieve a specific purpose: to comfort a friend, resolve a conflict, lead a group discussion, or deliver an informative presentation.

However, learning about strategies is not enough. Effective strategies are based on theories. If you don't understand theory, you won't know why strategies work in one situation and fail in another. Strategies based on theory help you understand when, where, why, and how to use a particular strategy most effectively.

Develop Effective Skills

Communication **skills** refer to your ability to accomplish communication goals through

> **"Theories are nets to catch what we call 'the world': to rationalize, to explain, and to master it."**
>
> Karl R. Popper, philosopher[17]

interactions with others. Communication skills are the tools or techniques you use to collaborate with a colleague, prepare a meeting agenda, and speak loudly enough to be heard by a large audience. Throughout this book, you will read about and practice many communication skills:

- How to be more assertive
- How to think critically
- How to resolve conflicts
- How to speak clearly
- How to organize a message
- How to explain complex concepts or persuade others

Like strategies, skills are most effective when grounded in theory. Without theories, you may not understand

Adapt to others

Prepare and deliver a presentation

COMMUNICATION SKILLS

Improve your personal relationships

Improve your professional relationships

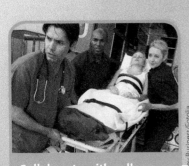

Collaborate with colleagues

Tim Pannell/Blink/Corbis

Konstantin Sutyagin/Fotolia

Jeanette Dietl/Fotolia

Chabruken/The Image Bank/Getty Images

Monkey Business/Fotolia

when and why to use a particular strategy or skill to its best advantage. For example, in the hope of improving group morale, you may be tempted to omit using a well-structured, problem-solving agenda at a critical meeting when, in fact, group morale is low because your approach to problem solving is disorganized and wastes their time. However, if you are familiar with group communication theory, you will know that using a standard agenda helps a group to follow a series of practical steps to solve problems. In our eagerness to communicate effectively, we may rely on ready-made, easy-to-use "tricks of the trade" that are inappropriate or ineffective. Enlisting skills without understanding the theories and strategies can make interpersonal communication inefficient and ineffective as well as frustrating for everyone.

Skilled speakers and listeners have made effective interpersonal communication into an enduring habit. As Stephen Covey notes, a habit has three components: knowledge, skills, and desire. Knowledge plays a role similar to theories and strategies: it describes *what* to do and *why* to do it. Skills represent *how* to do it. And desire is the motivation to communicate effectively and ethically: you *want* to do it. Effective and ethical communication relies as much on your attitude (*wanting* to do it) as it does on your knowledge and skills.

Learning to communicate is a complex challenge that requires more than simple rules and imitation. Highly successful communicators internalize the knowledge, skills, and motivation they need to communicate effectively and ethically.

MAKE **EFFECTIVE COMMUNICATION** AN **ENDURING HABIT**

STEPHEN COVEY is the author of *The 7 Habits of Highly Effective People*, one of the most popular self-help/business books ever published. Covey presents a principle-centred approach for solving personal and professional problems. Covey claims that effective people transform these principles into enduring habits. We believe the same is true about the principles of communication. Effective communicators transform communication principles into enduring habits, things you do so frequently and for so long that you've stopped thinking about why, when, how, and whether you do them.

In his book, Covey provides many examples that illustrate how knowledge, skill, and desire must all be considered when working with others. Knowledge provides the theoretical background for understanding problems, but alone it does not provide the entire picture. Skilful communicators will also take into consideration why an individual says or does something (his or her motivation), and then also consider if there is a willingness on the part of those involved to make changes. This willingness can be described as the desire to change.[18]

communication theories, strategies, and skills

Communicating Ethically

Why is ethical decision-making essential for respectful interpersonal communication?

How would you feel if you learned that …

- a corporate executive hid lavish, personal expenditures while laying off employees?
- a teacher gave higher grades to students he liked and lower grades to students who annoyed him?
- a close friend shared your most intimate secrets with people you don't know or don't like?
- a politician used a racial slur in private to describe a disgruntled group of voters?

Most of these behaviours are not illegal. They are, however, unethical.

Theories answer *why* (Why does communication work this way?), strategies answer *what* (What should work in this communication situation?), and skills answer *how* (How should I express myself?). An effective communicator also must be able to answer the *whether* questions—that is, whether you should communicate as planned: Is it right? Is it fair? Is it deceptive?[19]

Ethical issues arise whenever we communicate because communication has consequences. What we say and do can help or hurt others. Unscrupulous speakers have misled trusting citizens and consumers. Bigots have used hate speech to oppress and discriminate against those who are "different." Self-centred people have destroyed the reputations of their rivals by spreading cruel rumours among friends and colleagues.

Ethics requires an understanding of whether communication behaviours meet agreed-on standards of right and wrong.[20] The National Communication Association (NCA), which is the largest professional association of communication scholars, researchers, educators, students, and practitioners in the world, provides a Credo for Ethical Communication. In Latin, the word *credo* means "I believe." Thus, the NCA Ethics Credo is a set of belief statements about what it means to be an ethical communicator.

ETHICAL COMMUNICATION

The National Communication Association Credo for Ethical Communication[21]

Questions of right and wrong arise whenever people communicate. Ethical communication is fundamental to respectful, responsible thinking, decision making, and the development of relationships and communities within and across contexts, cultures, channels, and media. Moreover, ethical communication enhances human worth and dignity by fostering truthfulness, fairness, responsibility, personal integrity, and respect for self and others. We believe that unethical communication threatens the well-being of individuals and the society in which we live. Therefore we, the members of the National Communication Association, endorse and are committed to practicing the following principles of ethical communication:

- We advocate truthfulness, accuracy, honesty, and reason as essential to the integrity of communication.
- We endorse freedom of expression, diversity of perspective, and tolerance of dissent to achieve the informed and responsible decision making fundamental to a civil society.
- We strive to understand and respect other communicators before evaluating and responding to their messages.
- We promote access to communication resources and opportunities as necessary to fulfill human potential and contribute to the well-being of families, communities, and society.
- We promote communication climates of caring and mutual understanding that respect the unique needs and characteristics of individual communicators.
- We condemn communication that degrades individuals and humanity through distortion, intimidation, coercion, and violence, and through the expression of intolerance and hatred.
- We are committed to the courageous expression of personal conviction in pursuit of fairness and justice.
- We advocate sharing information, opinions, and feelings when facing significant choices while also respecting privacy and confidentiality.
- We accept responsibility for the short- and long-term consequences of our own communication and expect the same of others.

Are You an Effective Communicator?

How can you become a more effective communicator? Use the five-point scale below to rate the following competencies in terms of their importance. Circle only one number for each item.

Competencies	Extremely Important	Very Important	Somewhat Important	Not Very Important	Not at All Important
1. Reduce your speaking anxiety	5	4	3	2	1
2. Influence the attitudes and behaviour of others	5	4	3	2	1
3. Use humour appropriately	5	4	3	2	1
4. Listen effectively to others	5	4	3	2	1
5. Develop good interpersonal relationships	5	4	3	2	1
6. Hold an interesting conversation	5	4	3	2	1
7. Use your voice effectively	5	4	3	2	1
8. Resolve interpersonal conflicts	5	4	3	2	1
9. Use gesture, movement, and eye contact effectively	5	4	3	2	1
10. Interview for a job	5	4	3	2	1
11. Adapt to people from different cultures	5	4	3	2	1
12. Lead a group or work team	5	4	3	2	1
13. Present visual aids and slides effectively	5	4	3	2	1
14. Tell stories skilfully	5	4	3	2	1
15. Chair or conduct a meeting	5	4	3	2	1
16. Gain audience or listener attention and interest	5	4	3	2	1
17. Prepare and deliver an effective presentation	5	4	3	2	1
18. Explain complex ideas to others	5	4	3	2	1
19. Inspire or motivate others	5	4	3	2	1
20. Assert your ideas and opinions	5	4	3	2	1
21. Participate effectively in a group discussion	5	4	3	2	1
22. Organize the content of a presentation	5	4	3	2	1
23. Begin and end a presentation	5	4	3	2	1
24. Use appropriate and effective words	5	4	3	2	1
25. Develop strong, valid arguments	5	4	3	2	1
26. Interact in business and professional settings	5	4	3	2	1
27. Support and comfort others	5	4	3	2	1

Review your ratings: Circle the competency item numbers next to the skills that you scored as fives—skills that, in your opinion, are the most important and essential for effective communication. Why did you select these items?

1.1
Communication in Your Life
What is communication, and how does it affect your everyday life?

- Communication is the process of using verbal and nonverbal messages to generate meaning within and across various contexts, cultures, and channels.
- Effective interpersonal communication helps you achieve your personal, professional, educational, intercultural, intellectual, societal, and ethical goals.

1.2
Communication Principles
What do you need to know to become a more effective communicator?

- Effective communicators make critical decisions about the seven guiding principles of human communication represented by the key elements *self*, *others*, *purpose*, *context*, *content*, *structure*, and *expression*.
- The four types of communication context are psychosocial, logistical, interactional, and mediated.
- The three interactional contexts are interpersonal, group/team, and presentational communication.

1.3
Communication Models
How do communication models help you address interpersonal communication challenges?

- Unlike linear and interactional communication models, the transactional model depicts communication as a *simultaneous* transaction in which we continuously exchange verbal and nonverbal messages and share meanings.
- In an interpersonal transaction, communicators encode and decode messages at the same time.
- The components of a transactional communication model include all seven elements of effective communication as well as message, feedback, and noise.

1.4
Communication Theories, Strategies, and Skills
How do theories help you choose effective interpersonal communication strategies and skills?

- Your choices of communication strategies and skills are most effective when they are grounded in theory. Without theory, you may not understand when and why to use a particular strategy or skill to its best advantage.

- Make communication an enduring habit by knowing what to do and why to do it (knowledge), knowing how to do it (skills), and wanting to do it (desire).

1.5
Communicating Ethically
Why is ethical decision making essential for respectful interpersonal communication?

- Questions of right and wrong arise whenever people communicate. Ethical communication is fundamental to respectful, responsible thinking, decision making, and the development of relationships and communication within and across contexts, cultures, and channels.
- The National Communication Association Credo for Ethical Communication endorses principles of ethical communication for all communicators.

Mandy Godbehear/Shutterstock

TEST YOUR KNOWLEDGE

1.1 What is communication, and how does it affect your everyday life?

1 The textbook defines *communication* as the process of using verbal and nonverbal messages to generate meaning within and across various contexts, cultures, and channels. Which term in this definition refers to the various physical and electronic media through which we express messages?

a. messages
b. meaning
c. contexts
d. cultures
e. channels

2 Which of the following skills received the *lowest* ranking in the study of skills employers seek in college graduates?

a. computer skills
b. written communication skills
c. oral communication skills
d. leadership
e. proficiency in field of study

1.2 What do you need to know to become a more effective communicator?

3 Which communication principle seeks an answer to the following question: How well do you suspend *your* personal needs and attitudes when you listen?

a. Know Thy Self
b. Connect with Others
c. Determine Your Purpose
d. Adapt to the Context
e. Structure Your Message

4 Which communication principle seeks an answer to the following question: How can I adapt to the psychological circumstances and physical setting of the communication situation?

a. Know Thy Self
b. Select Appropriate Content
c. Connect with Others
d. Adapt to the Context
e. Structure Your Message

5 The logistical context of communication refers to

a. the cultural environment in which you live.
b. your emotional history, personal experiences, and cultural background.
c. the time, place, setting, and occasion in which you will interact with others.

d. whether communication occurs one to one, in groups, or between a speaker and an audience.
e. interpersonal, group, and presentational communication.

1.3 How do communication models help you address communication challenges?

6 Linear models of communication

a. include the concepts of noise and feedback.
b. function in only one direction: a source creates a message and sends it through a channel to reach a receiver.
c. recognize that we send and receive messages simultaneously.
d. illustrate the interrelationships among the key elements of human communication.
e. all of the above

7 The encoding process can be described as

a. the way you feel about others.
b. the process of minimizing internal noise.
c. effective listening.
d. converting a "code" sent by someone else into a meaningful message.
e. the decision-making process you use to create messages that generate meaning.

1.4 How do theories help you choose effective communication strategies and skills?

8 Stephen Covey defines a habit as the intersection of

a. theories, strategies, and skills.
b. theories, methods, and tools.
c. knowledge, cognition, and intellectual skills.

d. knowledge, skill, and desire.
e. preparation, practice, and performance.

9 Theories answer *why*, strategies answer *what*, skills answer *how*, and ethics answers *questions* of

a. who
b. where
c. when
d. whether
e. all of the above

1.5 Why is ethical decision making essential for effective communication?

10 Which principle in the NCA Credo for Ethical Communication is violated if a close friend shares your most intimate secrets with people you don't know or don't like?

a. We advocate truthfulness, accuracy, honesty, and reason as essential to the integrity of communication.
b. We strive to understand and respect other communicators before evaluating and responding to their messages.
c. We promote access to communication resources and opportunities as necessary to fulfill human potential.
d. We advocate sharing information, opinions, and feelings when facing significant choices while also respecting privacy and confidentiality.
e. We are committed to the courageous expression of personal conviction in pursuit of fairness and justice.

Answers found on page 330.

Key Terms

Channels	Interactive communication model	Presentational communication
Communication	Internal noise	Psychosocial context
Communication models	Interpersonal communication	Receiver
Context	Linear communication model	Skills
Culture	Logistical context	Source
Decoding	Mass communication	Strategies
Encoding	Media richness theory	Structure
Ethics	Mediated context	Symbol
External noise	Messages	Theories
Feedback	Noise	Transactional communication model
Group communication		
Interactional context		

Understanding
YOUR SELF

2

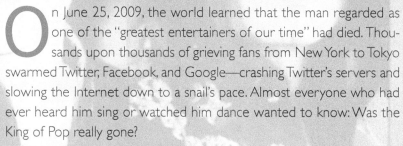

On June 25, 2009, the world learned that the man regarded as one of the "greatest entertainers of our time" had died. Thousands upon thousands of grieving fans from New York to Tokyo swarmed Twitter, Facebook, and Google—crashing Twitter's servers and slowing the Internet down to a snail's pace. Almost everyone who had ever heard him sing or watched him dance wanted to know: Was the King of Pop really gone?

Michael Jackson's death had a profound effect for many people and so we ask, "Who was Michael Jackson?" According to *Newsweek*'s David Gates, "He was a music legend and a legendary oddball.... He was the king of pop."[1] Michael Jackson was a superstar at age five, singing and dancing with his brothers in the Jackson Five. As a young man he won the Grammy award 18 times as a solo recording artist and innovator.

But from the 1990s, when Jackson's career and personal life began its decline, we also remember a troubling and tragic side to this former child star. Rumours of his "sleepovers" with young children at his Neverland ranch led to allegations of child abuse. He contracted vitiligo, an autoimmune disease that turned his skin from brown to white.[2] Literally, Jackson changed before our eyes. Eventually, his physical and emotional problems led to prescription drug dependence and ultimately his death.

Trying to answer the question, "Who was Michael Jackson?," British blogger *hysperia* writes that he was "a man who couldn't be known and who, most likely, could not know himself."[3] While reflecting on Michael Jackson and his life, we must acknowledge the importance of knowing one's own *self*. All communication begins with *you*. Who you are and how you think determines how you interact with others and how others interact with you.

THINK About... and ASK YOURSELF...

2.1
Who Are You?

How do your characteristics, perceptions, self-concept, and level of confidence affect the way you communicate?

Your **self-concept** represents the sum total of beliefs you have about yourself. It answers two simple questions: "Who am I?" and "What makes me, *me*?" Not only are you defined by characteristics such as your age, nationality, race, religion, and gender (as in "I am a 30-year-old, Japanese Canadian, Catholic female"). It also includes, your life experiences, attitudes, and personality traits that influence your opinion of yourself.

Your self-concept changes as you change; you are always *becoming*. A physically awkward child may eventually grow into a confident and graceful dancer. A middle school student with poor grammar may eventually become a celebrated author.

Sources of Self-Concept

Where does your self-concept come from? You certainly aren't born with one. Infants only begin to recognize themselves in a mirror between 18 and 24 months of age. Only then do they begin to express the concept of "me."[4] Although many factors influence how you develop a self-concept, the following are among the most significant: self-awareness, the influence of others, past experiences, and cultural perspectives.

Self-Awareness **Self-awareness** is an understanding of your core identity.[5] It requires a realistic objective appraisal of your traits, thoughts, and feelings. In his best-selling book *Emotional Intelligence*, Daniel Goleman identifies self-awareness as the first and most fundamental emotional competency: the keystone of emotional intelligence.[6] He also claims that "the ability to monitor feelings from moment to moment is crucial to psychological insight and self-understanding. An inability to notice our true feelings leaves us at their mercy."[7]

Awareness of your thoughts and feelings is referred to as **self-monitoring**. Effective self-monitoring helps you

SUDRES Jean-Daniel/Hemis /Alamy

realize, "This is anger I'm feeling." It gives you the opportunity to modify or control anger rather than allowing it to take over your mind and body. Self-monitoring also helps you differentiate emotional responses: love versus lust, disappointment versus depression, and anxiety versus excitement.

By becoming aware of your thoughts and feelings, you can avoid mistaking lust for everlasting love, avoid letting minor problems trigger anxiety, and avoid mistaking fear for anger. People who are *high self-monitors* constantly watch other people, what they do, and how they respond to the behaviour of others. They are also self-aware, like to "look good," and usually adapt well to differing social situations. On the other hand, *low self-monitors* often seem oblivious to how others see them and may "march to their own, different drum."[8]

> **❝** People with greater certainty about their feelings are better pilots of their lives, having a surer sense of how they really feel about personal decisions from whom to marry to what job to take. **❞**
>
> —Daniel Goleman[9]

The Influence of Others Self-awareness may be the keystone of emotional intelligence, but the influence of other people is a more powerful cause of your self-concept. These influences include significant others, the groups to which you belong, the roles you assume, and the rewards you receive from others (as shown below).

Past Experiences Without past experiences and personal memories, you would have little basis for a coherent self-concept. For example, vivid memories of traumatic events—the death of a loved one, a serious automobile accident, or life-threatening illness—can affect how you interpret and react to current events and personal circumstances. Who would you be if you could not remember the past experiences that define you?[10]

It is not surprising that you (and everyone else) have a tendency to distort memories. You tend to remember the past as if it were a drama in which you were the leading player.[11] When asked about high school, many people describe it as "terrible" or "wonderful" when they really mean it *seemed* terrible or wonderful *to them*. This is personalizing a situation or event. When we tell stories about the past, we cast ourselves at the center of action rather than as bit players or observers.

Cultural Background Culture plays a significant role in determining who you are and how you understand yourself. Intercultural communication scholar Min-Sun Kim explains that cultures have "different ways of being, and different ways of knowing, feeling, and acting."[12] For example, Western cultures typically emphasize the value of independence and self-sufficiency, whereas East Asian cultures often emphasize the value of group memberships. The

> Who would you be if you could not remember your parents or childhood playmates, your successes and failures, the places you lived, the schools you attended, the books you read, and the teams you played for?

"self" generally is not perceived outside its relationship to the "other." Chapter 3, "Adapting to Canada's Changing Faces," discusses how understanding cultural differences and similarities affects our communication.

THE **INFLUENCE** OF **OTHERS**

Significant others are people whose opinions you value, such as family members, friends, co-workers, and mentors. What do such people tell you about yourself? Equally important, how do you behave around them?

Reference groups are groups with whom you identify. Think about a high school group you may have belonged to (popular, smart, artistic, geeky, or athletic). How did that membership affect your self-concept and interaction with others? How do your current group memberships (work team, church group, civic association, professional, organization, social, or campus club) affect the way you see yourself?

Roles are adopted patterns of behaviours associated with an expected function in a specific context or relationship. Your behaviour often changes when you shift to a different role. For example, how does your public role (student, teacher, mechanic, nurse, manager, police officer) affect your view of yourself? How do your private roles (child, parent, spouse, lover, best friend) shape your self-concept? Not surprisingly, you learn how to behave in a role largely by modelling others in that role. For example, for better or worse, you learn the parenting role from your parents.

Rewards are recognitions received from others at home, at school, on the job, or in a community for good work (academic honour, employee-of-the-month award, job promotion, community service prize). Meaningful praise and words of encouragement from others affect your self-concept. Consider how you might feel about yourself if you never received encouraging feedback.

Assessing Yourself

Self-appraisals are evaluations of your self-concept in terms of your abilities, attitudes, and behaviours. "I'm not popular" or "I'm an excellent basketball player" are examples of self-appraisals. It is not surprising that when your appraisals are positive, you are more likely to succeed. Positive beliefs about your abilities can make you more persuasive when asking for a promotion, or assignment extension, or better able to deal with rejection. At the same time, your mind may try to protect you from potentially harmful or threatening feedback from others. These ego-defence mechanisms can mislead us into forming a distorted self-image:[13] "What's the big deal about being late to a meeting? She's just obsessed with time and took it out on me. It's no big deal." When actually, being late to the meeting happens often and shows a lack of respect for the other participants.

> **"Of all the judgments we pass in life, none is as important as the ones we pass on ourselves."**
> —Nathaniel Branden[14]

Examining and understanding self-concept is difficult because we tend to view ourselves favourably—often more favourably than we deserve. In his book *The Varnished Truth: Truth Telling and Deceiving in Ordinary Life*, David Nyberg writes, "Human self-deception is one of the most impressive software programs ever devised."[15] Most of us seem to be "wired" to fool ourselves about ourselves, often deceiving ourselves about things we want to be true (but aren't).[16] To minimize this kind of self-deception, you should enlist two forms of self-appraisals—*actual performance* and *social comparison*.

Actual Performance Your actual performance or behaviour is the most influential source of self-appraisals.[17] If you repeatedly succeed at something, you are likely to evaluate your performance in that area positively. For example, if you were an "A" student in high school, you probably

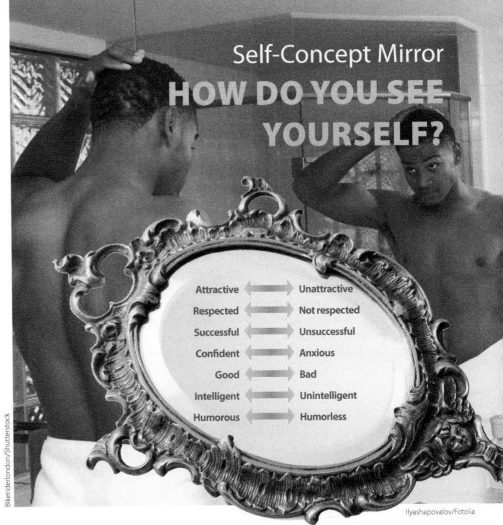

Self-Concept Mirror
HOW DO YOU SEE YOURSELF?

Attractive	⟷	Unattractive
Respected	⟷	Not respected
Successful	⟷	Unsuccessful
Confident	⟷	Anxious
Good	⟷	Bad
Intelligent	⟷	Unintelligent
Humorous	⟷	Humorless

expect to be a good student in college. Thus, you may be disappointed or distressed if you receive a low grade and, as a result, doubt your academic and intellectual abilities.

Social Comparison According to social psychologist Leon Festinger, **social comparison** is the process of you evaluating yourself in relation to the others in your reference groups.[18] The notion of "keeping up with the Joneses" is an example of our need to compare favourably with others. If you are the only one in the class who receives a failing grade on a test, you may conclude that you are less intelligent, less prepared, or less capable than your classmates. On the other hand, if everyone does poorly on the test, comparing yourself with your classmates may make you feel better about yourself because it means you did just as well as everyone else. We also compare ourselves with others in terms

of appearance and physical ability. When people compare themselves with fashion models, alluring movie stars, and professional athletes, however, they have chosen an almost impossible ideal.

Elite athletes and runway models are poor choices for social comparison. Their skills and body types are not representative of society as a whole and can lead to lower self-esteem.

Creating, Deceiving, and Revealing Yourself Online

Researchers disagree about whether online communication harms or promotes the development of a self-concept. Some suggest that the endless number of social media communities with constantly changing contexts, significant others, and reference groups make it difficult for anyone to develop a stable self-identity.[19] Others argue that social media provide opportunities to experiment with identities. For example, shy teenagers may feel more confident and comfortable communicating online than in face-to-face interactions. As they "try on" different selves online, positive feedback from virtual others can help them develop a stronger self-concept and a healthier self-esteem.[20]

Unfortunately, the absence of *real*, face-to-face interactions makes it easier to distort aspects of yourself, as well as to fabricate a false identity. A study of personal characteristics described by participants in online dating services uncovered gender-based misrepresentations. Men were more likely to misrepresent their personal assets (job status, income, intelligence, educa-

" Who are you online?"

tion). Women were more likely to misrepresent their weight as lower; men were more likely to misrepresent their age as older.[21]

Many people have been betrayed or seriously hurt by online deceptions—as in the tragic case of Megan Meier, who committed suicide after falling victim to the cruel torment of and rejection by a boy named Josh Evans, someone she'd met on MySpace. It turned out that Josh was actually a fictitious character created by Lori Drew, the mother of a former friend of Megan's. Drew, who created this false identity as a way of humiliating and punishing Megan for supposedly spreading rumours about Drew's daughter, was indicted on misdemeanour charges in November 2008. In July 2009, a federal judge threw out Drew's conviction and acquitted her of all charges.[22]

There are examples of online bullying in all provinces and territories in Canada. The following example occurred in the United States but is important to examine in Canada as well. It provides an important cautionary tale. Tyler Clementi, an 18-year-old first-year university student,

posted a suicide message on his Facebook page before jumping to his death from a bridge. He took his own life after his roommate, Dharun Ravi, used a webcam to videotape Clementi having sex with a man in his dorm room. In addition to video streaming the encounter on the Internet, the roommate posted Twitter messages about Clementi: "I saw him making out with a dude. Yay." and "Found out my roommate was gay." This public persecution may have precipitated Tyler Clementi's suicide.[23] Dharun was found guilty and was sentenced to 30 days in prison. He was released in June 2012. Tyler's family has started a foundation in support of suicide prevention.[24]

When you share aspects of yourself online—be they your opinions, your personal feelings, your photos, or the story of your wild summer vacation—remember that once you've hit the Send button, your communication is irreversible. Always ask yourself, Can this message embarrass or hurt me now or in the future? Will it hurt someone else? Would I want my family or a potential employer to read or see this posting?

How We Make Ourselves **LOOK GOOD**

In Order to Maintain a Positive Self-Concept, We Tend to

➡ attribute successes to our own abilities and blame our failures on external factors.

➡ view evidence depicting us unfavourably as flawed.

➡ forget negative feedback and remember positive feedback.

➡ compare ourselves to others who make us look good.

➡ overestimate how many people share our opinions and underestimate how many people share our abilities.

➡ believe our good traits are unusual while our faults are common.

COMMUNICATION

Exercise

Write a paragraph to answer the following questions based on this statement: You have been elected leader for your team or group.
1. Why do you think you were chosen?
2. What characteristics, perceptions of yourself, and self-awareness do you have that would make you the best candidate for leadership?

2.2
Building Self-Esteem

What communication strategies and skills can improve your self-esteem?

Igor Mojzes/Fotolia

Now that you know something about your self-concept, how do you *feel* about yourself? Are you satisfied, discouraged, delighted, optimistic, surprised, or troubled? **Self-esteem** represents your judgments about yourself. Nathaniel Branden puts it this way: "Self-esteem is the reputation we acquire with ourselves."[25] Not surprisingly, your personal beliefs, behaviour, and performance influence your level of self-esteem.

Studies consistently find that people with high self-esteem are significantly happier than people with low self-esteem. They are also less likely to be depressed. One especially compelling study surveyed more than 13,000 college students. High self-esteem emerged as the strongest factor in overall life satisfaction.[26]

If your self-esteem isn't very positive, you can take steps to improve it by self-monitoring and learning new ways of communicating with others.

There are several specific strategies you can try as well. Keep in mind that engaging in these practices requires persistence and effort.

Beware of Self-Fulfilling Prophecies

A prophecy is a prediction. A **self-fulfilling prophecy** is "an impression formation process in which an initial impression elicits behaviour . . . that conforms to the impression."[27] More simply, it is a prediction you make that you cause to happen or become true. For example, if young girls are told that boys do better in mathematics, they may believe it and stop trying to succeed. As a result, they won't do as well in math as boys, just as predicted.

In one study, researchers administered a math test to different groups of women. Before taking the test, one group of women was told that men and women do math equally well. Another group was told that there is a genetic difference in math ability that explains why women are not as good at math as men. The women in the first group got nearly twice as many right answers as those in the second group. The researchers concluded that people tend to accept genetic explanations as powerful and permanent, which can lead to self-fulfilling prophecies.[28]

High self-esteem will not solve all your personal problems, nor will it automatically improve your ability to communicate effectively and ethically.

Canada was instrumental in having October 11 declared International Day of the Girl Child. Girls are empowering each other to create a world where education and access to food, shelter, and medical care are provided for all girls in all countries.[29]

Factors That Affect YOUR SELF-ESTEEM

YOUR BELIEFS

Beliefs about yourself: "I am competent/incompetent."

Beliefs about your emotions: "I am happy/sad."

YOUR BEHAVIOUR

Positive behaviour: "I am assertive and appropriately ask for what I need or want."

Negative behaviour: "I'll start some juicy rumours that Gregory's been cutting out of work early."

YOUR PERFORMANCE

Skills: "I am a good writer and feel proud of that."

Character: "I am a good person and enjoy helping others."

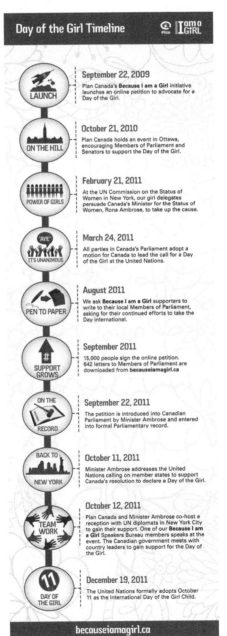

Day of the Girl Timeline

September 22, 2009
LAUNCH
Plan Canada's **Because I am a Girl** initiative launches an online petition to advocate for a Day of the Girl.

October 21, 2010
ON THE HILL
Plan Canada holds an event in Ottawa, encouraging Members of Parliament and Senators to support the Day of the Girl.

February 21, 2011
POWER OF GIRLS
At the UN Commission on the Status of Women in New York, our girl delegates persuade Canada's Minister for the Status of Women, Rona Ambrose, to take up the cause.

March 24, 2011
AYE IT'S UNANIMOUS
All parties in Canada's Parliament adopt a motion for Canada to lead the call for a Day of the Girl at the United Nations.

August 2011
PEN TO PAPER
We ask **Because I am a Girl** supporters to write to their local Members of Parliament, asking for their continued efforts to take the Day International.

September 2011
 # SUPPORT GROWS
15,000 people sign the online petition. 642 letters to Members of Parliament are downloaded from becauseiamagirl.ca

September 22, 2011
ON THE RECORD
The petition is introduced into Canadian Parliament by Minister Ambrose and entered into formal Parliamentary record.

October 11, 2011
BACK TO NEW YORK
Minister Ambrose addresses the United Nations calling on member states to support Canada's resolution to declare a Day of the Girl.

October 12, 2011
TEAM WORK
Plan Canada and Minister Ambrose co-host a reception with UN diplomats in New York City to gain their support. One of our **Because I am a Girl** Speakers Bureau members speaks at the event. The Canadian government meets with country leaders to gain support for the Day of the Girl.

December 19, 2011
11 DAY OF THE GIRL
The United Nations formally adopts October 11 as the International Day of the Girl Child.

becauseiamagirl.ca

Educators have learned this lesson, much to the detriment of students. For example, some well-meaning school systems tried to raise the self-esteem of disadvantaged and failing students by passing them to the next grade. Unfortunately, students' confidence was artificially raised, but soon the students realized they were not prepared for the work in the next grade and their self-esteem was damaged.[30]

STRATEGIES TO IMPROVE Your Self-Esteem[31]

STRATEGY	EXCEPTION
Practise self-acceptance ☑ **Self-acceptance** means recognizing, accepting, and "owning" your thoughts, feelings, and behaviour. You may not like your actions, but be willing to accept them as part of who you are. No one is perfect.	**But not as an excuse** ☒ Self-acceptance is not an excuse for bad behaviour. If a manager shouts at employees and justifies it by saying, "I'm a very emotional man. If you can't take it, quit," the manager is not displaying self-acceptance but rather is making excuses for yelling at the employees.
Practise self-responsibility ☑ **Self-responsibility** means taking responsibility for your own happiness and for achieving your goals. If you assume responsibility for what you do, you are more likely to be happy and satisfied.	**But don't try to control everything** ☒ Resist the urge to control everything so you don't end up feeling overburdened, frustrated, and angry with others. Ask for, and accept help when you need it.
Practise assertiveness ☑ Stand up for yourself in appropriate ways to satisfy your needs and pursue your goals. Don't become obsessed with getting approval from others.	**But respect the needs of others** ☒ Be assertive, not aggressive, when you pursue your goals. Don't stand in the way of others when you stand up for yourself.
Practise personal integrity ☑ **Personal integrity** means behaving in ways that are consistent with your values and beliefs. Don't simply think about what you should do; instead actually do "the right thing."	**But understand and respect others** ☒ "The right thing" for you may not be "the right thing" for someone else. Make sure your actions do not offend or hurt others and consider their beliefs and values.
Practise positive self-talk ☑ **Self-talk** represents the silent statements you make to yourself about yourself. Replace negative, self-defeating statements with more positive and productive statements.	**But listen to others, too** ☒ Listening to yourself should never substitute for, or prevent you from listening to others. It is important to balance our perception with the views of others.

Know Thy SELF

Assess Your Self-Esteem

The statements below describe different ways of thinking about your self. Read them carefully and choose the phrase that indicates how much you agree with each statement.[32]

Strongly Disagree (SD), Disagree (D), Agree (A), Strongly Agree (SA)

Scoring: Score items 1, 2, 6, 8, and 10 in a positive direction (i.e., strongly agree = 4, agree = 3, and so on) and items 3, 4, 5, 7, and 9 in a negative direction (i.e., strongly agree = 1, agree = 2, and so forth). The highest possible score is 40 points; the lowest possible score is 10 points. Higher scores indicate higher self-esteem. Please note that there are no good or bad scores; rather, the scale measures how you *perceive* your level of self-esteem.

_____ 1. I feel that I'm a person of worth.

_____ 2. On the whole, I am satisfied with myself.

_____ 3. I wish I could have more respect for myself.

_____ 4. I certainly feel useless at times.

_____ 5. At times I think I am no good at all.

_____ 6. I feel that I have a number of positive qualities.

_____ 7. Considering everything, I am inclined to feel that I am a failure.

_____ 8. I am able to do things as well as most other people.

_____ 9. I feel that I do not have much to be proud of.

_____ 10. I have a positive attitude toward myself.

Avoid the Self-Fulfilling Prophecy Trap

To minimize the chances of falling into the self-fulfilling prophecy trap, ask yourself the following questions:

- What prediction am I making about my own and/or the behaviour of others?
- Why am I making this prediction? Is it justified?
- Am I doing anything to cause the predicted response?
- What alternative behaviours could help avoid fulfilling my prophecy?

STOP&THINK

Practise Positive Self-Talk

Read the example of negative self-talk and its corresponding example of positive self-talk below. Then provide two examples of negative self-talk and corresponding examples of positive self-talk.

Negative Self-Talk

Example: *I won't be able to work as quickly as the other group members.*

Your example: _____

_____

Your example: _____

_____

Positive Self-Talk

Example: *I'll do my best and ask for help if I need it.*

Your example: _____

_____

Your example: _____

_____

2.3
Perception in Interpersonal Communication

How do your perceptions affect the way you select, organize, and interpret the world around you?

Why does one person experience great satisfaction in a job while another person in the same job dreads it? Why do you find a particular faculty inspiring, while another person finds the same faculty boring or difficult? The answer to these questions lies in one word: *perception*. Imagine that you and a colleague are chatting after a class. You say, "That was a good class. We got through all the content and ended early." Your friend responds with "Are you kidding? Didn't you notice that the instructor rushed us through the material to avoid any serious discussion or disagreement?" What happened here? You both attended the same class, but each of you perceived the experience quite differently. This is often described as your position.

From a communication point of view, we define **perception** as the process through which you select, organize, and interpret sensory stimuli in the world around you. The accuracy of your perceptions determines how well you interpret and evaluate experiences and people you encounter. At the same time, once you reach a conclusion, it's often difficult to change your perception. This is often described as your position.

Generally, we trust our perceptions and treat them as accurate and reliable. We say things such as, "Seeing is believing," "I call it as I see it," or "I saw it with my own eyes." However, as shown to the right, we can't always rely on what we see. Police officers know very well that three witnesses to a traffic accident may provide three different descriptions of the cars involved, the estimated speed they were travelling, and the physical characteristics of the drivers. In fact, eyewitness testimony, although

Old Woman or Young Woman?

What you see depends on how your eyes select graphic details, how you organize that information, and how you interpret the results.

persuasive, is often the least reliable form of courtroom evidence.

Even though you run the risk of drawing incorrect conclusions, you would be lost in a confusing world without your perceptions. Perception helps you make sense of other people's behaviour, and it also helps you decide what you will say or do. For example, suppose you notice that your boss keeps track of employees who arrive late and leave early, and that she rarely grants these employees the special privileges given to those who put in full workdays. These perceptions tell you that it is a good idea to arrive early and stay late if you want a positive evaluation or a future promotion.

There are three components to perception: **selection, organization**, and **interpretation.**

Selection

You use your senses (sight, sound, taste, smell, and touch) to notice and choose from the many stimuli around you. Your needs, wants, interests, moods, and memories largely determine which stimuli you will select. For example, when your eyes and ears detect something familiar or potentially interesting as you flip through television channels, you stop. Or, you may be daydreaming in class, but when your professor says, "The following chapters will be covered on the next test," you find yourself paying full attention again.

According to the **figure–ground principle** of perception: people focus on certain features (the figure) while deemphasizing less relevant background stimuli (the ground).[33] While walking down the street, if you notice someone standing against a building, that's what you would see first: a person standing against a building, not a building with a person-shaped hole in it.[34] When communicating, your friend may smile and tell you that everything is okay. However, you focus your attention on her red and swollen eyes, suspect that she has been crying, and conclude that she is upset. Her smile and verbal assurances are relegated to the background. Ultimately, what you select to focus

---

COMMUNICATION IN *ACTION*

Making Sense of Our Senses

Neuroscientists have discovered that what you see can influence what you taste. In other words, your senses "talk" to and influence one another because your brain "glues" your senses together.[35] Here are a few examples of how the boundaries between your senses are blurred:

- If you put red food colouring in a glass of white wine, some of the most accomplished wine experts will believe they're drinking red wine.
- If you show a friend a single flash on a computer screen while playing two beeps, she may swear she saw two flashes.

- If you ask someone to rub his hands together while listening to an audiotape of rubbing dry skin, his skin may feel rough and parched to him.
- If you dye a delicious strawberry blue, it's

Stolekg/Fotolia

Do blue strawberries taste and smell differently than red strawberries?

Stolekg/Fotolia

likely to smell strange as well as taste strange.

Neuroscientists have also observed that what you touch can change how you feel and how you interact with other people. For example, when you're holding a hot cup of coffee, you're more likely to view others as caring and generous. Sit in a comfy chair (rather than a hard one), and you may be more open to a compromise. Below are a few more examples of how different physical sensations affect your perceptions of people *and* their perceptions of you.[36]

Types of Touch	How Touch Affects Perceptions
Soft Touch	Touching something soft can make you more open to suggestion. When people touch smooth surfaces, they feel a sense of ease.
Rough or Smooth Touch	Rough textures are associated with friction. Smooth surfaces, such as a soft blouse or a soft leather binder, can influence a meeting outcome more positively than if you wear or bring along something with a rough surface.
Warm Feelings	When you're warm, you're more likely to both trust others and be trustworthy yourself. Heated rooms promote more social connections than cold rooms do.
Cold Feelings	The old phrase "She gave me the cold shoulder" now makes new sense. When people were asked to choose a gift for either them or a friend, those made to feel chilled were 75 percent more likely to keep the gift; those who felt warm were 54 percent more apt to offer it to a friend.
Hard or Soft Hearted	Research subjects who held hard blocks and met someone in the role of an employee, judged the employee to be strict. When those same employees were holding a soft blanket, the research subjects viewed them to be less strict.
Heavy Weight	Heaviness implies seriousness, importance, and status. Choosing heavier paper for your correspondence can give the impression that you're "weighty" and therefore more serious.

on will affect how you organize and interpret the events around you *and* how well you communicate in those situations.

Organization

Suppose you see a middle-aged woman wearing a suit walking across campus. You conclude that she is a professor. You also observe a young man entering a classroom wearing a school sweatshirt and carrying a backpack that appears to be loaded with books. You assume that he is a student. You took the information, or stimuli, you observed and categorized it into "professor" and "student." What these two scenarios demonstrate is how *context* influences the way you organize information. For example, you could conclude that a woman in a suit on campus is a professor, but in a different context, you might conclude that she is a business executive. You may conclude that a young man wearing a school sweatshirt and carrying books on campus is a student, but backstage in a theatre, you may decide that he is an actor or stagehand.

Is this woman a college student? An instructor? A store clerk? An attorney? A business executive?

Information Principles

You sort and arrange the sensory stimuli you select into useful categories based on your knowledge and past

In what ways does this photo illustrate how we select and organize stimuli to reach conclusions about their meaning?

experiences with similar stimuli. Four principles influence how you organize or categorize information: the **proximity principle**, the **similarity principle**, the **closure principle**, and the **simplicity principle**.[37]

The Proximity Principle The closer objects, events, or people are to one another, the more likely you will perceive them as belonging together.[38] You go to a restaurant to eat lunch alone, and another person whom you do not know gets in line behind you. The host asks, "Two for lunch?" When you don't want to be perceived as associated with an individual, you may move away from that person to create greater physical distance.

The Similarity Principle Similar elements or people are more likely to be perceived as part of a group. When two individuals share one characteristic or trait, you may conclude that they also have other things in common. For example, you meet a person from Nova Scotia and assume that she enjoys fiddle music because other Nova Scotians

you know listen to that kind of music. Unfortunately, the similarity principle can lead to stereotyping and inaccurate conclusions. Your new acquaintance may dislike fiddle music but love Drake's music.

The Closure Principle We often fill in missing elements to form a more complete impression of an object, person, or event. Look, for example, at the above figure.

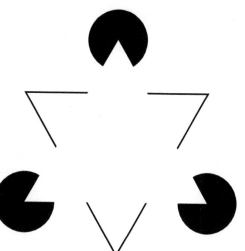

How Many Triangles Do You See?

Some people see as many as 11 triangles in this drawing. However, given that a triangle is a figure with three attached sides, there are no triangles. If you saw triangles, you mentally filled in or "closed" the image's elements.

The Simplicity Principle We tend to organize information in a way that provides the simplest interpretation. For example, on a cloudy day, you look out the window and see that the sidewalk is wet and think that it must have rained. This is a reasonable, simple conclusion. There may be other explanations for the wet sidewalk, like automatic sprinklers or a leak in a water pipe, but you chose the simplest one first.

COMMUNICATION&CULTURE

WEST IS WEST AND EAST IS EAST

The mental process of perception is the same across cultures. Everyone selects, organizes, and interprets stimuli. Psychologist Richard Nisbett argues that each culture can "literally experience the world in very different ways."[39] Look, for example, at the three objects depicted on your right. Which two objects would you pair together?

Studies indicate that people from Western cultures are more likely to put the chicken and cow together, because they are both animals. East Asians, however, are more likely to pair the cow and the grass because cows eat grass. According to Nisbett, East Asians perceive the world in terms of relationships, whereas

Your culture influences what you notice, how you organize that information, and how you interpret information and situations.

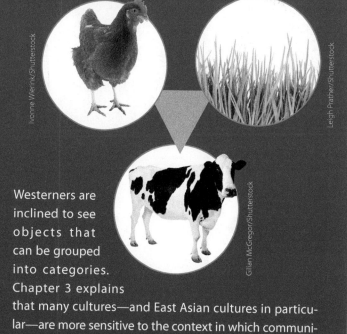

Westerners are inclined to see objects that can be grouped into categories. Chapter 3 explains that many cultures—and East Asian cultures in particular—are more sensitive to the context in which communication takes place. As Rudyard Kipling wrote in *The Ballad of East and West*, "Oh, East is East, and West is West, and never the twain shall meet."

Perception-Checking Guidelines:
The Martha and George Dilemma

Perception checking enlists the seven key elements of effective communication to assess and improve your ability to select, organize, and interpret sensory stimuli into more accurate perceptions. Read the following scenario carefully. Then examine how the perception-checking guidelines and application examples help a communicator respond fairly and appropriately to this particular situation.

Your best friend, Martha, has lived with George for three years. Everyone had been expecting them to get married, so you were shocked when Martha told you they'd broken up. Martha explained that she could no longer live with a man who made fun of her "menial" job as a receptionist, comparing it unfavourably to his position as a senior marketing manager. When he insisted that he control all their finances, and refused to tell her how he was spending their money, she couldn't take it anymore and left him. Yesterday, you learned that George has been hired as a consultant to develop a marketing plan for your office. Whether you like him or not, you will have to work with him for the next four weeks.

Principles of Effective Communication	Perception-Checking Guidelines	Applying Perception-Checking Guidelines
1 SELF	How could factors such as your personal biases, level of self-awareness, cultural background, or the influence of others affect your perceptions?	How do my feelings about Martha, my biases, my past experiences with George, and my gender affect my perceptions of their breakup and George's character?
2 OTHERS	Do you perceive a situation the same way others do? If not, how can you understand their perceptions?	Although I was shocked at George's behaviour, I know there are usually two sides to every story.
3 PURPOSE	How does the way you select, organize, and interpret information affect the way you communicate?	When I work with George, I may pay more attention to his mistakes or suggestions I don't like rather than to the job we need to do. I need to be aware of and guard against such assumptions and behaviour.
4 CONTEXT	How could the psychological, logistical, and interactional communication contexts affect your perceptions and the perception of others?	In the office environment, I will do my best to put aside my feelings about George and work with him to get the job done in a professional way.
5 CONTENT	How could your perceptions affect the content you choose for a message?	I won't make comments about Martha. Certainly, I need to avoid commenting about menial jobs, receptionists, and personal finances.
6 STRUCTURE	How could your perceptions affect the way you organize ideas and information in a message? Will others interpret your meaning differently based on the way you organize your content?	I will put the job first and, if George begins talking about Martha, I will tell him that discussing personal matters is inappropriate at work.
7 EXPRESSION	How could your perceptions affect the way you express your messages and choose communication channels?	I will avoid engaging in negative nonverbal behaviour such as frowning, avoiding eye contact, or putting more distance between us.

Interpretation

A number of factors influence your interpretation of experiences. Suppose a friend asks you to volunteer your time over the weekend to help build a house for Habitat for Humanity. The following factors may affect your interpretation and reaction to your friend's request:

- *Past experiences.* After volunteering at a soup kitchen last year, you felt really good about yourself.
- *Knowledge.* You spent a summer working as a house painter and have a useful skill to contribute.
- *Expectations.* It sounds like fun, and you might meet some interesting people.
- *Attitudes.* You believe that volunteering in the community is important.
- *Relational involvement.* This work is really important to your friend.

These same factors may also lead to inaccurate perceptions. For example, suppose you once volunteered at a homeless shelter and had a terrible experience. The coordinator assigned you the task of washing the sheets and towels every morning and cleaning the bathrooms. As a result, you didn't use your counselling skills and rarely talked to a homeless person.

Clearly, your previous experience may have created an unfair or erroneous perception of volunteer work. Would you be eager to volunteer this time?

Perception Checking

Psychologists Richard Block and Harold Yuker point out that "perception often is a poor representation of reality. Yet it is important to recognize that a person's behaviour is controlled less by what is actually true, than what the person believes is true. Perceptions may be more important than reality in determining behaviour!"[40]

You can improve the accuracy of your perceptions by pausing to check the basis for your conclusions. **Perception checking** involves noticing and analyzing how you select, organize, and interpret sensory stimuli, whether you consider alternative interpretations, and whether you try to verify your perceptions with others.[41]

In the Martha and George Dilemma on the previous page, you learned how perception checking can help you assess and make appropriate responses in a difficult communication situation. Perception checking is just as valuable in everyday life. Perception checking helps you decode messages more accurately, reduce the likelihood of misunderstanding or conflict, and respond fairly and appropriately to others.

ETHICAL COMMUNICATION

The Golden Rule May Not Apply

The Golden Rule, "Do to others what you would have them do to you," comes from the New Testament (Matthew 7:12).[42] Most of the major religions in the world have similar 'rules' in their scriptures. However, what *you* would do is not necessarily what another person wants you to do. In his *Maxims for Revolutionists*, playwright George Bernard Shaw wrote, "The golden rule is that there are no golden rules. . . . Do not do unto others as you would, that they should do unto you. Their tastes may not be the same."[43] Before speaking or acting:

- Consider how another person may perceive the same situation differently than you do.
- Look for solutions that would be appropriate and fair from someone else's point of view or culture.

2.4
Communicating with Confidence

How do you become a more confident communicator?

Your self-concept and level of self-confidence directly affect how successfully you communicate.[44] Most of us see ourselves as bright and hardworking. At the same time, all of us have occasional doubts and insecurities. If you lack confidence, you are less likely to share what you know or voice your opinions. On the other hand, when you feel good about yourself, you can engage in a conversation with ease, defend your ideas in a group, and give successful presentations.

Most people experience some anxiety when they are in an important communication situation. In fact, that "keyed-up" feeling is a positive and normal reaction and demonstrates that you care about what you have to say.

Communication Apprehension

The anxiety you may experience when speaking to others is referred to by many names: *communication apprehension*, *speech anxiety*, and *stage fright*. **Communication apprehension** is "an individual's level of fear or anxiety associated with either real or anticipated communication with another person or persons."[45] It occurs in a variety of communication contexts, such as group discussions, meetings, interpersonal conversations, public speaking, and job interviews.

Communication apprehension is not just "in your head"; it is a type of stress that manifests in real physiological responses. Physical reactions such as sweaty palms, perspiring, a fast pulse, shallow breathing, cold

> **Preparation**
> changes the unfamiliar into something familiar.

Communication Apprehension

Since the early 1970s, the study of communication apprehension has been a major research focus in the communication discipline. Leading researcher James C. McCroskey explains that "it permeates every facet of an individual's life," including major decisions such as career and housing choices, as well as affects the quality of our communication behaviour in a variety of interpersonal, small group, social, educational, work, and public settings.[46]

In the beginning, when McCroskey began studying communication apprehension, he believed that it was a "learned trait, one that is conditioned through reinforcements of the child's communication behavior."[47] More recently, he has argued that a person's environment or situation has only a small effect on that person's level of anxiety. He now believes that communication apprehension is a personality trait, "an expression of principally inborn neurobiological functioning."[48]

McCroskey believes that communication apprehension, can be reduced by a variety of methods.[49] In the remainder of this chapter we provide a deeper understanding of communication apprehension and a variety of methods for reducing its effects.

---

extremities, flushed skin, nausea, trembling hands, quivering legs, or "butterflies" in the stomach are the body's response to the release of hormones such as adrenaline.[50]

Surveys have discovered that fear of snakes and fear of speaking in public are the top two common fears among North Americans, way ahead of fear of heights, anxieties about financial problems, and even fear of death.

> **" The human brain is a wonderful thing; it works from the moment you are born until the moment you get up to give a speech!"**[51]

Strategies for Becoming a Confident Communicator

Always remember that in most cases, your anxiety is invisible. We can't see your pounding heart, upset stomach, cold hands, or worried thoughts. Most of us think we display more anxiety than listeners report noticing. However, the fact that your anxiety is often invisible to others does not make it feel any less real to you. Fortunately, there are a number of strategies to reduce your anxiety and help you become a more confident communicator.

Prepare Although you may not be able to predict unexpected situations or anticipate the nature of everyday conversations, you can prepare for many of the communication situations you encounter. For instance, you can prepare for a job interview or performance appraisal, a group meeting or professional seminar, and a public speech or presentation. When you are prepared, you know a great deal about the ideas you wish to discuss, the others who will be involved, the context of the situation, the content and structure of your message, and how you will express yourself.

Relax, Rethink, Re-vision By learning to relax your body, you can reduce your level of communication apprehension. However, physical relaxation is only half the battle; you also need to change the way you think about communication.[52] When you have confident thoughts ("I know I can persuade this group to join the Animal Rescue League"), you begin to feel more confident. Three strategies can help you rethink your attitudes, visualize your message, and relax your body:

- **Cognitive restructuring** is a method for reducing anxiety by replacing negative, irrational thoughts with more realistic, positive self-talk. The next time you feel anxious, repeat any one of these positive statements: "My message is important" or "I am a well-prepared, skilled communicator," "I know more about

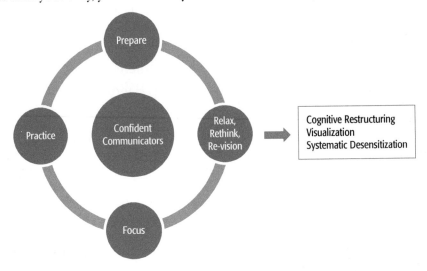

Cognitive Restructuring
Visualization
Systematic Desensitization

Sources of **COMMUNICATION APPREHENSION**

The process of managing communication apprehension begins with recognizing why you feel anxious when speaking to an individual, group, or audience. Although everyone has personal reasons for nervousness, researchers have identified some of the key fears that underlie communication apprehension.[53]

FEAR OF **FAILURE**

Many researchers claim that the fear of a negative evaluation is the number one cause of communication anxiety.[54] When you focus your thoughts on the possibility of failure, you are more likely to fail (self-fulfilling prophecy). Try to shift your focus to the positive feedback you see from others—a nod, a smile, or an alert look. When you sense that a listener likes you and your message, you may gain the extra confidence you need.

FEAR OF **OTHERS**

Do you get nervous when interacting with people who have more status or power, education or experience, fame or popularity? Fear of others can be heightened when talking to a powerful person, an influential group, or a large audience. Usually, this fear is based on an exaggerated feeling of being different from or inferior to others. If you don't know much about the people around you, you are more likely to feel apprehensive. Learning more about your listeners can decrease your anxiety. You may have more in common with them than you realize.

FEAR OF **BREAKING THE RULES**

"Three strikes and you're out" works in baseball, and "What goes up must come down" makes sense in physics, but the rules of communication are not as rigid and should not be treated as though they are enforceable laws. For example, novice speakers sometimes over rehearse to the point of sounding robotic because you fear saying "uh" or "um" in a presentation. Good communicators learn not to "sweat the small stuff" and that, sometimes, "rules" should be bent or broken.

FEAR OF **THE UNKNOWN**

Most people fear the unknown. Performing an unfamiliar or unexpected role can transform a usually confident person into a tangle of nerves. If you are attending an event as an audience member and suddenly are called on to introduce a guest to the audience, you can become very unsettled. Similarly, most people feel stressed when interviewing for a job in an office they've never been to and with a person they hardly know.

FEAR OF **THE SPOTLIGHT**

Although a little attention may be flattering, being the centre of attention makes many people nervous. Psychologist Peter Desberg puts it this way: "If you were performing as part of a choir, you'd probably feel much calmer than if you were singing a solo."[55] The more self-focused you are, the more nervous you become. This is especially true when giving a presentation to an audience. Staying focused on your purpose and message will help you to be less distracted by being in the "spotlight."

ZUMA Press, Inc./Alamy

Even successful and experienced rock stars like Sting practise meditation and other relaxation techniques to transform nervousness and anxiety into calmness and confidence.

Wolpe to reduce the anxiety associated with stressful situations.[56] You start with deep muscle relaxation. In this relaxed state, you then imagine yourself in a variety of communication contexts ranging from very comfortable to highly stressful. By working to remain relaxed while visualizing various situations, you gradually associate communication with relaxation rather than nervousness.

Focus One of the best ways to build confidence is to concentrate on your message. Anxiety only draws your attention away from your message and directs it to your fears. When you focus on getting your message across, you don't have time to think about how you might look or sound.

Practise The best way to become good at something is to practise, regardless of whether it's cooking, serving a tennis ball, or communicating. You can practise wording a request or expressing an emotion to another person, answering questions in an interview, stating your position at a meeting, or making a presentation to an audience.

In addition to enhancing your confidence, practice stimulates your brain in positive ways. As Daniel Goleman notes in *Social Intelligence*, "Simulating an act is, in the brain, the same as performing it."[57] Practising communication mentally and physically is as important as practising the piano or a gymnastics routine. At the very least, communicators should practise what they intend to say to others before they say it.

this than the audience does," or "I've done this before, so I'm not going to be as nervous as I've been in the past."

- **Visualization** is a powerful method for building confidence, and it allows you to imagine what it would be like to communicate successfully. Find a quiet place, relax, and imagine yourself walking into the room with confidence and energy. Think about the smiles you'll receive as you talk, the heads nodding in agreement, and the look of interest in the eyes of your listeners. By visualizing yourself communicating effectively, you are mentally practicing the skills you need to succeed while also building a positive self-image.

- **Systematic desensitization** is a relaxation and visualization technique developed by psychologist Joseph

Know Thy SELF

Work Toward Calm Through Systematic Desensitization

The following hierarchy of anxiety-producing communication situations[58] range from those least likely to, and most likely to produce stress. Assess your reactions to find out which of these situations produce the most anxiety; then, as you visualize each context, try to remain calm and relaxed.

1. You are talking to your best friend in person.

2. You are being introduced to a new acquaintance by your best friend.

3. You are talking to a small group of people, all of whom you know well.

4. You are at a social gathering where you don't know anyone but are expected to meet and talk to others.

5. You are asking someone to go to a party with you.

6. You are in a supervisory role talking to someone in a supervisory role about a problem at work or school.

7. You are presenting in front of a large group of people you do not know well.

8. You are going on a job interview.

9. You are appearing on a television show with other panelists to talk about a topic you know well.

10. You are appearing on a television show and debating another person.

Personal Report of Communication Apprehension

The Personal Report of Communication Apprehension (PRCA)[59] is composed of 24 statements. Indicate the degree to which each statement applies to you by marking whether you (1) strongly agree, (2) agree, (3) are undecided, (4) disagree, or (5) strongly disagree. Work quickly; record your first impression.

_____ 1. I dislike participating during group discussions.

_____ 2. Generally, I am comfortable while participating during group discussions.

_____ 3. I am tense and nervous while participating in group discussions.

_____ 4. I like to get involved during group discussions.

_____ 5. Engaging in a group discussion with new people makes me tense and nervous.

_____ 6. I am calm and relaxed while participating in a group discussion.

_____ 7. Generally, I am nervous when I have to participate in a meeting.

_____ 8. Usually, I am calm and relaxed while participating in a meeting.

_____ 9. I am very calm and relaxed when I am called on to express an opinion at a meeting.

_____ 10. I am afraid to express myself at meetings.

_____ 11. Communicating at meetings usually makes me feel uncomfortable.

_____ 12. I am very relaxed when answering questions at a meeting.

_____ 13. While participating in a conversation with a new acquaintance, I feel very nervous.

_____ 14. I have no fear of speaking up in conversations.

_____ 15. Ordinarily, I am very tense and nervous in conversations.

_____ 16. Ordinarily, I am very calm and relaxed in conversations.

_____ 17. While conversing with a new acquaintance, I feel very relaxed.

_____ 18. I'm afraid to speak up in conversations.

_____ 19. I have no fear of giving a speech.

_____ 20. Certain parts of my body feel very tense and rigid while I am giving a speech.

_____ 21. I feel relaxed while giving a speech.

_____ 22. My thoughts become confused and jumbled when I am giving a speech.

_____ 23. I face the prospect of giving a speech with confidence.

_____ 24. While giving a speech, I get so nervous I forget facts I really know.

Scoring: As you score each subcategory, begin with a score of 18 points. Then add or subtract from 18 based on the following instructions:

Subscores	Scoring Formula
Group discussions	18 + scores for items 2, 4, and 6; – scores for items 1, 3, and 5
Meetings	18 + scores for items 8, 9, and 12; – scores for items 7, 10, and 11
Interpersonal conversations	18 + scores for items 14, 16, and 17; – scores for items 13, 15, and 18
Public speaking	18 + scores for items 19, 21, and 23; – scores for items 20, 22, and 24

To obtain your total score for the PRCA, add your four subscores together. Your score should range between 24 points and 120 points. Then examine your score for each of the subcategories. If, for example, your score for the Group subcategory is 20 (which is higher than average), you are probably more anxious than most other people when participating in a group discussion.

Norms for PRCA

	Mean	Standard Deviation
Total score	65.5	15.3
Group	15.4	4.8
Meetings	16.4	4.8
Interpersonal	14.5	4.2
Public speaking	19.3	5.1

2.1
Who Are You?

How do your characteristics, perceptions, and confidence affect the way you communicate?

- Your self-concept is determined by your level of self-awareness, the influence of other people, past experiences, and your cultural perspectives.

- People-based factors (significant others, reference groups, your roles, and the acknowledgment you receive from others) are powerful factors of your self-concept.

- Beware of self-fulfilling prophecies, which are predictions that directly or indirectly true.

- You can minimize self-deception and trust your view of yourself by objectively assessing your behaviour compared to others in society.

2.2
Building Self-Esteem

What communication strategies and skills can improve your self-esteem?

- You can improve your self-esteem by practising self-acceptance, self-responsibility, self-assertiveness, personal integrity, and self-talk.

- Practise converting negative self-talk about yourself into positive self-talk.

2.3
Perception in Interpersonal Communication

How do your perceptions affect the way you select, organize, and interpret the world around you?

- Perception is the process through which you select, organize, and interpret sensory stimuli in the world around you.

- Your needs, interests, moods, wants, and memories largely determine which stimuli you will select.

- Four principles that influence how you organize information are the proximity, similarity, closure, and simplicity principles.

- Your past experiences, knowledge, expectations, attitudes, and relationships affect how you interpret and react to people and events.

- When you engage in perception-checking, apply perception-checking guidelines and skills linked to the seven key elements of effective communication for the specific situation.

2.4
Communicating with Confidence

How do you become a more confident communicator?

- *Communication apprehension* refers to an individual's level of fear or anxiety associated with real or anticipated communication with another person or persons.

- Sources of communication apprehension include fear of failure, fear of the unknown, fear of the spotlight, fear of others, and fear of breaking the supposed rules.

- Strategies for reducing your level of communication apprehension include (1) preparation, (2) physical relaxation, (3) cognitive restructuring, (4) visualization, (5) systematic desensitization, (6) focus, and (7) practise.

Shestakoff/Fotolia

TEST YOURKNOWLEDGE

2.1 How do your characteristics, perceptions, and confidence affect the way you communicate?

1 Most infants begin to recognize themselves in a mirror _____ months of age.
   a. by 6
   b. between 6 and 12
   c. between 12 and 18
   d. between 18 and 24
   e. after 24

2 If your parents or teachers tell you that you'll never become a doctor because you're not a good science student, you may not pursue this career goal. Which aspect of self-concept may be responsible for your decision?
   a. self-awareness
   b. self-monitoring
   c. self-assertiveness
   d. self-fulfilling prophecy
   e. self-disclosure

2.2 What communication strategies and skills can improve your self-esteem?

3 Which of the following techniques for improving self-esteem can help you stop blaming others for your failures?
   a. self-talk
   b. personal integrity
   c. self-assertiveness
   d. self-responsibility
   e. self-acceptance

4 As a member of the varsity team, Selena believes that she's a better soccer player than anyone on the intramural teams. What factor has influenced Selena about her self?
   a. reference groups
   b. significant others
   c. rewards
   d. personal memories
   e. actual performance

2.3 How do your perceptions affect the way you select, organize, and interpret the world around you?

5 Your textbook uses the example of eyewitness testimony to illustrate
   a. the power of self-concept.
   b. the inaccuracies in human perception.
   c. the role of selection in the perception process.
   d. the role of organization in the perception process.
   e. the role of interpretation in the perception process.

6 A mother sees blood on her daughter's sleeve and assumes that her daughter has been badly hurt in an accident. This is an example of
   a. the proximity principle.
   b. the similarity principle.
   c. the closure principle.
   d. the simplicity principle.
   e. the complexity principle.

7 Which guiding principle helps you check your perceptions?
   a. Know Thy Self.
   b. Connect with Others.
   c. Determine Your Purpose.
   d. Select Appropriate Content.
   e. all of the above

8 Neuroscientists have discovered that our brains link our perceptions closely to our senses. Examples of this include
   a. viewing others as caring and generous when you are holding a hot cup of coffee.
   b. blue strawberries taste strange.

   c. red water can trick some wine experts so that they believe they are drinking wine.
   d. a, b and c are correct.
   e. Only a and b are correct.

2.4 How do you become a more confident communicator?

9 Which communication scholar has done the most research on communication apprehension?
   a. Hermann Rorschach
   b. Daniel Goleman
   c. James McCroskey
   d. Min-Sun Kim
   e. Leon Festinger

10 Which strategy for reducing your level of communication apprehension involves replacing negative, irrational thoughts with more realistic, positive self-talk?
   a. Be prepared.
   b. Use cognitive restructuring.
   c. Imagine what it would be like to experience an entire communication act successfully.
   d. Use systematic desensitization.
   e. Focus on your message and practice that message.

Answers found on page 330.

Key Terms

Closure principle	**Reference groups**	**Self-responsibility**
Cognitive restructuring	**Rewards**	**Self-talk**
Communication	**Role**	**Significant others**
apprehension	**Self-acceptance**	**Similarity principle**
Figure–ground	**Self-appraisals**	**Simplicity principle**
principle	**Self-awareness**	**Social comparison**
Perception	**Self-concept**	**Systematic**
Perception checking	**Self-esteem**	**desensitization**
Personal integrity	**Self-fulfilling prophecy**	**Visualization**
Proximity principle	**Self-monitoring**	

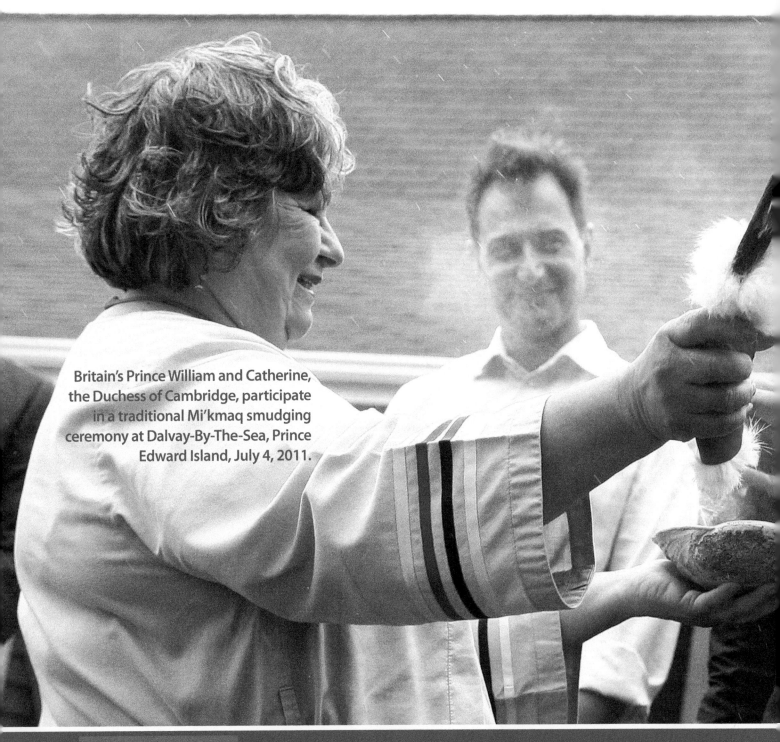

Britain's Prince William and Catherine, the Duchess of Cambridge, participate in a traditional Mi'kmaq smudging ceremony at Dalvay-By-The-Sea, Prince Edward Island, July 4, 2011.

Adapting to Canada's
CHANGING FACES

Not that many years ago, a white Canadian businessman could predict the gender, race, average age, and even religion of his neighbours, friends, and colleagues: They would look like him, speak like him, and share many of the same attitudes, beliefs, and values. Today, corporations are global communities in which a 35-year-old woman from India might be a CEO, a salesperson, an attorney, or a building engineer.

In the mid 1950s in Dresden, Ontario, black citizens were refused service in restaurants even though Canada had specific laws and regulations prohibiting this behaviour.[1] Interracial couples who married could be jailed for "mixing races." Same-sex couples hid—and in some cases, still hide—the fact that they are more than "just friends" in order to be welcomed by their families and to avoid verbal and physical harassment. But, in 2009, the son of an African immigrant and a white American woman became the forty-fourth president of the United States. And just as the laws and attitudes against interracial marriage took many years to change,[2] the laws and attitudes about same-sex marriages are also slowly changing. Same-sex couples have been openly and legally married in Canada since 2005.[3] The "other" we thought we knew now defies our expectations. Now, more than ever, we must understand, respect, and adapt to the many others we encounter every day.

Paul Darrow/Reuters/Corbis

3.1

Our Faces

How has the "changing face" of Canada affected your daily interactions?

msphoto/Fotolia

WONG SZE FEI/Fotolia

Canada's population is changing and growing. Just twenty years ago only one in five Canadian workers were born in another country. It is projected that by 2031, this will rise to one in three workers. In 1996, one in ten Canadian workers were from a visible minority group and it is expected that by 2031 this figure will most likely be one in three. [4]

Defining Culture

When some people hear the phrase *cultural diversity*, they think about skin colour and New Canadians. Words such as *nationality*, *race*, and *ethnicity* are often used synonymously with the term *culture*. However, culture comprises much more than a country of origin, race, or ancestral heritage. In Chapter 1, we defined *culture* as "a

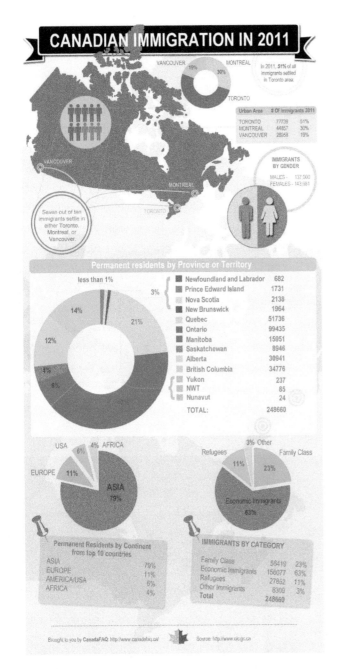

CANADIAN IMMIGRATION IN 2011

VANCOUVER 19% MONTREAL 30%

In 2011, **51%** of all immigrants settled in Toronto area.

TORONTO

Urban Area	# Of Immigrants 2011	
TORONTO	77739	51%
MONTREAL	44857	30%
VANCOUVER	28958	19%

IMMIGRANTS BY GENDER

MALES - 137,000
FEMALES - 143,081

Seven out of ten immigrants settle in either Toronto, Montreal, or Vancouver.

Permanent residents by Province or Territory

less than 1%

3%

14%

21%

12%

4%

6%

◼ Newfoundland and Labrador	682
◼ Prince Edward Island	1731
◼ Nova Scotia	2138
◼ New Brunswick	1964
◼ Quebec	51736
◼ Ontario	99435
◼ Manitoba	15951
◼ Saskatchewan	8946
◼ Alberta	30941
◼ British Columbia	34776
◼ Yukon	237
◼ NWT	85
◼ Nunavut	24
	TOTAL:	248660

USA 6% 4% AFRICA

EUROPE 11%

ASIA 79%

3% Other

Refugees 11% Family Class 23%

Economic Immigrants 63%

Permanent Residents by Continent from top 10 countries

ASIA	79%
EUROPE	11%
AMERICA/USA	6%
AFRICA	4%

IMMIGRANTS BY CATEGORY

Family Class	56419	23%
Economic Immigrants	156077	63%
Refugees	27852	11%
Other Immigrants	8309	3%
Total	248660	

Brought to you by **CanadaFAQ** http://www.canadafaq.ca/   Source: http://www.cic.gc.ca

Gabriel Blaj/Fotolia

learned set of shared interpretations about beliefs, values, and norms which affect the behaviours of a relatively large group of people."[5]

Within most cultures, there are also groups of people—members of **co-cultures**—who coexist within the mainstream society yet remain connected to one another through their cultural heritage.[6] In Canada, Aboriginal peoples are members of co-cultures, as are African Canadians, Hispanic/Latino Canadians, Asian Canadians, Arab Canadians, Irish Canadians, and members of large and small religious groups. Given our broad definition of culture, an Alberta rancher and a Montreal professor can have very different cultural perspectives, as would a native Egyptian, a Brazilian, an Indonesian, and a Mississauga Aboriginal Canadian.

Communication Exercise

In small groups, start with the word *culture*; then each member should decide on two words that he or she associates with the word *culture*. From the two words, add four more associations, all the way until the web has eight words. From the eight words, choose only four words, from the fours words, choose only two words, and then choose one word. At the end, a single word closes the web.[7]

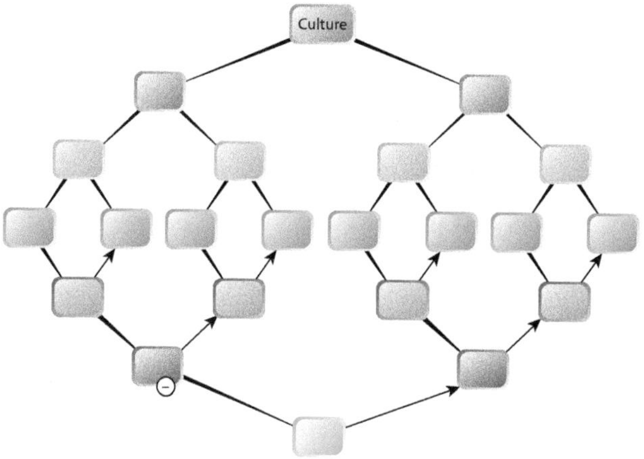

1. How does your perception of the word *culture* lead you to more and different meanings?
2. Does the single word you end with effectively describe culture? Why or why not?
3. When you have completed the discussion, watch this YouTube video and compare your group's ideas with those expressed in the video: www.youtube.com/watch?v=4484oUqLYYQ.

Know Thy SELF

What Do *You* Believe Is Culturally "Normal"?

Respond to each of the following items by putting a check mark in the column that indicates your evaluation of behaviours or customs on a continuum from "quite ordinary" to "quite strange."

Behaviours	Quite Ordinary	Ordinary	Neutral	Strange	Quite Strange
1. A man wearing a skirt in public					
2. A woman breast-feeding her child in public					
3. Talking with a person who does not look you in the eye					
4. A woman refusing to shake hands with a man					
5. A family taking a communal bath					
6. A man who stands so close you can smell his breath					
7. People who will not eat the food in your home					

Review your ratings. All seven behaviours are customary *and* normal in another culture or country. What are some of *your* culture's ordinary behaviours, and why might others consider them unusual or strange?[8]

3.2 Barriers to Understanding Each Other

How do ethnocentrism, stereotyping, prejudice, discrimination, and racism affect communication?

Learning to communicate effectively in the global village that characterizes our lives in the twenty-first century can be a significant challenge. In order to become a more effective and ethical communicator in a multicultural nation and world, you must recognize and overcome five obstacles that can inhibit your understanding of others: ethnocentrism, stereotyping, prejudice, discrimination, and racism.

Ethnocentrism

Ethnocentrism is the mistaken belief that your culture is a superior culture with special rights and privileges that are or should be denied to others.

Ethnocentric communicators offend others when they imply that they come from a superior culture with superior values. As an ethical and culturally sensitive communicator, you should examine your own ethnocentric beliefs.

BARRIERS
to Understanding Others

Ethnocentrism
Stereotyping
Prejudice
Discrimination
Racism

Begin by investigating how your culture and your culture-based perspectives may differ from others. By recognizing the ethnocentric beliefs that you hold, you will have the opportunity to change and become more culturally sensitive and inclusive. Then complete the GENE (Generalized Ethnocentrism) Scale at the end of this chapter to assess your level of ethnocentrism.

Stereotyping

Stereotypes are generalizations about a group of people that oversimplify the group's characteristics. When we stereotype others, we rely on exaggerated beliefs to make judgments about an entire group of people. Unfortunately, stereotyping usually attributes negative traits to all group members when, in reality, only a few people may possess those traits.[9] For example, believing that all Asian students are only interested in their studies may lead friends and teachers to hold unrealistic expectations and place undue pressure on students of Asian descent. Comments such as "Athletes are poor students," "Old people are boring," and "Native Indians are lazy" express stereotypical sentiments.

In addition to negative stereotypes, we may hold positive ones. Comments such as "Women are more compassionate than men" and "Gay men dress with style" may be viewed as a compliment but are actually all-inclusive generalizations. Although it may appear that positive stereotypes are not harmful, they can lead to unfair judgments and prevent you from seeing people's individual strengths and characteristics.

Prejudice

Stereotypes lead to **prejudices**: positive or negative attitudes about an individual or cultural group based on little or no direct experience with

Communication
Exercise

Canadian Rick Mercer discusses Canadian stereotypes with George Stroumboulopoulos in this YouTube video

www.youtube.com/watch?v=Z3EvS467JK0

After viewing the video, answer this question: "What stereotypes do you believe that may not be true?"

The Characteristics of PREJUDICE

- Biased beliefs about group members that are not based on direct experience and firsthand knowledge[10]
- Irrational feelings of dislike and even hatred for a group
- A willingness to behave in negative and unjust ways toward an individual or members of a group

COMMUNICATION IN *ACTION*

How Does Language Shape Stereotypes?

Intercultural communication scholars Stella Ting-Toomey and Leeva C. Chung claim that the nature of our language creates many stereotypes. Paired words, for example, encourage either/or thinking: *straight* or *gay*, *us* or *them*, *female* or *male*, *black* or *white*, *rich* or *poor*, *old* or *young*. Such either/or perceptions lead us to interpret the social world as good or bad, normal or abnormal, and right or wrong. When you think in either/or terms, you may overlook the fact that a person may not be a good *or* bad athlete, but like most of us, better at some sports than at others.[11]

Highlighting a cultural detail about someone while sharing a personal story can also contribute to stereotyping. Such details are usually meaningless and, rather than strengthening a point, promote a biased view, as in the following example:

Corrine: You know I have such a bad sense of direction, but I must look like I know where I'm going because people are always coming up to me to ask for directions. Last week, I was shopping in downtown Winnipeg and this young—(Corrine pauses at this point to lean in to her friend, raise her hand up to partially cover her mouth, and whisper) *black* guy came up to me and asked for directions to Powell's Books.

Clearly, the point of Corrine's story is that despite her poor sense of direction, people often ask her for directions. So, why did Corrine mention the race of the man who approached her? And why announce his race in such hushed tones? The unnecessary details and the manner in which Corrine expresses those details perpetuate stereotypes. Pay careful attention to your word choices—what you say, why you say it, and the way you say it.

Halifax Chronicle-Herald-Christian Laforce/THE CANADIAN PRESS

In 1946, Viola Desmond was charged with sitting in the "whites only" section of a theatre near Halifax, Nova Scotia.

STOP&THINK

Is There Such a Thing as Race?

According to many anthropologists, biologists, geneticists, and ethicists, race is "a social construct, not a scientific classification," and a "biologically meaningless" concept.[12] They emphasize that 99.9 percent of DNA sequences are common to all humans.[13] Extensive research clearly establishes that pure races never existed and that all humans belong to the same species, *Homo sapiens*, which originated in Africa.

Before the human genome was decoded, most systems of race classification were based on characteristics such as skin colour. The genetic definition of race, however, has absolutely nothing to do with any physical or behavioural characteristics.[14]

So what does all of this mean? Is there such a thing as race? The word *race* certainly has meaning and is very real to all of us. Those who believe that one race (depending on their ethnicity or background) is superior to another have an erroneous, misguided, or biased view of race. Rather, **race** should be viewed as a socially constructed concept *and* understood as the outcome of ancient population shifts that left their mark in our genes. When race is viewed in social and genetic contexts, it becomes a neutral human characteristic.

Jenner/Fotolia

How have human genome research and biological studies affected beliefs about race?

ETHICAL COMMUNICATION

Acknowledge Unconscious Biases

The National Communication Association's *Credo for Ethical Communication* includes the following principle: "We condemn communication that degrades individuals and humanity through distortion, intimidation, coercion, and violence, and through the expression of intolerance and hatred."[15] Practising this principle, however, is often more difficult than it seems. Despite claims of "I'm not prejudiced," most of us have positive and negative attitudes about cultural groups based on little or no direct experience with that group.

Two Harvard researchers, Mahzarin Banaji and Brian Nosek, have developed an implicit association test you can take for free on Harvard's website at http://implicit.harvard.edu. The results indicate that the majority of Americans, including people of colour and other minorities, show a variety of biases they believe they do *not* have. Banaji and Nosek recommend that when it comes to prejudice, it is less important how biased you are and more important how willing you are to confront your unconscious thoughts about others. When you acknowledge your unconscious biases, you can take steps to confront them.[16]

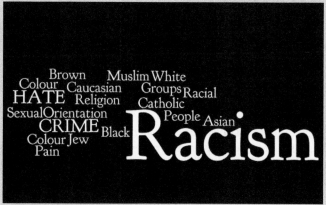

that person or group. The word *prejudice* has two parts: *pre*, meaning "before," and *judice*, as in "judge." When you believe or express a prejudice, you are making a judgment about someone before you get to know that person and learn whether your opinions and feelings are justified. Although prejudices might be viewed as positive—"He must be brilliant if he went to the University of Toronto"—they are still prejudicial. Statements such as "I don't want a disabled person working on our group project" or "He's too old to understand

barriers to understanding each other

45

cutting-edge technology" are examples of prejudice based on stereotypes.

Discrimination

Discrimination is how we act out and express prejudice. When we discriminate, we exclude groups of people from opportunities granted to others: employment, promotion, housing, political expression, equal rights, and access to educational, recreational, and social institutions.

Sadly, discrimination comes in many forms: discrimination against racial, ethnic, religious, and gender groups; discrimination based on sexual orientation, disability, age, and physical appearance; and discrimination against people from different social classes and political ideologies.

Racism

Racism emerges from ethnocentrism, stereotyping, prejudice, and discrimination. Racist people assume that a person with a certain inherited characteristic (often something superficial such as skin colour) also has negative characteristics and abilities. Racists also believe in the superiority of their own race above all others. In his book *Privilege, Power, and Difference*, Allan Johnson points out that racism is built into the system that

people live and work in. It goes beyond the personal and becomes a pattern of privilege and oppression within a society.[17]

Racism leads to the abuse of power. When racists acquire power, they may dominate, restrain, mistreat, and harm people of other races. In its cruelest form, racism results in the torture, humiliation, and extermination of others— for example, the internment of Japanese Canadians in WWII, the brutality of the Nazis against Jews and other ethnic minorities in Europe, and the genocide in Rwanda in which hundreds of thousands of Tutsi people were murdered by Hutu militia groups and gangs.

Extreme racism can lead and has led to a rise of hate crimes and hate groups. For example, in February 2010, in a small town in Nova Scotia, Canadians witnessed the impact of racist behaviour. Shayne Howe and his partner, Michelle Lyon, live in a small town where Shayne

> **Racism** is an attitude, a collection of stereotypes, a bad intention, a desire or need to discriminate or do harm, a form of hatred.
>
> —Allan Johnson, *Privilege, Power, and Difference*[18]

is the only black resident. The couple became victims of extreme racism when they awoke to find a 2-metre-high burning cross on their front lawn.[19] James W. von Brunn was a white supremacist who hosted a racist, anti-Semitic website and wrote a book entitled *Kill the Best Gentiles*, alleging a Jewish "conspiracy to destroy the white gene pool."[20] And in 2011, Norway's Anders Breivik justified his brutal massacre of 76 people in an online manifesto that described his hatred for Muslims and multiculturalism.[21]

In all of these examples, the poisonous hatred of "others" reflects the views of many hate groups. "Hate group membership," writes Judith Warner, of *The New York Times*, "has been expanding steadily over the course of the past decade— fuelled largely by anti-immigrant sentiment. But after President Barack Obama's election, it spiked. The day after the election, the computer servers of two major white supremacist groups crashed, because their traffic went through the roof."[22]

Canadian Perspectives[23]

65% believe minorities are treated equally in the workplace

46% say racism is increasing and 45% say racism is decreasing

38% say they observed a racist incident within the last year

Canadian views on racism in Canada

3.3

Understanding Cultural Diversity

Why is it so important to understand cultural diversity?

Each one of us has an ethnicity, gender, age, religious belief (including atheism), socio-economic position, sexual orientation, and abilities. We also live in, or come from a certain region or country. Consider the following examples:

- a sixth-generation, female, Lutheran teacher whose family still lives in the same midwestern town
- a 55-year-old Jewish male scientist living in Montreal whose family emigrated from Russia

- an Islamic, African Canadian woman working as a researcher for the federal government in Montreal, Quebec.

All these characteristics contribute to our **social identity**: our self-concept as derived from the social categories to which we see ourselves belonging.[24] Many of us, however, although we may identify ourselves as Irish, Korean,

Ethiopian, or Sioux, have lost touch with our family history and culture.

Understanding *Your* Culture

Culture affects your life in both obvious and subtle ways. The first step in understanding others is to understand your own culture. You derive a significant part of your social identity from the cultural groups to which you belong as well as the groups to which you do *not* belong: "I know who I am and that I am *not* you." This is a thoroughly natural feeling. However, we often divide our world into distinct and very opposite social groups (men and women, rich and poor, black and white, young and old, Canadian and foreign) in a way that sets us in opposition to others. A more constructive approach is to explore your own social identity and share it with people to create understanding and appreciation for our heritage.

For example, many white people don't think of their behaviour as characteristic of their culture. Because whiteness is a historical norm in some countries, many find it difficult to classify it as a culture. Yet as Dr. Rita Hardiman wrote,

> Like fish, whose environment is water, we are surrounded by Whiteness and it is easy to think that what we

20th Century Fox/Everett Collection

In *Avatar*, ex-Marine Jake Sully is transformed from a human into a Na'vi cat person. After infiltrating the cat people to gather intelligence for a military invasion, he falls in love with a cat woman. A "race traitor" to his fellow humans, Sully leads the cat people to victory over the human invaders. Are the Na'vi just blue versions of oppressed people of colour, or do they represent something more significant?

Know Thy SELF

Questions of Faith

According to Stephen Prothero, professor of religion at Boston University, many of us are illiterate about our own and others' religions. He defines **religious literacy** as "the ability to understand and use the religious terms, symbols, images, beliefs, practices, scripture, heroes, themes, and stories that are employed in American public life."[25] Test your knowledge about a few of the world's major religions by selecting "True," "False," or "I Don't Know" (?) for each of the items below:[26]

T	F	?	1.	Muslims believe in Islam and the Islamic way of life.
T	F	?	2.	Judaism is an older religion than Buddhism.
T	F	?	3.	Islam is a monotheistic religion (belief in one God) just like Christianity and Judaism.
T	F	?	4.	A Christian Scientist believes that disease is a delusion of the carnal mind that can be cured by prayer.
T	F	?	5.	Jews fast during Yom Kippur; Muslims fast during Ramadan.
T	F	?	6.	Jesus Christ was Jewish.
T	F	?	7.	Roman Catholics throughout the world outnumber all other Christians combined.
T	F	?	8.	Sunni Muslims compose about 90 percent of all adherents to Islam.
T	F	?	9.	Hindus believe in the idea of reincarnation.
T	F	?	10.	The Ten Commandments form the basis of Jewish religious laws.
T	F	?	11.	Mormonism is a Christian faith founded in the United States.[27]
T	F	?	12.	The Protestant reformer Martin Luther labelled the beliefs of Muslims, Jews, and Roman Catholics as false.
T	F	?	13.	One-third of the world's population is Christian.
T	F	?	14.	One-fifth of the world's population is Muslim.
T	F	?	15.	Hinduism is the oldest of the world's major religions, dating back more than 3,000 years.

Answers: All of the statements are true.

understanding cultural diversity

experience is reality rather than recognizing it as the particular culture of a particular group. And like fish who are not aware of water until they are out of it, White people sometimes become aware of their culture only when they get to know, or interact with, the cultures of people of color.[28]

Understanding *Other* Cultures

If you believe you can live a life in which you avoid people from other cultures, you are fooling yourself.

Religion is also a very important aspect of a culture, but what some people forget is that in many countries and for many groups, the religion *is* the culture, such as Buddhism in Tibet and Islam in Iran. Occasionally, when religious groups attempt to practise their culture in a secular country, they encounter intolerance. In France, for example, religious attire, including head-scarves for Muslim girls, skullcaps for Jewish boys, and crosses for Christian children, has been banned from public high schools.[29] Regardless of your individual religious beliefs, "you must remember that people feel strongly about their religion, and that differences between religious beliefs and practices do matter."[30]

You live in a pluralistic society; the more knowledge you gain about the people around you and the more you learn to respect others, the better you will be able to communicate. On a practical level, your willingness and ability to work in a diverse environment will likely increase your opportunities for success in any career choice you make.

3.4

The Dimensions of Culture

What cultural dimensions affect the way you communicate with others?

We owe a great deal to social psychologist Geert H. Hofstede and anthropologist Edward T. Hall for identifying several important dimensions of culture. Hofstede's ground-breaking research on cultural characteristics has transformed our

5 DIMENSIONS OF CULTURE

1 Individualism/Collectivism

2 Power Distance

3 Masculine/Feminine Values

4 High/Low Context

5 Monochronic/Polychronic Time

Photosindia/Getty Images

Goodluz/Fotolia

understanding of others. He defines **intercultural dimension** as "an aspect of a culture that can be measured relative to other cultures."[31] His work on cultural variability identifies several dimensions that characterize cultural groups. Here we look at three of those dimensions—individualism/collectivism, power distance, and masculine/feminine values—because they have received more research attention and support than the others.

Communication

Exercise

To learn more about dimensions of culture, conduct a Web search for intercultural dimensions or Geert Hofstede.

Hall adds a fourth and fifth dimension: high-context/low-context cultures and monochronic/polychronic time.

Individualism/Collectivism

Individualism/collectivism may be the most important factor distinguishing one culture from another.[32] According to Hofstede, and many contemporary researchers, most North Americans traditionally value **individualism** while **collectivism**, (interdependence) is valued by 70 percent of the world's population.[33] For instance, once

INDIVIDUALISTIC
Characteristics[34]

- "I" is important.
- Independence is worth pursuing.
- Personal achievement should be rewarded.
- Individual uniqueness is valued.

COLLECTIVIST
Characteristics[35]

- "We" is important.
- The needs, beliefs, and goals of the "in-group" (e.g., family, community members) are emphasized above those of the individual.
- Achievements that benefit and foster cooperation in the group should be rewarded.
- Individual uniqueness is not considered important.

MOST **INDIVIDUALISTIC** COUNTRIES

1. United States
2. Australia
3. Great Britain
*4/5. Canada/ The Netherlands

MOST **COLLECTIVIST** COUNTRIES

1. Guatemala
2. Ecuador
3. Panama
4. Venezuela
5. Colombia

*Tied rankings.

Figure 3.1 Individualism and Collectivism

HIGHEST **POWER- DISTANCE** COUNTRIES

1. Malaysia
*2/3. Guatemala Panama
4. Philippines
*5/6. Mexico/Venezuela

LOWEST **POWER- DISTANCE** COUNTRIES

1. Austria
2. Israel
3. Denmark
4. New Zealand
5. Ireland

*Tied rankings.

Figure 3.2 Power Distance

children have completed high school or higher education in the United States, many parents encourage them to strike out on their own—to pursue a career and find their own place to live. However, in many Asian countries, parents encourage their children to stay at home and work until they marry and, once they do, to work for the benefit of the immediate *and* extended family. Figure 3.1 ranks the top countries in each category.[36]

Despite the fact that Canada ranks in the top five in terms of individualism, not all Canadians are individualistic. In fact, many of our diverse co-cultures have the characteristics of collectivist societies. The focus on individual achievement and personal rewards in segments of Canada can make interaction with people from collectivist cultures and co-cultures harder to understand. For some of us, a person's communication style and behaviour may be viewed as arrogant, antagonistic, power hungry, ruthless, and impatient. Interestingly, as poor nations gain wealth, they begin to shift toward greater individualism.[37]

Power Distance

Is it easy to make a personal appointment with the president of your college or university? Can you simply walk into your boss's office, or do you have to navigate your way through an army of secretaries and administrative assistants? Does our society truly believe in the sentiments expressed in

the Canadian Charter of Rights that all people are created equal? These are the questions addressed in Hofstede's power distance dimension. **Power distance** refers to the physical and psychological distance between those who have power and those who do not in relationships, institutions, and organizations. It also represents "the extent to which the less powerful person in society accepts inequality in power and considers it normal."[38]

In cultures with **high power distance**, individuals accept differences in power as normal. It is accepted that all people are *not* created equal. In such cultures, the privileged have much more power and use it to guide or control the lives of people with less power. In a high-power-distance culture, you accept and do not challenge authority. Parents have total control over their children. Husbands may have total control over their wives. And government officials, corporate officers, and religious authorities dictate rules of behavior and have the power to ensure compliance.

In cultures with **low power distance**, power distinctions are minimized: supervisors work with subordinates, professors work with students, elected officials work with constituents. Figure 3.2 ranks the top countries in each category of this dimension. Despite the fact that the United States claims to be the greatest democracy on earth and an equal opportunity society, it is sixteenth on the list after low-power-distance countries such as Finland, Switzerland, Great Britain, Germany, Costa Rica, Australia, the Netherlands, and Canada.[39]

Power distance has enormous implications for communication. For example, in Australia (a low-power-distance country), students and professors are often on a first-name basis, and lively class discussions are the norm. However, in Malaysia (a high-power-distance country), students show up and are seated *before* class begins; almost no one comes late. Students are polite and appreciative but rarely challenge a professor's claims. In a high-power-distance culture, you do not openly disagree with teachers, elders, bosses, law enforcement officials, or government agents.

If you compare Figures 3.1 and 3.2, you will notice a strong correlation between collectivism and high power distance and between individualism and low power distance. If you are individualistic and strongly encouraged to express your own opinion, you are more willing to challenge authority. If, on the other hand, your culture is collectivist and your personal opinion is subordinate to the welfare of others, you are less likely to challenge the collective authority of your family, your employer, or your government.

Masculine/Feminine Values

Hofstede uses the terms *masculine* and *feminine* to describe whether masculine or feminine traits are *valued* by a culture. The terms are used to describe a societal perspective rather than individuals.

In **masculine societies**, men are supposed to be assertive, tough, and focused on material success, whereas women are supposed to be more modest, tender, and concerned with the quality of life. In **feminine societies**, gender roles overlap: Both men and women are supposed to be modest, tender, and concerned with the quality of life.[40] Figure 3.3 ranks countries in terms of masculine/feminine values.[41]

Hofstede ranks Canada as slightly more masculine in terms of values but still less masculine than Australia, New Zealand, and Greece. In masculine societies, personal success, competition, assertiveness, and strength are admired. Unselfishness and nurturing may be seen as weaknesses or feminine. Although women have come a long way from the rigid roles of past centuries, they have miles to go before they achieve genuine equality in cultures with high masculine values.

High/Low Context

In Chapter 1, we defined *context* as the psychosocial, logistical, and interactional environment in which communication occurs. Edward T. Hall sees context as the information that surrounds an event, inextricably bound up with the meaning of the event. He claims that a message's context—in and of itself—may hold more meaning than the actual words in a message.[42] Like Hofstede's dimensions, we can place cultures on a continuum from high context to low context.

In a **high-context culture**, very little meaning is expressed through words. In contrast, gestures, silence, and facial expressions, as well as the relationships among communicators, have meaning. In high-context cultures, meaning can also be conveyed through status (age, gender, education, family background, title, and affiliations) and through an individual's informal network of friends and associates.

In a **low-context culture**, meaning is expressed primarily through language. As members of a low-context culture, people in North America tend to speak more, speak more loudly, and speak more rapidly than a person from a high-context culture. Americans and Canadians "speak up," "spell it out," "just say no," and "speak our mind." Figure 3.4 contrasts the characteristics of high- and low-context cultures.[43]

High-context communication usually occurs in collectivist cultures in which members share similar attitudes, beliefs, and values. As a result, spoken communication can be indirect, implied, or vague because everyone *gets* the meaning by understanding the context, the person's nonverbal behaviour, and the significance of the communicator's status.

Visiting dignitaries congratulate newlyweds at an Islamic mosque. How does Secretary Clinton demonstrate her understanding and respect for this country and its people's values?

COUNTRIES WITH THE HIGHEST
MASCULINE VALUES

1. Japan
*2/3. Austria / Venezuela
*4/5. Italy / Switzerland

COUNTRIES WITH THE HIGHEST
FEMININE VALUES

1. Sweden
2. Norway
3. The Netherlands
4. Denmark
*5/6. Costa Rica / Yugoslavia (now the republics of Serbia and Montenegro)

*Tied rankings.

Figure 3.3 Masculine and Feminine Values

Muted Group Theory

Cheris Kramarae's **muted group theory** observes that powerful, wealthy groups at the top of a society determine who will communicate and be listened to. For this reason, women, the poor, and people of colour may have trouble participating and being heard.[44] The following three assumptions in muted group theory explain how women's voices are subdued or silenced in many cultures:

1 Women perceive the world differently than men because of tradi-

tional divisions of labour. Examples: homemaker versus breadwinner, nurses versus doctors.

2 Women's freedom of expression is limited by men's dominance in relationships and institutions. Examples: Women in Canada only gained the right to vote in federal elections in 1919. The "glass ceiling" still prevents women from achieving professional goals.

3 Women must transform their thinking and behaviour to participate fully in society. Example: Women have become politically active and even militant to make sure that sexual harassment, date and marital rape, and spousal abuse are seen as serious crimes rather than practices that may be excused or tolerated.

Although muted group theory focuses on women, its assumptions apply to many groups. The voices of people of colour, recent immigrants, the disabled, and the poor are also muted.

Kapil Sethi/AP Photos

Figure 3.4 Characteristics and Examples of High- and Low-Context Cultures

HIGH-CONTEXT CULTURES

Examples
Chinese
Japanese
South Korean
Native American
African American
Mexican American
and Latino

Characteristics
Implicit meaning
Nonverbal communication
Reserved reactions
Strong in-group bonds
High level of commitment
Time open and flexible

LOW-CONTEXT CULTURES

Characteristics
Explicit meaning
Verbal communication
Reactions on the surface
Flexible group memberships
Low level of commitment
Time highly organized

Examples
German
Swiss
White American
Scandinavian
Canadian

j.woothisak/Shutterstock

Thomas Stankiewicz/LOOK Die Bildagentur der Fotografen GmbH/Alamy

the dimensions of culture

Shirley van der Veur, a former Peace Corps volunteer and now a university professor, relates the following illustration of this concept: A scholar from Kenya was invited to dinner at an American colleague's home. Even though he ate ravenously, not leaving a morsel of food on his plate, the American hosts were not convinced that he liked his dinner because he had not *said* so. In Kenya, if his hosts saw him appreciatively eating his meal, they would know that he was enjoying it without necessarily needing him to express his pleasure verbally.[45]

Monochronic/Polychronic Time

In most parts of northern Europe and North America, time is a very valuable commodity. As a result, we fill our days and nights with multiple commitments and live a fast-paced life. However, the pace of life in India, Kenya, and Argentina, for example, is driven less by a need to "get things done" than by

a sense of participation in events that create their own rhythm.[46]

Edward T. Hall classifies time as a form of communication and claims that cultures treat time in one of two ways: as monochronic or polychronic.[47] In **monochronic time**, or M-time, events are scheduled as separate items—one thing at a time. M-time people like to concentrate on one job before moving to another and may become irritated when someone in a meeting brings up a personal topic unrelated to the purpose of the meeting.

In **polychronic time**, or P-time, schedules are not as important and are frequently broken. People in polychronic cultures are not slaves to time and are easily distracted and tolerant of interruptions. P-time people are frequently late for appointments or may not show up at all.[48] If you are a P-time person, you probably find it stimulating to think about several different problems at the same time and feel comfortable

holding two or three conversations simultaneously.

Hall maintains that these two time orientations are incompatible. When monochronic and polychronic people interact, the results can be frustrating. Hall notes that monochronic North Americans become distressed by how polychronic people treat appointments. Being on time in some countries simply doesn't have the same significance as it does in Canada. For P-time people, schedules and commitments, particularly plans for the future, are not firm, and even important plans may change right up to the last minute.[49]

If you are an M-time person, you can try to modify and relax your obsession with time and scheduling. If you are a P-time person, you can do your best to respect and adapt to a monochronic person's need for careful scheduling and promptness. Figure 3.5 depicts several differences between monochronic and polychronic perspectives and cultures.

Figure 3.5 Monochronic and Polychronic Time: Characteristics and Cultures

MONOCHRONIC CULTURES

Examples

German
Austrian
Swiss
White American and Canadian

Characteristics

Do one thing at a time
Concentrate on the job
Take all time commitments (deadlines, schedules) seriously
Adhere to plans
Emphasize promptness
Engage in short-term relationships

POLYCHRONIC CULTURES

Characteristics

Do many things at once
Are easily distracted
Take time commitments less seriously
Often change plans
Base promptness on the importance of a relationship
Build lifetime relationships

Examples

Latin American
Arab
African
African American

Pressmaster/Shutterstock

AfriPics.com/Alamy

Intercultural Communication Strategies

What strategies can help you understand, respect, and effectively communicate with "others"?

In our increasingly global world, simply learning about people from different cultures is not enough; instead we must find ways to embrace our differences and similarities and build the skills and attitudes needed to effectively communicate within and beyond our own cultural communities.

Be Mindful

Mindfulness is both a very old and a very new concept. The ancient concept can be traced back to the first millennium B.C.E. to the foothills of the Himalayas, when it is believed that Buddha attained enlightenment through mindfulness.[50] **Mindfulness** involves being fully aware of the present moment without making hasty judgments.

Before explaining mindfulness in more detail, let's take a look at its opposite: mind*less*ness. **Mindlessness** occurs when you allow rigid categories and false distinctions to become habits of thought and behaviour.[51] For example, you approach a sales counter and say, "Excuse me" to the salesperson. Why did you say that? Did you really mean to beg his or her pardon, or were you apologizing for interrupting someone who should have been paying more attention to you in the first place? All of us engage in some mindless behaviour without any serious consequences. But when mindlessness occurs in a sensitive situation, the results can be detrimental to a relationship or damaging to an important project. For example, after the 9/11 tragedy, many patriotic Muslim Americans suffered mindless stereotyping, prejudice, and discrimination as a result of a larger ignorance about the Islamic faith and culture. If you are mindless, you are trapped in an inflexible, biased world in which your religion is always right and good; people from other cultures are inferior and untrustworthy; boys will always be boys, and girls will always be girls; and change is a terrible and scary thing.[52]

Mind*ful*ness, in contrast, requires paying attention to how you and another person communicate. It asks you to observe what is happening as it happens, without forming opinions or taking sides as you learn more about someone else.[53] When you are mindful, you recognize stereotypical thinking and prejudices and try to overcome them. Mindfulness gives you the freedom and motivation to understand, respect, and adapt to others.

Be Receptive to New Information Mindful communicators learn more about others and their cultures by being open to new information. Too often, we dismiss another person's belief or behaviour as irrational or bizarre when more information about that belief or behaviour would help

Mindful communicators understand what they experience *inside themselves* (body, mind, heart, spirit) and pay full attention to what is happening *around them* (people, the natural world, surroundings, events).[54]

us understand it. Once you learn why observant Muslims and Jews won't eat pork products or why Hindus won't eat the meat of sacred cows even under famine conditions, you have the opportunity to become more mindful and tolerant of their customs. Canadian First Nations elder Albert Marshall describes this concept as **Etuaptmumk** (two-eyed seeing), which occurs when we look with one "eye" toward the Aboriginal ways of learning and with the other "eye" to the Western knowledge. This ability to see from two-eyes or perspectives is beneficial to everyone because it weaves together multiple views to create deeper understanding and knowledge.[55]

Respect Others' Perspectives In addition to being open to new information, mindful communicators are open to other points of view. Psychologist Richard Nisbett credits a graduate student from China with helping him understand such differences. When he and the student were trying to work and communicate with each other, his Chinese student said, "You know, the difference between you and me is that I know the world is a circle, and you think it's a line. The Chinese believe in constant change, but with things always moving back to some prior state. . . . Westerners live in a simpler world . . . and they think they can control events because they know the rules that govern the behaviour of objects."[56]

When you cling to one way of seeing a person or interpreting an event, you have stopped being mindful. Every idea, person, and object, can be many things depending on the perspective from which it is viewed.

RANGE OF THINKING

WESTERN

Focuses on discovering the basic and predictable nature of objects and events

Tries to control objects, events, and environments

Puts things in discrete categories

Uses formal logical rules

Insists on the correctness of one belief vs. another

EAST ASIAN

Focuses on the interacting, unpredictable relationships among events

Doubts that objects, events, and environments are controllable

Describes relationships and connections, not categories

Accepts contradictions and dissimilar beliefs

COMMUNICATION&CULTURE

WHY DON'T HUNGRY HINDUS EAT SACRED COWS?

Among India's Hindus, cows are a sacred symbol of life. There is no greater sacrilege for a Hindu than killing a cow. At first, this belief may seem irrational, particularly in light of India's food shortage and poverty. If you have visited or seen pictures of India, you've seen cows wandering city streets and sidewalks, highways and railroad tracks, gardens, and agricultural fields. You've also seen pictures of extreme poverty and hunger.

In his book *Cows, Pigs, Wars, and Witches: The Riddles of Culture,* Marvin Harris offers an explanation for Hindus' treatment of cows.[57] Cows give birth to oxen, which are the principal source for ploughing fields. Unfortunately, there are too few oxen for India's 60 million farms. Without oxen to plough fields, farmers cannot farm; food shortages result, and people go hungry.

JeremyRichards/Fotolia

If you kill a cow, you eliminate your source of oxen. During the worst famines, killing a cow only provides temporary relief. Once a cow is killed, there will be no more oxen to plough the field in future years. The long-term effect may be a much more devastating famine. Harris offers this conclusion:

> What I am saying is that cow love is an active element in a complex, finely articulated material and cultural order. Cow love mobilizes the latent capacity of human beings to persevere in a low-energy ecosystem in which there is little room for waste or indolence.[58]

In light of Harris's anthropological explanation, you can begin to understand and respect why hungry peasants in India refuse to eat the cows that surround them.

A cow is steak to a rancher, a sacred creature to a Hindu, a collection of genes and proteins to a biologist, and a mistreated animal to members of PETA (People for the Ethical Treatment of Animals).[59]

Adapt to Others

You probably feel most comfortable when you "fit in" with the people around you. To fit in, you may modify the way you talk to family members, friends, colleagues, authority figures, and strangers. For example, two people may be from different areas of the country, one from St. John's and the other from Whitehorse. When they go "home," their dialects, vocabulary, sentence structure, rate of speech, and even volume change to accommodate their home culture. Yet, in professional settings, their speech may be more formal in style and substance.

Professor Howard Giles explores these adaptive tendencies in **communication accommodation theory**,[60] which states that in every communication situation, we compare ourselves with speakers from other groups. If we believe that another group has more power or has desirable characteristics, we tend to "accommodate" or "adapt" our conversations to the accepted speech behaviours and norms of that group. The following ideas are central to communication accommodation theory:

1. *Communication similarities and differences exist between participants in all conversations*. Whether you talk to an international student or your grandmother, you will encounter differences.

2. *The manner in which we perceive the communication of others will determine how we evaluate our interaction with others*. Effective communicators avoid stereotyping by carefully listening to others and attentively observing what they do.

3. *Language and behaviour convey information about social status and group membership*. Usually, the person or group with more status and power establishes the "accepted" type of talk and behaviour. For example, if during a job interview the interviewer's behaviour is very formal, you are likely to be more formal in your behaviour.

4. *Accommodation varies in its degree of appropriateness, and there are norms that guide the accommodation process*. When a situation is awkward, you will try to accommodate (adapt) the behaviour of the group in that situation. Thus, if you interact with a culture that respects its elders; you may hesitate questioning the views of an older person or senior official. Or when you learn that a particular behaviour is *inappropriate*, you will not engage in that behaviour. For example, if you and your colleagues are on a deadline for group work and they decide to leave the meeting before they complete the project, you may not leave with them.

Actively Engage Others

Direct, face-to-face interaction with people from culturally diverse backgrounds benefits everyone. You and others may transform and let go of long-held negative beliefs about each other's cultures into understanding and acceptance.

One of the most interesting and exciting ways to actively engage others is to explore your community. Canada has a rich, vibrant cultural mosaic that provides opportunities to meet, learn about and understand people from many countries. Traveling abroad is just as engaging and has long-term benefits. A survey of students who studied abroad found a positive link to career success, a more tolerant worldview, and increased self-confidence. When questioned about their intercultural development and understanding, 98 percent reported that study abroad helped them to better understand their own cultural values and biases.[61] Combining domestic and global exploration and travel helps you to become a true global citizen, capable of effectively communicating with all people.

If you succeed in minimizing your level of anxiety and uncertainty when encountering others, you may discover new worlds with fascinating people who can enrich your life. The fact is, regardless of culture, nationality, gender, religion, age, and ability, all of us share the traits unique to the amazing human condition.

Development Model of Intercultural Sensitivity (DMIS)

Denial ▶ Defense ▶ Minimization ▶ Acceptance ▶ Adaptation ▶ Integration

Milton J. Bennett developed this DMIS model after many years of observing how people dealt with cultural differences.[62] The DMIS considers six distinct stages that occur as we develop intercultural sensitivity.

Denial	At this stage, people avoid noticing or acknowledging cultural differences.
Defense	On the one hand, this involves focusing only on the common characteristics of all humans. The opposite response involves attempting to correct stereotypes and failed attempts at multiculturalization of communities.
Minimization	This occurs when you become immersed in another culture for a limited amount of time. It can be misinterpreted as cultural sensitivity, but in reality lacks depth of understanding. An example of this can be found in some exchange student programs.
Acceptance	This takes places when you are able to understand another culture and use that knowledge and skill in culturally appropriate contexts. You are able to value another culture and acknowledge the levels of complexity within that culture.
Adaptation	This is a big shift in both understanding and actions. When you adapt, you keep your beliefs and values and add to these the parts of other cultures' values and beliefs that fit within your life. Becoming authentic in your sensitivity occurs when you broaden your definition of who you are.
Integration	The ability to see people, cultures, and world contexts through a variety of perspectives. You are able to move easily with confidence and sensitivity between various cultures.

Read each of the following statements and decide which stage of the DMIS is being described.

_____ 1. I know a lot about foreign countries and cultures.

_____ 2. If they don't want to be Canadian, they should just go back home!

_____ 3. It makes sense to learn about the people, cultures, and customs of the society before visiting another country.

_____ 4. All families want the same things for their children.

_____ 5. I am a global citizen in my beliefs.

_____ 6. I don't see any differences; live and let live is my motto.

_____ 7. The people of the Caribbean share the same customs, whether they are from Cuba, the Dominican Republic, or Haiti.

_____ 8. The more time I spend with my group member from India, the more I am able to see things from her perspective.

_____ 9. It is important to share Canadian values, customs, and beliefs and to understand the values, beliefs, and customs of the new immigrant family when working alongside them.

_____ 10. How they parent their children is wrong. We should do something to make them more Canadian.

Answers: (1) minimize, (2) denial, (3) acceptance, (4) minimize, (5) acceptance, (6) denial, (7) defense, (8) adaptation, (9) integration, (10) denial.

3.1
Our Faces

How has the "changing face" of Canada affected your daily interactions?

- Effective communicators learn how to understand, respect, and adapt to cultural diversity.
- By 2031, one in three workers in Canada will be from a visible minority.
- Culture is a learned set of shared interpretations about beliefs, values, and norms that affect the behaviours of a relatively large group of people.
- Co-cultures exist within the mainstream of society yet remain connected to one another through their cultural heritage.

3.2
Barriers to Understanding Others

How do ethnocentrism, stereotyping, prejudice, discrimination, and racism affect communication?

- Ethnocentrism is a belief that your culture is superior to others; stereotypes are generalizations about a group of people that oversimplify their characteristics.
- Stereotypes lead to prejudices, which can be perceived as positive or negative attitudes about an individual or cultural group based on little or no direct experience.
- Prejudice leads to discrimination, the exclusion of groups of people from opportunities granted to others.
- In the extreme, prejudice and discrimination lead to racism, which justifies dominating and mistreating people of other races.

3.3
Understanding Cultural Diversity

Why is it so important to understand cultural diversity?

- When we view race as a socially constructed concept, it becomes a very neutral and natural characteristic.
- Many people are not literate about others' religions or about their own religion. This lack of knowledge can affect their ability to communicate effectively with others.

3.4
The Dimensions of Culture

What cultural dimensions affect the way you communicate with others?

- The individualism/collectivism cultural dimension contrasts independence and personal achievement with interdependence and group values.
- The power distance cultural dimension examines the physical and psychological distance between those with power and those without power.
- The masculine/feminine values cultural dimension contrasts an assertive and tough perspective with a more modest and tender perspective.

- The high-/low-context cultural dimension focuses on whether meaning is expressed in words or through nonverbal communication and the nature of personal relationships.
- The monochronic/polychronic time cultural dimension contrasts cultures that value time and concentrate on one job at a time and cultures that are not controlled by time and are easily accept interruptions and distractions.

3.5
Intercultural Communication Strategies

What strategies can help you understand, respect, and effectively communicate with "others"?

- Effective communicators are mindful; that is, they are receptive to new information and are responsive to and respectful of other perspectives.
- Communication accommodation theory provides principles to help understand, respect, and successfully adapt to others without stereotyping.
- Finding ways to interact and actively engage people who are different than you are can help you become a better communicator.

Mikhail Kozlovsky/ITAR-TASS Photo Agency/Alamy

3.1 How has the "changing face" of Canada affected your daily interactions?

1 You could use the following words to define culture.
- a. nationality
- b. race
- c. ethnicity
- d. a, b, and c are correct.
- e. None of these words define culture accurately.

3.2 How do ethnocentrism, stereotyping, prejudice, discrimination, and racism affect communication?

2 Jack sincerely believes that most people would be better off if their government and country were more like Canada. Which barrier to understanding others does Jack exemplify?
- a. ethnocentrism
- b. stereotyping
- c. prejudice
- d. discrimination
- e. racism

3 When the courts examined a supermarket's hiring record, they found that the company never hired nonwhite applicants for the better-paying job of working cash registers. Which barrier to understanding others does this example exemplify?
- a. ethnocentrism
- b. stereotyping
- c. prejudice
- d. discrimination
- e. racism

4 Which of these barriers to understanding was evident when a 2-metre-high cross was set fire on the front lawn of a Nova Scotia family?
- a. ethnocentrism
- b. stereotyping
- c. prejudice
- d. discrimination
- e. racism

5 When someone seeks the advice of a gay friend when they want to decorate their home they are exhibiting this behaviour.
- a. ethnocentrism
- b. stereotyping
- c. prejudice
- d. discrimination
- e. racism

3.3 Why is so important to understand cultural diversity?

6 Which of the following contributes to your social identity?
- a. ethnicity
- b. socioeconomic position
- c. sexual orientation
- d. gender
- e. all of the above

3.4 What cultural dimensions affect the way you communicate with others?

7 Which of the following countries exhibits the most individualism?
- a. Australia
- b. Indonesia
- c. Taiwan
- d. Peru
- e. Pakistan

8 There is a strong correlation between collectivist cultures and cultures in which there is _____.
- a. individualism
- b. high power distance
- c. low power distance
- d. high-context communication
- e. monochronic time

9 Which behaviour is characteristic of a society with feminine values?
- a. Men are assertive, tough, and focused on success, whereas women are more modest and tender.
- b. Men's and women's gender roles overlap.
- c. Women assume most homemaking and child-rearing responsibilities.
- d. Men assume most homemaking and child-rearing responsibilities.
- e. Women are assertive, tough, and focused on success, whereas men are more modest and tender.

3.5 What strategies can help you understand, respect, and effectively communicate with "others"?

10 Which behaviour demonstrates mindfulness when communicating with people from other cultures?
- a. You pay attention to how you and another person are communicating.
- b. You recognize your personal prejudices and try to overcome them.
- c. You understand and respect different cultural values.
- d. You are receptive to new ideas and respect other people's perspectives.
- e. You do all of the above.

Answers found on page 330.

Key Terms

Co-cultures	High-context culture	Polychronic time
Collectivism	Individualism	Power distance
Communication accommodation theory	Intercultural dimension	Prejudices
	Low power distance	Race
Discrimination	Low-context culture	Racism
Etuaptmumk	Masculine societies	Religious literacy
Ethnocentrism	Mindfulness	Social identity
Feminine societies	Mindlessness	Stereotypes
High power distance	Monochronic time	
	Muted group theory	

LISTENING, Critical THINKING, and Reflective Practice

Y ou're walking down the street with a friend when she sees a man she knows. Your friend waves at him and pulls you over to meet him. You extend your hand and smile while your friend introduces the two of you, and says each of your names clearly. After a couple of minutes, you realize that you cannot recall his name. You don't want to appear rude by asking for his name again, especially because he's said your name several times during the conversation. Two weeks later, you bump into him and he greets you by name. You cannot return the honour.

Why do so many of us forget names? In *How to Start a Conversation and Make Friends*, Don Gabor suggests that it is because we're not *listening* effectively. We're too busy thinking about what we're going to say, whether we will make a good impression, and how other people will react to us.[1]

Remembering names—as well as the many more complex messages you hear every day—requires two communication skills: effective listening *and* critical thinking. When you listen effectively, you do much more than hear and recognize the words in a message. Regardless of why, where, when, and to whom you listen, you should always think critically about what you hear. After all, if no one will listen to you, why communicate? And if you have not given serious thought to your message, why *should* anyone listen?

An important skill in learning to listen and think critically is your ability to reflect on experiences and situations. Reflecting provides you with opportunities to understand how and why you listen and think as you do, and is crucial to effective interpersonal communication.

Gennadiy Poznyakov/Fotolia

The Nature of Listening

Why is listening essential for effective communication?

The International Listening Association defines **listening** as "the process of receiving, constructing meaning from, and responding to a spoken and/or nonverbal message."[2] This definition describes what effective listeners *do*; however, it does not explain *how* the listening process works. Listening—just like speaking, reading, and writing—is a complex process that goes beyond "you speak, I listen." Because many people do not appreciate this complexity, listening may appear to be easy and natural. In fact, just the opposite is true. Hearing only requires physical ability; listening requires complex thinking ability.

Although communication occurs in a variety of ways and through a variety of modalities, listening is our number one communication activity. A study of college students that accounted for Internet and social media use found that listening still occupies more than half of their communicating time.[3] Additionally, effective listening skills are a significant factor in predicting a student's academic success and survival.[4] In contrast, poor listening is a significant factor in predicting student failure.

> *Although most of us can hear, we often fail to listen to what others say.*

COMMUNICATION

Exercise

www.ted.com/talks/julian_treasure_5_ways_to_listen_better.html

1. How can you use the five ways discussed in this video to improve your interpersonal communication?
2. Which will be the most difficult for you to apply? Why?

In the business world, many executives devote more than 60 percent of their workdays to listening to others.[5] Moreover, listening is often cited as the communication skill most lacking in new employees.[6]

How Well Do You Listen?

In *The Lost Art of Listening*, Michael P. Nichols writes that "Listening is so basic that we take it for granted. Unfortunately most of us think of ourselves as better listeners than we really are."[7] For example, immediately after listening to a short talk, most of us cannot accurately report 50 percent of what was said. Without training, we listen at about 25 percent efficiency.[8] And of that 25 percent, most is distorted or inaccurate.[9]

A study of Fortune 500 company training managers concludes "ineffective listening leads to ineffective performance or low productivity." These same problems also appear in studies of sales professionals, educators, health practitioners, lawyers, and religious leaders.[10]

Listening at home is just as—or more—important. In families the common cry "Nobody around here listens to me!" may come from a frustrated mother, father, or any of the children. But good parenting necessitates good listening. Nichols notes that "adolescents need their parents to listen to their troubles, their hopes, and ambitions, even some of their farfetched plans."[11]

Effective listening is hard work. Researchers note that active listeners register an increase in blood pressure, a higher pulse rate, and even more perspiration.[12] Active listeners try to understand what a speaker is saying, the emotions behind the content, and the conclusion the speaker is making without stating it openly.[13] Effective listening requires the kind of preparation and concentration required of

Bikeriderlondon/Shutterstock

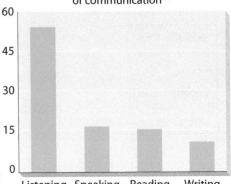

Average time spent in each aspect of communication[14]

60
45
30
15
0

Listening Speaking Reading Writing

attorneys trying a case and psychologists counselling a client.

Assess Your Listening Habits

In Chapter 1 we highlighted Stephen R. Covey's claim that an enduring habit must have three components: *knowledge*, *skills*, and *desire*. Here we briefly summarize how he applied this claim to listening:

1. *Knowledge.* Unless you understand the principles of human interaction, you may not even know you need to listen.
2. *Skills.* Even if you know you need to listen, you may not have the skill.
3. *Desire.* Knowing you need to listen and knowing how to listen are not enough. Unless you *want* to listen, listening won't be an enduring habit.

An interesting study expands and applies Covey's listening competencies to college students and people working in organizational settings. Research by Lynn Cooper and Trey Buchanan identified the "big five" of listening competencies (Figure 4.1). Notice how they reflect Covey's criteria for an enduring habit.[15]

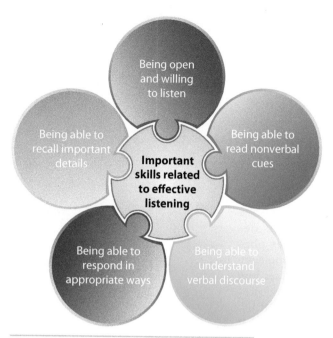

Figure 4.1 The "Big Five" of Listening Competencies

Know Thy SELF

Do You Have Poor Listening Habits?[16]

Examine the poor listening habits below and circle the response that best reflects how you listen. Notice that we have not included a "never" option because no one is a perfect listener 100 percent of the time.

Poor Listening Habits	How Frequently Do You Listen This Way?		
Defensive Listening. Do you feel threatened or humiliated by critical remarks from others? Do you focus on how to respond to or challenge another person's questions and criticisms rather than listening objectively?	Often	Sometimes	Rarely
Disruptive Listening. Do you interrupt others while they're speaking? Do you exaggerate your responses by sighing audibly, rolling your eyes, shaking your head in a *no*, or obviously withholding your attention?	Often	Sometimes	Rarely
Pseudolistening. Do you fake attention or pretend to listen when your mind is elsewhere, you're bored, or you think it pleases the speaker? Do you nod or smile even though your response has nothing to do with the message?	Often	Sometimes	Rarely
Selective Listening. If you don't like or agree with someone, do you avoid listening or look for faults in what that person says? Do you avoid listening to complex or highly technical information?	Often	Sometimes	Rarely
Superficial Listening. Do you pay more attention to the way other people look or how they speak rather than to what they say? Do you draw conclusions about others' intentions or claims before they've finished talking?	Often	Sometimes	Rarely

If you answered with an honest *rarely* to all of the questions, you are probably a good listener. If you answered *often* or *sometimes*, you have a lot to learn about listening.

The Listening Process

What are the key components of the listening process?

Listening researchers, cognitive scientists, and neurologists describe listening as a complex phenomenon. To address the complexity of listening, Judi Brownell, a leading listening researcher and author, presents a six-component HURIER listening model. The letters in HURIER represent six interrelated listening processes: **H**earing, **U**nderstanding, **R**emembering, **I**nterpreting, **E**valuating, and **R**esponding. Brownell links each of these six components to appropriate listening attitudes, relevant listening principles, and methods for improving your listening skills[17] (see Figure 4.2).

The HURIER model "recognizes that you are constantly influenced by both internal and external factors that color your perceptions and subsequent interpretations." These listening filters include your attitudes, values, biases, and previous experiences.[18] For example, if you know that your instructor's exams include questions based on her lectures, you are more likely to listen attentively to what she says.

The HURIER model also recognizes that different listening skills become more or less important depending on both your purpose and the

communication context.[19] For instance, when you're listening to a topic expert, you may be "all ears" and be open to learning and agreeing. In contrast, you may listen more judgmentally when a less informed speaker presents a poorly structured presentation. And if you are listening to someone in a hot, noisy room at a late hour of the day, it may be very difficult to focus your attention and energy on the task.

Brownell's HURIER listening model highlights six types of listening to ensure that you accurately and appropriately hear, understand, remember, interpret, evaluate, and respond

to spoken and/or nonverbal messages. In this section, we take a more detailed look at the different kinds of listening in the HURIER model to investigate which ones best meet your own and others' listening needs and abilities.

Listening to Hear

Hearing, the ability to make clear, aural distinctions among the sounds and words in a language, is the "prerequisite to all listening."[20] Your hearing ability also determines whether you can detect the meaning of non-word sounds such as a groan or a laugh.

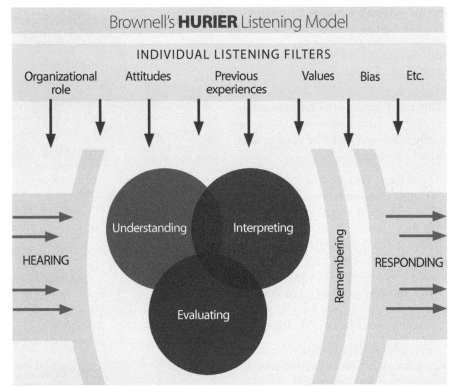

Figure 4.2 The HURIER Model of Listening

Table 4.1
Hearing limitation rates by age, 2006[21]

Age group	Total Canadian population	Population with hearing limitations	Hearing limitation rate
	counts		percent
Total - aged 15 and over	**25,422,280**	**1,266,120**	**5.0**
15 to 24	4,147,070	21,810	0.5
25 to 34	3,942,260	27,070	0.7
35 to 44	4,747,620	71,800	1.5
45 to 54	4,912,800	179,020	3.6
55 to 64	3,623,390	231,130	6.4
65 to 74	2,239,630	265,740	11.9
75 and over	1,809,500	469,560	25.9

TYPES OF LISTENING in the HURIER Listening Model

TYPE OF LISTENING	DEFINITION	EXAMPLE
Hearing	Your ability to make clear, aural distinctions among the sounds and words in a language	I sometimes have trouble hearing a soft-spoken person, particularly if there's background noise.
Understanding	Your ability to accurately grasp the *meaning* of someone's spoken and nonverbal messages	When you say *wait*, do you mean we should wait a few more minutes or wait until Caleb gets here?
Remembering	Your ability to store, retain, and recall information you have heard	Hi George. I remember meeting you last month. Did you end up selling your old truck?
Interpreting	Your ability to empathize with another person's feelings without judging the message	It must be frustrating and discouraging to have such an unsympathetic instructor.
Evaluating	Your ability to analyze and make a judgment about the validity of someone's message	I see two reasons why that proposal won't work. They are …
Responding	Your ability to respond in a way that indicates you fully understanding someone's meaning	You seem to be saying that it's not a good time to confront Mercedes. Am I right?

Hearing ability differs from person to person. Statistics Canada (2006) reports that 5% of Canadians aged 15 and older report some degree of hearing loss (see Table 4.1).[22] Given that hearing loss is usually gradual and cumulative throughout your life, older adults have greater hearing losses than children and young adults.

Table 4.1 reflects information gathered in the last long form census. Limited information is now available as many Canadians complete the short census form, which does not capture all of the details.

Later in this chapter, we describe the ways in which people with hearing loss listen.

Answering the following questions can help you understand why hearing is the gateway to effective listening.

- Do you often ask others to repeat what they've said or misunderstand what they've said because you did not hear them accurately?

- Do you notice nonverbal messages expressed in people's facial expressions, gestures, posture, movement, and vocal sounds (sighs, groans, laughter, gasps)?

Listening to Understand

Listening to understand, also known as comprehensive listening, focuses on accurately grasping the *meaning* of someone's spoken and nonverbal messages. After all, if you don't understand what someone means, how can you respond in a reasonable way? For example, an after-class discussion might begin as follows: "Let's get a drink and go over today's notes" says Samantha. If you are *listening to understand* Samantha's message you will need to decide if Samantha means coffee or wine, or if she needs to borrow your notes because she didn't take any during class. What you do and say next in response to Samantha may be very different depending on your understanding of Samantha's intentions.

Asking questions is one of the best ways to make sure you understand the meaning of someone's words and nonverbal behaviour.[23] The strategies discussed in "Ask Good Questions to Ensure Understanding" on the next page create a template to assist with clarity.

Listening to Remember

How good is your memory? How well do you store, retain, and recall information? Do you ever forget what you're talking about during a discussion? Can you remember a person's name or a phone number if you haven't written it down? Occasionally, everyone experiences memory problems. As we noted earlier in this chapter, most people cannot recall 50 percent of what they hear immediately after hearing it. At the same time, your ability to remember directly affects how well you listen.

When we ask people "How good is *your* memory?" they often answer, "It depends." For example, if you're very interested in what someone's saying you're more likely to remember the conversation, discussion, or presentation. You may not remember anything, however if you are under a lot of stress or preoccupied with personal problems. Here are just a few suggestions that, with practice, can improve your memory:

- **Repeat.** Repeat an important idea or piece of information after you hear it; say it aloud if you can. For example, if you've just learned that your class project group report is due on the 22nd, use this date in a sentence several times ("Let's see how many meetings we need to have before the 22nd"; "We'll need to have our first draft done a week ahead of time—22 minus 7 is 15"). If you're in a situation where it's not appropriate to do this aloud, repeat the information in your mind.

- **Associate.** Associate a word, phrase, or idea with something that describes it. For example, when you meet someone whose name you want to remember, associate the name with the context in which you met the person (Jamal in biology class) or with a word beginning with the same letter that describes the person (Blonde Brenda).

- Visualize. Visualize a word, phrase, or idea. For example, when a patient was told she might need to take calcium channel blockers, (a medication) she visualized a swimmer trying to cross the English Channel filled with floating calcium pills.

- Use mnemonics. A *mnemonic* is a memory aid that is based on something simple like a pattern or rhyme. For example, the HURIER

Ask **GOOD QUESTIONS** to Ensure Understanding

1. **Have a plan.** Make sure your question is clear and appropriate so it will not be misunderstood or waste time.
2. **Keep the questions simple.** Ask one question at a time and make sure it's relevant to the original message you received.
3. **Ask nonthreatening questions.** Avoid questions that begin with "Why didn't you … ?" or "How could you … ?" because they can create a defensive climate in responders.
4. **Ask permission.** If a topic is sensitive, explain why you are asking the question and ask permission before continuing. "You say you're fearful about telling Sharon about the mistake you made. Would you mind helping me understand why you're so apprehensive?"
5. **Avoid biased or manipulative questions.** Tricking someone into giving you the answer you want can destroy trust. There's a big difference between "Why did we miss the deadline?" and "Who screwed up?"
6. **Wait for the answer.** In addition to asking good questions, respond appropriately to the response you receive. After you ask a question, give the other person time to think and then wait for the answer using effective listening skills.

FACTS **THINK** ABOUT THEORY

TEST IDEA PLAN EXPERIMENT METHOD KNOWLEDGE

Listening and Working Memory

People with more working memory capacity are more likely to **understand** what others mean, to **analyze** complex issues and discussion threads, to **track** relevant and irrelevant interactions, and to **develop** appropriate responses.

Wavebreakmedia/Shutterstock

Early studies of listening focused on understanding **short-term memory,** the content you remember immediately after listening to a series of numbers or words. Psychologist Samuel Wood and colleagues note that this kind of "short-term memory has a very limited capacity—about seven (plus or minus two) different items or bits of information at one time. This is just enough for phone numbers and ordinary postal codes."[24] We use something much more complex than short-term memory to engage in effective listening.

Working memory theory recognizes that listening involves more than the ability to tap your short-term memory. Listening engages your **working memory.** Psychologists define working memory as the memory subsystem we use to comprehend, remember, and form a mental image of what is going on around us; we use working memory to learn new things, solve problems, and form and act on goals.[25] Listening researcher Laura Janusik describes working memory as "a dual-task system involving processing and storage functions. The processing function is synonymous with attention, and the storage function is synonymous with memory. Attention is allocated, and resources not used for attention are available for storage."[26] Your working memory does more than store what you've heard; it allows you to shift what you've heard and understood "from and into long-term memory" as a way to create new meanings.[27]

Peter Desberg, author of *Speaking Scared Sounding Good*, describes working memory as a clearinghouse where you have fewer than 30 seconds to decide if the information is worth keeping and storing in your long-term memory. If your brain is preoccupied or doesn't take the time to process the information, the information disappears.[28]

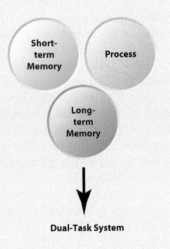

Short-term Memory — Process

Long-term Memory

Dual-Task System

in Brownell's Model of Listening is an acronym (the first letters for the six components of listening). Many people remember which months of the year have 30 days with the poem that begins "Thirty days hath September . . . ." For instance, by rearranging the above memory suggestions, you might be able to remember MARV (mnemonics, associate, repeat, visualize).

Remembering Names

At the beginning of this chapter, we described the frequent challenge of recalling a new acquaintance's name even a few minutes after hearing it. In *How to Start a Conversation and Make Friends*, Don Gabor suggests six strategies for remembering someone's name:

> **"I'm sorry, I forgot your name."**

poet who wrote the *Iliad* and *Odyssey*. If you meet someone who looks like a childhood friend, teachers, relative, or even celebrity with the same name, associate the new person with the name of that person.

1. Focus on the moment of introduction—rather than on yourself.

2. Don't think about what to say—listen for the name and information about the person.

3. Repeat the name out loud when you hear it.

4. Think of someone you know or someone famous with the same name. For example, if you meet someone named Homer, think about Homer Simpson or the epic

5. Link the person's name to a unique characteristic such as a word that begins with the same letter (Strong Sergio, Laughing Lewis, Cooking Cathy), a characteristic word that rhymes with the person's name (Curley Shirley, Slim Jim), or a word that reminds of you of an event (Tom's Toe because you met him the night he broke his toe).

6. Use the name during and at the end of the conversation.[29]

Listening to Interpret

Judi Brownell equates the ability to understand what someone says as "a primary factor in empathic listening, where your ability to recognize and respond appropriately to emotional meanings is critical."[30] Empathic listening answers this question: How does the other person feel? **Empathic listening** goes beyond comprehending what a person means; it involves focusing on understanding someone's situation, feelings, or motives. Can you see the situation through the other person's eyes? How would you feel in a similar situation?

By not listening for feelings, you may overlook the most important part of a message. Even if you understand every word a person says, you can still miss the anger, enthusiasm, or frustration in someone's voice. As an empathic listener, you don't have to agree with or feel the same way as others, but you do have to try to understand the type and intensity of feelings they are experiencing. For example, the after-class discussion mentioned earlier might continue as follows: "I don't want to go for a drink!" exclaims Kim. An empathic listener may wonder whether Kim means that (1)

> **"[Listening] involves learning how to suspend your own emotional agenda and then realizing the rewards of genuine empathy."**
>
> —Michael Nichols, *The Lost Art of Listening*.[31]

she has more important things to do during exam week, (2) she doesn't drink wine or liquor, or (3) she doesn't want to share her notes.

Empathic listening is difficult, but it also is "the pinnacle of listening" because it demands "fine skill and exquisite tuning into another's mood and feeling."[32]

Answering the following questions can help you understand the scope of empathic listening:

- Do you show interest and concern about the other person?
- Does your nonverbal behaviour communicate friendliness and trust?
- Do you avoid highly judgmental reactions to others?
- Do you avoid talking about your own experiences and feelings when someone else is describing theirs?[33]

Listening to Evaluate

Evaluative listening requires that you employ critical thinking skills to analyze what someone says. Once you are sure you've comprehended the meaning of a message, ask yourself whether your reasoning is sound and the conclusion is reasonable. Evaluative listeners understand why they accept or reject someone's ideas and suggestions. They make judgments based on their evaluation of another person's message: Is the speaker right or wrong, logical or illogical? Should I accept or reject the speaker's ideas and suggestions? Evaluative listeners are open-minded. They put aside biases or prejudices about the speaker or message when they analyze what they hear in order to arrive at a rational conclusion or decision.

Recognizing that someone is trying to persuade—rather than merely inform—is one of the first steps in improving your evaluative listening.

Best Practices When Listening

Listen to others, as you would have them listen to you. Unfortunately, this rule can be difficult to follow. It asks you to suspend your own needs and opinions to listen to someone else's.[34]

This best practice is also an ethical listening practice. It reflects a principle in the National Communication Association's Credo for Ethical Communication: "We strive to understand and respect other communicators before evaluating and responding to their message."[35] When you follow the golden listening rule, you communicate your interest, patience, and open-mindedness.

Best practices when listening is also a positive listening attitude. If you aren't motivated to listen, you won't listen. Effective listeners have made listening an enduring habit by recognizing the importance of good listening, learning effective listening skills, and—perhaps most important of all—*wanting* to listen. An appropriate listening attitude does not mean that you know exactly what another person thinks or feels. Rather, it requires a strong motivation to listen and discover.[36] The six positive listening attitudes that follow have six negative counterparts:[37]

How Positive Is Your Listening Attitude?	
Positive Listening Attitudes	**Negative Listening Attitudes**
Interested	Uninterested
Responsible	Irresponsible
Group-centred	Self-centred
Patient	Impatient
Equal	Superior
Open-minded	Closed-minded

Ask yourself the following questions to determine your ability to listen and evaluate what you hear:[38]

- Do you recognize persuasive communication strategies?
- Can you tell when someone is appealing to your emotions and/or to your critical thinking ability?
- Can you assess the quality and validity of arguments and evidence?

The ability to think critically as you listen and carefully evaluate what someone is saying is a difficult but learnable skill. The next section of this chapter focuses on the critical thinking skills you need to enhance the quality of communication and to separate the valid from invalid claims you hear.

Listening to Respond

When you listen to others (and especially if you listen to hear, understand, remember, interpret, and evaluate), you are likely to respond verbally and/or nonverbally. You may ask a question, provide support, offer advice, or share your opinion. You may frown, smile, laugh, shrug, or look confused. Fortunately, there is a key responding skill that can help you make sure you fully understand someone else's meaning. That skill is called paraphrasing, and it is essential to becoming a highly effective listener.

The Nature of Paraphrasing
Paraphrasing is the ability to restate what people say in a way that indicates you understand them. When you paraphrase, you go beyond the words you hear so that you understand the feelings and underlying meanings that accompany the words. Too often, we jump to conclusions and incorrectly assume that we know what a speaker means and feels.

Paraphrasing is a form of feedback—a listening check—that asks, "Am I right—is this what you mean?" Paraphrasing is not repeating what a person says; it requires finding *new* words to describe what you have heard.

The Complexities of Paraphrasing
Paraphrasing is difficult. Not only are you putting aside your own interests and opinions, but you are also finding *new* words that best match someone else's meaning. Figure 4.3 shows how a paraphrase can vary in four important ways: content, depth, meaning, and language.[39]

Paraphrasing says, "I want to hear what you have to say, and I want to understand what you mean." If you paraphrase accurately, the other person will appreciate your understanding and support. Even if you don't get the paraphrase right, your feedback provides another opportunity for the speaker to explain.[40]

Functions of PARAPHRASING

- To ensure comprehension before evaluation
- To reassure others that you want to understand them
- To clear up confusion and ask for clarification
- To summarize lengthy comments
- To help others uncover their own thoughts and feelings
- To provide a safe and supportive communication climate
- To help others reach their own conclusions[41]

Effective paraphrasing requires mindful listening. Paraphrasing says, "I want to hear what you have to say, and I want to understand what you mean."

Type of Paraphrase	Effective Paraphrase Example	Ineffective Paraphrase Example
Susan: "I never seem to get anywhere on time and I don't know why."		
Paraphrase Content: Find new words to express the same meaning. Paraphrase, don't parrot.	"Sounds as though you've tried to figure out the reasons why you're often late but can't. Is that what you're saying?"	"Ah, so you don't know why you never seem to get anywhere on time?" Susan's response: "Yeah, that's what I just said."
Susan: "People, including my boss, bug me about being late, and sometimes I can tell that they're pretty angry."		
Paraphrase Depth: Match the emotions to the speaker's meaning. Avoid responding lightly to a serious problem and vice versa.	"When you say that people are angry, you sound as though it's become serious enough to put your job at risk or damage your relationships with your boss and co-workers; is that right?"	"In other words, you worry that other people are upset by your lateness."
Susan: "I really don't know . . ."		
Paraphrase Meaning: Match the overall meaning. Avoid adding unintended meaning or completing the speaker's sentences.	"Let me make sure I understand what you're saying. Is it that you don't know why you're always late, or that you wish you had a better idea of how to manage your time?"	". . . how to manage your time?" (Susan was intending to finish her sentence with "what to do.")
Susan: "So I still can't figure out why I'm always late getting to the office."		
Paraphrase Language: Use clear, simple language to ensure the person's understands your paraphrase.	"It sounds as though being late has become a big problem at work and you're looking for ways to fix it. Right?"	"Ahh, your importunate perplexities about punctuality are inextricably linked." Susan's response: "Huh?"

Figure 4.3 Types of Paraphrasing

STOP&THINK

Paraphrase This

Read the following three statements and write a response that paraphrases their meaning, as demonstrated in the following example:

Group member: "I get really annoyed when André yells at one of us during our meetings."

Paraphrase: *"You sound as though you become very upset when André shouts at you or other group members. Is that what's bothering you?"*

1. **Friend:** I have the worst luck with computers. The computer I have now has crashed again, and I lost all of my documents. Maybe I'm doing something wrong. Why me?

Paraphrase: _____

_____

2. **Colleague:** I dislike saying *no* to anyone who asks me for help, but then I have to rush or stay up late to get my own work done. I want to help, but I also want to do my own work.

Paraphrase: _____

_____

3. **Classmate:** How on earth am I going to get an A on this exam if I can't even find time to read the textbook?

Paraphrase: _____

_____

4.3
Listening Strategies and Skills

What listening strategies and skills can help you communicate more effectively?

At this point, you should know *why* good listening is essential for effective and ethical communication. You should also have some ideas about how to better hear, understand, remember, interpret, evaluate, and respond appropriately to others. In this section, we introduce several general listening strategies and skills that can improve your listening ability in most situations and help you develop effective listening habits. When and how you use these strategies depends, in part, on whether you are the speaker or the listener (or both) and whether you are speaking to one person or a large group of people.

Thinking Faster Than Speaking: How to Use Your Extra Thought Speed

Most people talk at about 125 to 150 words per minute. But most of us can *think* at three to four times that rate.[42] This means, we have about 400 extra words of spare thinking time during every minute a person talks to us.

Thought speed is the speed (words per minute) at which most people can think compared with the speed at which they can speak. Poor listeners use their extra thought speed to daydream, engage in side conversations, take unnecessary notes, or plan how to respond to a speaker. Conscientious listeners use their extra thought speed to enhance all types of listening.

You can use your extra thought speed to:

- make sure you hear what someone says.
- determine the meaning of a message.
- identify and summarize key ideas.
- remember what someone says.
- empathize with a person's expressed feelings.
- analyze and evaluate arguments.
- determine the most appropriate way to respond to what you hear.

Listen to Feedback

One of the most important and challenging communication skills is listening to and providing appropriate feedback to others during a conversation, meeting, or presentation. Feedback, the verbal and nonverbal responses others communicate as they listen, reveals how listeners react—negatively or positively—to you and your message.

All listeners react in some way. They may smile or frown or nod "yes" or "no." They may break into spontaneous applause or not applaud at all. They may sit forward at full attention or sit back and look bored. Analyzing your listeners' feedback helps you determine how your message is being received. As you speak, look and listen to the ways

in which people react to you. Do they look interested or uninterested, pleased or displeased? If you can't see or hear reactions, ask for feedback. You can stop in the middle of a conversation, meeting, or presentation to ask whether others understand you. Soliciting feedback helps you adapt to your listeners and tells your listeners that you value your audience. It also helps others focus their attention and listen more effectively to your message.

Listen to Nonverbal Behaviour

Very often, another person's meaning is expressed through nonverbal behaviour (see Chapter 6). For example, a change in vocal tone or volume may be another way of saying, "Listen up! This is very important." A person's sustained eye contact may mean, "I'm talking to you!" Facial expressions can reveal whether a person is experiencing joy, scepticism, or fear. Nonverbal behaviour also reveals others' intentions. A recent study found that children as young as three are less likely to help a person at a later point in time after seeing them harm someone else. What's intriguing about this finding is that "the toddlers judged a person's intention" by observing their nonverbal behaviour. In other words—just like most three-year-olds—most of us can determine others' intentions without hearing them say a single word.[43]

Gestures express emotions that words cannot convey. For example, at the moment during a trial when an attorney makes his final argument to the jury that his client should be acquitted, one juror, almost imperceptibly, moves her head back and forth, signifying "no." When the attorney states that his client had no idea that a crime had been committed, another juror raises one eyebrow with a look that says, "Okay, you've done your best to defend your client, but you and I know he's guilty as sin." In the end, the jury finds the defendant guilty as charged.

> ... next to the words you say, your face is the primary source of information about you and the meaning of your message.
>
> —Mark Knapp and Judith Hall[44]

Listen Before You Leap

Ralph Nichols, often-called the "father of listening research," counsels listeners to make sure they understand a speaker's message *before* reacting, either positively or negatively. This strategy requires taking time to

Elena Elisseeva/Shutterstock

bring your emotions under control. You may comprehend a speaker perfectly but be infuriated or offended by what you hear. If an insensitive speaker refers to women in the room as "chicks" or a minority group as "those people," you may need to count to 20 to collect your thoughts and refocus your attention on comprehensive listening.

When you listen before you leap, you are using your extra thought speed to decide how to react to controversial, prejudiced, or offensive comments.

> **"We must always withhold evaluation until our comprehension is complete."**
> —Ralph Nichols[45]

Listening before you leap gives you time to adjust your reaction and to clarify and correct a statement rather than making a quick decision. In a class discussion, if someone uses offensive language you may feel angry or uncomfortable. Try to use your listening time to separate the message of the speaker from your emotional response.

Minimize Distractions

Have you ever attended a lecture where the room was too hot, the seats were uncomfortable, or people in the hallway were talking loudly?

FACTS TEST IDEA PLAN EXPERIMENT METHOD KNOWLEDGE

THINK ABOUT THEORY

The Personal Listening Styles Controversy

Communication research on listening is dynamic and continues to evolve. In 1995, communication researchers Kittie Watson, Larry Barker, and James Weaver theorized that each of us prefers and uses one or more of four distinct listening styles. They claimed that by understanding your preferred listening style or styles, you "can explore other styles and learn how to adapt [your] behaviours accordingly to maximize communication."[46]

In 2010 and 2011, researchers Graham Bodie, Debra Worthington, and Christopher Gearhart analyzed the personal listening styles concept proposed by Watson, Barker, and Weaver and concluded that the four styles cannot be validated as distinct or separate from one another and do not represent a reliable explanation of listening styles.[47] They also provided substantive evidence supporting an alternative set of listening styles as well as a statistically validated instrument to measure those styles. The table in this box lists each set of listening styles.

At first glance, these two sets of listening styles may seem very similar. What makes them different is the definition for each listening style and the

Which style or styles do you generally prefer and use when listening to others?

tools used to uncover and measure each style. In light of the original research by Watson, Barker, and Weaver and the analysis by Bodie, Worthington, and Gearhart do your best to answer the following questions:

1. If you have a preferred listening style or styles, what are the benefits and drawbacks of that style?
2. How, if at all, can understanding these four styles help you adapt how you listen to others?
3. Which of the two lists makes the most sense to you? Why? How can continued research help us better understand the complex task of listening to others?

Personal Listening Styles Research	
Watson, Barker, and Weaver	**Bodie, Worthington, and Gearhart**
Action-oriented: Focuses on objectives and results; prefers clear and structured messages; focuses on what will be done and who will do it	**Task Listening:** Focuses on completing simple communication transactions effectively and efficiently; describes listeners who need structure
Time-oriented: Focuses on the clock; time and listening are organized in neat segments; wants short answers to question	**Critical Listening:** Focuses on noting inconsistencies and errors when others speak; listens to evaluate what others say
People-oriented: Focuses on feelings, emotions, and understanding others; responds with "we" statements; Interested in understanding, not criticizing	**Relational Listening:** Focuses on understanding emotions and connecting with others; empathic listening
Content-oriented: Focuses on what is said, not who says it; not concerned about feelings; interested in facts, evidence, logic, and complex ideas	**Analytical Listening:** Focuses on withholding judgment about others' ideas in order to consider all sides of an issue before responding

What are students "telling" this instructor (who is reading from his lecture notes)?

Distractions such as loud and annoying noises, poor seating arrangements, foul odors, frequent interruptions, and unattractive decor can make listening very difficult.[48] Other forms of distraction include a speaker's delivery that is too soft, fast, slow, or monotone; an accent that is unfamiliar; or mannerisms and appearance that seem unconventional or distracting.

You can help people listen better by taking action to overcome distractions. For example, when a distraction is physical, you are well within your rights as a listener or speaker to shut a door, open a window, or turn on more lights. In large groups, you may want to ask permission to improve the group's surroundings. Depending on the circumstances and setting, you can also take direct action to reduce behavioural distractions. If someone is talking or fidgeting while the speaker is addressing the audience, ask that person to stop. If someone is speaking too quietly, kindly ask the presenter to speak more loudly.

Take Notes That Matter

Given that most of us only listen at 25 percent efficiency, why not take notes and write down important facts and big ideas? Research has found that note takers recall messages in more detail than non–note takers.[49]

Taking notes makes a great deal of sense but *only* when it is done skillfully. If you are like most listeners, only one-fourth of what is said may end up in your notes. Even if you copy every word you hear, your notes will not include the nonverbal cues that often tell you more about what a person means and feels. And if you spend all your time taking notes, when will you put aside your pen and ask or answer an important question?

Ralph Nichols summarizes the dilemma of balancing note taking and listening when he concludes, "there is some evidence to indicate that the volume of notes taken and their value to the taker are inversely related."[50] This does not mean you should stop taking notes, but you should learn how to take useful notes—the key to which is adaptability. Effective listeners adjust their note taking to the content, style, and organizational pattern of a speaker.

If someone tells stories to make a point, jot down a brief reminder of the story and its point. If a professor lists tips, dos and don'ts, or recommendations, include those lists in your notes. If someone asks and answers a series of questions, your notes should reflect that pattern. If someone describes a new concept, try to paraphrase the meaning in your notes or jot down questions you want to ask.

Good listeners are flexible and adaptable note takers.

4.4
Listening to Gender and Culture
How do gender and culture affect the way we listen?

Understanding and adapting to the diverse listening skills, types, and levels of others can be a challenging task, particularly when gender and cultural differences are taken into account. Keep in mind that there are many exceptions to the research summaries we present about listening differences. As you read, you may say, "But I know women who don't listen this way." The existence of exceptions does not mean that the general claim is false. Diversity research provides useful insights that help explain common differences in listening behaviour.

Gender and Listening

The listening behaviours of women and men often differ. In general, men are more likely to listen to the content of what is said, whereas women focus on the relationship between the speaker and listener. Males tend to hear the facts, whereas females are more aware of the mood of the communication. In other words, men generally focus on comprehensive and analytical listening, whereas women are more likely to be empathic and appreciative listeners.

Culture and Listening

In Chapter 3, we introduced the concept of high- and low-context cultures. In comparison to low-context countries, in high-context countries such as Japan, China, and Korea and in African Canadian, Canadian Aboriginal, and Arab cultures, not all meaning is expressed through words. Much more attention is given to

Exercise

Canadian Aboriginal Context

Circles represent important principles in the Aboriginal world view and belief systems—namely, interconnectedness, equality, and continuity. In the circle, an object that symbolizes connectedness to the land—for example, a stick, a stone, or a feather—can be used to facilitate the circle. Only the person holding the "talking stick" has the right to speak. Participants can indicate their desire to speak by raising their hands. Going around the circle systematically gives everyone the opportunity to participate. Silence is also acceptable; any participant can choose not to speak.

1. In small groups, discuss how the importance of listening and understanding is evident in Canadian Aboriginal culture.
2. How can you incorporate some of the benefits of this type of listening practice into your culture?

nonverbal cues and the relationships among the communicators. As a result, listeners from high-context cultures "listen" for meanings in your behaviour and in who you are rather than in the words you say. However, most listeners from Germany, Switzerland, Scandinavia, Canada, and the United States focus on words. They expect speakers to be direct. When high-context speakers talk to low-context listeners—and vice versa—misunderstanding, offence, and even conflict may result. In many Asian cultures, the amount of time spent talking and the value placed on talking are very different than they are in the United States and Latin America.

COMMUNICATION IN *ACTION*

How Men and Women Listen to Each Other

Some women complain that their male partners and colleagues don't listen to them. Interestingly, some men sometimes make the same complaint about women. Linguist Deborah Tannen explains that the accusation "You're not listening" often means "You don't understand what I said" or "I'm not getting the response I want."[51]

Tannen offers an explanation for why it may *seem* that men don't listen. Quite simply, many men don't *show* they are listening, whereas most women do. In general, women provide more feedback when listening: They provide listening responses, like *mhm*, *uh-huh*, and *yeah*. And women respond more by nodding and laughing. To a man (who may expect a listener to be quiet and attentive), a woman giving off a stream of feedback and support will seem to be "talking" too much for a listener. To a woman (who may expect a listener to be active and show interest, attention, and support), a man who listens silently will seem to have checked out of the conversa-

tion. The bottom line is this: Many women may get the impression that men don't listen when, in fact, they are listening. Unfortunately, there are also men who really don't want to listen because they believe that it puts them in a subordinate position to women.[52]

Researchers also note that men often tune out things they can't solve or wonder why they should even listen if there isn't a

problem to solve. Women may become more involved and connected to the speaker and see listening as something important to do for the other person.[53] Although men use talk to establish status, women are more likely to use listening to empower others. Unfortunately, people who listen much more than they talk are often viewed as subordinate and subservient rather than powerful.[54]

Mike Good/DK Images

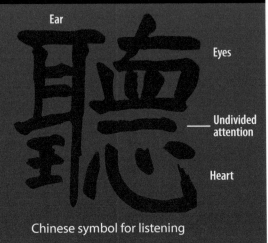

COMMUNICATION & CULTURE

THE ART OF EXCEPTIONAL LISTENING

Exceptional communicators listen beyond a person's words understand meaning by paying close attention to nonverbal cues. Interestingly, the Chinese symbol for "to listen" includes characters for eyes, ears, and heart.

For the Chinese, "it is impossible to listen ... without using the eyes because you need to look for nonverbal communication." The Chinese listen with their ears as well because they speak a tonal language in which intonation determines meaning. They claim that "you listen with your heart because ... [you must sense the] emotional undertones expressed by the speaker." In Korean, the word *nunchi* means that you communicate through your eyes. "Koreans believe that the environment supplies most of the information that we seek, so there is little need to speak."[55]

Ear

Eyes

Undivided attention

Heart

Chinese symbol for listening

4.5
The Nature of Critical Thinking

How does critical thinking enhance the quality of communication?

Critical thinking is the thought process you use to analyze what you read, see, or hear to arrive at a logical conclusion or decision. It is a conscious process when used effectively, can result in a conclusion, decision, opinion, or behaviour.[56] It can also result in a more meaningful conversation, group discussion, or presentation. Good critical thinkers know how to develop and defend a position on an issue, ask probing questions, be open-minded, and draw reasonable conclusions.[57] They are also highly skilled listeners who know how to accurately hear, understand, remember, interpret, and evaluate messages as well as appropriately respond to others.

The rest of this chapter focuses on critical thinking strategies and skills are essential to help you analyze the claims, facts, inferences, arguments, and thinking errors you encounter every day.

Critical Thinking About Claims

A **claim** is a statement that identifies your belief or position on a particular issue or topic. For example, claims answer the question "What am I trying to explain or prove?" Here, we describe several types of claims, as shown below: **claims of fact**, **conjecture**, **value**, and **policy**. You might claim that something is true or false, probable or improbable, good or bad, or reasonable or unreasonable.

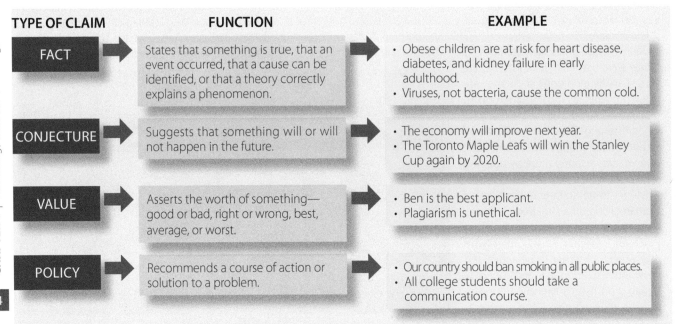

TYPE OF CLAIM	FUNCTION	EXAMPLE
FACT	States that something is true, that an event occurred, that a cause can be identified, or that a theory correctly explains a phenomenon.	• Obese children are at risk for heart disease, diabetes, and kidney failure in early adulthood. • Viruses, not bacteria, cause the common cold.
CONJECTURE	Suggests that something will or will not happen in the future.	• The economy will improve next year. • The Toronto Maple Leafs will win the Stanley Cup again by 2020.
VALUE	Asserts the worth of something— good or bad, right or wrong, best, average, or worst.	• Ben is the best applicant. • Plagiarism is unethical.
POLICY	Recommends a course of action or solution to a problem.	• Our country should ban smoking in all public places. • All college students should take a communication course.

COMMUNICATION

Exercise

www.youtube.com/watch?v=-85-j7Nr9i4

This video provides some insight into the factors that shape our opinions and challenges you to evaluate your critical thinking skills. After watching the video, consider the critical thinking questions listed above.

For more suggestions and information visit www.criticalthinking.org

1. Consider the following statement:
Immigrants to Canada are taking all of the good jobs.

2. Choose one of the critical thinking questions above and explore your thinking about this statement.

> Critical thinking puts your mind to work on complex communication problems—from applying for a job promotion to solving a family crisis, from making an effective classroom presentation to critiquing a politician's campaign commercial.[58]

Critical Thinking About Facts and Inference

In addition to understanding the different types of claims, critical thinkers know how to separate claims of fact (a statement that can be proved true or false) from inferences. An **inference** is a conclusion based on claims of fact. For example, "Julia has been late to the last three project meetings" is a claim of fact. You can document the truth of this statement. However, the statement "Julia does not care about our team's project" is an inference that may or may not be true.

Critical thinking helps you separate objective verifiable facts from questionable subjective inferences. When you accept an inference as a fact, you are jumping to conclusions that may not be accurate. When you assume that an inference is true, you may be led down a path that leads to a poor decision. Julia's tardiness might instead be the result of car trouble, unreliable childcare, or the needs of an elderly parent. More facts are needed to make a justifiable an accurate inference.

Some examples of critical thinking questions[59]

- What are the strengths and weaknesses of _____?
- Explain why/how _____?
- What would happen if _____?
- Why is _____ happening?
- How could _____ be used to _____?
- What are the implications of _____?
- What do I already know about _____?
- How does _____ affect _____?
- How does _____ tie in with what I have learned before?
- Why is _____ important?
- What is a solution to the problem of _____?
- What do you think causes _____? Why?
- Do I agree or disagree with this statement? What evidence is there to support my answer?
- What is another way to look at _____?

Critical Thinking About Fallacies

If you listen effectively and think critically about the content of conversations and quarrels, group discussions and meetings, speeches and presentations, media reports, and books, you will encounter valid and invalid claims. One way to recognize invalid arguments is to look for fallacies. A **fallacy** is an error in thinking that has the potential to mislead or deceive others. Fallacies can be intentional or unintentional.

After you've learned to identify a variety of fallacies, don't be surprised if you begin noticing them everywhere—in television commercials, in political campaigns, on talk radio, and in everyday conversations. As you learn about fallacies, ask yourself what is fallacious about advertisers' claims that "no other aspirin is more effective for pain than ours" and appeals to "buy Canada's best-selling pickup truck"? Are fallacies involved when a political candidate talks about an opponent's past as a pro-choice protester or a recovering alcoholic? We highlight six of the most common fallacies below.

Attacking the Person The fallacy of **attacking the person** also has a Latin name—*ad hominem*—which means "against the man." An *ad hominem* argument makes irrelevant attacks against a person rather than against the content of a person's message. Responding to the claim "Property taxes should be increased" with "What would you know? You don't own a home!" attacks the person rather than the argument. Name-calling, labelling, and attacking a person rather than the substance of an argument are unethical, *ad hominem* fallacies. Political campaign ads are notorious for attacking candidates in personal ways rather than addressing their positions on important public issues.

Appeal to Authority So-called expert opinion is often used to support arguments. However, when the supposed expert has no relevant experience on the issues being discussed, the fallacy of **appeal to authority** occurs, as in "I'm not a doctor, but I play one on TV, and I recommend Nick's Cough Syrup." Unless the actor has expert credentials on medical issues, the argument is fallacious. You see television and magazine advertisements in which celebrities praise the medicines they use, the companies that insure them, and the beauty

> When an unethical communicator misuses evidence or reasoning or when a well-meaning person misinterprets evidence or draws flawed conclusions, the result is still the same—inaccuracy and deception.

STOP&THINK

Can You Tell a Fact from an Inference?[60]

Read the following story carefully and assume that all the information presented is accurate and true while understanding that the story has ambiguous parts purposely designed to lead you astray. Then read the statements about the story and for each, select one of the following options:

T: The statement is definitely true on the basis of the information presented.

F: The statement is definitely false.

?: The statement may be true or false, but it is unclear from the information available.

Answer each statement in order, and do not go back to change previous answers. Once you have completed and counted the number of correct answers you have, take time to analyse the answers you selected and why.

STORY: A businessperson had just turned off the lights in the store when a man appeared and demanded money. The owner opened the cash register. The contents of the cash register were scooped up and the man sped away. A member of the police force was notified promptly.

Statements About the Story:

T	F	?	1. A man appeared after the owner had turned off his store lights.
T	F	?	2. The robber was a man.
T	F	?	3. The man who appeared did not demand money.
T	F	?	4. The man who opened the cash register was the owner.
T	F	?	5. The store owner scooped up the contents of the cash register and ran away.
T	F	?	6. Someone opened the cash register.
T	F	?	7. After the man who demanded the money scooped up the contents of the cash register, he ran away.
T	F	?	8. While the cash register contained money, the story does not state how much.
T	F	?	9. The robber demanded money of the owner.
T	F	?	10. A businessperson turned off the lights when a man appeared in the store.
T	F	?	11. It was broad daylight when the man appeared.
T	F	?	12. The man who appeared opened the cash register.
T	F	?	13. No one demanded money.
T	F	?	14. The story concerns a series of events in which only three persons are referred to: the owner of the store, a man who demanded money, and a member of the police force.
T	F	?	15. The following events occurred: someone demanded money, a cash register was opened, its contents were scooped up, and a man dashed out of the store.

Answers: (1) ?, (2) ?, (3) F, (4) ?, (5) ?, (6) T, (7) ?, (8) ?, (9) ?, (10) ?, (11) ?, (12) ?, (13) F, (14) F, (15) ?.

COMMON **FALLACIES**

FALLACY	DEFINITION	EXAMPLE
ATTACKING THE PERSON	Claiming that a person's opinions and arguments are wrong or untrue by attacking the person rather than what they are saying	Of course she supports universal child care for everyone—she's a socialist!
APPEAL TO AUTHORITY	Basing a claim on the opinion of a supposed expert who has no relevant experience on the issues being discussed	Look at all the celebrities who support him for governor. He must be the best candidate.
APPEAL TO POPULARITY	Claiming that an action is acceptable or excusable because many people are doing it	The Kindle is much better than the Nook because more people buy Kindles.
APPEAL TO TRADITION	Claiming that a certain course of action should be followed because it has always been done that way in the past	Grandma says that drinking brandy with a little honey is the best way to cure a cold.
FAULTY CAUSE	Claiming that a particular situation or event is the cause of another event before ruling out other possible causes	In our family we rarely get sick because we drink brandy with honey when we feel a cold coming on.
HASTY GENERALIZATION	Claiming that something is true based on too little evidence or too few experiences	My neighbour told me that vaccines cause autism and other disabilities in children.

products that make them look young and attractive. Just because someone is a good actor or good looking does not make her or him an expert on these topics.

Appeal to Popularity An **appeal to popularity** claims that an action is acceptable or excusable because many people are doing it. "Most of your neighbours have agreed to support the rezoning proposal" is an appeal to popularity. Just because a lot of people hold a particular belief or engage in an action does not make it right. If most of your friends overindulge on alcohol, should you? If lots of people tell

Szasz-Fabian Erika/Fotolia; Valdis Torms/Fotolia; Juniors Bildarchiv/Alamy; Jürgen Falchle/Fotolia

Superstitions are faulty cause fallacies.

Nancy Kaszerman/ZUMA Press/Alamy

Oprah Winfrey is viewed as an authority by her fans. When her talk show was still on the air and she chose a book for her book club, it sold millions. When she talked about her favorite products, stores were swamped with eager shoppers. When she raved about a film, it became a hit.

STOP&THINK

Do Emotions Matter in Critical Thinking?

Sometimes, emotions trigger a response that defies rational thinking. In such cases, instincts may be more reliable than a conclusion based on detailed analysis. Antonio Damasio, a neurologist, maintains that emotions play a crucial role in critical thinking. In his studies of patients with damage to the emotional centers of their brains, Damasio found that a lack of feelings actually impaired rational decision making.[61]

Emotions, gut feelings, instincts, hunches, and practical wisdom can help you make good decisions. They help you understand how decisions affect others and provide a way of assessing value when considering competing options.

Although you should pay attention to your emotions, they can also act as a barrier to critical thinking and decision making. Your intuitions and hunches are not always correct. For this reason, emotions must be balanced with critical thinking. Think about these popular sayings: "Opposites attract" and "Absence makes the heart grow fonder." Are these statements true? As much as your personal experiences or conventional wisdom may confirm both of these maxims, social science research suggests that both are usually wrong.

the nature of critical thinking

you that penicillin can cure a common cold, should you demand a prescription from your doctor? Unfortunately, appeals to popularity have also been used to justify discrimination, unscrupulous financial schemes, and dangerous behaviour.

Appeal to Tradition Claiming that a certain course of action should be followed because it was done that way in the past is an **appeal to tradition**. "We must have our annual company picnic in August because that's when we always schedule it" appeals to tradition. Just because a course of action has been followed for a time does not mean it is the best option.

Faulty Cause "We are losing sales because our sales team is not working hard enough." This statement may overlook other causes for low sales, such as a price increase that made the product less affordable or a competitor's superior product. The **faulty cause** fallacy occurs when you claim that a particular situation or event is the cause of another event before considering other possible causes. Will you catch a cold if you don't bundle up when you go outside? Will you have bad luck if you break a mirror? If you answer yes to either of these questions, you are not thinking critically. *Viruses*

cause colds, although a chill can weaken your immune system. Beliefs about breaking a mirror or walking under a ladder or allowing a black cat to cross your path are simply superstitions.

Hasty Generalizations You commit a **hasty generalization** fallacy when you jump to a conclusion based on too little evidence or too few experiences. The fallacy argues that if it is true for some, it must be true for all. "Don't go to that restaurant. I went once and the service was awful" is a hasty generalization. One negative experience does not mean that other visits to the restaurant would not be enjoyable.

The Nature of Reflective Practice

How does reflective practice enhance the quality of interpersonal communication?

Reflection refers to critically thinking about an experience as it occurs or after it occurs. Donald Schön (1983) describes this as *reflection-on-action* and *reflection-in-action*. Reflection is also part of our learning process and, like communication, takes time and practice.

In order to reflect meaningfully, you use the effective listening and critical thinking skills discussed in this chapter, combined with objective observations. We all think about our experiences, and intentional reflection encourages us to use analytical questions to examine experiences in more depth. The intention of reflective practice is to gain clearer and deeper understanding of our experiences. **Reflective practice** involves taking the time to review and ask questions to understand yourself and others. Reflective practice questions are designed to unravel a situation so that you can examine the experience from a variety of perspectives. This can help you to think critically, and as you have already read in this chapter, critical thinking can assist you in making appropriate decisions.[62]

Some Examples of Reflective Practice Questions
- What did I observe?

- What did I hear?
- Who was involved?
- What role did each person play?
- What words were spoken?
- What body language/nonverbal cues did I observe?
- What did I learn in this situation?
- What was the outcome of this situation or experience?
- How does this experience affect my future interpersonal interactions?
- What could I do differently next time?

Gibbs' Reflective Cycle[63]

DESCRIPTION
What happened?

FEELINGS
What were you thinking and feeling?

EVALUATION
What was good and bad about the experience?

ANALYSIS
What sense can you make of the situation?

CONCLUSION
What else could you have done?

ACTION PLAN
If it arose again what would you do?

COMMUNICATION

Exercise

1. Recall an incident, experience, or interpersonal interaction that you were involved in recently.
2. Using Gibbs' reflective cycle (above) and the critical thinking questions listed on this page, write your personal reflection of the events to better understand your role and participation in the events.

Student Listening Inventory[64]

Use the following numbers to indicate how often you, as a student, engage in the following listening behaviours. The "speaker" can refer to the instructor or another student.

1 = almost never   2 = not often   3 = sometimes   4 = more often than not   5 = almost always

Scoring: Add up your scores to assess how well you think you listen.

Listening Behaviour

1. When someone is speaking to me, I purposely block out distractions such as side conversations and personal problems. _____

2. I ask questions when I don't understand something a speaker has said. _____

3. When a speaker uses words I don't know, I jot them down and look them up later. _____

4. I assess a speaker's credibility while listening. _____

5. I paraphrase and/or summarize a speaker's main ideas in my head as I listen. _____

6. I concentrate on a speaker's main ideas rather than the specific details. _____

7. I try to understand people who speak both directly and indirectly. _____

8. Before reaching a conclusion, I try to confirm fully with the speaker my understanding of the message. _____

9. I fully concentrate when a speaker is explaining a complex idea. _____

10. When listening, I devote my full attention to a speaker's message. _____

11. I apply what I know about cultural differences when listening to someone from another culture. _____

12. I watch a speaker's facial expressions and body language for meaning. _____

13. I give positive nonverbal feedback to speakers—nods, eye contact, vocalized agreement. _____

14. When listening to a speaker, I establish eye contact and stop doing nonrelated tasks. _____

15. I avoid tuning out speakers when I disagree with or dislike their message. _____

16. When I have an emotional response to a speaker or the message, I try to set aside my feelings and continue listening to the message. _____

17. I try to match my nonverbal responses to my verbal responses. _____

18. When someone begins speaking, I focus my attention on the message. _____

19. I try to understand how past experiences influence the ways in which I interpret a message. _____

20. I attempt to eliminate outside interruptions and distractions. _____

21. When I listen, I look at the speaker, maintain some eye contact, and focus on the message. _____

22. I avoid tuning out messages that are complex, complicated, and challenging. _____

23. I try to understand the other person's point of view when it is different from mine. _____

24. I try to be nonjudgmental and noncritical when I listen. _____

25. As appropriate, I self-disclose personal information similar to the information the other person shares with me. _____

Score	Interpretation
0–62	You perceive yourself to be a poor listener.
63–86	You perceive yourself to be an adequate listener.
87–111	You perceive yourself to be a good listener.
112–125	You perceive yourself to be an outstanding listener.

4.1
The Nature of Listening
Why is listening essential for effective communication?

- We spend most of our communicating time engaged in listening.
- Most people cannot accurately recall 50 percent of what they hear after listening to a short talk. Without training, we listen at about 25 percent efficiency.

4.2
The Listening Process
What are the key components of the listening process?

- The six types of listening in the HURIER listening model—hearing, understanding, remembering, interpreting, evaluating, and responding—call for unique listening skills.
- Effective paraphrasing involves restating what others say in a way that indicates you understand their meaning.
- Asking well-planned, appropriate questions can help you understand another person's meaning.
- Working memory is your brain's processing centre for deciding if information is worth keeping and storing in your long-term memory.

4.3
Listening Strategies and Skills
What listening strategies and skills can help you communicate more effectively?

- Conscientious listeners use their extra thought speed to enhance listening.
- Effective communicators skilfully listen to feedback and nonverbal behaviour while also making sure that they withhold evaluation until their comprehension is complete.

- Effective listeners avoid and minimize distractions to themselves and others.
- Adaptability and flexibility are keys to listening and taking useful notes.

4.4
Listening to Gender and Culture
How do gender and culture affect the way we listen?

- Adjusting to diverse listening styles, particularly those involving differences in gender, culture, and hearing ability, is a challenging task that requires an understanding, respect, and adaptation to others.

4.5
The Nature of Critical Thinking
How does critical thinking enhance the quality of communication?

- Critical thinking is the kind of thinking you use to analyze what you read, see, or hear to arrive at a justified conclusion or decision.
- Critical thinking requires an understanding of the nature and types of claims, including claims of fact, conjecture, value, and policy.
- Critical thinkers understand and can separate verifiable facts from unsubstantiated inferences.

- Effective communicators identify and avoid using fallacies such as attacking the person, appeal to authority, appeal to popularity, appeal to tradition, faulty cause, and hasty generalizations.
- In addition to thinking critically, emotional responses in the form of gut feelings, instincts, hunches, and practical wisdom can help you make good decisions.

4.6
The Nature of Reflective Practice
How does reflective practice enhance interpersonal communication?

- Reflection involves thinking critically about an experience as it is occurring or after it takes place.
- Reflection is an important part of the learning process
- The purpose of reflection is to gain deeper and clearer understanding of an experience.
- Reflection can help you to be a more effective communicator.
- Reflective practice is complex and involves the use of probing questions to explore events, situations, and experiences.

Jaimie Duplass/Shutterstock/Pearson

TEST YOUR KNOWLEDGE

4.1 Why is listening essential for effective communication?

1 In general, we spend 40 to 70 percent of our communicating time engaged in _____.
   a. writing
   b. speaking
   c. reading
   d. listening
   e. reading and writing

2 Immediately after listening to a short talk or lecture, most people cannot accurately report _____ percent of what was said.
   a. 10
   b. 30
   c. 40
   d. 50
   e. 70

4.2 What are the key components of the listening process?

3 Listening to interpret refers to
   a. how accurately you understand the meaning of another person's message.
   b. your ability to distinguish auditory and/or visual stimuli in a listening situation.
   c. how you act out ethnocentrism and stereotyping of others.
   d. your ability to evaluate the validity of a message.
   e. how well you focus on understanding and identifying with a person's situation, feeling, or motives.

4.3 What listening strategies and skills can help you communicate more effectively?

4 Read the following statement and a listener's paraphrase that follows. What characteristic of paraphrasing has the listener failed to take into account?

Grace: My whole family—parents, sisters, and Aunt Ruth—bug me about it, and sometimes I can tell they're very angry with me and how I'm overdrawn at the bank.

Listener: In other words, your family is angry because you're overdrawn at the bank; am I right?
   a. The listener is not mindful.
   b. The listener is not using new words to express Grace's message.
   c. The listener has not heard Grace's words correctly.
   d. The listener has not asked for confirmation.
   e. all of the above

5 Which of the following listening strategies involves using your extra thought speed productively?
   a. Identify the key ideas in a message.
   b. Pay attention to the meaning of a speaker's nonverbal behaviour.
   c. Analyze the strengths and weaknesses of arguments.
   d. Assess the relevance and ethics of a speaker's comments.
   e. all of the above

4.4 How do gender and culture affect how we listen?

6 In general, men are more likely to listen comprehensively and analytically, whereas women are more likely to listen _____.
   a. only comprehensively
   b. empathically
   c. empathically and appreciatively
   d. appreciatively and comprehensively
   e. only emotionally

4.5 How does critical thinking enhance the quality of communication?

7 "The economy will improve next year" is an example of which type of argumentative claim?
   a. fact
   b. conjecture
   c. value
   d. policy
   e. emotion

8 Which of the following statements is an inference?
   a. I must have the flu.
   b. It is now flu season.
   c. I have a fever and ache all over.
   d. Both of my sisters had the flu two weeks ago.
   e. No one in my immediate family has had a flu shot.

9 What fallacy is committed in this statement: "Congestion and nausea! Oh, my God. John must have the swine flu!"
   a. hasty generalization
   b. appeal to authority
   c. attacking the person
   d. appeal to tradition
   e. faulty cause

10 What is the purpose of reflection?
   a. to understand an experience more deeply
   b. to think about which movie we want to see
   c. Neither of these answers is correct.

Answers found on page 330.

Key Terms

Appeal to authority	**Fallacy**	**Listening to respond**
Appeal to popularity	**Faulty cause**	**Listening to understand**
Appeal to tradition	**Gibbs' reflective cycle**	**Mnemonic**
Attacking the person	**Hasty generalization**	**Paraphrasing**
Claims	**Hearing**	**Reflection**
Claims of conjecture	**Inference**	**Reflective practice**
Claims of fact	**Listening**	**Short-term memory**
Claims of policy	**Listening to evaluate**	**Thought speed**
Claims of value	**Listening to hear**	**Working memory**
Critical thinking	**Listening to interpret**	**Working memory theory**
Empathic listening	**Listening to remember**	

"Did you see the brown girl over there?"

"STUPID QUEER!"

"That's a retarded thing to say!"

You would look so much better if you wore clothes that fit your body type.

THOSE people work like dogs!

5 VERBAL Communication

"Dress like a Canadian!! Lose the veil."

"Go back to your own country!!"

What is that smell? Do you people really EAT that stuff?

There is no denying the power of language, but it also comes with potential hazards. Once the words are out of your mouth, you cannot take them back.

A survey of college students enrolled in basic communication courses ranked "choosing appropriate and effective words" as one of the top 10 speaking skills. When asked to justify their rankings, students explained, "I'm afraid that right in the middle of speaking, I'll have trouble finding the words I need." "Sometimes, when someone asks me a question at work, I fumble with the answer—not because I don't know the answer but because I can't find the right words to explain what I know." "When someone disagrees with me, I can't seem to explain my position. I can't find the right words."[1]

Well-chosen words lie at the heart of electrifying, memorable presentations and at the core of meaningful and long-lasting interpersonal relationships. The right words explain, teach, support, comfort, persuade, inspire, and delight.

5.1
Human Language
What makes human language unique?

Humans do not share the remarkable sensory skills of many animals. You cannot track a faint scent through a forest trail or camouflage your skin colour to hide from a predator. Many mammals do a much better job of interpreting body movement than you do.[2] Yet you can do something that no other animal can: You can speak.

Even though other animals use sophisticated communication systems, they do not use a language as complex and powerful as the one you are reading right now. The ability to learn words and to combine, invent, and give meaning to new words makes humans unique among animals.[4]

Researchers estimate that the first humans to speak language as we know it lived in East Africa about 150,000 years ago.[5] In a 100,000-year-old skull, anthropologists found a modern-shaped hyoid bone, which fits right at the top of the windpipe and resembles part of the modern apparatus we need to speak. Fully modern language probably evolved only 50,000 years ago.[6] Thus, the ability to speak is relatively new given that our earliest known ancestors lived about 3.3 million years ago in what is now Ethiopia.[7]

Our early ancestors also walked upright rather than hunched over like apes. Standing upright made it possible for humans to use their hands to carry things, make tools, and gesture in complicated ways. Equally important, it contributed to physiological changes in the larynx, lungs, throat, and vocal cavity that enabled speech. As a result, we are the only species whose anatomy allows for speech and complex language development.[8]

> **"The difference between the almost right word and the right word is really a large matter—'tis the difference between the lightning bug and the lightning."**
> —Mark Twain[3]

Human **language** is a system of arbitrary signs and symbols used to communicate thoughts and feelings. Every language spoken on this planet is a *system*: an interrelated collection of words and rules employed to construct and express messages that generate meaning. In addition to determining the meanings of words, all languages impose a grammar that arranges words in a meaningful way. "The went store he to" makes no sense until you rearrange the words: "He went to the store." And although "Him go to store" may be understandable, it breaks several grammatical rules.

Career paths can be affected by the ability to communicate in a professional manner. Well-chosen words are at the centre of effective communication, whether you are chatting with a friend, leading a group, addressing an audience, or writing a novel. In this chapter, we focus on **verbal communication**—the ways in which we use the words in a language to generate meaning, regardless of whether we communicate face-to-face, text-to-text, cell-phone-to-cell-phone, or email-to-email.[9] In Chapter 6, we focus on nonverbal communication—the ways in which we use message components *other than words* to generate meaning.

> **"Whatever else people do when they come together—whether they play, fight, make love, or make automobiles—they talk. We live in a world of language."**
> —Victoria Fromkin and Robert Rodman, linguists[10]

Paylessimages/Fotolia

Language and Meaning

How do the characteristics of language affect meaning?

When you don't know the meaning of a word, you may look it up in a dictionary. Depending on the word, however, you may find several definitions. Likewise, no two people share exactly the same meaning of the same word. Even when a single word is used, different people may have different perceptions shaped by their values, experiences and knowledge.

> Words do not have meanings; people have meanings for words.[11]

Signs and Symbols

As noted earlier, all languages are human inventions composed of signs and symbols: The words we speak or write, and the system that underlies their use, have all been made up by people.[12] A **sign** stands for or represents something specific and often looks like the thing it represents. Thus, it has a visual relationship to that thing. For example, the graphic depictions of jagged lightning and dark clouds on a weather map are signs of a storm.

Unlike signs, **symbols** do *not* have a direct relationship to the things they represent. Instead, they are an *arbitrary* collection of sounds that in certain combinations stand for concepts. Nothing in the compilation of letters that make up the word *lightning* looks or sounds like lightning. The letters making up the word *cloud* are neither

Exercise

Do this exercise with a partner. One of you will read the following list of words; the other will say the first word or phrase that comes to your mind when you hear the word.

A. Preacher, teenager, farmer, prostitute, librarian, prime minister, soldier, hockey captain, feminist, dad, son, daughter, student, teacher.

B. Next switch roles. Why do you think there are differences in responses?

C. Read the quote above. Do you see the connection to this statement?

The Many Meanings of **LOVE**

Ruth Jenkinson/DK Images

Consider the many ways in which people define the word *love*.

Romantic **love**

Love for family and friends

Love for a pet

Love for a hobby or sport

Love of country

Common **SIGNS**

Rain

Rain and Lightning

Partly Cloudy

language and meaning

white and puffy nor dark and gloomy. You cannot be struck by the word *lightning* or get wet from the word *rain*.

When you see or hear a word, you apply your prior knowledge, experience, and feelings to decide what the word means. For example, if someone talks about a steak dinner, you may have very different reactions to the word *steak* depending on whether you are a rancher, a gourmet chef, a vegetarian, or an animal rights activist.

Language scholars C. K. Ogden and I. A. Richards provide an explanation of this phenomenon. They employ a triangle to explain the three elements of language: the thinking person, the symbol (or sign) used to represent something, and the actual thing, idea, or feeling being referenced.[13] The triangle does not have a solid base because the symbol and the referent are *not* directly related. The symbol must be mentally processed before it has meaning.

Denotative and Connotative Meaning

One of the great myths about language is that every word has an exact meaning. The truth is just the opposite: Just as no two communicators or communication contexts are exactly

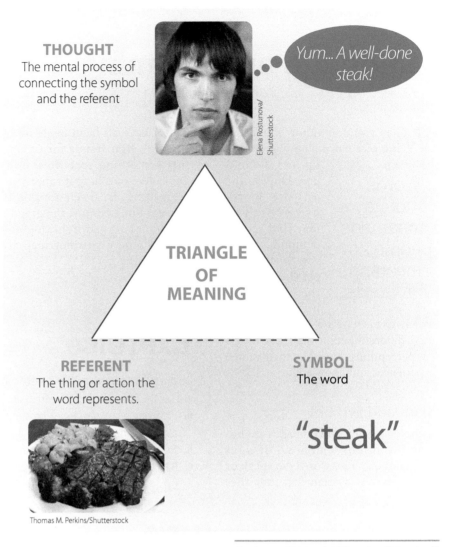

THOUGHT The mental process of connecting the symbol and the referent

Elena Rostunova/ Shutterstock

Yum... A well-done steak!

TRIANGLE OF MEANING

REFERENT The thing or action the word represents.

Thomas M. Perkins/Shutterstock

SYMBOL The word

"steak"

Ogden and Richards's Triangle of Meaning[14]

STOP&THINK

What's in a Name?

Our ability "to name" is uniquely human. It has been considered a holy privilege as well as a magical gift. According to Judaism and Christianity, the first honour God confers on Adam is that of naming the animals.[15]

Many names also have interesting histories as well as special meanings. For example, the English name *Dianna* is probably derived from an old Indo-European root meaning "heavenly"

and "divine" and is related to Diana, the Roman goddess of the moon, hunting, forests, and childbirth. The name *John* comes from the Greek name meaning "gracious." This name owes its popularity to John the Baptist and the apostle John in the New Testament. All cultures have their own naming traditions.

Now consider *your* name. Why did your parents choose this name? Does their choice say something about your family's history or your culture? How has your name affected your life?

HELLO my name is

Violet

Tran-Photography/Fotolia

CHAPTER 5 | verbal communication

alike, no two word meanings can ever be the same.[16]

Two linguistic concepts—denotation and connotation—help explain the elusive nature of word meanings. **Denotation** refers to the specific and objective-dictionary-based meaning of a word. For example, most of us would agree that a *snake* is a scaly, legless, sometimes venomous reptile with a long, cylindrical body. Plumbers have their own version of a *snake*—a flexible metal wire or coil used to clean out pipes. Each of these "snakes" has a denotative meaning.

Connotation refers to the emotional response or personal thoughts

> ❝CONNOTATION is the aura of feeling, pleasant or unpleasant, that surrounds practically all words.❞[17]
>
> —S. I. Hayakawa, semanticist

connected to the meaning of a word. Connotation, rather than denotation, is more likely to influence your response to words. For example, just the thought of a snake is enough to make some people who have a fear of snakes tremble. Yet a serpentologist—a scientist who studies snakes—would try to convince you that snakes are among the most intriguing and magnificent of animals.

For most people, a word's connotation has much more significance than its denotation. Whereas you may tell someone that a *cop* pulled you over and gave you an undeserved ticket, a *police officer* may have helped you with a flat tire. What seems like a neutral word to you can have strong connotations to others.

the serpent / the plumbing tool

Jupiterimages/Stockbyte/Getty Images

Vlue/Shutterstock

Concrete and Abstract Words

Your choice of concrete or abstract words significantly affects whether and how well others understand the intended meaning of your message. **Concrete words** refer to specific things you perceive with your senses—things you can smell, taste, touch, see, or hear. The words *table*, *Paris*, *giraffe*, and *red rose* are concrete because, unlike *furniture*, *city*, *animal*, and *flower*, they narrow the number of possible meanings and decrease the likelihood of misinterpretation. **Abstract words** refer to ideas or concepts that usually cannot be observed or touched and often require

interpretation. The word *animal* is more abstract than *giraffe* because there are a huge number of different kinds of animals. Moreover, you can see a giraffe in your mind, but what image does an animal conjure up? Both a crayfish and a giraffe are animals. Similarly, words such as *fairness*, *freedom*, and *evil* can have an almost endless number of meanings and don't specifically refer to something you can see, hear, smell, taste, or touch. The more abstract your language is, the more likely it is that your listeners may interpret your meaning other than the way you intended.[18]

Language has three general levels of meaning that range from highly abstract to very concrete.[19] **Superordinate terms** group objects and ideas together very generally; *vehicle*, *animal*, or *location* are superordinate terms. **Basic terms** further describe a superordinate term, such as *car*, *van*, *truck*; *cat*, *chicken*, *mouse*; or *New England*, *Deep South*, *Appalachia*. **Subordinate terms** offer the most concrete and specialized descriptions. The vehicle parked outside is not just a *car*. It is a 1988 red Mercedes sports car convertible. The cat purring on your lap is not just a cat; it is a blue-eyed male Siamese cat named Gatsby.

language and meaning

Three Levels of MEANING

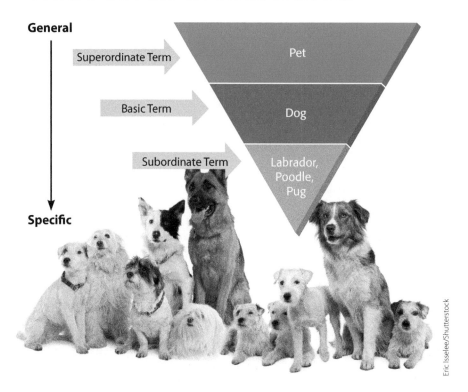

General

Superordinate Term → Pet

Basic Term → Dog

Subordinate Term → Labrador, Poodle, Pug

Specific

Eric Isselee/Shutterstock

5.3
Language and Culture

How do language and culture affect one another?

There are approximately 5,000 to 6,000 languages spoken in the world, all of them with different vocabularies and rules of grammar.[20] Have you ever tried to talk to or understand someone who speaks very little English? The experience can be frustrating, comical, enlightening, or even disastrous.

The words in a language often reflect what is important to the people in a specific culture. Just as there are dozens of words used to describe camels in Arabic languages and snow in Eskimo languages, there are many English words to describe the many kinds of vehicles driven in Canada as well as for coffee drinks served at a café. In many countries, there are significant regional differences in vocabulary. For example, a sandwich on a large roll with a variety of meats and cheeses on it may be a *grinder*, a *hero*, a *sub*, a *hoagie*, or a *po'boy*, depending on the region of the country.[21]

> "Let's go to Timmies for a double-double and be sure to Roll Up the Rim."

Pronouns

As we noted in Chapter 3, individualism-collectivism is the most significant cultural dimension and the factor that best distinguishes one culture from another. Individualistic cultures have an "I" orientation; collectivist cultures have a "we" orientation. Interestingly, English is the only language that capitalizes the pronoun *I* in writing. English does not, however, capitalize the written form of the pronoun *you*.[22] By contrast, people of the Athabaskan-speaking community in Alaska speak and think in a collective plural voice. The word for *people, dene,*

CHAPTER 5 | verbal communication

The Whorf Hypothesis

One of the most significant and controversial language theories attempts to explain why people from different cultures speak and interpret messages differently from one another. Linguist Edward Sapir and his student Benjamin Whorf spent decades studying the relationship between language, culture, and thought. Whorf's most controversial theory contends that the structures of a language *determines* how we see, experience, and interpret the world around us. For example, if you don't have a word for *red*, will you be able to see red or separate it from other colours you do recognize?

In English, we understand the grammatical differences between "I saw the girl," "I see the girl," and "I will see the girl." Whorf observed that the Hopi Indians of Arizona make no past-, present-, and future-tense distinctions in their language. Therefore, he concluded, they must perceive the world very differently. He also noted that the Hopi have a single word, *masa'ytaka*, for everything that flies, from insects to airplanes. Does that mean the Hopi cannot think about tomorrow and cannot see the differences between an airplane and a fly? Originally, many linguists believed that the answer was *yes*. Now linguists understand that the Hopi *do* think about tomorrow, even if they may lack a specific word for it.

Like many controversial theories, the Whorf hypothesis (also referred to as the Sapir-Whorf hypothesis) has been accepted, rejected, resurrected, and amended—several times. Today, most linguists accept a more moderate

While language does not determine everything we think, it does influence the way we perceive others and the world around us.[23]

version of the **Whorf hypothesis**: Language *reflects* cultural models of the world, which in turn influence how the speakers of a language come to think, act, and behave.[24] For example, in English, terms that end with *man*, such as *chairman*, *fireman*, and *policeman*, may lead us to view certain roles and jobs as only appropriate for men. Substituting words such as *chairperson*, *firefighter*, and *police officer* may change perceptions about who can work in these careers.

---

is used as a kind of *we*, and is the subject for almost every sentence requiring a personal pronoun.[25]

When speaking to others, pay attention to the individualistic or collectivist tendencies in the way they use languages. Although frequent use of the words *I*, *me*, and *you* may be common for a group of ambitious and individualistic corporate executives in Canada, the words *we* and *us* might be heard more frequently from African Canadians or people from Central and South America and Africa who are more collectivist.

Verbal Directness

Most people living in the United States have a low-context, direct way of speaking. In the eyes of other cultures, they get to the point with blunt, straight talk. Many other cultures view this direct use of language as a disregard for others that can lead to

Exercise

Do You Think?

To dig deeper into the Whorf hypothesis and cultural influence, view this YouTube video.

www.youtube.com/watch?v=GRMNrEo7CRw&list=PL52A8C98342181508

embarrassment and injured feelings.[26] For example, at a news conference, President George W. Bush acknowledged that his all-American speaking style may have been too direct when dealing with the leaders of other nations. "'I explained to the prime minister [Tony Blair of Great Britain] that the policy of my government is the removal of Saddam.' Catching himself,

Bush added: 'Maybe I should be a little less direct and be a little more nuanced, and say we support regime change.'"[27]

Most North Americans learn to say yes or no when expressing their opinions; however, a Japanese person may say yes to a suggestion or business proposal because it is what she or he believes you want to hear when, in fact, the real response may be no.

5.4

Language and Gender

How does language reflect gender differences?

Most languages reflect a gender bias. These differences can be minor or major depending on the language and context in which communication takes place.[28] In English, we struggle with the words *he* and *she*. For many years, the pronoun *he* was used to refer to an unspecified individual. Older English textbooks used sentences such as:

How do you talk about a couple when using their first names? Is it Juliet and Romeo or Romeo and Juliet?

Every speaker should pay attention to his words. Other languages have gender-related challenges as well. French, for example, has separate third-person plurals: masculine and feminine versions of *they* (*ils, elles*). Japanese distinguishes gender in both the first and the second person; they use a different version of *you* for men and women. The language of Finland may have the best solution. All pronouns are gender neutral; there is a single word that means both *he* and *she* (*hän*).[29]

Although some languages, such as Finnish, make very few distinctions between men and women, English favours men over women. Most gender-related word pairings begin with the male term: male and female, boys and girls, husband and wife, Jack and Jill, Romeo and Juliet, Mr. and Mrs.[30] If you doubt this preference, think about the married couples you know. Would you address a letter to Mrs. and Mr. Smith?

Unfortunately, because of the male bias in English and in North American society, female terms tend to take on demeaning connotations. The connotations of the second word in the following pairings are negative or outdated for women: *governor/governess, master/mistress,* and *sir/madam*. Women are also compared with animals: *chick, bitch, fox, cow, shrew, and dog*. One study lists more than 500 English slang terms for *prostitutes* but only 65 for the men who are their willing clients.[31]

Robin Lakoff, one of the first linguists to write about gender differences, in *Language and Woman's Place*, contends that women tend to use language that expresses uncertainty, lack of confidence, and excessive deference or politeness.[32] For example, women tend to use questions tagged onto sentences to gain approval, such as "don't you agree?" and "haven't you?"

> When the communication goal is significant and personally important, *both* men and women use highly powerful language.

They are more likely to avoid direct requests, using superpolite phrases instead such as "Could you please close the door?" or "Would you mind closing the door?" Women's speech is also described as more tentative, using such hedges or "fillers" as *like, you know, well,* and *kind of.*

We would be guilty of stereotyping if we didn't note the exceptions to such tendencies. Certainly, many men speak tentatively and co-operatively, and many women speak directly and assertively.

Strategies for AVOIDING GENDER BIAS WITH PRONOUNS

- **Use plural forms.** Instead of saying, "Every speaker should pay attention to his words," consider, "All speakers should pay attention to their words."

- **Avoid using any pronoun.** Instead of using a pronoun at all, consider, "Good speakers pay careful attention to language."

- **Use variations on the phrase "he or she" as well as "his and hers."** Instead of saying, "Every speaker should pay attention to his or her words," consider, "Every speaker should pay attention to her or his words."

GENDER-NEUTRAL TERMS for Jobs and Professions

Gender-BIASED Terms	Gender-NEUTRAL Terms
Stewardess	*Flight attendant*
Fireman	*Firefighter*
Female soldier	*Soldier*
Chairman	*Chairperson*
Male nurse	*Nurse*

Use gender-neutral terms to describe jobs and professions. In the theatre and film industries, for example, the word *actor* is replacing *actress* for female performers.

Oleg_Zabielin/Fotolia

BlueSkyImage/Shutterstock

COMMUNICATION&CULTURE

DO WOMEN TALK MORE THAN MEN?

One language myth is that women talk more than men. This belief is neither new nor confined to the Canada.[33] Most research studies, however, paint a different picture. A recent study of 400 college students found that the number of words uttered by males and females were virtually the same. An analysis of 63 studies of gender differences in talkativeness found that men actually "yakked slightly more than women, especially when interacting with spouses or strangers and when the topic was non-personal." Women talked more with classmates, with parents and children, and in situations where the topic of conversation required disclosure of feelings.[34]

In work settings, men do most of the talking. Even when women hold influential positions, they often find it hard to contribute to a discussion as much as men do. This pattern is also evident in educational settings (from kindergarten through university), where males usually dominate classroom talk. Sadly, when women talk as much as men do, they may be perceived as talking "too much."[35]

When linguist Janet Holmes answers the question "Do women talk more than men?" she concludes, "It depends." It depends on the social context, the kind of talk, and the confidence of the speaker, the social roles, and the speaker's expertise. Generally, men are more likely to dominate conversation in formal, public contexts where talk is highly valued and associated with status and power. Women, on the other hand, are likely to contribute more in private, informal interactions, when talk functions to maintain relationships and in situations where women feel socially confident.[36]

Jameschipper/Fotolia

COMMUNICATION

Exercise

Rewrite the following passage using gender-neutral words.

New faculty hired to work in the Fireman Foundation Studies Program undergo intensive training to help them to evaluate their students' assignments. The average college student is worried about his grades. When he has an assignment returned, he can decide to accept the grade, or to launch an appeal. There is often a middleman, a student liaison, who can assist the student with the appeal process. If this is not satisfactory, the next step is often to involve the chairman of the program.

5.5

Language and Context

How does context affect language choices?

What kind of language would you use in a college classroom, at a family member's funeral, at a critical job interview, at a political or pep rally, at home with your parents, or at a party with your friends? There would be subtle and not-so-subtle differences in your choice of words and grammar. We naturally change the way we use language based on our relationships with other communicators, their psychological traits and preferences, and the extent to which they share our cultural attitudes, beliefs, values, and behaviours.

The phrase *code switching* refers to a common strategy for adapting to the many contexts in which we communicate. If you can speak more than one language, you already code switch as you move from one language to another. Here we use the term **code switching** in a broader sense: to describe how we modify our verbal and nonverbal communication in different contexts.

Effective communicators learn to adapt their language to the communication context. Although a swear word would never pass your lips at a job interview, during a church service, or in a formal public speech, you may curse in the company of close friends and like-minded colleagues.

How do context and culture affect the way we choose and use language?

5.6

Overcoming Common Language Barriers

How do bypassing, exclusionary language, and offensive language affect communication?

Despite our best efforts to understand the complex relationship between language and meaning, misunderstandings are inevitable.

Bypassing, exclusionary language, and offensive language are three common barriers to effective communication.

Bypassing

When two people assign different meanings to the same word or phrase, they risk bypassing each other. **Bypassing** is a form of miscommunication that occurs when people "miss each other with their meanings."[37] If you have ever found yourself saying, "But, that's not what I meant," you have experienced bypassing.

Note the problem created in the following example of bypassing: A high school graphic design teacher wrote a letter to Randy Cohen, a former "ethicist" for *The New York Times Magazine*. The teacher explained that students were assigned the task of creating a guitar using Photoshop. A few asked if they could use an online tutorial. The teacher said *yes*, assuming and quite sure they'd merely consult it for help. Three students handed in identical work because they'd carefully followed the tutorial to the letter. The teacher wanted to give each student a C on the assignment because the other students created their

work from scratch. Thus his question: Should he give them the C, or is he bound by having given them the okay to use the tutorial?

The ethicist wrote back, saying, "There's something not quite right about penalizing these students for doing what you explicitly permitted them

> Remember that it's not what words mean to *you*, but what others mean when they use those words.

to do. It's a teacher's obligation to be clear about what is and what is not acceptable."[38] The students clearly believed they had permission to use the tutorial to create the guitar graphic, whereas the teacher assumed they would only consult the tutorial for help.

COMMUNICATION IN *ACTION*

Tiptoeing Around Words

When you use a **euphemism,** you substitute a bland, mild, vague, or unobjectionable word or phrase for one considered too direct, indecent, harsh, offensive, or hurtful. Rather than say someone has died, we may say he or she has "passed away." In Victorian England, the word *limb* was used for *leg*, a word that had sexual connotations. Even a chair leg wasn't referred to as such because it might spark thoughts of sexuality. In U.S. restaurants, we usually ask for directions to the restroom rather than the toilet.[39] Some euphemisms also substitute letters in a word to make it less offensive.

You frequently hear people say "jeeze" instead of "Jesus," "darn" instead of "damn," and "heck" rather than "hell." Can you "translate" the following words and phrases into their non-euphemistic meaning: *doggone, freaking, oh my goodness*, and *shoot*?

Euphemisms, however, can be used to mask the truth. The Pentagon referred to the information-seeking techniques Americans used on Iraqis in the Abu Ghraib prison as *interrogation*, whereas many described these techniques (food and sleep deprivation, water boarding, stress positioning, hooding, and attacking with dogs) as *torture*.[40]

What Slanguage Do You Speak?

Slanguage is the language of slang, which is nothing new. It's been around since we began creating and speaking words. Although there is disagreement about the origins of the word **slang**, most linguists agree that slang is a short-lived, group-related, ever-changing, creative and innovative, often playful and metaphorical, colloquial language variety that is below the level of stylistically neutral language.[41] Huh? In other words, slang consists of informal, nonstandard words or phrases that tend to originate in subcultures (such as teenagers, musicians, athletes, inner-city gangs, railroad workers, prisoners) within a society.

Slang helps language change and renew itself.[42] Many words that began as slang—*cool*; *Uncle Tom* and *Mr. Charley*; *booze*, *bread* and *dough*; and lots of words for toilet (*john*, *head*, *can*, *loo*)—have ended up in standard usage dictionaries. Just about every surviving slang word has an interesting history. Why, for example, do people say "I have to use the john?" Could it be that the inventor of the first toilet in a home (as opposed to an outhouse) was Sir John Harrington, a member of Queen Elizabeth I's court in England?[43]

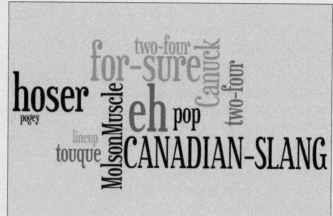

> ## Slang is language, which takes off its coat, spits on its hands—and goes to work.
>
> —Carl Sandburg, American poet[44]

Most slang, however, doesn't last long. As Kathryn Lindskoop writes in *Creative Writing*, "It looks foolish when it gets old, when it is slightly misused, and when it is used by the wrong people in a futile attempt to sound hip."[45] In other words, we see nothing wrong with using slang in the right place at the right time with the right people and for the right reasons.

As in most cultures, Canadians have developed national and regional slang words. The table below identifies and explains those most frequently used in our casual conversations.

William Haney, an organizational communication scholar, maintains that effective "communicators who habitually look for meanings in the people using words, rather than in the words themselves, are much less prone to bypass or be bypassed."[46]

Exclusionary Language

Exclusionary language uses words that reinforce stereotypes, belittle other people, or exclude others from understanding an in-group's message. Exclusionary language widens the social gap by separating the world into *we* (to refer to people who are like you) and *they* or *those people* (to refer to people who are different from you). Such terms can offend others. You don't have to be excessive about being "politically correct," using *vertically challenged* for *short*, but you should avoid alienating others and use language that includes rather than excludes. Specifically, avoid mentioning anything about age, health or mental and physical abilities, sexual orientation, or race and ethnicity unless these

COMMUNICATION

Exercise

In small groups, answer the following questions.

- Have you heard friends and fellow students use the slang terms listed in the above box? If not; why not? Is it because your geographic location is different, because you're not an 18- to 21-year-old college student, or because the terms are already dated?
- What would you add to this list? What other slang terms do you and your friends use?
- Which term or terms do you believe is the most frequently used slang term on your campus or in your neighbourhood?

characteristics are relevant to the discussion.

- **Age.** Instead of *old lady*, use *older woman* or just *woman*.
- **Health and Abilities.** Instead of the word *retarded* in reference to *mental ability* or *physical ability* use people-first language such as, "he has a learning disability," or "she uses a wheelchair."[47]
- **Sexual Orientation.** Never assume that the sexual orientation of others is the same as your own. *Homo*, *fairy*, *fag*, *butch*, and *dyke* are unacceptable; instead, use *gay* or *lesbian*.
- **Race and Ethnicity.** Avoid using stereotypical terms and descriptions based on a person's race, ethnicity, or region, such as *hick*. Use the names people prefer to describe their racial or ethnic affiliations, such as black, African Canadian, Latino/Latina, Muslim, and Asian. Rather than saying "That Polish guy down the

block owns several repair shops," say instead, "That man down the block owns several repair shops."

In her book, *Poor Bashing: The Politics of Exclusion* (2001), Canadian activist and author, Jean Swanson discusses the exclusionary words unfairly used to describe those living in poverty. Poor people in Canada are often described as being lazy, drunk, stupid, uneducated, having large families, and not looking for work.[48]

In addition to stereotyping others, exclusionary language can prevent some people from participating in or joining a discussion that relies on specialized jargon. **Jargon** is the specialized or technical language of a profession or homogeneous group. English professor William Lutz points out that groups use jargon as "verbal shorthand that allows members to communicate with each other clearly, efficiently, and quickly."[49] In some settings and on some occasions, such as at a meeting of psychiatrists, attorneys, information technology professionals, or educators, the ability to use jargon properly is a sign of group membership, and it speeds communication among members.

Some speakers use jargon to impress others with their specialized knowledge. For example, a skilled statistician may bewilder an audience by using unfamiliar terms to describe

cutting-edge methodologies for establishing causality. In other situations, people use jargon when they have nothing to say; they just string together a bunch of nonsense and hope no one notices their lack of content.[50] Such tactics fail to inform others and often result in misunderstandings and resentment.

Offensive Language and Swearing

During the first half of the twentieth century, many words were considered inappropriate, particularly those that referred to private body parts and functions. Women went to the *powder room* and men to the *lavatory*. Even the word *pregnant* was once considered improper. Instead, a woman was "in a family way" or "with child." In 1952, Lucille Ball became the first pregnant woman to appear on a television show. The scripts called her an "expectant mother," never using the word *pregnant*. All of the *I Love Lucy* scripts were reviewed by a priest, a rabbi, and a minister to make certain they were in good taste.[51] Not that long ago, swear

"What the @*^$%! ^*@$?"

Daniel Smith/Universal Pictures/AP Images

Cursing and using sexually explicit language were once taboo on television and not considered "ladylike." Although some women now believe swearing is "liberating," it remains a stigma in many contexts—for both women *and* men. Pictured here is the foul-mouthed character Hit Girl from the cult film *Kick-Ass*.

ETHICAL COMMUNICATION

Sticks and Stones May Break Your Bones, but Words Can Hurt Forever

Movie director Spike Lee rejects being labeled as a "black" filmmaker. "I want to be known as a talented filmmaker. That should be first. But the reality today is that no matter how successful you are, you're black first."

Two problems occur when you label someone or accept a label you hear or see. First, you reduce an entire person into a label: black filmmaker, dumb blonde, female doctor, or rich uncle. Second, the label can affect your perceptions or relationship with that person. For example, if you label a person as inconsiderate, you may dismiss an act of kindness: "I wonder what prompted her to do that?" When you label someone as near perfect, you may go to great lengths to justify or explain less-than-perfect behaviour: "Nicole is still the best player on the softball team; she's just having an off year." Labels also influence how we interpret the same behaviour:

- I'm energetic; you're overexcited; he's out of control.
- I'm laid-back; you're untidy; she's a slob.
- I'm smart; you're intelligent; Chris is brilliant!

words were literally unheard of on radio and television. Today you may hear dozens of swear words on cable television shows, and you might easily witness steamy sexual scenes that would have given the *I Love Lucy* censors heart attacks. And then there's the Internet, where swearing and pornography are only a few clicks away.

Researchers who study the evolution of language report that swearing or cursing is a human universal.[52]

How would you define swearing? Is it bad language, embarrassing language, profane language? **Swearing** refers to using words that are taboo or disapproved of in a culture that should *not* be interpreted literally and can be used to express strong emotions and attitudes.[53] When we use swear words, we rarely wish that someone would literally "go to hell" or be "damned." Rather, we are using the words as a coping mechanism to express a strong emotion or to release stress.[54] In some cases, swearing may be a sign of a neurological disorder, as is the case with the small percentage of people with Tourette's syndrome who cannot control their tendency to swear.[55]

There are good reasons to stop swearing or, at least, to control where, when, and with whom you use such language. For example, swearing frequently offends others. One study reported that 91 percent of respondents ranked foul language as "the most ill-mannered type of workplace behavior."[56] People who do *not* swear are seen as more intelligent (because they can find more accurate and appropriate words) and more pleasant (because they don't offend anyone). They are also perceived as effective communicators who have greater control over their emotions.

If swearing is a problematic habit of speech for you, you can take steps to break it. Like any habit—biting your nails, overeating, swearing—you must *want* to stop doing it. When you feel like swearing, use a euphemism such as *darn* or *good grief*. Look for better, more interesting words. Rather than saying, "This place looks like *&%#!" try something like "This place looks like it needs a makeover."

> **"Every language, dialect or patois ever studied, living or dead, spoken by millions or by a small tribe, turns out to have its share of forbidden speech."**
>
> —Natalie Angier, science writer for *The New York* Times[57]

Idioms

Idioms are words or phrases that develop as informal or conversational language. The difficulty with idioms,

---

STOP&THINK

How's Your Netspeak, Netlingo, and leet (133t)?

Netspeak, Netlingo, and leet are three types of Internet slang. Unless you are a *n00b* (newbie—as in new and inexperienced or uninformed), you're probably familiar with the new language forms used in email, text messages, and increasingly in everyday writing.

David Crystal, who writes about language, claims "Netspeak is a development of millennial significance. A new medium of linguistic communication does not arrive very often in the history of the [human] race."[58] Check out these brief descriptions of three of these languages, Netspeak, Netlingo, and leet:

NETSPEAK includes common typographic strategies used to achieve a more sociable, oral, and interactive communication style:

- *Letter homophones.* Examples: RU (are you); OIC (oh, I see); CUL8R (see you later)
- *Capitalization or other symbols used for emphasis.* Examples: YES, * yes *
- *Sound-based and/or stylized spelling.* Examples: cooooool, hahahahahah
- *Keyboard-generated emoticons.* Examples: :-) = smiley; @>—;— = rose; ;-) = winking; ;-o = shocked, uh-oh, oh-no

NETLINGO refers to a variety of language forms used in Internet communication, such as the familiar FYI (for your information) and FAQ (frequently asked questions):

- *Compounds and blends.* Examples: shareware, netiquette, e- and cyber- anything
- *Abbreviations and acronyms.* Examples: BTW = by the way; THX = thanks; IRL = in real life; F2F = face to face; IMHO = in my humble opinion; GMTA = great minds think alike; BBL = be back later; WDYT = what do you think?

- *Less use of capitalization, punctuation, and hyphenation.* Examples: internet and email
- *Less use of traditional openings and closings.* Examples: *Hi* or *Hey* instead of *Dear* or using no greeting phrase at all[59]

LEET, also known as *eleet* or *leetspeak*, can be found in the comic world and uses an alternative alphabet to create words. In many cases the new alphabet's symbols visually resemble our standard alphabet. So *leet* can become 133t, or 1337. *Leetspeak* becomes 133tspeek. Commonly replaced letters include *A* = (4), *E* = (3), *I* = (1), *O* = (0), However l33t is a very flexible "language" and you can go from this very basic l33t, to ultra 1337 by being creative; a few examples: *O* = () *U* = |_| *T* = 7 *D* = |) *W* = \/\/ *S* = $[60] Leet also uses common misspellings or letters and symbols that correspond to the sound of a word as in *skillz* or skills as well as a variety of symbols for sounds as c@tL0vr, and (@ L0V3r for cat lover.

Be careful when using netlingo, netspeak, and especially leet. Some readers may not "get it" and will become confused or exasperated. The changing trends in Internet language even have some people in their 20s feeling old or slightly out of touch. As a 23-year-old technology consultant complained about his 12- and 19- year-old siblings' messages, "I have no idea what they're saying. . . . I may not text in full sentences, but at least there's punctuation to get my point across. I guess I'm old school."[61]

If you send difficult-to-understand netspeak, netlingo, or leet messages to people who will have to translate your "words" into recognizable English, they may not make the effort or may ignore what you're saying. Don't load your messages with unnecessary or "show-off" symbols. Too many in one message can make reading difficult and annoying, as well as make you and your writing appear immature.[62]

is that both the sender and the receiver must know the 'informal meaning' of the words or phrases. Every language has these idioms, but for many English idioms tend to pose real challenges. For example, some of you may be familiar with the saying "when the rubber meets the road" and others of you may have never heard the expression before. Other common ones we have been known to say in Canada include:

"It's just sour grapes" when something doesn't turn out like someone expected, or "It's raining cats and dogs" to describe when the rain is very heavy. [63]

5.7

Improving Your Way with Words

What strategies can improve your way with words?

In the previous section, we emphasized what *not* to do if you want to be understood and respected by others. Here we take a more positive approach by examining five ways in which you can use language to express messages clearly and appropriately: expand your vocabulary, use oral language, use active language, use *I* and *you* pronouns wisely, and know your grammar.

Expand Your Vocabulary

How many words do you know? By the age of five, you probably knew about 10,000 words, which means that you learned about 10 words a day. Children have an inborn ability for learning languages that diminishes at around age 12 or 13. Although children can learn a second or third language with relative ease, adults struggle to become fluent in a second language.[64]

By the time you are an adult, your vocabulary has expanded to include tens of thousands of words. Not surprisingly, finding the "right" word is a lot easier if you have many words from which to choose. When your only ice cream choices are vanilla or chocolate, you miss the delights of caramel butter pecan, mocha fudge swirl, and even simple strawberry. When you search for words in the English language, you have more than a million choices.

As you learn more words, make sure you understand their meaning and usage. For example, you should be able to make distinctions in meaning among the words in the following groups:[65]

- Absurd, silly, dumb, ridiculous, ludicrous, idiotic
- Pretty, attractive, gorgeous, elegant, lovely, cute, beautiful

Remember, the difference between the almost-right word and the right word is significant. You may not mind being called "silly" but may have serious objections to being called "idiotic." Improving your vocabulary is a lifelong task—and one that will be much easier if you are an avid reader.

Use Oral Language

Usually, there is a big difference between the words we use for written documents and the words we use orally in conversations, group discussions, and presentations. In his book *How to Win Any Argument*, Robert Mayer writes, "The words you'll craft for a listener's ears are not the same as the words you'll choose for a reader's

eyes. Readers can slow their pace to reread, to absorb, and to understand—luxuries listeners don't have."[66] This is an important consideration if you are speaking to someone when English is not his or her first language or to someone who, is hearing impaired or has a learning disability.

Use Active Language

Effective communicators use active language: vivid, expressive verbs rather than passive forms of the verb vivid, expressive verbs that describe the immediate action. Consider the difference between "Cheating is *a* violation of the college's plagiarism rules" and "Cheating *violates* the college's plagiarism rules." The second sentence is stronger and draws attention to the subject by focusing the reader on the word '*violates*'.

Voice refers to whether the subject of a sentence *performs* or *receives* the

Know Thy SELF

How Broad Is Your Vocabulary?

We generally assume that most of you know and can define the words we use in this textbook. We also understand that this may not always be the case. Consider the following, non–key term words from this chapter. Can you write a coherent definition of each and use it in a sentence? If you cannot, we urge you to look up and learn the words you do not know.

Arbitrary	**Demeaning**	**Regime**
Causality	**Hypothesis**	**Semanticist**
Colloquial	**Linguist**	**Stigma**
Deference	**Nuanced**	

Crafting Language **FOR THE EAR**

Oral Style	When You Speak, Say This	Do Not Say This
Shorter, familiar words	Large	Substantial
Shorter, simple sentences	He came back.	He returned from his point of departure.
Contractions	I'm not going and that's that.	I am not going and that is that.
Informal, colloquial expressions	Give it a try.	You should attempt it first.
Incomplete sentences	Old wood, best to burn; old wine, best to drink	Old wood burns the best, and old wine is best to drink.

Say what you mean by speaking the way you talk, not the way you write.

action of the verb. If the subject performs the action, you are using an **active voice**. If the subject receives the action, you are using a **passive voice**. A strong, active voice makes your message more engaging, and dynamic. A passive voice takes the focus away from the subject of your sentence.

"The mystery book *was read* by the student" is passive. This sentence emphasizes the book, not what the student is doing. "The student read the mystery book" is active. This sentence states clearly what the student is doing: reading a mystery book.

An active voice requires fewer words, it also keeps sentences short and direct. Simply state who is doing what, not what was done by whom.

Less committed and confident speakers often have trouble using the active voice because they worry about sounding too direct. Look at the differences in these sentences:

Active verb: Sign this petition.

Passive verb: The petition should be signed by all of you.

A passive sentence conveys a less powerful message.

Use *I* and *You* Language Wisely

The pronouns you use can affect the quality and meaning of your verbal communication. Understanding the nature and power of pronouns can help you improve your way with words.

When you use the **I language**, you take responsibility for your own feelings and actions: *I* feel great. *I* am a good student. *I* will not vote for someone who cuts spending on education. Some people avoid using the word *I* because they think it may seem like they are showing off, being selfish, or bragging. Other people use the

---

The Three Components of *I* Language

1. Identify your feelings.

2. Describe the other person's behavior.

3. Explain the potential consequences.

---

word *I* too much and appear self-centred or oblivious to those around them.

Unfortunately, some people avoid *I* language when it is most important. Instead, they shift responsibility from themselves to others by using the word *you*. **You language** can express judgments about others. When the judgments are positive—"You did a great job" or "You look marvellous!"—there's rarely a problem. When *you* is a tool to accuse, blame, or criticize, it can produce defensiveness, anger, and even revenge. Consider the following statements: "You make me angry." "You embarrass me." "You drive too fast."

When you use *you* language, you are saying that another person makes you feel a certain way rather than accepting that you control how you feel. To take personal responsibility and decrease the probability of defensive reactions, use *I* language even when your impulse tells you to use *you*. Ethical interpersonal communication requires each of us to be responsible for our word choices as well as our actions.

The following examples demonstrate how the three components of *I* language listed to the lower left can help you express yourself by describing someone's behaviour and explaining how it affects you. Also note that the *you* statements are short. The *I* statements are longer because they offer more information to explain the speaker's feelings.

You versus *I*

You Statement
You embarrassed me last night.

I Statement
I was really embarrassed last night when you interrupted me in front of my boss and contradicted what I said. I'm afraid she'll think I don't know what I'm doing.

Gobbling Gobbledygook

Semanticist Stuart Chase defines **gobbledygook** (the sound of which imitates the nonsense gobbling of a turkey) as "using two or three or ten words in place of one, or using a five-syllable word where a single syllable would suffice." He cites the example of the single word *now* being replaced by the five-word, 17-letter phrase "at this point in time."[67]

In his book *Say What You Mean*, Rudolf Flesch contends that long words are a curse, a special language that comes between a speaker and listener.[68]

To demonstrate the value of clear, plain language, Nipissing University offers some examples of gobbledygook. Read over the examples in the Communication Exercise box below and then check to see what the author really was trying to say.

You Statement
What a stupid thing to do!

I Statement
I am afraid the gas grill will explode when you leave the gas on for a long time before you light the grill.

Use Grammatical Language

In his book *If You Can Talk, You Can Write*, Joel Saltzman notes that when you're talking to someone, you rarely worry about grammar or let it stand in the way of getting your point across. You probably never say to yourself, "Because I don't know if I should use *who* or *whom*, I won't even ask the question." According to Saltzman, when you're talking, 98 percent of the time, your grammar is fine and not an issue. For the 2 percent of time your grammar is a problem, many of your listeners won't even notice your mistakes.[69]

We are not saying that grammar isn't important. However, worrying about it all the time may make it impossible for you to write or speak. If you have questions about grammar, consult a good writing handbook or website. Although most listeners miss or forgive a few grammatical errors, consistent grammatical problems can distract listeners and seriously harm your credibility. Your ability to use grammar correctly makes a public statement about your education, confidence, and even intelligence.

COMMUNICATION Exercise

Can you interpret these famous sayings that have been gobbledygooked?
- It's important to effect the verbalization of concepts through the utilization of unsophisticated terminology.
- Precipitation entails negation of economy.
- He who expresses merriment subsequent to everyone else expresses merriment of most superior quality.
- Pulchritude is not evinced below the dermal surface.
- Exclusive dedication to necessitous chores without interlude of hedonist diversion renders John an unresponsive fellow.

Answers:
- Speak simply.
- It never rains but it pours.
- He who laughs last laughs best.
- Beauty is only skin deep.
- All work and no play makes John a dull boy.

COMMUNICATION Exercise

Role Play

In small groups, assign roles and use the following situation to create a three- to four-minute skit to illustrate verbal communication skills.

A customer comes into a store with a T-shirt in her hand. She goes up to the checkout register and drops the T-shirt on the counter and tells the clerk she wants her money back. The clerk asks for a receipt, but the customer just looks away. The clerk tells the customer that no refund can be given without a receipt. What happens next?

Consider the words chosen, voice tone, quality of voice, and context of the exchange.

Writing Apprehension Test (WAT)[70]

Writing apprehension is the fear or anxiety associated with writing situations and topic-specific writing assignments. The following statements will help you to gauge how you feel about writing. Indicate the degree to which each statement applies to you by marking whether you (1) strongly agree, (2) agree, (3) are uncertain about, (4) disagree, or (5) strongly disagree with the statement. Although some of these statements may seem repetitious, take your time and try to be as honest as possible.

_____ 1. I avoid writing.

_____ 2. I have no fear of my writing being evaluated.

_____ 3. I look forward to writing down my ideas.

_____ 4. My mind seems to go blank when I start to work on an essay.

_____ 5. Expressing ideas through writing seems to be a waste of time.

_____ 6. I would enjoy submitting my writing to magazines for evaluation and publication.

_____ 7. I like to write my ideas down.

_____ 8. I feel confident in my ability to express my ideas clearly in writing.

_____ 9. I like to have my friends read what I have written.

_____ 10. I'm nervous about writing.

_____ 11. People seem to enjoy what I write.

_____ 12. I enjoy writing.

_____ 13. I never seem to be able to write down my ideas clearly.

_____ 14. Writing is a lot of fun.

_____ 15. I like seeing my thoughts on paper.

_____ 16. Discussing my writing with others is an enjoyable experience.

_____ 17. It's easy for me to write good compositions.

_____ 18. I don't think I write as well as other people write.

_____ 19. I don't like my compositions to be evaluated.

_____ 20. I'm not good at writing.

Scoring: To determine your score on the WAT, complete the following steps:

1. Add the scores for items 1, 4, 5, 10, 13, 18, 19, and 20.
2. Add the scores for items 2, 3, 6, 7, 8, 9, 11, 12, 14, 15, 16, and 17.
3. Determine your score using the following formula:

WAT score = 48 – total from step 1 + total from step 2
Your score should be between 20 and 100 points. If your score is less than 20 or more than 100 points, you have made a mistake in computing the score. The higher your score, the more apprehension you feel about writing.

Score	Level of Apprehension	Description
20–45	Low	Enjoys writing; seeks writing opportunities
46–75	Average	Some writing creates apprehension; other writing does not
76–100	High	Troubled by many kinds of writing; avoids writing in most situations

5.1 Human Language

What makes human language unique?

- The ability to learn words and to combine, invent, and give meaning make humans different from other animals.

- Language is a system of arbitrary signs and symbols used to communicate with others.

5.2 Language and Meaning

How do the characteristics of language affect meaning?

- Whereas signs often look like the thing they represent, symbols are arbitrary collections of sounds that in certain combinations stand for concepts.

- Words have both denotative and connotative meanings and also differ in terms of whether they are concrete or abstract.

5.3 Language and Culture

How do language and culture interact with one another?

- The Whorf hypothesis claims that the nature of your language reflects your culture's view of the world.

- Individualistic cultures have an "I" orientation, whereas collectivist cultures have a "we" orientation.

- People living in low-context cultures rely on words to convey meaning. In high-context, collectivist cultures, people rely on nonverbal behavior and the relationship between communicators to generate meaning.

5.4 Language and Gender

How does language reflect gender differences?

- Most languages have a gender bias that privileges men more than women.

- Men tend to talk more than women even though many people believe the opposite.

- Avoid gender bias by avoiding male and female pronouns when possible.

5.5 Language and Context

How does context affect language choices?

- Code switching refers to modifying verbal and nonverbal communication during interaction with people from other cultures.

5.6 Overcoming Common Language Barriers

How do bypassing, exclusionary language, idioms and offensive language affect communication?

- Communicators who look for meaning in words rather than in the people using words are more likely to bypass and be bypassed.

- Exclusionary language uses words that reinforce stereotypes, belittle other people, or exclude others from understanding an in-group's message.

- People who rarely swear or use offensive language are seen as more intelligent, more pleasant, and more skilled at controlling their emotions.

- Idioms are words or phrases that develop as informal or conversational language.

5.7 Improving Your Way with Words

What strategies can improve your way with words?

- You can improve your way with words by expanding your vocabulary, using oral language when you speak, speaking in an active voice, using the pronouns *I* and *you* wisely, and avoiding gobbledygook.

- An excessive number of grammatical errors in your speech can derail a career or create a negative personal impression.

Paylessimages/Fotolia

TEST YOUR KNOWLEDGE

5.1 What makes human language unique?

1 _____ are an arbitrary collection of sounds that in certain combinations stand for concepts.
  a. Signs
  b. Symbols
  c. Denotations
  d. Connotations
  e. Vocalized grunts

5.2 How do the characteristics of language affect meaning?

2 Which of the following words is a superordinate term?
  a. liquid
  b. water
  c. rain
  d. ocean
  e. Caribbean Sea

5.3 How do language and culture affect one another?

3 Approximately how many languages are currently spoken on planet Earth?
  a. 50–60
  b. 500–600
  c. 5,000–6,000
  d. 50,000–60,000
  e. 500,000–600,000

4 According to the more modern version of the Whorf hypothesis,
  a. People without a word for "airplane" cannot see airplanes.
  b. Primitive people, even with training, cannot understand modern technology.
  c. Language reflects cultural models and influences how people think and act.
  d. People without a word for "tomorrow" or "future" cannot plan.
  e. all of the above

5 The only language that capitalizes the first-person singular pronoun is
  a. English.
  b. Finnish.
  c. French.
  d. Hopi.
  e. Korean.

5.4 How does language reflect gender differences?

6 Which of the following demonstrates the male bias in the English language?
  a. Grammar books advising using the pronoun *he* to describe both men and women.
  b. Words such as *stewardess* instead of *flight attendant* and *mankind* instead of *human beings*.
  c. Gender word pairings such as *Mr. and Mrs., men and women,* and *husband and wife.*
  d. Word pairings such as *wizard and witch* as well as *master and mistress.*
  e. all of the above

5.5 How does context affect language choices?

7 Code switching includes
  a. switching from one language to another.
  b. adapting your language to the communication context.
  c. understanding when and where it may be acceptable to use swearing.
  d. modifying non-verbal language to suit the situation.
  e. all of the above

5.6 How do bypassing, exclusionary language, and offensive language affect communication?

8 All of the following are examples of exclusionary language except:
  a. The man who served us at lunch was very professional.
  b. A little old lady tipped the young man.

  c. Even though she's a cancer victim, she has a very positive attitude.
  d. What do you expect from such a right-wing nut?
  e. Asian women are quiet and polite.

9 Which of the following strategies can help you control cursing?
  a. When you feel like swearing, bite your tongue until it hurts.
  b. Ask a friend to hold her nose if she hears you swearing.
  c. Do not participate in an argument or a heated exchange with others.
  d. Describe what you see or hear rather than swearing.
  e. Swear in another language so no one understands what you are saying.

5.7 What strategies can improve your way with words?

10 Effective oral language
  a. uses shorter, familiar words.
  b. uses shorter, simpler sentences.
  c. uses an informal speaking style.
  d. uses colloquial expressions.
  e. uses all of the above.

Answers found on page 330.

Key Terms

Abstract word	**Gobbledygook**	**Slang**
Active voice	*I* **language**	**Subordinate terms**
Basic terms	**Jargon**	**Superordinate terms**
Bypassing	**Language**	**Swearing**
Code switching	**Leet**	**Symbol**
Concrete word	**Netlingo**	**Verbal communication**
Connotation	**Netspeak**	**Whorf hypothesis**
Denotation	**Passive voice**	**Writing apprehension**
Euphemism	**Sign**	*You* **language**
Exclusionary language		

NONVERBAL
Communication

In April 2009, the world met Susan Boyle, the unfashionable, unmarried, unemployed, 47-year-old church volunteer from Scotland who sang her way to instant fame on the television show *Britain's Got Talent*. When she walked onto the stage, the judges' faces registered skepticism. Camera pans of the audience revealed looks of disdain and disbelief. After Susan announced that she would sing, "I Dreamed a Dream," a song from the musical *Les Miserables*, the judges smirked and the audience snickered. When the music started, the judges sat back and braced themselves for what judge Simon Cowell would later describe as "something extraordinary."

And then Susan Boyle began to sing. The judges' skeptical gazes turned into expressions of delight; these, coupled with their hands held ready to applaud, said it all. At the conclusion of her song, everyone rose in a standing ovation. The rest of Ms. Boyle's story is entertainment history.

Susan's story illustrates that communication is more than just words; our nonverbal communication is at least as important as our verbal communication. What does a hug from a friend, a raised eyebrow from a co-worker, tears from a child, or the applause of an audience tell you? The answer to this question depends on many factors—the communicators; their purpose; the context, content, and structure of their message; *and* how their nonverbal behaviour enhances the words they say.

Peter Stroh/Alamy

6.1
Communicating Without Words
What is nonverbal communication, and how does it affect your everyday life?

Nonverbal communication refers to message components other than words that generate meaning. Some researchers estimate that 60 to 70 percent, or about two-thirds, of the meaning we generate may be conveyed through nonverbal behaviours.[1] Whereas verbal communication depends on words, nonverbal communication is more multidimensional, depending on such things as physical appearance, body movement, facial expressions, touch, vocal characteristics, and the communication context.

Everyone uses nonverbal communication. When you are aware of your own nonverbal behaviour and are sensitive to others' unspoken messages, you are more likely to experience academic and occupational success, satisfying social relationships, a more satisfying marriage, and less stress, anxiety, and hypertension.[2]

Functions of Nonverbal Communication

Because nonverbal communication allows you to send and receive messages through all five of your senses, you have more information to draw on when generating or interpreting a message. You can achieve many interpersonal communication goals through nonverbal behaviour, ranging from creating a positive impression to detecting deception.

Create an Impression As soon as you walk into a room, your physical appearance, clothing, posture, and facial expression create an impression. When attorneys prepare witnesses to testify in court, they tell them how to dress and teach them how to look and sound sincere and confident. Experienced courtroom lawyers know that jurors begin forming their opinions of witnesses before witnesses utter a word. Whether it's a first date, a job interview, or a meeting with your study group, nonverbal messages create strong impressions.

Identify and Express Emotions We rely on nonverbal communication to identify and express the emotional components of a message. For example, if Jason says, "I'm angry," he simply labels an emotion, but his nonverbal behaviour—vocal intensity, facial expression, and body movement—tell you how to interpret his anger. Expressing emotions by smiling, laughing, frowning, crying, grimacing, and even walking away from an encounter can make words unnecessary, provided the other person accurately interprets the meaning of the nonverbal cues they see or hear. Understanding the relationship between interpersonal communication and our emotions is explored fully in Chapter 8.

Define Relationships The nature of a relationship is often expressed nonverbally. For example, the closeness and duration of a hug can reveal the level of intimacy between friends. Or a group member may take a central position at the head of a conference table to establish leadership. The simple act of holding hands in public or a first kiss signifies "we are more than just friends."

Establish Power and Influence Do you know people who are powerful and persuasive? What kind of nonverbal characteristics do they display? Powerful people often take up more space by having a bigger office or desk. They often touch others more than they are touched. They look at others less frequently unless they want to convey a strong message. By using a powerful voice and confident posture, they command attention and influence.

COMMUNICATION
Exercise

This video at Vimeo.com looks at nonverbal communication, exploring what non-verbal communication includes, and acknowledging its importance.

https://vimeo.com/63270281

nikOs/Fotolia

Interpret Verbal Messages Nonverbal communication provides us with a message about a message, or a **metamessage**, by offering important clues about how to interpret its verbal aspects. For example, you may doubt a person who says he's feeling fine after a fall if he winces when he walks. If someone says she's glad to see you but is looking over your shoulder to see who else is in the room, you may distrust her sincerity.

Deceiving Others and Detecting Deception Have you ever tried to hide your feelings from others—whether you're denying wrongdoing or keeping a secret? Of course you have. Great poker players have mastered this skill. However, most of us are amateurs. Our "innocent" smile may seem false, our gestures may look awkward, our voice may sound shaky, and our persistent toe tapping or knee jiggling may broadcast our anxiety.

> **❝He that has eyes to see and ears to hear may convince himself that no mortal can keep a secret. If his lips are silent, he chatters with his fingertips; betrayal oozes out of him at every pore.❞**
> —Sigmund Freud[3]

STOP&THINK

Can You Detect a Lie?

Most of us aren't very good at detecting a lie. According to Judee Burgoon, a noted researcher in human deception, most people's ability to detect deception accurately is equivalent to the flip of a coin: about 50/50.[4] Paul Ekman, another leading researcher in deception and nonverbal communication, points out that accurately identifying when someone is lying is further complicated by the fact that there is no single facial expression or body movement that serves as a reliable sign of deceit.[5]

Yet many liars do give themselves away by displaying **leakage cues**, unintentional nonverbal behaviours that may reveal deceptive communication. These cues, which fall into three categories, are what you need to look for when trying to detect a lie.

Monkey Business Images/Shutterstock

1. *Displays of nervousness*: More blinking, higher pitch speech, vocal tension, less gesturing, more fidgety movements, longer pauses, fewer facial changes
2. *Signs of negative emotions*: Reduced eye contact, fewer pleasant facial expressions, agitated vocal tone
3. *Incompetent communication*: More speech errors, physical rigidity, hesitations, and exaggerated movements, lack of spontaneity[6]

Keep in mind that leakage cues are not the same for everyone. Rather than reduce or eliminate eye contact, a skilful liar may look you in the eye. Some nonverbal behaviours, however, are better lie indicators than others. For instance, since facial muscles are generally easier to control than other muscles in the body, facial expressions can be managed and therefore don't necessarily reveal a liar. But, vocal pitch is less controllable, so any noticeable changes may well give a liar away.

It is important to remember that there are important cultural differences in nonverbal behaviours, so behaviours in one context and culture may indicate deceit while having a completely different meaning in another context and culture.

Mark Knapp, another prominent researcher in lying and deception, acknowledges that a small minority of people are highly skilled lie detectors. These human "lie detectors" pay close attention to what nonverbal communication tells them; they look for discrepancies between verbal and nonverbal behaviour.[7] So pay attention to what people say as well as how they act. For example, researchers have noted that people telling the truth tend to add 20 to 30 percent more external detail to their stories and explanations than do those who are lying.[8]

THE NATURE OF NONVERBAL COMMUNICATION

MORE CONVINCING
Nonverbal communication is more believable because it seems spontaneous and revealing. CAUTION: Perceptions can deceive. Think of the times you've heard, "He *seemed* so honest when I met him," or "She acted like she really cared."

HIGHLY CONTEXTUAL
The meaning of nonverbal messages depends on a situation's psychosocial, logistical, and interactional context. CAUTION: Depending on the context, a laugh can be interpreted as amusement, approval, contempt, scorn, or embarrassment.

CONTINUOUS
Whereas verbal communication may stop and start, nonverbal communication usually continues uninterrupted. CAUTION: People interpret your opinions and feelings even when you are not talking.

LESS STRUCTURED
Unlike verbal communication, nonverbal communication has few agreed-upon rules. CAUTION: Nonverbal behaviour can communicate multiple and ambiguous meanings, and can be difficult to interpret.

LEARNED INFORMALLY
You learn to communicate nonverbally by watching others and interpreting feedback about your nonverbal behaviour. CAUTION: Failure to learn appropriate nonverbal behaviour can embarrass you and result in misunderstanding and confusion.

Photo credits (clockwise from top): Jupiterimages/ FoodPix/Getty Images; Ryan McVay/Stone+/Getty Images; Mark Kolbe/Getty Images; Beowulf Sheehan/ Getty Images; David Buzzard/Alamy

Is Your Teenage Brain to Blame?

For decades, parents, teachers, and psychologists "threw up their hands and cried, 'Hormones!' when asked why children become so nutty around the time of adolescence."[9] Scientists now claim that hormones are only part of the answer.

Using neuroimaging, neuropsychologist Deborah Yurgelun-Todd and her colleagues found that teenage brains work differently than adult brains when processing nonverbal emotional information.[10] Before explaining more about this research, look at the image above.

Kim Schneider/Fotolia

What emotion do you see on this person's face?

The answer is: fear. While 100 percent of adults who were shown this photo guessed this woman's emotion correctly, only 50 percent of teenagers got it right. Many teens identified the emotion as shock, confusion, or sadness.[11] It turns out that teens and adults use different part of their brains to identify emotions.

The results of these studies are significant for communicators of all ages. It means that what we see as teenage indifference to emotions is, in fact, an inability to recognize emotions correctly, particularly the feelings in an adult's face. According to Dr. Yurgelun-Todd,

[Teenagers] see anger when there isn't anger, or sadness when there isn't sadness. And if that's the case, then clearly their own behaviour is not going to match that of the adults. So you'll see miscommunication, both in terms of what they think the adult is feeling, but also what the response should then be to that.[12]

In Chapter 2, we explained how effective self-monitoring helps you identify your own feelings and the feelings of others, particularly when they're expressed nonverbally. People who are high self-monitors astutely watch other people; correctly interpret the meaning of their facial expressions, body language, and tone of voice; and then appropriately respond to their behaviour. Research on the teenage brain helps us understand why many teenage brains need to "grow up" and physically mature in order to develop and practise self-monitoring skills.

6.2

Linking Verbal and Nonverbal Communication

How do verbal and nonverbal communication interact to create meaning?

Verbal communication and nonverbal communication often rely on each other to generate and interpret the meaning of a message. When you verbally congratulate someone, you may smile, shake hands, or hug that person. When you verbally express anger, you may frown, stand farther away, or use a harsh voice.

Psychologist Paul Ekman notes that most nonverbal behaviours repeat, complement, accent, regulate, substitute for, and/or contradict verbal messages.[13]

Repeat

Repetitive nonverbal behaviours visually repeat a verbal message. For example, when a server asks if anyone is interested in dessert, Elaine nods as she says, "Yes." She then points at a selection on the dessert tray and says, "I want the cheesecake." Ralph says he would like

the same, so Elaine holds up two fingers and says, "Make it two pieces."

Complement

Complementary nonverbal behaviours are consistent with the verbal message. During a job interview, your words tell the interviewer that you are a confident professional, but what you say will be more believable if nonverbal elements such as posture, facial expressions, and vocal quality send the same message. Even the meaning of a simple *hello* can be strengthened if your facial expression and tone of voice communicate genuine interest and pleasure in greeting someone.

Accent

Accenting nonverbal behaviours emphasize important elements in a message by highlighting its focus or

emotional content. Saying the words "I'm angry" may fail to make the point, so you may couple this message with louder volume, forceful gestures, and piercing eye contact. Stressing a word or phrase in a sentence also focuses meaning.

Regulate

We use **regulating nonverbal behaviours** to manage the flow of a conversation. Nonverbal cues tell us when to start and stop talking, whose turn it is to speak, how to interrupt other speakers, and how to encourage others to talk more. If you lean forward and open your mouth as if to speak, you are signalling that you want a turn in the conversation. In a classroom or large meeting, you may raise your hand when you want to speak. When your friend nods her head as you speak, you may interpret her nod as a sign to continue what you're saying.

Substitute

Nonverbal behaviour can take the place of verbal language. This is called **substituting nonverbal behaviours.** When we wave hello or good-bye, the meaning is usually clear even in the absence of words. Without saying anything, a mother may send a message to a misbehaving child by pursing her lips, narrowing her eyes, and moving a single finger to signal "stop."

Contradict

Contradictory nonverbal behaviours conflict with the meaning of spoken words. On receiving a birthday gift from a co-worker, Sherry says, "It's lovely. Thank you." However, her forced smile, flat vocal expression, and lack of eye contact suggest that Sherry does not appreciate the gift. This is a classic example of a **mixed message:** a contradiction between verbal and nonverbal meanings. When nonverbal behaviour contradicts spoken words, messages are confusing and difficult to interpret. Nonverbal channels can carry more information than verbal ones, and we usually rely on the nonverbal cues to help us determine the true meaning of a message.

FACTS **THINK** ABOUT THEORY
TEST IDEA PLAN EXPERIMENT METHOD KNOWLEDGE

Expectancy Violation Theory

The following two scenarios are quite similar but may produce significantly different reactions.

Scenario 1. You stop at a local convenience store for a cup of coffee on your way to work, and you notice a poorly dressed man looking at you as you walk into the store. You've never seen him before. While you are preparing your coffee, he approaches and stands right next to you, smiling. As he reaches for a cup, his hand brushes against your arm. You turn to leave. Now he is standing directly behind you to pay for the coffee—and smiles again. As you leave, he follows you out the door.

Scenario 2. You stop at the office break room to get a cup of coffee, and your colleague, Henry, from your department is looking at you. He's a valued friend and colleague and you've worked with him for many years. While you are preparing your coffee, he approaches and stands right next to you, smiling. As he reaches for a cup, his hand brushes against your arm. You turn to leave. Now he is walking directly behind you. As you leave, he follows you out the door.

Both scenarios are similar. Yet in the first case, you probably react with suspicion and disapproval, whereas in the second case you may feel more relaxed and positive. According to **expectancy violation theory**, your expectations about nonverbal behaviour have a significant effect on how you interact with others and how you interpret the meaning of nonverbal messages. When you enter an elevator, you probably conform to nonverbal expectations: You turn around and face front, avoid eye contact with others, avoid movement, refrain from talking or touching others, and stare at the numbers as they go up or down. But how would you react if someone entered a cramped elevator with three unruly dogs and lit a cigar? You'd most likely disapprove or object because this is not the kind of behaviour you'd expect in a confined public space.

At least three characteristics influence your expectations and reactions to the nonverbal behaviour of another person.[14] Think of the previous two scenarios as you consider these characteristics.

1. *Communicator Characteristics.* Personal characteristics, such as age, gender, ethnicity, and physical appearance, as well as personality and reputation
2. *Relational Characteristics.* Level of familiarity, past experiences, relative status, and type of relationship with others, such as close friend, romantic partner, business associate, service provider, or stranger
3. *Contextual Characteristics.* Physical, social, psychological, cultural, and professional settings and occasions, such as football games, stores, religious services, classrooms, or business meetings

The first scenario clearly highlights differences in communicator, relational, and contextual characteristics, whereas the second scenario highlights similarities. In the first scenario, the man violates a number of nonverbal expectations: don't stare, follow, or touch strangers. In the second scenario, the man is "allowed" to violate the same nonverbal "rules" because you know him well.

Exercise

To view expectancy violation theory in action, and without words, watch this Vimeo short movie created by college students.

https://vimeo.com/61740282

6.3
Types of Nonverbal Communication

What types of nonverbal communication should you pay attention to when interacting with others?

Nonverbal communication is undeniably complex. To interpret nonverbal meaning accurately, you must pay attention to multiple nonverbal dimensions. To be an effective communicator you must consider the totality of your own and others' nonverbal behaviour.

Daniel Staniszewski/Alamy

Types of
NONVERBAL CUES

Physical Appearance

Body Movement and Gestures

Touch

Facial Expressions

Eye Behaviour

Vocal Expressiveness

Silence

Space and Distance

Time

Environment

Aikon/Fotolia

Almost 90 percent of Canadian women and girls are not happy with the way they look![15]

Physical Appearance

When you first meet someone, you automatically analyze his or her physical appearance to form an impression. Although it seems unfair to judge a person's personality and character based on physical characteristics such as weight, attractiveness, clothing, and hairstyle, these factors strongly influence how we interact with others.

Attractiveness For better or worse, attractive people are perceived as kinder, more interesting, more sociable, more successful, and sexier than those considered less attractive. One study found that good-looking people tend to make more money and get promoted more often than those with average looks.[16]

In addition to weight, height influences how people perceive each other. Generally, taller people are viewed as more attractive, powerful, outgoing, and confident than shorter people. A 2009 study found that tall people report more enjoyment of life and less pain and sadness. These findings reflect the positive association between height and both income and education, both of which are positively linked to better lives.[17]

In their quest to be more attractive, many people try to change their physical appearance. Dieting, healthy eating, and fitness training can change a person's weight, figure, and overall build. Some people alter the colour of their skin by tanning or with cosmetics. Hair colour and style are easily changed. Plastic surgery and chemical enhancements alter individuals' facial structure and body shape.

types of nonverbal communication

Can Tattooing and Body Piercing Hurt Your Image?

In many cultures, both past and present, people have pierced and tattooed their bodies. These markings often commemorated a rite of passage such as puberty, marriage, or a successful hunt. For many in Western cultures, tattoos have been associated with people of lower social status, gangs, "bikers," and lower-ranked military personnel.

But in recent decades the popularity of tattoos has grown among all age groups. In 2011, the police service commissioned a community survey, conducted by Framework Partners Incorporated, to gauge resident views on a number of policing issues including appearance standards (tattoos, piercings, unusual hair colour). The results were quite clear, as noted in the report below.

- Public respect for the police would drop—69 percent of the respondents either agree or strongly agree with this statement.
- The public would have less pride in the police—66 percent of respondents either agree or strongly agree with this statement.
- I would have less pride in the police—60 percent of the respondents either agree or strongly agree with this statement.
- Public trust in police would drop—54 percent of respondents either agree or strongly agree with this statement.
- I would have less respect for the police—53 percent of the respondents either agree or strongly agree with this statement.
- I would trust the police less—45 percent of the respondents either agree or strongly agree with this statement.[18]

Many people are also divided about the social impact of body piercing, particularly piercings of ear edges as well as the nose, tongue, lips, face, nipples, naval, and genitals.

The *Canadian Human Rights Act* doesn't protect Canadian employees' rights to have and show tattoos, unless they are for religious or cultural reasons.[19]

Ear gauging (stretching) is also popular despite the fact that many people (especially parents) find the practice appalling and even repulsive. When the mother of a 14-year-old inquired on an online chat whether she should let her son gauge his ears, claiming she thought "ear gauging looks disgusting and weird," the answer voted as "best" by the

anetlanda/Fotolia

blog visitors was "I definitely agree with you about ear gauging being disgusting. If I was a mother, I would NEVER let my child get their ears gauged."[20]

David Brooks, political and cultural commentator for the *New York Times*, observes that "a cadre of fashion-forward types thought they were doing something to separate themselves from the vanilla middle class but are now discovering that the signs etched into their skins are absolutely mainstream."[21] There's no question that "tattoos have become more acceptable for men and women of all socio-economic classes in today's society."[22] Regardless of whether *you* like or dislike them, the popularity of tattoos and piercings has made it more difficult and often unfair to negatively stereotype those who tattoo and pierce their bodies.

Couperfield/Fotolia

Certainly the images of attractive men and women on television and in popular magazines and film influence how we see others. Most of us were not born with movie-star features and never will meet those standards of "beauty." Yet there is no question that physical attraction plays a significant role in selecting romantic partners, getting and succeeding in a job, and persuading others.

Clothing and Accessories Your clothing and accessories send messages about your economic status, education, trustworthiness, social position, level of sophistication, and moral character. For example, a person wearing a stylish suit and carrying an expensive leather briefcase suggests a higher income, a college education, and more status within a company than a person wearing a uniform and carrying a mop. Accessories such as a college ring, a wedding band, or a religious necklace reveal a great deal about another person.

However, judging others based on their clothing can lead to inaccurate assumptions. For example, what type of clothing does a millionaire wear? In their book *The Millionaire Next Door: The Surprising Secrets of America's Wealthy*, marketing researchers Thomas Stanley and William Danko note that the vast majority of millionaires do not wear expensive suits, shoes, or watches. "It is easier to purchase products that denote superiority than to actually be superior in economic achievement."[23]

Hair Hair is something of an obsession in the United States.

In *Reading People*, jury consultant Jo-Ellan Dimitrius and attorney Mark Mazzarella use hair as a predictor of people's self-image and lifestyle. They claim that your hairstyle can reveal, "How you feel about aging, how extravagant or practical you are, how much importance you attach to impressing others, your socio-economic background, your overall emotional maturity, and sometimes even the part of the country where you were raised or now live."[24] If you doubt their claim, think about the ways in which very long hair on men communicated antiwar rebellion and hippie lifestyles in the late 1960s and early 1970s, what multicoloured spikey hair said about a young person in the 1980s, or what a Justin Bieber flip meant in 2010.

In his recent documentary, *Good Hair*, comedian Chris Rock took a serious look at the high price that black women pay (in harsh chemical treatments, hours of tight braiding, and dollars) to have "good hair," a colloquial phrase in the African-American community that describes the straight or soft-curly hair of non-black women.

Rock exposed a $90 billion (that's right, billion dollar) industry that profits by transforming "nappy" hair into hair more like that of European women or into elaborate weaves.[25]

Ultimately we should remember to be careful when drawing conclusions about others based on their hairstyle. A man who wears short hair may be an ultraconservative or a rebel, an athlete or a cancer patient, a police officer or a fashion model. A short and chic haircut on a woman can signify an artistic, creative, and expressive nature or may indicate a more practical nature.

Body Movement and Gestures

Jamal points to his watch to let the chairperson know that the meeting time is running short. Karen gives a thumbs-up gesture to signal that her friend's speech went well. Robin stands at attention as the Canadian flag is raised. How you sit, stand, position your body, or move your hands generates nonverbal messages. Even your posture can convey moods and emotions. Slouching back in your chair may be perceived as lack of interest or dislike, whereas sitting upright and leaning forward communicates interest and is a sign of active listening.

Gestures are body movements that communicate an idea or emotion. They can emphasize or stress parts of a message, reveal discomfort with a situation, or convey a message without the use of words. The hands and arms are used most frequently for gesturing, although head and foot movements are also considered types of gestures.[26]

Many people have difficulty expressing their thoughts without using gestures. Why else would we gesture when speaking to someone on the phone? Gesturing can also ease the mental effort required when communication is difficult. For example, we tend to gesture more when using a language that is less familiar or when describing a picture that a listener cannot see. Paul Ekman and Wallace Friesen classify hand movements as **emblems**, **illustrators**, and **adaptors**.[27]

TYPES OF **GESTURES**

TYPE OF GESTURE	CHARACTERISTICS	EXAMPLES
EMBLEM	Expresses the same meaning as a word in a particular group or culture	• Forming a V with your index and middle finger as a sign of victory or peace • Raising your hand in class to indicate "I want to speak" • Placing your index finger over your lips to mean "be quiet" • Extending the middle finger to offend someone or declare "up yours"
ILLUSTRATOR	Used with a verbal message that would lack meaning without the words	• Pointing as a way of identifying an object or person. • Holding your hands two feet apart and saying, "The fish I caught was this big" • Counting out the steps of a procedure with your hand while orally describing each step • Snapping your fingers while saying, "It happened just like that," to indicate that an event occurred quickly
ADAPTOR	Habitual gestures that help manage and express emotions	• Scratching your head to signify confusion or an inability to answer • Chewing your nails because you are worried or anxious • Drumming your fingers on a table because you are impatient • Wringing your hands because you are distressed • Playing with your hair or an object to relieve stress or impatience

chunumunu/Fotolia

Tatiana Popova/Shutterstock

camrocker/Fotolia

types of nonverbal communication

COMMUNICATION&CULTURE

IS THE OK SIGN ALWAYS OK?

Keep in mind that the examples of emblems, illustrators, and adaptors discussed in this chapter are gestures commonly used in Canada and have very specific meanings. Therefore, before interacting with people from other countries and cultures, think before you gesture. For example, the emblem that means "OK" to most Canadians (forming a circle with the thumb and index finger) is considered an obscene gesture to Brazilians and signifies money to the Japanese.[28] When describing the height of a person, we may hold an arm out, palm down, and say, "My friend is this tall." In some South American countries, this same gesture is fine for describing a dog but would not be used for describing a person. To designate a person's height, a South American would hold her arm out with her palm sideways. Even putting your hands in your pockets can offend others, as a professor learned when he spent a year teaching in Indonesia.

Viorel Sima/Shutterstock

Touch

Touch is one of the most potent forms of physical expression. It not only has the power to send strong messages, but it also affects your overall well-being. Being deprived of touch can have a negative effect on your physical and psychological health.[29] For example, we know that babies need human touch to survive and develop. When new parents and hospital nurses engage in more touching behaviour, infant death rates decrease.

Many people have difficulty expressing their thoughts without using gestures. An encouraging pat on the shoulder from a co-worker or a lover's embrace can convey encouragement, appreciation, affection, empathy, or sexual interest. Playful touches tend to lighten the mood without expressing a high degree of emotion. Lightly punching a friend in the arm or covering another's eyes and asking, "Guess who?" are forms of playful touch.

Know Thy SELF

Are You Touchy?[30]

How touchy are you? Indicate the degree to which each statement below applies to you using the following rating scale: (5) strongly agree, (4) agree, (3) undecided or neutral, (2) disagree, or (1) strongly disagree.

_____ 1. I don't mind if I am hugged as a sign of friendship.

_____ 2. I enjoy touching others.

_____ 3. I seldom put my arms around others.

_____ 4. When I see people hugging, it bothers me.

_____ 5. People should not be uncomfortable about being touched.

_____ 6. I really like being touched by others.

_____ 7. I wish I were free to show my emotions by touching others.

_____ 8. I do not like touching other people.

_____ 9. I do not like being touched by others.

_____ 10. I find it enjoyable to be touched by others.

_____ 11. I dislike having to hug others.

_____ 12. Hugging and touching should be outlawed.

_____ 13. Touching others is a very important part of my personality.

_____ 14. Being touched by others makes me uncomfortable.

Scoring:

1. Add up the responses you put next to the following items: 1, 2, 5, 6, 7, 10, and 13. Your Step 1 score = _____.

2. Add up the responses you put next to the following items: 3, 4, 8, 9, 11, 12, and 14. Your Step 2 score = _____.

3. Complete the following formula: 42 + Step 1 score – Step 2 score = _____

Your score should be between 14 and 70 points. A score of more than 53 points suggests that you are a touch approacher. A score of less than 31 points indicates that you tend to avoid touch.

Touch can also be used to express control or dominance. In some instances, only a minor level of control is needed, such as when we tap someone on the shoulder to get her or his attention. In other cases, touch sends very clear messages about status or dominance. Research shows that individuals with more power and status are more likely to touch someone of lesser status and subordinates rarely initiate touch with a person of higher status.[31]

Some people are more comfortable with touch than others as demonstrated in the *Know Thy Self: Are You Touchy?* feature on the previous page. **Touch approachers** are comfortable with touch and often initiate touch with others. A touch approacher is more likely to initiate a hug or a kiss when greeting a friend. Some touch approachers even touch or hug people they don't know very well. At the extreme end of the continuum are touch approachers who touch too much and violate nonverbal expectations.

Touch avoiders are less comfortable initiating touch or being touched. They are also more conscious of when, how, and by whom they are touched.

> We use touch to express a wide range of emotions.

Extreme touch avoiders avoid any physical contact even with loved ones. Most of us are somewhere in the middle of the continuum. Obviously, misunderstandings can result when touch approachers and avoiders meet. Approachers may view avoiders as cold and unfriendly, and avoiders may perceive approachers as invasive and rude.

Not surprisingly, norms for touch depend on the context. For example, violating touch norms in the workplace can result in misunderstandings or allegations of sexual harassment. Norms for touch also vary according to gender and culture. In some cultures men hug each other as part of a greeting, but most North American men avoid this type of embrace with the exception of expressing happiness in a sporting event such as football or hockey.

Facial Expression

Your face is composed of complex muscles capable of displaying well over a thousand different expressions.

COMMUNICATION
Exercise

This YouTube video discusses aspects of nonverbal communication and cultural considerations:

www.youtube.com/watch?v=ORkRTb0LJPA

Are you aware of your personal nonverbal messages? Are you sensitive to different cultural expectations?

Share with someone else (in pairs or groups) a time when you were not immediately aware of your nonverbal message until someone else pointed out your lack of sensitivity. How did you respond when you realized you may have made another person uncomfortable?

ADAPTING FACIAL EXPRESSIONS

TECHNIQUE	CHARACTERISTICS	EXAMPLES
Masking	Conceals true emotions by displaying expressions considered more appropriate in a particular situation	• Smiling and congratulating a colleague for getting a promotion you wanted • Looking stern when reprimanding a toddler who has dumped a bowl of spaghetti on his head
Neutralization	Eliminates all displays of emotions	• Avoiding any display of emotion when serving as a juror during a trial • Displaying a "poker face" during a card game
Intensification	Exaggerates expressions to meet other people's needs or to express strong feelings	• Hugging someone a few more seconds than usual to communicate how much you care • Pouting dramatically when you do not get your way
Deintensification	Reduces or downplays emotional displays to accommodate others	• Looking mildly disapproving when a group member rudely interrupts another speaker during a meeting • Subduing smiles of happiness after defeating a highly competitive friend in a tennis match

spaxiax/Fotolia

types of nonverbal communication

113

:)   Happiness, sarcasm, joking

:P   Sticking out your tongue

;)   Wink

:(Unhappy or sad

:o   Surprise

:D   Laughing

XD Hysterical laughter

:S   Indecision or disappointment

:3   coy/cutesy/self-conscious smile

Holly Harris/Stone/Getty Images

Facial expressions let you know if others are interested in, agree with, or understand what you have said. Generally, women tend to be more facially expressive and to smile more often than men. But although men are more likely to limit the amount of emotion they reveal, everyone relies on facial expressions to comprehend the full meaning of a message.

In order to add emotional flavour to online messages, some people use **emoticons,** typographical characters such as :-) or :-(that serve as substitutes for expressing emotions nonverbally. However, current research claims that emoticons have become less useful as nonverbal cues and have little or no effect on the interpretation of a typed message.[32]

We learn to manage facial expressions in order to convey or conceal an emotion and to adapt our facial expressions to particular situations. The most common techniques for adapting facial expressions are **masking,** **neutralization, intensification,** and **deintensification.**[33]

Eye Behaviour

Your eyes may be the most revealing and complex of all your facial features.

Our eyes can signify social position, express both positive and negative

COMMUNICATION
Exercise

Why is it so important to make sure your message is clear when sending email? How does the lack of nonverbal communication affect the receiver's ability to fully know what the sender's intentions are?

WHAT DO WE KNOW ABOUT **EYE Behaviour?**

Researchers have arrived at several conclusions about eye behaviour.[34] Rate each of the following behaviours as generally true or false. Keep in mind that factors such as personality, gender, culture, and context influence our eye behaviour.

True/False

_____ 1. We look at people and things we like.

_____ 2. We avoid looking at people and things we do not like.

_____ 3. We look more at another person when seeking approval or wanting to be liked.

_____ 4. When we avert our gaze from someone, it's an intentional act.

_____ 5. Deception can rarely be detected by looking solely at another person's eye behaviour.

_____ 6. Our pupils dilate when we look at someone or something that is appealing or interesting to us.

_____ 7. Our pupils constrict when we look at someone or something that is not appealing or interesting to us.

_____ 8. Women often look longer at their conversational partners than men do.

Answers: All are true.

emotion, and indicate willingness to relate.[35] When we try to understand what someone else is saying, most of us will look at a speaker more than 80 percent of the time. A group member who wants to be viewed as a leader may choose a seat at the head of the table to gain more visual attention. We tend to increase gaze in response to positive emotions such as surprise and avert our eyes in response to negative experiences like disgust or horror. We use eye contact to get a server's attention in a restaurant and avert our eyes when we don't want the instructor to call on us in class.

As with all nonverbal behaviour, norms for eye contact vary according to gender and culture. Women tend to engage in more eye contact when listening than men. In North America, lack of eye contact is frequently perceived as rudeness, indifference, nervousness, or dishonesty. This is not true across all cultures. For example, "direct eye contact is a taboo or an insult in many Asian cultures. Cambodians consider direct eye contact an invasion of one's privacy."[36]

Vocal Expressiveness

How you *say* a word significantly influences its meaning. Your vocal quality also affects how others perceive you. For example, it can be difficult to listen to a person with a very high-pitched or monotone voice.

Some of the most important vocal characteristics are volume, pitch, and word stress. **Volume** refers to the loudness of the voice. Whispering can indicate that the information is confidential; yelling suggests urgency or anger. **Pitch** refers to how high or low your voice sounds. Men and women with deeper voices are seen as more authoritative and effective. Men with a naturally high pitch may be labelled effeminate or weak, and women with very high pitches may be labelled as childish, silly, or anxious.

Rate is the speed at which you speak. A speaking rate that is too fast makes it difficult for others to understand your message. On the other hand, we become bored by or stop listening to a person who speaks too slowly.

When volume, pitch, and rate are combined, they can be used to

Silence is also speech. (African proverb)

A loud voice shows an empty head. (Finnish proverb)

Those who know, do not speak. Those who speak, do not know. Lao Tzu, *Tao Te Ching*

Silence is a friend who will not betray. (Confucius)

vary the stress you give to a word or phrase. **Word stress** refers to the "degree of prominence given to a syllable within a word or words within a phrase or sentence."[37] Notice the differences in meaning as you stress the italicized words in the following sentences:

> Is **that** the report you want me to read?

> Is that the report you want **me** to read?

> Is that the report you want me to **read**?

Although the same words are used in all three sentences, the meaning of each question is quite different.

Silence

The well-known phrase "silence is golden" may be based on a Swiss saying, "*Sprechen ist silbern; Swchweigen ist golden*," which means "speech is silver; silence is golden." This metaphor contrasts the value of speech and silence. Although speech is important, silence may be even more significant in certain contexts.

Understanding the value of silence is important because we use silence to communicate many things: to establish interpersonal distance, to put our thoughts together, to show respect for another person, or to modify others' behaviours.[38]

Space and Distance

The ways in which we claim, use, and interpret space and distance are significant dimensions of nonverbal communication.

In nonverbal terms, **territoriality** is the sense of personal ownership attached to a particular space. For instance, most classroom students sit in the same place every day. If you have ever walked into a classroom to find another person in "your" seat, you may have felt that your territory had been violated. Ownership of territory is often

COMMUNICATION

The Dark Side of Nonverbal Behaviour

Unfortunately, some people use violent nonverbal communication to express negative emotions or exert power over others. Sometimes a pat on the back is encouraging; a shove on the back is violent. Violence occurs in the home, between spouses, as well as in the workplace between co-workers and by frustrated customers.

Physical intimidation and violence includes acts such as hitting, restraining, and shoving as well as behaviour that stops short of physical contact, such as throwing objects, pounding on a desk, or destroying property. Intimidating nonverbal communication can also take more subtle forms, such as physically blocking another's path, moving aggressively and too close, or creating a threatening presence. Both the *Canadian Human Rights Act* and the *Canada Labour Code* protect employees from harassment related to work. The *Criminal Code* protects all people from physical or sexual assault.[39]

designated by objects acting as **markers** of territory. Placing a coat on a chair or books on a table can send a clear message that a seat is taken or saved.

Anthropologist Edward T. Hall uses the term **proxemics** to refer to the study of spatial relationships and how the distance between people communicates information about their relationship. Hall maintains that we have our own personal portable "air bubble" that we carry around with us. This personal space is culturally determined. For example, the Japanese, who are accustomed to crowding, need less space around them, whereas North Americans need "wide open spaces" around them to feel comfortable.[40]

Most North Americans interact within four spatial zones or distances: **intimate**, **personal**, **social**, and **public**.[41]

Not surprisingly, we reduce the distance between ourselves and others as our relationships become more personal. Intimate distance is usually associated with love, comfort, protection, and increased physical contact. In most situations, you encounter a mixture of distances. You may feel comfortable using an intimate or personal distance with a good friend at work or in college but use social distance with other acquaintances.

Time

In Chapter 3, we introduced the cultural dimension known as monochronic-polychronic time. We noted that people with these two time orientations might not be compatible. Monochronic people want things to run on schedule because time is valuable. Polychronic people who tolerate interruptions in a schedule frustrate monochronic people.

Although researchers have studied how people make use of and respond to time, making rules about it proves difficult. For example, it's unforgivable to be late for a job interview but okay to be late for a party. And what, according to some research, do students see as the *most* disruptive thing in a classroom? The answer: students walking in after the class has begun.[42] As you pay attention and observe

Hall's FOUR Spatial Zones

Tyler Olson/Fotolia

Intimate Distance
(0–18 inches)

Nicholas Piccillo/Fotolia

Personal Distance
(18 inches–4 feet)

StockLite/Shutterstock

Social Distance
(4–12 feet)

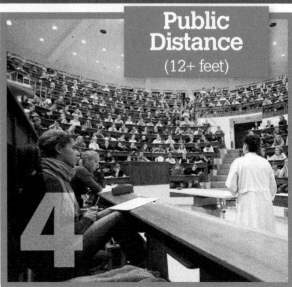

Boelkow/vario images GmbH & Co.KG/Alamy

Public Distance
(12+ feet)

others' nonverbal behaviour, try to learn what their attitudes are about time and punctuality and compare it to yours.

Environment

Do you behave the same way in the classroom as you do at work?

Context, or the environment, does more than influence nonverbal communication; it is a part of nonverbal communication. In other words, context alone can communicate a message. For example, an office with unorganized stacks of papers, a stale smell, uncomfortable chairs, and ugly orange walls may create a negative impression of the occupant. It also may also affect how comfortably you interact in that space. Environmental elements, such as furniture arrangement, lighting, colour, temperature, and smell, communicate.

Most environments are designed with a purpose in mind. An expensive restaurant's dining room may separate tables at some distance to offer diners privacy. The restaurant's atmosphere may be comfortable, quiet, and only subject to the mouth-watering aroma of good food. How does this differ from the environment of your local fast-food restaurant?

6.4
Improving Nonverbal Skills

How can you improve your ability to recognize, use, and adapt to nonverbal communication?

Most children learn to communicate nonverbally by imitating others and by paying attention to and adapting to feedback. When someone responds positively to a particular nonverbal behaviour, you tend to keep using it. If you receive negative reactions, you may choose a more effective behaviour next time. As an adult, awareness and practice can help you develop more effective nonverbal communication skills.

Be Other Oriented

Other-oriented people are effective self-monitors and sensitive to others. They give serious, undivided attention to, feel genuine concern for, and focus on the needs of other people. You can pay attention during a casual phone conversation, note whether your friend's tone of voice communicates more than the words you hear. During face-to-face encounters, observe and "listen" to the nonverbal messages; that is, *look* while you listen. The more of your five senses you use, the more nonverbal cues you will notice.

As you make your own observations of people, ask yourself some of these questions:

- Does their nonverbal behaviour repeat, complement, accent, regulate, or substitute for what they say, or does it contradict their verbal messages?

- How does the use of emblems, illustrators, or adaptors affect the meaning of their messages?
- Do facial expressions mask, neutralize, intensify, or deintensify their thoughts and feelings?
- Do they maintain or avoid eye contact?
- Do they display leakage cues that may reveal a lie or deceptive communication?

Not only should you look at someone *while* you are listening, but you should also look as though you *are* listening. Nodding your head, leaning forward, and engaging in direct eye contact are just some of the nonverbal cues that indicate to others that you are paying attention and interested. Furthermore, your nonverbal feedback lets others sense your response to a message. For example, if your nonverbal behaviours suggest you don't understand or that you disagree with what is being said, the other person may try to clarify information or present a better argument.

If, as you listen, you have difficulty interpreting the meaning of nonverbal behaviour,

ask for help. Describe the message, as you understand it. For example, if someone tells you about a tragic event while smiling, you might say, "George, you don't seem very upset by this. Maybe your smile is just a sign of nervousness?" If you are having trouble setting up a meeting with someone and sense a problem, approach him or her and ask "You seem to be avoiding me—or is it just my imagination?" In Chapter 7, we discuss several techniques for ensuring that you understand the meaning of verbal and nonverbal messages.

Use Immediacy Strategies

Generally, we avoid individuals who appear cold, unfriendly, or hostile. Similarly, we tend to feel more comfortable and want to approach people who seem warm and friendly.

Immediacy is the degree to which a person seems approachable or likable. Imagine approaching a customer service counter where you see two workers, both available to help you. One of the workers leans away from the counter, does not make eye contact with you, and is frowning. The other worker

> Not only should you look at someone while you are listening, you should also look like you are listening.

looks directly at you and smiles. The principle of immediate communication suggests that you will walk up to the worker who appears friendly.

A variety of nonverbal behaviours can promote immediacy.[43] Neat, clean, and pleasant-smelling people are, understandably, more approachable than those who are dirty, sloppy, and smelly. The degree to which you are perceived as likable and approachable may be the difference between a smile and a frown, leaning toward rather than away from another person, direct eye contact versus looking away, a relaxed rather than a rigid body posture, or animated instead of neutral vocal tones. When you use nonverbal immediacy behaviours, other people are more likely to want to communicate with you, and those interactions are warmer and friendlier for everyone involved.

STOP&THINK

How Immediate Are Your Teachers?

Think of your favourite and least favourite teachers—now or in the past. Which ones were most effective? Which teachers left the most indelible impressions? How would you describe their nonverbal behaviours? Were their bodies glued to their desk or lectern, or did they come from behind that barrier, gesture openly, and move closer to you and the other students? Did they smile and look at you directly, use an expressive voice, and listen actively? Did you like them more and learn more from them?[44]

Several studies find positive links between immediacy and learning. Teachers who are immediate generate more interest and enthusiasm about the subject matter.[45] Some of the nonverbal characteristics of high immediacy include the following:

- Consistent and direct eye contact
- Warm voice
- Nodding head approvingly
- Using expressive hand gestures
- Smiling
- Appropriate and natural body movement
- Vocal variety
- Maintaining closer physical distance[46]

Communication researchers conclude "immediacy is the overriding factor in a teacher's overall effectiveness."[47] Now consider the following question: To what extent is immediacy a factor in a student's overall effectiveness? Unfortunately there hasn't been much research on this question. At the same time, you have many years of experience as a student

Angie D'Amico/Shutterstock

and as an observer of other students. Consider the following list of student behaviours and the extent to which you could use such nonverbal immediacy behaviours to create a positive impression on your instructors:

1. Do you make direct eye contact when communicating with your instructors in or outside of class?

2. Do you smile at your instructors?

3. Do you nod your head thoughtfully as you listen to instructors?

4. Do you approach and stand at an appropriate distance from your instructors before or after class?

5. Do you participate in class using direct eye contact, a warm voice, vocal variety, and/or appropriate gestures?

If you answer yes to these questions, your nonverbal immediacy behaviours have made a positive and lasting impression on your instructors.

Role Plays to Assess Your Nonverbal Skills

Scenario #1: A person is out in the local mall, shopping. She hears someone calling her name but can't see who it is. She turns around and sees someone she knows from school but doesn't really like, but can do little about it now because they have made eye contact. They begin a conversation, but one of them appears to be angry, the other in a hurry.

Scenario #2: You have just received a telephone call on your cell. You didn't get to answer it in time, and now you are checking your voice mail. The message is from your father, and he never leaves messages unless it is really important. You listen carefully and your face and body language tells your friend who is with you everything. You haven't said a word.

Scenario #3: You and your friends are out after work and meet at a local restaurant for something to eat. Tonight the newest employee is coming along too. You don't him very well, or what he does yet at your work, but you know he isn't going to fit in well. You sit down at the table and the new guy sits down next to you and pulls his chair in right beside you. You try to move over a little bit, but there isn't much room. He moves his upper body closer to you and starts a conversation. You were right; he isn't fitting in at all.

Scenario #4: A friend walks by your desk and trips, just catching herself before falling over. You weren't paying attention because you were thinking about the movie you saw last night, and you are not aware she almost fell. You look up and see her now, smile, and actually laugh a little when you remember the joke from the movie you wanted to tell her. She scowls at you and walks away.

After you have completed the role plays consider the following questions:

1. Are nonverbal messages stronger when combined with verbal messages? Why or why not?

2. Do you trust nonverbal messages more than verbal messages? Why or why not?

3. How can recognizing nonverbal communication cues make you a better communicator?

6.1
Communicating Without Words

What is nonverbal communication, and how does it affect your everyday life?

- Nonverbal communication refers to message components other than words you use to generate and respond to meaning.

- Nonverbal communication accounts for between 60 and 70 percent of the meaning in a face-to-face message.

- In everyday life, you use nonverbal communication to express emotions, define relationships, establish power and influence, interpret verbal messages, deceive, and detect deception.

6.2
Linking Verbal and Nonverbal Communication

How does verbal and nonverbal communication interact to create meaning?

- Nonverbal communication differs from verbal communication in that it is more convincing, highly contextual, learned informally, less structured, and continuous.

- Nonverbal behaviour can repeat, complement, accent, regulate, substitute, and/or contradict verbal messages.

- Expectancy violation theory demonstrates how your expectations about nonverbal behaviour significantly affect how you interact with others and how you interpret the meaning of nonverbal messages.

6.3
Types of Nonverbal Communication

What types of nonverbal communication should you pay attention to when interacting with others?

- Nonverbal communication has many dimensions, including physical appearance, body movement and gestures, touch, facial expressions, eye behaviour, vocal expressiveness, silence, space and distance, time, and environment.

- Physical appearance includes nonverbal elements such as attractiveness, the presence or absence of tattoos and body piercings, clothing and accessories, and hairstyles.

- Hand movement can be classified as emblems, illustrators, and adaptors.

- Facial expressions can function to mask, neutralize, intensify, or deintensify an emotion.

- *Proxemics* is the study of how the distance between people communicates information about the nature of their relationship.

- Edward Hall's four spatial zones—intimate, personal, social, and public distances—are culturally determined.

6.4
Improving Nonverbal Skills

How can you improve your ability to recognize, use, and adapt to nonverbal communication?

- By observing others' nonverbal behaviour and confirming your interpretation of its meaning, you can become more other oriented.

- Nonverbal immediacy strategies such as maintaining eye contact, smiling, using vocal variety and appropriate body movements, and maintaining close physical distance can enhance your interactions with others.

Monkey Business Images/Shutterstock

6.1 *What is nonverbal communication, and how does it affect your everyday life?*

1 The textbook defines *nonverbal communication* as message components other than words that generate meaning. Which of the following answers is *not* an example of nonverbal communication?

a. using :-) in an email to highlight your feelings

b. reading an old letter from a good friend who was living abroad

c. putting on perfume or cologne before going to a party

d. brightening up your apartment with flowers before your parents come over for dinner

e. sitting in a middle position at the side of a table during a staff meeting

2 Even though Fiona has nothing but good things to say about her boyfriend, her family can tell she's angry at him. Which nonverbal characteristic best explains this experience?

a. Nonverbal communication is more convincing.

b. Nonverbal communication is highly contextual.

c. Nonverbal communication is learned informally.

d. Nonverbal communication is less structured.

e. Nonverbal communication is continuous.

3 Which of the following nonverbal communication goals could Sigmund Freud have been describing when he wrote that "He who has eyes to see and ears to hear may convince himself that no mortal can keep a secret"?

a. to express emotions

b. to define relationships

c. to establish power and influence

d. to interpret verbal messages

e. to deceive and detect deception

4 Most people can detect deception accurately about_____ percent of the time.

a. 25 b. 30 c. 50 d. 75 e. 80

5 According to research reported by Mark Knapp, the small minority of people who are *highly* skilled lie detectors look for

a. higher voice pitch and vocal tension in a speaker.

b. exaggerated movements and longer pauses.

c. discrepancies between verbal and nonverbal behaviour.

d. more blinking and less eye contact.

e. fidgety movements and less gesturing.

6.2 *How do verbal and nonverbal communication interact to create meaning?*

6 Which of the following nonverbal hand movements is an example of an illustrator?

a. making a circle with your thumb and index finger to indicate "OK"

b. holding your thumb and fingers about two inches apart as you describe how much shorter your hair was after your last haircut

c. putting your face in the palms of your hands when you realize that you've forgotten to buy your spouse a Valentine's present

d. raising your hand in class so the instructor will call on you

e. crossing your index and middle fingers as a good-luck signal

6.3 *What types of nonverbal communication should you pay attention to when interacting with others?*

7 If one of your co-workers tells you that she got the promotion that both of you applied for, you may smile at the news even though you feel awful. Which technique for adapting facial expressions are you using?

a. masking

b. neutralizing

c. intensification

d. unmasking

e. deintensification

8 If the speaker stresses the word indicated in italics, which of the following statements means "I was born in Nova Scotia, not in Newfoundland as you seem to think."

a. "*I* was born in Nova Scotia."

b. "I *was* born in Nova Scotia."

c. "I was *born* in Nova Scotia."

d. "I was born *in* Nova Scotia."

e. "I was born in *Nova Scotia.*"

9 According to research, how close to a good friend does the average person in North America stand?

a. 0 to 6 inches

b. 6 to 18 inches

c. 18 inches to 4 feet

d. 4 feet to 12 feet

e. more than 12 feet

6.4 *How can you improve your ability to recognize, use, and adapt to nonverbal communication?*

10 _____ refers to the degree to which you seem approachable and likable.

a. Other oriented

b. Immediacy

c. Observant

d. Confirming

e. Conversational

Answers found on page 330.

Key Terms

Accenting nonverbal behaviour	**Immediacy**	**Public distance**
Adaptors	**Intensification**	**Rate**
Complementary nonverbal behaviour	**Intimate distance**	**Regulating nonverbal behaviour**
	Leakage cues	
Contradictory nonverbal behaviour	**Marker**	**Repetitive nonverbal behaviour**
	Masking	
Deintensification	**Metamessage**	**Social distance**
Emblems	**Mixed message**	**Substituting nonverbal behaviour**
Emoticons	**Neutralization**	
Expectancy violation theory	**Nonverbal communication**	**Territoriality**
	Other oriented	**Touch approachers**
Gesture	**Personal distance**	**Touch avoiders**
Illustrators	**Pitch**	**Volume**
	Proxemics	**Word stress**

Understanding
INTERPERSONAL
RELATIONSHIPS

7

What do most popular films, novels, and television series have in common? They tell stories. Now go one step further: What do these stories have in common? They are stories about interpersonal relationships. For example, are the *Harry Potter* books and films about wizards and magic, or are they about Harry's relationships with his friends, his foes, his teachers, and his dysfunctional Muggle family?

The close and supportive relationships Harry enjoys with his Hogwarts classmates confirm psychologist David Myers's claim that "there are few stronger predictions of happiness than a close, nurturing, equitable, intimate, lifelong companionship with one's best friend."[1] Like all deeply satisfying stories with happy endings, from *The Wizard of Oz* and *Star Wars* to *Slumdog Millionaire* and *Avatar*, the films in the *Harry Potter* series reaffirm this universal truth: Interpersonal relationships—between friends, and colleagues—are central to the human condition.

Interpersonal Communication and Relationships

What are the characteristics and benefits of effective interpersonal communication?

Your ability to communicate effectively in close personal relationships influences your psychological and physical health, your identity and happiness, your social and moral development, your ability to cope with stress and misfortunes, and the quality and meaning of your life.[2] In this chapter we examine the interpersonal communication theories, strategies, and skills that lead to healthy and satisfying relationships.

Interpersonal communication occurs when a limited number of people, usually two, interact and generate meaning through verbal and nonverbal messages. This interaction typically results in sharing information, achieving a goal, and/or maintaining a relationship. When we use the word **relationship** in this textbook, we are referring to a continuing and meaningful attachment or connection to another person. There are many types of interpersonal relationships—perhaps as many as there are people you know.

In addition to the emotional connections and commitments you have in close **personal relationships** with friends, romantic partners, and family members, you also have work-based relationships. **Professional relationships** involve connections with people you associate and work with to accomplish a goal or perform a task. Many relationships fall into both categories. One of your best friends may also be a colleague at work.

John Gottman, who studies the value and consequences of close personal relationships and strong marriages, offers several conclusions drawn from his own and others' research:

- People with good friends usually have less stress and live longer.
- Longevity is determined far more by the state of people's closest relationships than by genetics.
- People who have good marriages live longer than those who don't.
- Loners are twice as likely to die from all causes over a five-year period as those who enjoy close friendships.[3]

Some people mistakenly believe that Gottman is urging us to make as many friends as possible and (if not

Medical researchers have found "a link between relationships and physical health. . . . People with rich personal networks—who are married, have close family and friends, are active in social and religious groups—recover more quickly from disease and live longer."[4]

already married) to get married as soon as possible in order to live longer. But Gottman's essential point is that meaningful and lasting personal relationships lead to a happy life. Quality relationships do not just happen. *You* make them happen, and the success of those relationships depends largely on how well you communicate.

What types of relationships are shown in these photos?

goodluz/Fotolia

WavebreakmediaMicro/Fotolia

THINK ABOUT THEORY

Schutz's Interpersonal Needs Theory

Psychologist William Schutz's **fundamental interpersonal relationship orientation (FIRO) theory** asserts that people interact with others in order to satisfy one or all of three basic interpersonal needs: (1) the need for inclusion, (2) the need for control, and (3) the need for affection.[5]

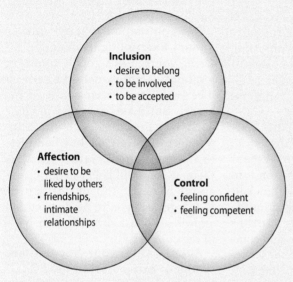

Inclusion
- desire to belong
- to be involved
- to be accepted

Affection
- desire to be liked by others
- friendships, intimate relationships

Control
- feeling confident
- feeling competent

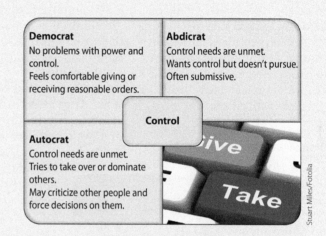

Democrat
No problems with power and control.
Feels comfortable giving or receiving reasonable orders.

Abdicrat
Control needs are unmet.
Wants control but doesn't pursue.
Often submissive.

Autocrat
Control needs are unmet.
Tries to take over or dominate others.
May criticize other people and force decisions on them.

Control

Stuart Miles/Fotolia

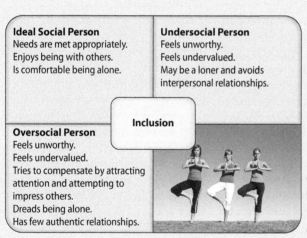

Ideal Social Person
Needs are met appropriately.
Enjoys being with others.
Is comfortable being alone.

Undersocial Person
Feels unworthy.
Feels undervalued.
May be a loner and avoids interpersonal relationships.

Oversocial Person
Feels unworthy.
Feels undervalued.
Tries to compensate by attracting attention and attempting to impress others.
Dreads being alone.
Has few authentic relationships.

Inclusion

Biocreative/Fotolia

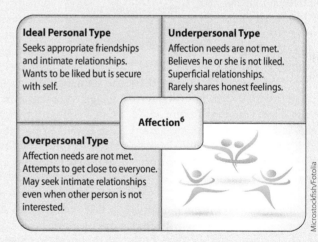

Ideal Personal Type
Seeks appropriate friendships and intimate relationships.
Wants to be liked but is secure with self.

Underpersonal Type
Affection needs are not met.
Believes he or she is not liked.
Superficial relationships.
Rarely shares honest feelings.

Overpersonal Type
Affection needs are not met.
Attempts to get close to everyone.
May seek intimate relationships even when other person is not interested.

Affection[6]

Microstockfish/Fotolia

Schutz's Fundamental Interpersonal Relationship Orientation (FIRO) Theory[7]

COMMUNICATION

Exercise

In small groups discuss the following:
1. How would you define the word *friend*?
2. Brainstorm the most important characteristics of a friend.
3. Identify which characteristics of friendship can be seen in Schutz's fundamental interpersonal relationship orientation theory in each category: inclusion, control, and affection.

Developing Interpersonal Relationships

How do you form positive and lasting relationships with others?

Do you make a good impression on others? Do people seem to enjoy talking to you? Are you understood or misunderstood, seen as interesting or boring, and generally liked or merely tolerated?

The answers to these questions say a great deal about how you communicate, particularly when you want to initiate or further develop a relationship. Research tells us that significant and meaningful relationships develop when you make a positive impression and have satisfying conversations with others.

Impression Management

You know from experience that first impressions count. If you don't make a good impression on a first date, it may be your last with that person. Someone you meet on an airplane may eventually offer you a job. If you get off to a good start with someone sitting next to you in class, you may become close friends. And, once you've made a good initial impression on someone, your subsequent behaviour can reinforce and maintain that impression or can weaken and even reverse it.

Sociologist Erving Goffman claims that we assume a social identity that others help us to maintain.[8] This perspective is useful in understanding **impression management**, the strategies we use to shape and control the way other people see us. These impressions affect how others perceive us in social interactions as well as how they interpret our ability to gain influence, power, sympathy, or approval.[9]

The section that follows presents five impression management strategies—ingratiation, self-promotion, exemplification, supplication, and intimidation—as related to a communicator's desired goal and the emotions sought in others.[10]

Ingratiation (But Not Phony Flattery) Ingratiation is the most common impression management strategy; the goal of ingratiation is to be liked by others. Ingratiation skills include giving compliments, doing another person a favour, and comforting someone. Complimenting someone with whom you disagree can ease tensions and reopen communication channels. Insincere ingratiation, however, has the potential to damage rather than enhance your image. Whereas honest flattery ingratiates you with others, phony flattery can have the opposite effect.

Self-Promotion (But Not Bragging) Self-promotion is a strategy for being seen as competent. The goal is to be respected by others. Announcing, "I'm a fast writer" can earn you a place on an important work team that has short-deadline projects and reports. At the same time, *over self-promotion*— exaggerating your achievements and skills in order to impress others—may create a negative impression that is difficult to change. And if your actual performance does not live up to your self-promotion, you can create a bad, lasting impression. Promote yourself with honest and integrity, because no one likes a show-off.

Exemplification (But Not Just in Public) Exemplification entails offering yourself as a good example or a model of noteworthy behaviour. The goal is to be seen as honest and moral. But make sure you practise what you preach. If you claim it's wrong to pirate CDs but you photocopy entire books rather than buy them, no one will believe your claims about honesty and moral values. Don't declare you're on a strict diet and then get caught with your hand in the cookie jar.

Supplication (But Not Endless Whining) Supplication describes a humble request or appeal for help. The goal of supplication is compassion from others. Appropriate supplication causes other people to feel resourceful and valued. But don't rely on supplication to get someone else to do your work or to earn admiration and respect; if you cry out for help when you have the resources to handle something on your own, you will soon be ignored. In other words, ask for help when you truly need it, not when you just don't want to do the work.

Intimidation (But Not Brutality) The goal of **intimidation** is to provoke fear. In order to be seen as powerful, an intimidating person demonstrates a willingness and ability to cause harm. Intimidation strategies

> You don't get a second chance to make a first impression.

Steve Jobs (co-founder and chief executive of Apple, Inc.) and Bill Gates (co-founder and chairman of Microsoft) created unique public images that differ from each other. What is your overall impression of each man?

Peer Grimm/Peter Stroh/Alamy

Benjamin Stansall/Alamy

involve threats to subdue or control others. "If you speak to me that way again, I will file a formal grievance against you." We do not recommend using intimidation in communication situations. In some instances, however, you may need to establish appropriate willingness to use power. If others are taking advantage of you, you may need to stand up for yourself—demonstrating that you won't be intimidated.

Effective Conversations

A **conversation** is an interaction, often informal, in which we exchange speaking and listening roles with another person. In his book *A Good Talk*, Daniel Menace regards conversation as a human art of great importance produced by all people everywhere.[11]

On any given day, you may have a conversation with a close friend from childhood on the phone, a classmate in the hallway, a co-worker at the next desk, or someone you've just met at a party. Conversations differ depending on where they take place and the type of relationship. For example, you may wait until others aren't around or until a championship game on television is over to have a serious and private conversation with a close friend. You may discuss highly personal issues with your life partner, but you probably won't share as much with someone you've just met.

Starting a Conversation Introducing yourself and sharing some superficial information is the most obvious way to begin a conversation with someone you do not know: "I'm Ahmad; my family and I are here on vacation from Montreal." The other person will usually reciprocate by offering similar information or following up on what you've shared: "I have cousins in Montreal and visited them one summer when I was a kid." A second approach to opening a conversation is to ask simple questions: "Do you know anything about this movie?"

Maintaining a Conversation One of the best ways to keep a conversation going is to ask **open-ended questions** that encourage specific or detailed responses. "What do you think of Dr. Pearson's course

We negotiate conversational turn-taking primarily through our nonverbal behaviour.

StockLite/Shutterstock

and assignments?" invites someone to share an observation or opinion. A **closed-ended question**, "Is this class required for your major?" requires only a short and direct response and can generally be answered with a yes or no.

Funnelling questions start with a broad question, "What did you do while visiting India?" The next question then begins to become more specific and funnels the conversation to find out more specific information and detail and to extend the conversation. A possible next question in this example is "Were you in one area only?"[12]

When you answer questions during a conversation, give a response that provides the other person with more information about your thoughts or experiences. An engaging conversation requires the effort and commitment of two people. Without work, a conversation can quickly deteriorate into an awkward silence.

Finally, make sure you balance talking with listening. A successful conversationalist takes turns listening and speaking. Watch for nonverbal cues to find out when it's your turn to listen or speak. **Turn-requesting cues** are verbal and nonverbal messages that signal a desire to speak, such as leaning forward, providing direct eye contact, and lifting one hand as if beginning to gesture. **Turn-yielding cues** are verbal and nonverbal messages that signal that you are completing your comments and are preparing to listen, such as slowing down your speaking rate, relaxing your

posture or gestures, and leaning slightly away. Good conversationalists are sensitive to turn-taking cues.

Listening in Conversations Effective listening promotes a genuine conversation rather than a one-way speech.

In a good conversation, you must be able to suspend your own needs and opinions to listen to someone else's. Daniel Menaker explains that both parties in a conversation must "listen very closely, not only to the loud notes, but to the quiet one . . . as well—to what sounds as though it's being downplayed or skipped over. Such attention is, for one thing, flattering, but it also yields insights that the people we're talking to sometimes don't even know they have."[13] Review Chapter 4 to make sure that you listen to understand, remember, interpret, evaluate, and appropriately respond to what you hear.

Ending a Conversation Ending a conversation abruptly can send a rude message to the other person. Look for a moment in the conversation where an ending seems natural—either when the topic seems fully exhausted or when someone shifts to the edge of a chair, stands up, looks away, leans away, or picks up personal belongings.[14] Try to end every conversation on a positive and courteous note. If, however, your companion is ignoring your attempts to end the conversation, you may need to be direct but firm: "I hate to cut our conversation short, but I have to get going."

Exercise

1. Watch this video clip about questions:

   www.youtube.com/watch?v=cvsMOw6D1M0

2. In pairs, create sample closed, open, and funnelling questions for these situations: meeting someone in your class for the first time, getting to know your study group members, and interviewing a tutor for a subject you are struggling with in college.

7.3
Strengthening Personal Relationships

How does interpersonal communication affect your relationships with friends colleagues?

Igor Mojzes/Fotolia

Everyone has a multitude of personal relationships—with family members and friends, with teachers and students, with business associates and service providers, and with that special person who is your beloved partner or spouse. Unfortunately, we lack the space in this chapter and

COMMUNICATION&CULTURE

GIRL-FRIENDS AND BOY-FRIENDS DIFFER

In adolescence as well as in young, middle, and older adulthood, men report less intimacy, less complexity, and less contact in same-gender friendships. In contrast, women report greater continuity in their long-term, same-sex friendships than men and see these friendships as important in their lives over time. One interesting study notes that throughout middle and older adulthood, women often value talk with their friends more than talk with their husbands.[15]

Mutual and confirming talk is both the substance and central feature of many women's friendships. Male friendships, on the other

Phase4Photography/Fotolia
oliveromg/Shutterstock

hand, tend to focus on common interests, shared activities, and sociability. In his book *Friendship Matters*, William Rawlins notes that male friendships are "often geared toward accomplishing things and having something to show for their time spent together—practical problems solved, the house painted or deck completed . . . cars washed or tuned, poker, or music played, and so on."[16]

Despite these differences, both adult men and women view close friendship as a mutually dependent, accepting, confidential, and trusting relationship.

textbook to examine all these relationships in detail. Instead, we focus on two of the most significant personal relationships you develop in your lifetime: friends and lovers. The distinct context and importance of these relationships requires special communication strategies and skills to enhance their quality and longevity.

Friendship

Although just about everyone has friends, not all friendships are alike. Several factors influence the kind of friendship you have with another person. For example, for young children, a friend is simply someone with whom a child shares toys and plays; when these activities are absent, so is the friendship.[17]

In adolescence and young adulthood, we often establish enduring and intimate relationships with best friends. **Intimacy**, the feeling or state of knowing someone deeply, occurs in many forms. For example, in most romantic relationships, physical intimacy is a way of expressing affection and love. In romantic and friend relationships, intimacy takes a different form. It can be emotional (sharing private thoughts and feelings), intellectual (sharing attitudes, beliefs, and interests), and/or collaborative (sharing and achieving a common goal).[18]

Close friends learn that it's okay to share personal thoughts, secrets, hopes, and fears, but whether we do so depends on our ability (1) to disclose personal information in a way that maintains the relationship; (2) to recognize that most of these disclosures center on mundane, everyday issues; and (3) to respect that some topics are taboo, such as

negative life events and serious relationship issues.[19]

During late adolescence and young adulthood, most of us leave home—to work, to go to college, or to marry and raise a family. The dual tasks of developing new friendships while adapting to a new job, new living conditions, or new academic settings are stressful. Adolescents and young adults have more opportunities to make friends, but this stage in their development often proves to be one of their loneliest times.[20]

Being Mindful

In the rush of today's multi-tasking societies, it is often very difficult to stay "in the moment" or to slow down enough to be mindful of the conversations we are having with each other. When you commit to being mindful, it forces you to be aware and to participate. This in turn allows you to focus on the interpersonal relationships in your life.

> **"** In today's rush we all think too much—seek too much—want too much—and forget the joy of just being. **"**[21]

Mindful listening is critical to effective interpersonal communication. As discussed in Chapter 4, listening

attentively and with purpose increases understanding, but when you listen mindfully it creates an atmosphere of trust that may lead to deeper, more appropriate relationships.

Mindfulness impacts all of your interactions, and paying attention in your future career will be very important. Consider for a moment the work of 911 emergency operators. As they answer a call, they must be able to be mindful of what is and is not being said. They need to listen to the caller's concern, ask important questions, respond to the emotional tone of the caller, listen to interpret what information the caller may be leaving out, and assess the risks for the emergency personnel who will be attending to the call. If the operator is not "in the moment" during the phone call, he or she could easily make an error that could cause stress or danger for those involved.

Mindful of the Environment
• eliminate distractions
• make eye contact

Mindful of Others
• pay attention
• appropriate listening strategy

Mindful of Yourself
• physical health
• emotional health
• learn to listen to your body

COMMUNICATION

Exercise

What other careers require high degrees of mindfulness in order to assure safety, quality, and effective interpersonal communication?

How does mindfulness in interpersonal communication affect your own career choice?

For further exploration of mindfulness, view this YouTube video.

www.youtube.com/watch?v=wPNEmxWSNxg

7.4

Sharing Your Self with Others

How do self-disclosure and sensitivity to feedback affect your interpersonal relationships?

Sharing your self with others is essential for developing meaningful relationships. Whether you are talking about your favourite smartphone app with a new acquaintance or revealing your deepest fears to someone you love, both of you must be able and willing to share personal information and feelings.

Self-disclosure is the process of sharing with others personal information, opinions, and emotions that would not otherwise be known to them. This is *not* to say you should reveal the most intimate details of your life to everyone you meet. Instead, you must judge if and when sharing is appropriate by understanding and accepting the other person's attitudes, beliefs, and values.[22] One of the most difficult communication challenges you face in a personal relationship is deciding what, where, when, how, and with whom to self-disclose.

The Johari Window Model

Psychologists Joseph Luft and Harrington Ingham provide a useful model for understanding the connections between self-disclosure and feedback.[23] They authors use the metaphor of a window, calling their model the **Johari Window** (the name is a combination of their first names).[24] The model looks at two interpersonal communication dimensions: willingness to self-disclose

Scott Griessel/Fotolia

and receptivity to feedback. *Willingness to self-disclose* describes the extent to which you are prepared to disclose personal information and feelings to other people. *Receptivity to feedback* describes your awareness, interpretation, and response to someone else's self-disclosure about you.[26] When these two dimensions are graphed against one another, the result is a figure that resembles a four-paned window as illustrated. Each pane means something different, and each pane can vary in size.

Four Different Panes The *open area* of your Johari Window contains

RECEPTIVITY TO FEEDBACK

Known to Self — Unknown to Self

WILLINGNESS TO SELF-DISCLOSE

Known to Others — Unknown to Others

Open area | Blind area

Hidden area | Unknown

Springfield Gallery/Fotolia

The Johari Window[25]

information you are willing to share with others as well as information you have learned about yourself by accurately interpreting others' feedback. For example, suppose you wonder whether it's okay to tell an embarrassing but funny personal story to a group of new colleagues. You decide to take the risk. If your listeners laugh and seem to appreciate your sense of humour, you've learned two things: that it's safe to share personal stories with this group and that you are, in fact, funny.

The *hidden area* represents your private self, which includes information you know about yourself ("I am attracted to that person," "I was once arrested") but that you are not yet willing to share with others. The hidden area contains your secrets. Some people retain a lot of personal information in this area that could enhance their personal relationships and likability if that information were shared.

The *blind area* contains information others know about you but that you do *not* know about yourself because you don't pay attention to or correctly interpret feedback from others. If you don't notice that someone disapproves of your behaviours or wants your praise for a job well done, you may not develop or maintain a close relationship with that person.

Information unknown to *both* you and others exists in the *unknown area*. For example, suppose you have always avoided doing any writing at work because you don't think you're a good writer. And yet, when working with a group of colleagues on an interesting project, you end up doing most of the writing. As time passes, you and your co-workers recognize and appreciate your writing talent. This "discovery" about yourself now moves from your unknown area to your open area.

Varying Size of Panes Depending on how willing you are to self-disclose and how receptive you are to feedback, each of the four panes in the Johari Window differs in size. Although this makes a very unusual-looking window, it does a good job of reflecting your level of self-awareness. As a relationship develops, you should disclose more, which enlarges your open area and reduces the amount of information in your hidden area. As you become more receptive to feedback, you reduce your blind area and enlarge your open area.[27] As your open area expands, your unknown area gets smaller.

Exercise

For an illustration of the Johari Window, view this video:

www.youtube.com/watch?v=-7FhcvoVK8s

7.5

Expressing Your Self Appropriately

How should you express your personal thoughts and feelings to others?

As you get to know yourself and others better you may find yourself engaging in more intimate self-disclosure and responding more to feedback. Both of these communication skills help to increase your self-awareness and the overall quality of your personal relationships. Social penetration theory (see p. 132) and the Johari Window model help explain the need for appropriate self-disclosure and receptivity to feedback; this section describes communication strategies and skills that can help you express yourself appropriately and thereby strengthen and preserve your relationships with others.

Although it can be painful and risky, when the emotional stakes are high, self-disclosure can benefit a relationship in significant ways.

STRATEGIES FOR **EFFECTIVE SELF-DISCLOSURE**

STRATEGY	RATIONALE
Focus on the present, not the past.	Obsessing about past problems may not help or enlighten either person.
Be descriptive, not judgmental.	Criticizing someone's behaviour can end up in a hostile argument.
Disclose your feelings, not just the facts.	Explaining how you feel about what is happening clarifies and justifies your reactions.
Adapt to the person and context.	Revealing intimate personal information to the wrong person at the wrong time in the wrong place benefits no one.
Be sensitive to others' reactions.	Modifying or discontinuing self-disclosure is essential if the other person's reaction is extreme (rage, crying, hysteria).
Engage in reciprocal self-disclosure.	Modifying or discontinuing self-disclosure is appropriate if the other person does not disclose as well.
Gradually move disclosure to a deeper level.	Increasing the breadth, depth, and frequency of your self-disclosure should occur as your level of comfort with the other person increases.

FACTS THINK ABOUT THEORY
TEST IDEA PLAN EXPERIMENT METHOD KNOWLEDGE

Social Penetration Theory

Social penetration theory, developed by Irwin Altman and Dalmas Taylor, describes the process of relationship bonding that occurs when individuals move from superficial communication to deeper, more intimate communication.[28] According to Altman and Taylor, the process of developing an intimate relationship is similar to peeling an onion. The outer skin of the onion represents superficial and mostly public information about yourself, and the inner layers—those closest to the core—represent your most intimate information.

Social penetration theory explains that self-disclosure has three interconnected dimensions: depth, breadth, and frequency.[29] *Deep* self-disclosure is intimate and near the core of the onion; for example, there's a big difference between telling someone "You're OK" and telling someone "I love you." When self-disclosure is *broad*, it covers many topic areas, some very personal, some impersonal. In addition to sharing information about your hobbies and job, you may also share your strong beliefs and values about family and religion. Self-disclosure becomes more *frequent* as the depth and breadth of your relationship expands.

The animated film *Shrek* captures the underlying premise of Social penetration theory. As Shrek, the large, lumbering, green ogre, and his hyperactive companion, Donkey, trek through fields and forests, Shrek tries to explain himself to Donkey:

Shrek:	For your information, there's a lot more to ogres than people think.
Donkey:	Example?
Shrek:	Example? Okay. Um. Ogres are like onions.
Donkey:	They stink?
Shrek:	No.
Donkey:	Oh, they make you cry?
Shrek:	No.
Donkey:	Oh, you leave them out in the sun and they get all brown and start sprouting little white hairs?
Shrek:	No! Layers. Onions have layers. Ogres have layers. You get it? We both have layers![30]

Social penetration theory contends that as two people get to know one another better, they reveal personal information, feelings, and experiences below the public image layer. Relationships develop when this process is reciprocal—that is, one person's openness leads to another's openness, and so on.

EXAMPLES OF LAYERS

Layer A: Most impersonal layer (music, clothing, food preferences)

Layer B: Impersonal layer (job, politics, education)

Layer C: Middle layer (religious beliefs, social attitudes)

Layer D: Personal layer (personal goals, fears, hopes, secrets)

Layer E: Most personal layer (inner core, self-concept)

EXAMPLES OF TOPICS

Topic 1: Leisure activities

Topic 2: Career

Topic 3: Family

Topic 4: Health

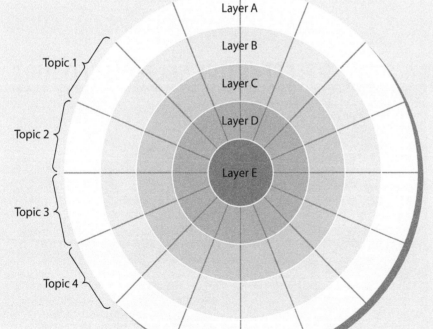

The Social Penetration Process

Effective Self-Disclosure

When you self-disclose, you reveal how you are reacting to a situation while sharing relevant information about yourself and your experiences. Successful self-disclosure is not a solo activity. If the

Giving and Asking for FEEDBACK

- Focus on behaviour, not on the person.
- Make it specific, not general or abstract.
- Use "I" rather than "you" statements.
- Focus on what was said and done, not on why it was said and done.
- Focus on current behaviour, not behaviour from the past.
- Share information, perceptions, and feelings, not advice.
- Provide feedback at an appropriate time and place.
- Focus on actions that both of you able to change.[31]

Exercise

Role Play

In pairs, create a short (two-minute) scene. One person self-discloses to the other. Before each pair presents their scene, they must set the setting and describe the type of relationship being role-played (romantic, business, friendship, etc.).

After each pair presents, discuss the level of risk associated with the self-disclosure displayed in the scene.

other person does not self-disclose or respond to your self-disclosures, you may want to rethink the relationship or stop sharing your thoughts and feelings.[32]

Effective Feedback

Effective interpersonal communication relies on giving and receiving feedback from others. No matter where or when you provide feedback, it should not be threatening or demanding. At the same time, remember that there is only so much that you and another person can comprehend

and process at one time. Too much personal information can overwhelm and overload the best of listeners.

Defensive and Supportive Communication

Communication scholar Jack Gibb asserts that there are six behaviours that create a supportive climate for communication and six that cause defensiveness.[33] **Defensive behaviours** reflect our instinct to protect ourselves when someone is physically or verbally attacking us. Even though

DEFENSIVE BEHAVIOURS

EVALUATION: Judges another person's behaviour. Makes critical statements. "Why did you insult Sharon like that? Explain yourself!" "What you did was terrible."

CONTROL: Imposes your solution on someone else. Seeks control of the situation. "Give me that report and I'll make it better." "Since I'm paying for the vacation, we're going to the resort I like rather than the spa you like."

STRATEGY: Manipulates others. Hides or disguises personal motives. Withholds information. "Frankie's going to Florida over spring break." "Remember when I helped you rearrange your office?"

NEUTRALITY: Appears withdrawn, detached, or indifferent. Won't take sides. "You can't win them all." "Life's a gamble." "It doesn't matter to me." "Whatever."

SUPERIORITY: Implies that you and your opinions are better than others. Promotes resentment and jealousy. "Hey—I've done this a million times—let me have it. I'll finish in no time." "Is this the best you could do?"

CERTAINTY: Believes that your opinion is the only correct one. Refuses to consider the ideas and opinions of others. Takes inflexible positions. "I can't see any other way of doing this that makes sense." "There's no point in discussing this any further."

SUPPORTIVE BEHAVIOURS

DESCRIPTION: Describes another person's behaviour. Makes understanding statements. Uses more *I* and *we* language. "When we heard what you said to Sharon, we were really embarrassed for her." "I'm sorry about that."

PROBLEM ORIENTATION: Seeks a mutually agreeable solution. "Okay. Let's see what we can do to get that report finished to specifications." "Let's figure out how both of us can enjoy our vacation."

SPONTANEITY: Makes straightforward, direct, open, honest, and helpful comments. "I'd like to go to Florida with Frankie over spring break." "Would you help me move some heavy boxes?"

EMPATHY: Accepts and understands another person's feelings. "I can understand how you are feeling. No wonder you're upset." "It sounds as though you're having a hard time deciding."

EQUALITY: Suggests that everyone can make a useful contribution. "If you don't mind, I'd like to explain how I've handled this before. It may help." "Let's tackle this problem together."

PROVISIONALISM: Offers ideas and accepts suggestions from others. "We have a lot of options here—which one makes the most sense?" "I feel strongly about this, but I would like to hear what you think."

Gibb's Defensive and Supportive Behaviours[34]

expressing your self appropriately

such reactions are natural, they also discourage reciprocal self-disclosure. On the other hand, **supportive behaviours** create a climate in which self-disclosure and responsiveness to feedback benefit both parties.

The paired behaviours in Gibb's model are not necessarily "good" or "bad" behaviours. For example, you may behave strategically when you have important and strong personal motives. You may behave with certainty when your expertise is well recognized and a critical decision must be made. And you may respond neutrally when the issue is of little consequence to you or others.[35]

7.6

Developing Assertiveness

How can you assert yourself and also respect the rights and needs of others?

What should you do if your boss wants you to work longer hours, but you want more time with your family? What if your friend wants to go to a party, but you need to stay home and study? How do you balance these competing needs and resolve potential conflicts? The answer may lie in how ready you are to be assertive. **Assertiveness** is the willingness and ability to stand up for your own needs and rights while also respecting the needs and rights of others.

Passivity and Aggression

Assertiveness is best understood by considering three alternatives to assertiveness: passivity, aggression, and passive aggression. **Passivity** is characterized by giving in to others at the expense of your own needs in order to avoid conflict and disagreement. For example, Jackson's boss asks him to work over the weekend. Jackson agrees and says nothing about his plans to attend an important family event. Not surprisingly, passive individuals often feel taken advantage of by others and blame them for their unhappiness. As a result, they fail to take responsibility for their own actions and the consequences of those actions.[36]

The opposite of passive behaviour is **aggression**, in which communicators put their personal needs first while violating someone else's needs and rights. Aggressive individuals demand compliance from others. Although aggressive behaviour can be violent, it is usually displayed in more subtle behaviour, such as a raised voice, rolled eyes, or a withering glance.[37]

Sometimes people may *seem* passive when, in fact, their intentions are aggressive. Although **passive-aggressive** individuals may *appear* cooperative and willing to accommodate the needs of others, their actions are a subtle form of aggressive behaviour. Passive-aggressive communicators manipulate others to get what they want. For example, when you refuse to do a favour for your brother, he mopes around the house until you finally give in to his request. While aggressive, passive, and passive-aggressive behaviour may initially seem effective, in the long run, they damage interpersonal and professional relationships.

Assertiveness Skills

Assertiveness can be difficult to learn, particularly if you become passive or aggressive when challenged. Being assertive may involve breaking old communication habits while recognizing that in some contexts those styles may be appropriate. Initially, assertive behaviour may feel strange or uncomfortable because asserting your rights can open the door to discomfort. Sharon and Gordon Bower, the authors of *Asserting Yourself*, have developed what they call a **DESC script**—a four-step process that relies on communication skills for becoming more assertive. DESC is an acronym for Describe, Express, Specify, and Consequences. This scripting method can be used in both personal and professional

> Assertive behaviour can improve your self-esteem, your ability to resolve conflict, and the quality of your relationships.

relationships.[38] In some cases, you may want to write out your DESC script in advance and practise it before you have to confront someone. A DESC script can be used in both personal and professional relationships.

DESC Scripting

D: Describe. Describe the unwanted situation or offensive behaviour as completely and objectively as you can. Describe the other person's action, not his or her perceived motive. **Example:** "The last time we had a group project due, I did most of the work."

E: Express. Express your feelings clearly and calmly. Use "I" and not "you" in order to avoid eliciting a defensive reaction. **Example:** "As a result, I was exhausted and angry."

The Benefits of Asserting Yourself

- Expressing your feelings appropriately
- Accepting compliments graciously
- Speaking up for your rights when appropriate
- Enhancing your self-esteem and self-confidence
- Expressing disagreement on important issues
- Asking others to change their inappropriate or offensive behaviour[39]

S: Specify. Specify what you want to happen or the behaviour you want from the other person. Take into account whether the other person can do what you request and what changes you're willing to make. **Example:** "For this next project, I would like the two of us to work together."

C: Consequences. Consequences (both positive and negative) of accepting or denying your request are outlined. Ask yourself: What rewarding consequences can I provide? **Example:** "If we work together on this project, the report will be done better and faster—and hopefully we'll earn a good grade."

PETER COSGROVE /AP Images

COMMUNICATION IN *ACTION*

Just Say No.

Saying "no" to someone can very difficult—even scary. In his book *The Anxiety and Phobia Workbook*, Edmund Bourne writes that "an important aspect of being assertive is your ability to say no to requests you don't want to meet. Saying no means that you set limits on other people's demands for your time and energy when such demands conflict with your own needs and desires."[40]

In some cases, you may need to say no to a family member, good friend, or close colleague. Here are the four steps Bourne recommends:

1. Acknowledge the other person's request by repeating it. "I'd love to have lunch with you tomorrow."
2. Explain your reason for declining. "But, I have a deadline on Friday, so I have lots of work to do and can't take the time this week."
3. Say no. "So I'll have to say no."
4. (Optional) Suggest an alternative proposal in which both your needs and the other person's needs will be met. "I'd love to do this another time. How about next Tuesday or Wednesday?"[41]

When there isn't a reasonable alternative proposal that works for both parties, leave out the fourth step. Bourne offers this example:

"I hear that you need help with moving" (acknowledgment). "I'd like to help out but I promised my boyfriend we would go away this weekend (explanation), so I'm not going to be around" (saying no).. "I hope you can find someone else."[42]

Saying no means setting limits.

There are times, however, when you must say no to a person you don't want to be friends with, don't like, or who seems "unsafe." In such cases, simply say "No" or "No thank you" in a polite and firm manner. If the other person persists, say no again without apologizing.

COMMUNICATION

Exercise

In pairs, work through the situations below, using Edmund Bourne's four-step model (acknowledge, explain, say no, and suggest alternatives), record your ideas, and share them with other pairs in the class.

1. Someone in your class asks for your notes because they were absent.

2. A member of your class asks to join your study group, but you have already had a negative experience with this person during group work.

3. A friend is in a different section of the same course as you, but you have the class earlier in the day. The friend asks you to meet after you take the test and share the questions with him.

4. An acquaintance from class overhears you making plans to meet later in the cafeteria for coffee and asks to join you. This person often wants to dominate the conversation.

7.1
Interpersonal Communication and Relationships

What are the characteristics and benefits of effective interpersonal communication?

- Good personal relationships positively affect your psychological and physical health, your happiness, your social and moral development, and your ability to cope with stress.
- William Schutz's fundamental interpersonal relationship orientation (FIRO) theory identifies three interpersonal needs: inclusion, control, and affection.

7.2
Developing Interpersonal Relationships

How do you form positive and lasting relationships with others?

- Impression management strategies that help you shape your image in positive ways include ingratiation, self-promotion, exemplification, supplication, and intimidation.
- Effective communicators know how to initiate, maintain, and end conversations as well as how to listen with interest and empathy.

7.3
Strengthening Personal Relationships

How does interpersonal communication affect your relationships with friends and colleagues?

- Strong friendships increase life satisfaction and help increase your life expectancy.

- There are 10 common stages in most romantic relationships, divided into five coming-together steps and five coming-apart steps.

7.4
Sharing Yourself with Others

How does self-disclosure and sensitivity to feedback affect your interpersonal relationships?

- Self-disclosure is the process of sharing personal information, opinions, and emotions.
- The Johari Window model displays the extent to which you are willing to self-disclose and are receptive to feedback from others.
- Social penetration theory describes the process of relationship bonding in which individuals move from superficial communication to deeper, more intimate communication.

7.5
Expressing Yourself Appropriately

How should you express your personal thoughts and feelings to others?

- Effective self-disclosure requires the ability to focus on the present, be descriptive and understanding, respect and adapt to others, reciprocate self-disclosure, and move disclosure to deeper levels as appropriate.

- Effective feedback requires giving and asking for information about behaviour, actions, perceptions and feelings, that you and others can change.
- Gibb's defensive-supportive communication behaviours are evaluation-description, control-problem orientation, strategy-spontaneity, neutrality-empathy, superiority-equality, and certainty-provisionalism.

7.6
Developing Assertiveness

How can you assert yourself and also respect the rights and needs of others?

- Assertive communicators promote their own needs and rights while respecting the needs and rights of others.
- Passivity is characterized by giving in to others at the expense of your own needs; aggression involves putting your own needs first, often at the expense of someone else's needs; passive aggression may appear to accommodate others, but it is a subtle form of aggressive behaviour.
- DESC scripting is a four-step process (describe, express, specify, and consequences) for becoming more assertive.

Igor Mojzes/Fotolia

7.1 What are the characteristics and benefits of effective interpersonal communication?

1 According to Schutz's FIRO theory, a(n) _____ is a submissive person who wants and needs control, but is reluctant to pursue it.
   a. autocrat
   b. abdicrat
   c. democrat
   d. undersocial type
   e. underpersonal type

7.2 How do you form positive and lasting relationships with others?

2 What impression management strategy is Collette using if, in a conversation with a colleague, she says, "Let's work on your part of this report together so you can get home at a decent hour."
   a. ingratiation
   b. self-promotion
   c. exemplification
   d. supplication
   e. intimidation

7.3 How does interpersonal communication affect your relationships with friends and romantic partners?

3 Close friends learn that it's okay to share personal thoughts, secrets, hopes, and fears, but whether we do so depends on our ability _____.
   a. to disclose personal information in a way that maintains the relationship
   b. to recognize that most of these disclosures centre on mundane, everyday issues
   c. to respect that some topics are taboo, such as negative life events and serious relationship issues
   d. a, b, and c are correct.
   e. a and b are correct.

7.4 How do self-disclosure and sensitivity to feedback affect your personal relationships?

4 In the Johari Window model, the more receptive and adaptive you are to feedback from others, the larger your _____ window pane is.
   a. open
   b. hidden
   c. blind
   d. unknown
   e. private

5 Social penetration theory explains that relationships are closest when communication is _____.
   a. friendly, frequent, and fair
   b. deep, broad, and frequent
   c. open, hidden, and unknown
   d. private, patient, and powerful
   e. personal, social, and public

6 In terms of Gibb's categories of behaviour for creating a positive communication climate, how would you classify the following statement? "Let's find a way for both of us to go where we want on our vacation."
   a. description
   b. strategy
   c. problem orientation
   d. empathy
   e. neutrality

7.5 How should you express your personal thoughts and feelings to others?

7 All of the following are effective ways to give and respond to feedback except _____.
   a. focusing on behaviour, not on the person
   b. making your statements specific, not general or abstract
   c. using "you" rather than "I" statements
   d. focusing on what was said and done, not on why it was said and done
   e. focusing on current rather than past behaviour

8 All of the following behaviours are characteristics of effective self-disclosure except _____.
   a. focusing on the person's past behaviour
   b. disclosing your feelings as well as facts

   c. adapting to the person and context
   d. describing rather than judging
   e. engaging in reciprocal self-disclosure

7.6 How can you assert yourself and also respect the rights and needs of others?

9 Which of the following behaviours characterizes passive-aggressive behaviour?
   a. You advance your own needs and rights while also respecting the needs and rights of others.
   b. You give in to others at the expense of your own needs in order to avoid conflict and disagreement.
   c. You put your personal needs first often at the expense of someone else.
   d. You appear to go along with others but sabotage their plans behind their backs.
   e. all of the above

10 The letters in DESC scripting are an acronym for
   a. Describe, Express, Specify, and Consequences.
   b. Decide, Empathize, Self-Disclose, and Conflict.
   c. Dialectic, Expression, Separation, and Change.
   d. Decider, Extrovert, Sensor, and Controller.
   e. Decide, Explain, Sympathize, and Communicate.

Answers found on page 330.

Key Terms

Abdicrat	**relationship**	**Personal**
Affection need	**orientation (FIRO)**	**relationship**
Aggression	**theory**	**Professional**
Assertiveness	**Impression management**	**relationship**
Autocrat	**Inclusion need**	**Relationship**
Closed-ended question	**Ingratiation**	**Self-disclosure**
Control need	**Interpersonal**	**Self-promotion**
Conversation	**communication**	**Social penetration**
Defensive behaviours	**Intimacy**	**theory**
Democrat	**Intimidation**	**Supplication**
DESC script	**Johari Window**	**Supportive behaviours**
Exemplification	**Open-ended question**	**Turn-requesting cue**
Fundamental	**Passive-aggressive**	**Turn-yielding cue**
interpersonal	**Passivity**	

Exploring **Emotional Intelligence**

During the 2010 Winter Olympics, Canadian figure skater Joannie Rochette faced a very emotional and stressful time. Her mother passed away from a heart attack just a few days before Joannie was scheduled to compete in the Women's Figure Skating event.

Joannie was faced with an emotional roller-coaster as she tried to understand her own emotions, helped her father and other family members, and considered her responsibility to the Canadian Olympic team. Joannie decided to go ahead and compete, partly to demonstrate respect for her mother and partly to honour her mother's wish that she compete. Joannie won a Bronze medal for Canada with an amazing, emotional performance.

We are often faced with circumstances and decisions that require not only our ability to think critically, but also our ability to recognize, understand, interpret, and incorporate our emotional responses to the circumstances effectively. In this chapter, we will define and explore emotions, and examine emotional intelligence and the importance of appropriately managing and regulating emotions when communicating with others.

Nuccio DiNuzzo/Chicago Tribune/MCT/Getty Images

THINK About…

and ASK YOURSELF…

Emotions: Types and Functions
What are emotions and how are they categorized?

Emotions play a major role in all relationships. An **emotion** is the physical feeling you have when reacting to a situation. Emotions are fundamental to effective and ethical communication. They also play a significant role in how you develop, maintain, and strengthen interpersonal relationships.

The Basic Emotions

Everyone experiences basic, primary emotions, although researchers disagree on the number of such emotions. Robert Plutchik's **psychoevolutionary emotion theory** illuminates the development and meaning of emotions.[1] According to this theory; each basic emotion has a range of feelings (from mild to intense). Plutchik further explains that some emotions blend two or more emotions. As the infographic on the right shows, love is a combination of joy and trust. Despair is a combination of fear and sadness. Emotions that occur at a primary level, such as anger in response to being hit, can be described as instinctive. These responses are **primary emotions**. Primary emotions include feeling happy, sad, angry and afraid.

Secondary emotions are developed through socialization and cultural education. For example, feeling guilty for sharing gossip is learned from our parents and communities. This is partially why we don't all feel guilty about the same situations or experiences. This learned response to our emotions creates opportunities for misunderstanding to occur. Perception, based on our experiences, values, and beliefs, as discussed in Chapter 3, shapes the emotional responses that are expected. If your family views displaying anger as a negative behaviour, then you may feel guilty for feeling angry. If you have been raised in a society that values acknowledging success, then you may feel pride and outwardly celebrate your success. Secondary emotions are more involved and require you to take into consideration the

> Emotional responses are a complex process.

primary emotion (happiness, sadness, anger, fear) and then consider how to interpret the emotion. One of the methods we use is to think about prior experiences and how we have responded

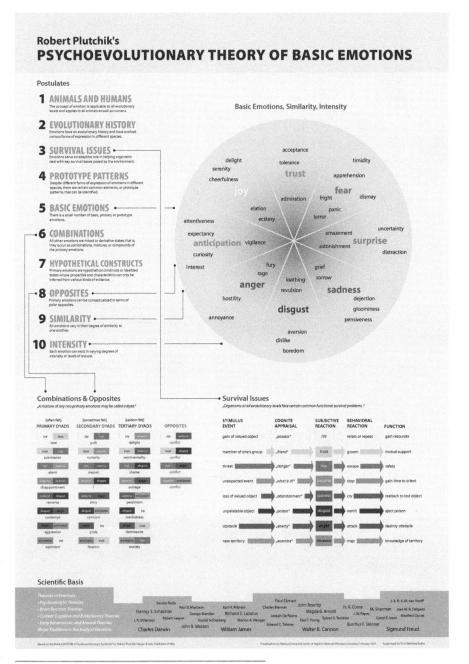

Robert Plutchik's Psychoevolutionary Emotion Theory[2]

Naomi Hasegawa/Fotolia

Minerva Studio/Fotolia

Jürgen Fälchle/Fotolia

JackF/Fotolia

in the past. For example, as a child you may have resorted to pushing or yelling when you were angry. The response you received from others (family, peers, community) provided feedback to you. As an adult, self-regulation and experience, combined with cultural expectations, have taught you that it is better to control aggression and anger and that you may express them as disappointment instead.

Emotional responses are a complex process that author Sally Planalp breaks down into four sections.[3] These include the **physiological response**, **nonverbal reactions**, **cognitive interpretations**, and **verbal expression** that occur in each situation that provokes an emotional response (see figure to the left). Combining emotions changes the way each emotion is experienced. In every situation there is the potential for our emotions to be manifested in a variety of ways, and as we become more aware of our own personal reactions to the stimuli that provoke an emotional response, we become better able to manage our emotions during interpersonal communication.

The Complexity of Emotional Responses[4]

Physiological Response	Heart rate, adrenalin, dilation of pupils, upset stomach, muscle tensing
Nonverbal Reactions	Blushing, sweating, facial expression, posture, vocal tone
Cognitive Interpretations	Shyness, awkwardness, happiness, sadness, awareness, recognition, impulse control
Verbal Expression	Anger, tone of voice, emotional intelligence, social competence

COMMUNICATION

Exercise

In pairs, brainstorm the physiological response, nonverbal reaction, cognitive interpretation, and verbal expression you would expect to take place when a close friend lies to you.

What other scenarios can you create to illustrate the complexities of emotions?

Important Functions of Emotions

Emotions serve a number of functions in our everyday lives. In fact, appropriate emotional response can be one sign a physician looks for when diagnosing illnesses such as stress, depression, and mental illness.[5] Authors Moshe Zeidner, Gerald Matthews, and Richard D. Roberts (2009) describe six functions of our emotions:[6]

- Signalling meaning of events to self and to others ⟶ Is this event important to you or others?

- A tool to enlist emotional support ⟶ Would you help someone who is fearful or upset?

- Regulating behaviour ⟶ Can you change or modify emotional responses to engage in interpersonal communication effectively?

- Maintaining social control and hierarchy ⟶ Are you a calm, patient leader who maintains status quo when faced with challenges?

- Organizing activity ⟶ When feeling or observing a particular emotion, do you quickly organize your response based on prior knowledge, memory, or cultural expectations?

- Influencing cognitive processing ⟶ Do feelings of excitement, passion, or anger inspire you to be creative or to change your behaviour?

8.2
Shaping Your Emotional Responses
How do our cultures and roles influence our emotional communication?

The Function of Emotions

Happiness, sadness, anger, and fear are the primary emotions we all experience. So why, then, do we not all experience and express them in the same way? In previous chapters, we have explored **values**, **beliefs**, **perceptions**, and **cultural diversity** as they relate to **interpersonal communication**. Their importance is again evident when exploring the impact of emotions within all aspects of our communication with each other.

The Potential Impact of Culture on Emotional Expression

Generally speaking, **high-context cultures** and **low-context cultures**, as discussed in Chapter 3, display differing characteristics. It is not surprising, then, that cultural conventions in Japanese, Native Canadian, Chinese, and South Korean communities dictate that members of these communities are more reserved in their display of emotions, whereas, per their cultural conventions, Canadians, Germans, and Americans more readily show their reactions and feelings to situations and people. Social scientist Steven Gordon (1981) included emotion culture in his definition of emotions.[7] This is important because it suggests that while some emotions seem to be hardwired responses for survival, some are learned and influenced by the environment, including culture.

COMMUNICATION IN *ACTION*

Recognize Emotional Cues

Communication is part of every interpersonal interaction and using dimensions of emotional intelligence can create an environment that is productive, collaborative, and inclusive. Emotionally intelligent communicators are able to use their skills of perception to observe and notice the "emotional cues" of others. They can then use these insights to match their communication style, the content of their message, and their nonverbal communication skills to communicate in a meaningful way with others.

Do you possess the following emotionally intelligent communication skills? If not, what can you do to develop them?

- An ability to work toward shared understanding
- Willingness to participate in conversational give and take

- An ability to have honest and open conversations with others
- An ability to compromise with others
- Awareness of barriers to communication
- An ability to clearly identify and label emotional reactions and responses
- Awareness of nonverbal communication behaviour
- Awareness of cultural perceptions

FACTS **THINK ABOUT THEORY**
TEST IDEA
EXPERIMENT
METHOD
KNOWLEDGE

Cultural Theory and Emotions

In their essay "Cultural Theory and Emotions," Kaplan, Stets, Turner, and Peterson examine theories of emotion as they strive to explain the intertwined relationship between our cultures and our emotions, and the reasons for differences and similarities in how we internalize and express them. The authors note that "Culture plays a role in defining our emotions, connecting emotions and our sense of self, dictating our interactional scripts, determining our emotional reactions to our relationship, [and] using emotion management techniques . . ."[8]

The chart below offers some insight into the importance of culture as an influence on emotions.

Stimulus or Situation That Affects Expression of Emotions	Cultural Influence on Expression of Emotions	Reasons for Expression of Emotions
Immersion in a specific culture	Stronger beliefs and customs aligned with culture	Familiarity with cultural norms and rewards for conformity may encourage expression.
Intensity of emotions	Expectations of culture	Strong emotions may be more challenging to control, but culture may dictate behaviour.
Types of emotions	Primary emotion Secondary emotion	Anger is a more physical response. Pride and shame are more culturally constructed and learned responses, based on cultural norms and values.
Social situations	Presence of physical or mental reminders of culture	Other members of the same culture, at the same event can remind us of expectations. May include food, language, and symbols.

8.3

Emotional Intelligence

How does our emotional intelligence affect our effectiveness in interpersonal communication?

Emotional Intelligence

Science writer Daniel Goleman defines **emotional intelligence** as "the capacity for recognizing our own feelings and those of others, for motivating ourselves, and for managing emotions well in ourselves and in our relationships."[9] His influential book *Emotional Intelligence: Why It Can Matter More Than IQ* credits two psychologists, Peter Salovey and John Mayer, who coined the term emotional intelligence in 1990.[10] You can examine emotional intelligence as a set of interpersonal communication competencies summarized and described in Figure 8.1 on the next page.

Communication Strategies	As an Emotionally Intelligent Communicator, You . . .
Intrapersonal Communication Strategies	
Develop Self-Awareness	Monitor and identify your feelings in order to guide your decision making. Example: Noticing whether you have raised your voice because you are angry or surprised.
Manage Your Emotions	Restrain or release your emotions when the situation is appropriate. Practice relaxation to recover from emotional distress. Example: Deciding whether expressing strong emotions will facilitate or interfere with your goals.
Motivate Yourself	Persevere in the face of disappointments and setbacks. Seek the support of friends, colleagues, and family members to stay motivated, improve your mood, and bolster your confidence. Example: Seeking help from a trusted mentor.
Interpersonal Communication Strategies	
Listen to Others	Engage effective listening skills to ensure you understand what another person means. Use effective, empathic listening. Example: Paraphrasing what you hear to make sure you understand someone before responding emotionally.
Develop Interpersonal Skills	Use self-disclosure, assertiveness, and appropriate verbal and nonverbal communication. Try to resolve conflicts. Example: Deciding whether and how to share your emotions with a close friend.
Help Others Help Themselves	Help others become more aware of their emotions. Help them speak and listen more effectively. Example: Providing emotional support to a distressed friend.

Figure 8.1 Emotionally Intelligent Communication

EMOTION

Emotions are coordinated responses to changes in the environment that involve:

- invoking specific subjective experiences
- activating relevant cognitions, especially related to taking action in relation to the self and environment
- coordinating bodily states so as to prepare for certain reactions (e.g., fight or flight)
- appraising the ongoing situation for changes

EMOTIONAL INTELLIGENCE

Emotional intelligence is an ability to understand and to problem-solve that involves:

- managing emotional responses
- understanding emotions and emotional meanings
- appraising emotions from situations
- using emotion for reasoning
- identifying emotions in faces, voices, postures, and other content

INTELLIGENCE

Intelligences are abilities to understand and problem-solve about information that involve:

- reasoning about abstract relationships (fluid intelligence)
- storing material in an organized fashion in memory (crystallized intelligence)
- learning targeted material
- inputting material through sensory and perceptual channels
- processing information quickly

The Scope of Emotional Intelligence[11]

Self-Awareness	Recognize emotions and their impact
Self-Regulation	Emotional and impulse control Adaptability
Motivation	Drive to achieve Optimism Willingness to accept group goals
Social Empathy	Understanding others' views and perspectives Diversity awareness
Social Skills	Listening Conflict resolution Advocacy Team/group cooperation Leadership

Dimensions of Emotional Intelligence

What happens when people cannot make emotions work for them? Neurologist Antonio Damasio, who studies patients with damage to the emotional centre of their brains, reports that these patients may make terrible decisions even though their IQ scores stay the same. So even though they test as "smart," they "make disastrous choices in business and their personal lives, and can even obsess endlessly over a decision as simple as when to make an appointment." Their decision-making skills are poor because they have lost access to their emotions.[12] Damasio's claims make sense when you consider whether you could answer any of the following questions without taking emotions into account: Whom should I marry? What career should I pursue? Should I buy this house? What should I say to a bereaved relative?

> **" ... feelings are indispensable for rational decision making. "**[13]
> —Antonio Damasio, Neurologist

COMMUNICATION

Exercise

Watch this short video about emotional intelligence testing.

www.emotionwisegroup.org/emotion-test/quick-test

Daniel Goleman created a matrix that examines five dimensions of emotional intelligence: self-awareness, self-regulation, motivation, social empathy, and social skills.[14] Each dimension is then divided into specific competencies to help individuals understand and develop stronger emotional intelligence.

Self-awareness is more than just acknowledging that you feel happy or jealous, for example. It also involves understanding how your emotional state affects others in your communication with them. **Self-regulation** is the second dimension, and in order to become emotionally intelligent you learn to control what you do when you feel emotions such as anger, sadness, or fear. This is a skill that takes considerable practice for children as they learn to use their verbal skills to express frustration rather than biting one of their playmates.[15]

Emotionally intelligent people have **motivation** to become self-aware and to self-regulate their emotional responses in order to become active, willing participants in relationships with others including family, friends, and social groups. When an individual is able to view situations through another's perspective and understand how the situation would make the other person feel, he or she has achieved **social empathy.** This is a skill that many people experiencing autism spectrum disorder have difficulty achieving. The fifth and final dimension of Goleman's matrix is the area of **social skills.** This dimension combines the earlier four dimensions to enable an individual to be self aware, to self-regulate, to be motivated in interpersonal interactions, and to display social empathy in order to fully participate in teams and groups. Individuals with strong social skills are able to bring an emotional awareness to their problem-solving strategies. They can listen empathetically and lead a team with clear understanding of the perspectives of its members.

Emotional and Social Competence

How do emotions affect work and school success?

Emotional Intelligence in the Workplace

In October 2012, Canadian market research company Ipsos Reid published survey results for Great-West Life Centre for Mental Health in the Workplace. The results noted that 9 of 10 Canadian managers recognize the importance of emotional intelligence in the workplace.[16] "Emotional intelligence in the workplace encompasses skill areas such as the ability to deal with other people's negative emotions and reactions, to understand and manage our personal reactions, and to communicate effectively, including resolving conflict," notes Mike Schwartz, senior vice-president of group benefits for Great-West Life and executive director of the centre.[17]

The work environment creates a dynamic situation where there is a reciprocal relationship between emotions experienced and the work itself. In *What We Know About Emotional Intelligence*, authors Zeidner, Matthews, and Roberts look at emotions as either positive or negative within the contexts of task-related work and social-related work. Their findings show that emotional responses greatly affect our ability to view work and work situations as either positive or negative as noted in the chart below.[18]

The level of emotional intelligence an individual has, as represented by Goleman's five dimensions, may be one important factor contributing to his or her overall job satisfaction. Understanding, recognizing, and adapting your emotional responses in a work environment will help your achieve your career goals.

Management training and development specialist company MTD Training published *Emotional Intelligence Training* in 2010. The authors clearly recognized that company managers would greatly benefit from understanding and implementing strategies to develop emotional intelligence in the workforce.[19] Consider the kind of environment that could be possible if emotional intelligence was emphasized to the same degree as cognitive intelligence. Listed below are some of the workplace benefits associated with emotionally intelligent employees. Can you see how these qualities are valued by you and others in your academic classes?

- Everyone's ideas are respected.
- Teams work to their fullest potential.
- Gossip and other negative behaviour stops.
- Everyone celebrates and encourages others' success.
- Stumbling blocks can be overcome.
- Decisions are based on what is best for all involved.
- Integrity is valued.
- Work relationships are rewarding.
- Your personal potential is continually developed.[20]

As shown in this infographic, Canadian managers value emotional intelligence.

Focus	Positive	Negative
TASK-RELATED	Enjoyment Hope Relief Pride Gratitude	Anger Sadness Shame or guilt Boredom Jealousy
SOCIAL-RELATED	Empathy Admiration Sympathy	Contempt Social anxiety Embarrassment

STOP&THINK

How Can You Become an Emotionally Intelligent Leader?

Leadership relies heavily on the leader's ability to influence, guide, and mentor members of the team. Emotionally intelligent leaders capitalize on their abilities to work well with other team members. They are open to the suggestions of others and actively seek input from all members. Leaders who are self-aware and able to regulate their own emotional responses are also able to share recognition with all involved without feelings of anger or frustration. These abilities are critical to leaders as they help move the team or group toward successfully achieving a workplace or academic goal. You can become an emotionally intelligent leaders by doing the following:

- Actively take on leadership roles and use your communication strengths.
- Always lead by example, demonstrating self-regulation of your emotional responses.
- Encourage enthusiastic participation.
- Motivate others by recognizing the goals of the team and optimistically expecting success.
- Guide others with awareness of their strengths and the ways in which they can actively contribute to the process or task.
- Insist on appropriate behaviour from all members of the team. Use your skills to actively listen to others, think critically, and solve problems.

COMMUNICATION

Exercise

How would task-related and social-related emotional responses apply to your life as a post-secondary student? In your future career? Are you creating opportunities to build your emotional intelligence? Which of Goleman's five dimensions do you continue to develop as an emotionally intelligent adult?

8.5

Supportive Interpersonal Communication

How can you effectively manage your emotions and provide emotional support to others?

Constructing Emotionally Supportive Messages

Emotionally supportive communication strategies can help you comfort and support others. These strategies include being clear about your intentions, protecting the other person's self-esteem, and centring your messages on the other person.

Communicate Your Intentions Clearly When someone is in great distress, you may think this person knows you want to be helpful and supportive. You may assume that just "being there" tells the other person that you care. In some cases, your assumptions are correct. In other

The Ethics of Caring

The National Communication Association Credo for Ethical Communication includes a principle that speaks directly to interpersonal relationships: "We promote communication climates of caring and mutual understanding that respect the unique needs and characteristics of individual communicators."[22] The ethical value of care focuses on the responsibilities we have for others in our interpersonal relationships.[23]

Philosopher and educator Nel Noddings believes we make moral choices based on an ethic of caring. For example, a mother picks up a crying baby, not because of a sense of duty or because she is worried about what others will say if she doesn't but because she cares about the baby. Relationship theorists emphasize that this is not a gender-based ethic. Rather, it is based on a way of thinking that honours two fundamental characteristics of ethical behaviour: avoiding harm and providing mutual aid.[24]

oksun70/Fotolia

In what way does this scene depict an ethic of caring, and how does such behaviour promote effective communication?

situations, a person in distress needs to know that you *want* to help or provide assistance.

You can enhance the clarity of your supportive messages by stating them directly ("I want to help you") and by making it clear you care ("I'm here for you"). You can also intensify the perceived sincerity of your response by emphasizing your desire to help ("I really want to help however I can"), by reminding the person of the personal history you share ("You know we've always been there for each other"), and by indicating what you feel ("Helping you is important to me; I'd feel terrible if I weren't here to help").[25]

The Importance of Empathy

In order to be fully empathetic, it is necessary to have experienced life. The more experience we have with living in a variety of day-to-day situations, the more likely we will be able to practise emotional intelligence when we are confronted with a friend, co-worker, or classmate who is experiencing a difficult time in his or her life.[26] When you are able to listen, acknowledge, and remain aware of the other person's feelings, then you will be more emotionally intelligent.

Protect the Other Person's Self-Esteem Make sure that your offer of help does not imply that the other person is incapable of solving the problem or dealing with the situation. Otherwise, you may damage someone's self-esteem. Even with the best of intentions, expressions of sympathy ("Oh, you poor thing . . .") can convey judgments about the person's lack of competence and lack of independence. Try to encourage and praise the other person.[27]

Offer Person–Centred Messages Messages that reflect "the degree to which a helper validates [a] distressed person's feelings and encourages him or her to talk about the upsetting event" are **person-centred messages**.[28] Rather than focusing on helping someone feel better, your goal is helping the person develop a deeper understanding of the problem so that they may take on the task of solving or coping with it. You can help someone in distress understand the problem by encouraging her or him to tell an extended, personal story about the problem or upsetting event. People in need of emotional support may want nothing more than to share the details with a trusted friend.

While these communication strategies express your willingness to help, your supportive feelings, and your personal commitment, take care to

Comforting Message STRATEGIES

- Communicate Your Intentions Clearly
  "I'm here to help because I care."
- Protect the Other Person's Self-Esteem
  "I can see you're trying very hard to deal with this problem."
- Offer Person-Centred Messages
  "Tell me all about what happened and how you're feeling."

Bryan Creely/Fotolia

avoid counterproductive strategies. For example, do not focus on or share *your* emotional experiences, as in "I know exactly how you feel. Last year, I went through a similar kind of problem. It all started when . . ." Not only does this stop the other person from sharing, but it also shifts the focus to yourself. You should also avoid messages that criticize or negatively evaluate another person because these can hurt more than help. Do not tell others that their feelings are wrong, inappropriate, immature, or embarrassing.

Encourage Coping Through Storytelling

Making Sense Through Stories Think back to your childhood and chances are you remember stories—perhaps stories read to you, or perhaps the simple telling of stories by your family members, often recalling details of events. **Storytelling** provides a framework to make sense of events, problems, worries, and all sorts of the daily interactions in our lives.[29] Understanding the importance of making sense of what is happening or has happened is another important ability of emotionally intelligent people.

Catharsis Through Storytelling Describing the events or situations that are affecting us can provide an outlet for strong feelings and emotions.[30] This release of emotional strain can be described as **cathartic**, and can help to make sense of a situation.

Strategies to Engage Someone in Telling Their Story

- Ask for your friend's version of the situation. ("What happened here?")
- Create a supportive environment and provide enough time for the person to talk. ("Take your time. I want to hear the whole story.")
- Ask about the person's feelings, not just the events. ("How did you feel when that happened?" "What was your reaction when she said that?")
- Legitimize the expression of feelings. ("I certainly understand why you'd feel that way.")
- Indicate that you connect with what the other person is saying. ("If that happened to me, I'd be furious too.") [31]

COMMUNICATION&CULTURE

STORYTELLING

Our earliest stories told to us by our parents, and perhaps our grandparents, were meant to help us make sense of or understand our lives within the context of our culture. Our personal history cannot be shared without considering our culture, values, ethnicity, traditions, and beliefs. These are all influenced by our emotional responses to new situations and the events that take place in our lives. Some of these milestones are common to all cultures, while some are specific to geography, language, and traditional practices. In every culture, babies are born and relatives and friends become ill or die. We all become frustrated, angry, happy, and sad, so it makes sense that every culture has stories and uses storytelling to explain events and provide guidance for managing our emotions.

Stories for preschool children include *Momma Do You Love Me?*, *The Name Jar*, *Everywhere Babies*, *Mama's Saris*, and *Somewhere in the World Right Now.*

What stories were told to you when you were young to help you make sense of your world?

How Emotionally Intelligent Are You?

Daniel Goleman proposes five basic emotional competencies that are expressed in the five headings below.[32] Use this rating scale listed to assess your level of competence for each question:

5 = Always   4 = Usually   3 = Sometimes   2 = Rarely   1 = Never

Know Thy Self

_____ 1. Can you accurately identify the emotions you experience and why you experience them?

_____ 2. Do you have a strong self-concept?

_____ 3. Are you aware of your strengths and limitations?

Control Your Emotions and Impulses

_____ 4. Can you keep disruptive emotions under control?

_____ 5. Do you take responsibility for your emotions and resulting actions?

_____ 6. Are you open-minded and flexible in handling difficult situations?

Persevere

_____ 7. Do you strive to improve or meet high standards of excellence?

_____ 8. Do you persist in the face of obstacles and setbacks?

_____ 9. Can you postpone gratification and regulate your moods?

Empathize

_____10. Do you accurately interpret others' feelings and needs?

_____11. Do you provide appropriate emotional support to others?

_____12. Do you paraphrase appropriately?

Interact Effectively

_____13. Do you listen appropriately and effectively?

_____14. Do you make a positive social impression?

_____15. Do you work effectively with others to achieve shared goals?

Scoring: Add up your ratings. The higher your score, the more emotionally intelligent you are. Keep in mind that your ratings are only your *perceptions* of your feelings and behaviours. For example, despite what you think, you may not interpret others' feelings and needs accurately or persist in the face of obstacles. On the other hand, you may not recognize that you provide appropriate emotional support to others, even though your friends often turn to you when they need someone to listen empathetically.

When you are aware of your level of emotional intelligence in each dimension, you then have the opportunity to assess your skills; develop a strategy to enhance areas noted as *sometimes, rarely* or *never* and to continue to practise those elements you indicated were your *usual* or *always* responses.

8.1

Emotions: Types and Functions

What are emotions and how are they categorized?

- Emotions are fundamental to effective and ethical communication.
- Robert Plutchik's psychoevolutionary emotion theory describes the development and meaning of emotions.
- Primary emotions include happiness, sadness, anger, and fear.
- Secondary, or learned, emotions are often shaped by culture, values, and beliefs.

8.2

Shaping Your Emotional Responses

How do our cultures and roles influence our emotional communication?

- Some cultural communities tend to be more reserved in their display of emotions, while other cultures more readily show their reactions and feelings to situations and people.
- Culture influences the intensity of emotion, the display of secondary emotions, and the social contexts of emotional expression.

8.3

Emotional Intelligence

How does our emotional intelligence affect our effectiveness in interpersonal communication?

- Emotional intelligence is the capacity for recognizing your own feelings and those of others, for motivating yourself, and for effectively managing your emotions in relationships.
- There are 5 dimensions of Emotional Intelligence: self awareness, self-regulation, motivation, social empathy, and social skills.

8.4

Emotional and Social Competence

How do emotions impact work and school success?

- Emotional responses greatly affect our ability to view work and work situations as either positive or negative.
- The level of emotional intelligence a person has may be one important factor contributing to overall job satisfaction.

8.5

Supportive Interpersonal Communication

How can you effectively manage your emotions and provide emotional support to others?

- When comforting another person, you should make your intentions clear, protect the other person's self-esteem, and centre your message on the other person, not on yourself.
- Encouraging another person to tell his or her story will provide an opportunity for the person to share, and give you an opportunity to listen empathetically.

Bryan Creely/Fotolia

TEST YOUR KNOWLEDGE

8.1 What are emotions and how are they categorized?

1 In Plutchik's psychoevolutionary emotion theory, which two basic emotions combine to create the emotion of love?

a. submission and surprise

b. anticipation and awe

c. acceptance and joy

d. optimism and pessimism

e. acceptance and tolerance

2 The physiological manifestations of our emotions include all but

a. changes in heart rate.

b. upset stomach.

c. dilation of pupils.

d. vocal tone.

e. muscle tensing.

8.2 How do our cultures, and roles influence our emotional communication?

3 Sally Planalp argues that

a. when emotions combined, this creates a change in how each emotion is experienced.

b. when emotions are combined, they remain the same.

c. when emotions are combined, there is little change in how they are expressed.

d. it is important to manage our emotions.

4 In *Cultural Theory and Emotions*, Kaplan, Stets, Turner, and Peterson state that

a. emotions are intertwined relationships between cultures.

b. emotions are the reasons that we see differences and similarities in our cultures

c. relationships do not affect our cultural expression of emotions

d. a, and b are correct.

8.3 How does our emotional intelligence affect our effectiveness in interpersonal communication?

5 Self-regulation is

a. the second dimension in Goleman's theory and is a skill that takes practice to control strong emotions like anger.

b. a theory that involves demonstrating empathy toward others.

c. the third dimension in Goleman's theory and not necessary for emotional intelligence

6 Social skills are the fifth dimension in Goleman's theory of emotional intelligence. It combines the earlier four dimensions which are

a. to be able to be self-aware

b. to self-regulate

c. to be motivated in interpersonal interactions

d. to display social empathy in order to fully participate in teams and groups

e. intelligence determined by IQ

8.4 How do emotions affect work and school success?

7 According to Mike Schwartz, social skills in the workplace

a. are necessary for strong work teams and groups.

b. assist employees with managing negative reactions to job situations.

c. are important to effective solving problems.

d. are not important interpersonal communication skills.

e. a, b and c are correct.

8 Job-related tasks could provoke a wide variety of emotional responses. These might include

a. primary emotional responses.

b. secondary emotional responses.

c. Both a and b are correct.

d. Neither of these types of emotion would be expressed in a work environment.

9 Which of the following statements communicates your desire to help and support a person dealing with emotional distress?

 a. I'm here for you.

 b. I really want to help however I can.

 c. You know we've always been there for each other.

 d. I'd feel terrible if I weren't here to help.

 e. all of the above

10 An effective strategy to use when supporting a friend in a crisis is

 a. giving them advice.

 b. analyzing their emotions.

 c. using storytelling.

 d. solving their problems for them.

Answers found on page 330.

Key Terms

Beliefs	Motivation	Self-awareness
Cathartic	Nonverbal reaction	Self-regulation
Cognitive interpretation	Perceptions	Social empathy
Cultural diversity	Person-centred messages	Social skills
Emotion	Physiological response	Storytelling
Emotional intelligence	Primary emotion	Values
High-context culture	Psychoevolutionary Emotion theory	Verbal expression
Interpersonal communication	Secondary emotions	
Low-context culture		

PROFESSIONAL
RELATIONSHIPS

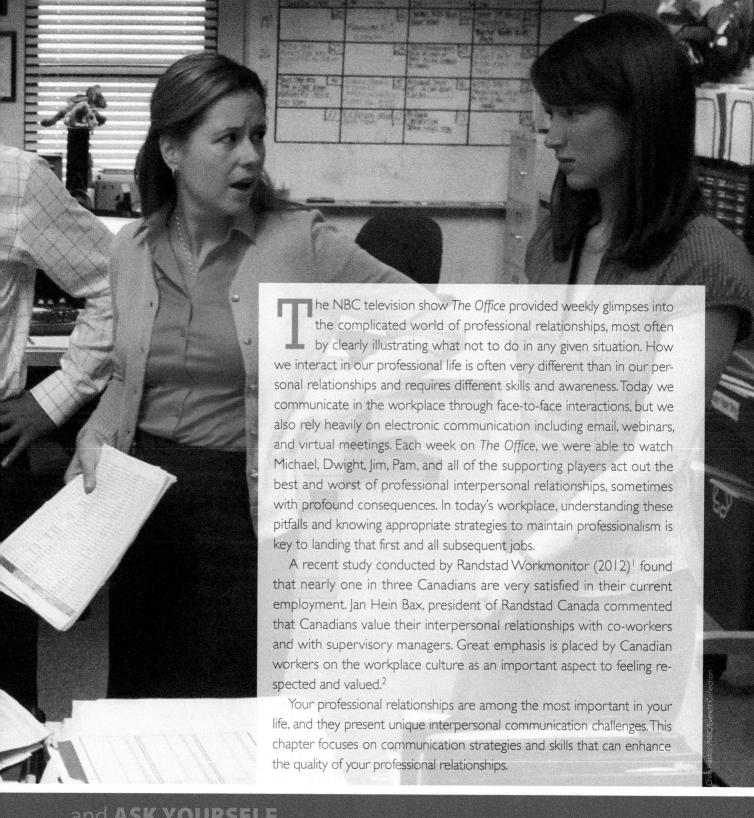

The NBC television show *The Office* provided weekly glimpses into the complicated world of professional relationships, most often by clearly illustrating what not to do in any given situation. How we interact in our professional life is often very different than in our personal relationships and requires different skills and awareness. Today we communicate in the workplace through face-to-face interactions, but we also rely heavily on electronic communication including email, webinars, and virtual meetings. Each week on *The Office*, we were able to watch Michael, Dwight, Jim, Pam, and all of the supporting players act out the best and worst of professional interpersonal relationships, sometimes with profound consequences. In today's workplace, understanding these pitfalls and knowing appropriate strategies to maintain professionalism is key to landing that first and all subsequent jobs.

A recent study conducted by Randstad Workmonitor (2012)[1] found that nearly one in three Canadians are very satisfied in their current employment. Jan Hein Bax, president of Randstad Canada commented that Canadians value their interpersonal relationships with co-workers and with supervisory managers. Great emphasis is placed by Canadian workers on the workplace culture as an important aspect to feeling respected and valued.[2]

Your professional relationships are among the most important in your life, and they present unique interpersonal communication challenges. This chapter focuses on communication strategies and skills that can enhance the quality of your professional relationships.

The Nature of Professional Relationships

How can you improve your professional relationships?

The nature of your professional relationships reflects your work responsibilities, the quality of your relationships with colleagues, and the organizational culture in which you work. You also have professional relationships beyond traditional workplace settings. For example, you may have professional interactions with the members of a labour union, an academic association, a community organization, a volunteer group, or a medical team.

Types of Professional Relationships

The quality and success of your professional relationships depend on how well you communicate with your boss, your co-workers, and your customers or clients. For example, a corporate attorney may communicate differently when interacting with a paralegal or assistant (superior–subordinate relationship), when resolving a dispute with a colleague (co-worker

relationship), or when counselling a client (customer relationship).

Superior–Subordinate Relationships In **superior–subordinate relationships**, the superior (supervisor) has formal authority over the productivity and behaviour of subordinates (workers).[3] Superiors direct activities, authorize projects, interpret policies, and assess subordinates' performance. Subordinates provide information about themselves, about co-workers, and about the progress of their work as well as "what needs to be done and how it can be done" to supervisors.[4]

Poor superior–subordinate relationships negatively affect productivity, job satisfaction, and employee retention. In addition to considering interactions with a supervisor the most stressful part of their jobs, the majority of employees who quit their jobs do so because they are unhappy with their boss.

For supervisors/managers, success largely depends on their ability to establish trust with subordinates, convey

closeness and caring, and give useful feedback about work and progress.[5] Although some superior–subordinate relationships are formal and distant, others flourish in informal, friendly, and nonthreatening interactions without sacrificing respect and productivity.

Co-Worker Relationships Interactions among people who have little

Can you tell who the supervisor is and who the frontline workers are in this photo? What nonverbal cues might help you decide?

auremar/Fotolia

Supervisory Strategies for PROMOTING TRUST AND OPENNESS[6]

- **Behave** in a consistent and predictable manner.
- Be **honest** and keep your promises.
- **Share** control of decision making.
- Clearly **explain** policies, procedures, and decisions.
- Express **concern** for employee well-being.

wavebreakmedia/Shutterstock

Exercise

Professional communication requires you to be able to choose the correct language and tone. Respond to each of these circumstances with (a) friends, (b) family, (c) other professionals.

1. Saying goodbye
2. Asking for help
3. Emailing or texting
4. Showing enthusiasm or excitement

What are the consequences of choosing the incorrect approach to communication as a professional?

Criteria for a SATISFYING Co-Worker Relationship[7]

- **Individual Excellence.** Do both of you perform well in the job?
- **Interdependence.** Do you have complementary skills and need one another to successfully complete the work?
- **Investment.** Do both of you devote time and resources to helping one another succeed?
- **Information.** Do both of you share information openly?
- **Integration.** Do you have compatible values about and styles of work?
- **Integrity.** Do you treat each other with respect?

> Workplace relationships are affected by hierarchy and by the perceptions of those involved.

or no official authority over one another but who must work together to accomplish the goals of an organization are known as **co-worker relationships**.

A co-worker who won't share important information or who has a different work style can derail your performance. A colleague who does a poor job or is uncooperative won't be respected. Satisfying co-worker relationships make the difference between looking forward to and dreading another day at work.

COMMUNICATION IN *ACTION*

Difficult Behaviour at Work

Supervisors and co-workers who are difficult to work with can negatively affect your ability to do your job and to enjoy what you're doing. They engage in counterproductive behaviours, such as chronic lateness, poor performance, derogatory emailing, persistent negativity, resisting needed change, putting down new ideas, complaining constantly, and neglecting commitments, including more serious forms of behaviour, such as harassment, work sabotage, and even physical abuse.[8]

> **Dealing with difficult behaviour at work is, not surprisingly, difficult.**

Failure to remedy such behaviour, however, perpetuates a work environment that takes its toll on everyone. There are many models used for solving problems, and they all will include some basic guidelines that can be adapted for individual situations.

1. Be specific and focus on the exact issue when confronting problems.
2. Remember that an excellent communicator listens more than he or she speaks. This is an opportunity to look at the problem from another perspective.
3. Explain clearly the impact the problem or behaviour is having on team members. Use concrete examples whenever possible.
4. Try to include a "big picture" view in the discussion; helping people to see where changes can lead in the future creates a more inclusive environment.
5. In any situation, talking about it isn't enough; action and accountability must be clearly outlined.

Robert Kneschke/Fotolia

Does *customer relationship* describe the interaction between teachers and students? Or are these relationships more like superior–subordinate or co-worker relationships?

applicants believed that customers should follow company policies if they want help and be told when they are wrong. Approximately 10 percent of would-be employees would not help a customer if it was not part of their jobs and would not volunteer to assist a customer unless the customer asked for help.

Effective employees understand that, in a typical customer relationship, the customer has several basic communication needs.[11]

1. The customer or client needs to feel welcome. Many retail staff members are trained to greet customers the moment they enter a store or business.

2. Customers need enough information to make a decision or solve a problem regarding a service or product. Sales and customer service representatives must be product experts who offer information and ask insightful questions.

3. Customers need to be treated with respect, especially because they have the power to take their business elsewhere and to encourage others to do the same.

Customer Relationships The success of any business or organization depends on effective and ethical communication with customers and clients.[9] **Customer relationships** are interactions between someone communicating on behalf of an organization and an individual who is external to the organization. This category of relationships includes the way colleges treat students, the way medical professionals take care of patients, and the way police officers respond to crime victims.

Unfortunately, some employees lack appropriate training or have inaccurate assumptions about customer service. One study checked thousands of applications for grocery store workers and identified several false assumptions about customer service.[10] Almost half the

> ### The quality of customer relationships affects the financial health of a business and employee job security.

STOP&THINK

Is the Customer Always Right?

Dealing with dissatisfied and angry customers can be difficult and stressful, especially when customers with legitimate complaints behave in inappropriate ways. When a customer is rude or disrespectful, you may become angry. Expressing your anger, however, may only escalate the conflict. The Better Business Bureau points out that even when a customer isn't happy with the solution, an employee who listens and attempts to help will be perceived as cooperative.[12] The following strategies can help calm an unruly customer and promote effective problem solving:[13]

- Don't take a complaint personally.
- Listen attentively and ask questions.
- Try to separate the issues from the emotions. A rude customer may have legitimate complaints and

may only be expressing well-founded frustrations inappropriately.

- Make statements that show you empathize: "I can understand why you're upset."
- Share information or explain the reasons for a decision but do not argue with a customer.
- If the company is at fault, acknowledge it and apologize.
- Ask the customer how she or he would like the problem to be resolved.

> Customers may not always be right, but they should always be treated with courtesy and respect.

FACTS THINK ABOUT THEORY

TEST IDEA PLAN EXPERIMENT METHOD KNOWLEDGE

Organizational Culture Theory

Many workplaces are organized in a structured hierarchy that establishes levels of authority and decision-making power. That hierarchy may influence who talks to whom, about what, and in what manner. In large organizations, employees are often expected to convey information and voice concerns to their immediate supervisor. Only when a problem cannot be remedied at that level do employees have the "right" to speak to the next person up the hierarchy.

In general, the more levels within an organization's structure, the more likely it is that information will be distorted as communication goes up or down the "chain of command." The accuracy of information can be reduced by up to 20 percent every time a message passes through a different level.[14]

In addition to an organizational structure, every organization has a unique culture that influences member communication. According to Michael Pacanowsky and Nick O'Donnell-Trujillo, **organizational culture theory**[15] describes the ways in which shared symbols, beliefs, values, and norms affect the behaviours of people working in and with an organization. For example, one company may expect their employees to wear suits, spend much of their time working silently in their offices, arrive and leave promptly, and get together in small groups to socialize only after hours. Just as cultural beliefs, norms, and traditions change when you travel from one country to another, organizational culture can vary from job to job. Customs in an organizational culture include personal, celebratory, and ritual behaviours (responding to email, celebrating birthdays, attending department meetings), social behaviours (politeness, thanking customers, supporting worried colleagues), and communication behaviours (retelling legendary stories, using in-house-only jargon, giving colleagues nicknames).

Organizations also have subcultures. An **organizational subculture** consists of a group of people who engage in behaviours and share values that are, in part, different from that of the larger organizational culture. For example, the marketing department in an organization may develop different customs than the accounting department across the hall. The regional sales office in St. John's may have different traditions than the Winnipeg office.

Classic Organizational Hierarchy

BOARD OF DIRECTORS
Makes policy and key decisions

UPPER MANAGEMENT
Senior executives who implement board policies and decisions

MIDDLE MANAGEMENT
Managers who link upper management to supervisors and their workers

LOWER MANAGEMENT
Supervisors or team leaders who have regular and direct contact with workers

SUPPORT STAFF
Secretaries, administrative assistants, project directors

FRONTLINE WORKERS
People who do the fundamental tasks of the organization

How would you describe the organizational culture depicted in this photo?

Picture-Factory/Fotolia

the nature of professional relationships

159

Exercise

This YouTube video further explains organizational culture theory.

www.youtube.com/watch?v=sO2vNyBroco

9.2

Professional Communication Challenges

How should you deal with office rumours and gossip, working with friends, and leaving a job?

Reesa didn't want anyone at work to know that she was dating her co-worker James. Unfortunately, her officemate overheard her talking with James on the phone and told several other people in the office about the relationship. Soon there was a buzz about it. Reesa was worried that their boss would disapprove and that their co-workers would tease or harass them.

Ineffective and inappropriate communication in professional settings can result in serious consequences: tension in the workplace, limited advancement opportunities, and even job loss. In this section we examine some of the difficult communication situations that occur within organizations: office gossip, sexual harassment, working with friends, and quitting or losing a job.

Office Rumours and Gossip

Whereas a **rumour** is an unverified story or statement about the facts of a situation, **gossip** is a type of rumour that focuses on the private, personal, or even scandalous affairs of other people. Nicholas DiFonzo of the Rochester Institute of Technology describes gossip as a rumour that is "more social in nature, usually personal and usually derogatory." When spreading "gossip, truth is beside the point. Spreading gossip is about fun."[16]

Most of us listen to rumours because we want to have as much information as everyone else. Typically, we spread gossip because we want to be perceived as "in the know."[17] In one survey of office workers, more than 90 percent of

Strategies for MANAGING OFFICE GOSSIP

▶ Do not spread malicious rumours. If you don't know if the information is accurate or if someone else will be hurt if the information is shared, don't repeat it.

▶ Evaluate the reliability of a rumour or gossip by asking questions and checking facts.

▶ When others gossip, change the subject, tell them you prefer not to discuss certain topics, or say that you're too busy to talk at the moment.

▶ Consider the potential consequences of divulging confidential information or spreading a rumour.

▶ Before self-disclosing to a co-worker, assume that your secret *will* be told to others.

▶ If you believe that gossip has created a serious problem, talk to someone with more power or influence.[18]

When organizations learn that misinformation is making its way through the rumour mill, they should address and correct it quickly before any more harm is done.

Bikeriderlondon/Shutterstock

In some workplaces, malicious gossip infects the workplace and creates a climate of hostility and distrust.

Scott Griessel/Fotolia

employees admitted that they have engaged in gossip.[19] The same study also found that after learning information about a colleague that was intended to be secret, 75 percent of employees revealed that secret to at least two other employees the same day.

While rumours and gossip have the potential to be harmful, they can also serve an important social function. Consultant Annette Simmons observes, "A certain amount of small talk—sharing small details of your life—helps people feel closer to co-workers. It is what humanizes the workplace and helps people bond."[20] However, unchecked or malicious

gossip can have serious consequences. Private and potentially embarrassing information, even if untrue, can damage your professional credibility. Divulging company secrets can get you fired. Time spent gossiping is time not spent doing your job.

An organization can take measures that prevent the *need* for gossip by keeping employees well informed.[21] For example, when a larger corporation purchases a company, many employees worry about losing their jobs and spend hours talking about who will stay and

STOP&THINK

Are You Twittering the Hours Away at Work?

Do you send and respond to personal emails at work? Do you tweet, text, or visit friends on Facebook while being paid to do a job? If your answer is *yes*, check the rules where you work before doing it again.

According to a study commissioned by Robert Half Technology, an information technology staffing firm, "54% of companies ban workers from using social networking sites like Twitter, Facebook, LinkedIn and MySpace while on the job. . . . Only 10% of the 1,400 surveyed companies said they allowed employees full access to social networks during work hours."[22]

The problem of on-the-job social networking involves more than concerns about employee productivity. What if employees use social media to send discriminatory statements, racial slurs, or sexually explicit messages to coworkers or clients? What if employees reveal, either intentionally or unintentionally, confidential company information? What should a company do if an information technology worker reports finding child pornography on a company computer they're servicing? Employees and corporate officers may be fired, the company may be sued, and/or law enforcement officials may prosecute.[23]

Most companies and organizations have formal or informal policies or guidelines to restrain social network-

ing at work. At the same time, they may permit certain employees—depending on their job—to use social media during work hours. In either case, more and more companies are monitoring how you use computers at work.

Do you agree that your personal email, tweets, and social networking at work decrease your productivity? If your answer is *no*, then you are not alone. Many feel that taking a short break from work to be involved in social conversations via media such as Facebook and Twitter can actually make you more productive. Perhaps this type of interaction is replacing the lunchroom coffee break?[24]

Before deciding to redesign your Facebook page or get involved in a controversial political debate online, make sure you know the "rules."

who will be asked to leave. If no personnel cutbacks are planned, employees should be told. When cutbacks are anticipated, an organization should inform everyone about how and when those decisions will be made—this way, everyone will have more accurate information.

Sexual Harassment

Workplace romances should not be confused with sexual harassment. Romance in the workplace involves two individuals who want a close, personal relationship, whereas **sexual harassment** is characterized by unwanted sexual advances for sexual favours, inappropriate verbal or physical conduct of a sexual nature, or an intimidating, hostile, or offensive work environment.[25] Sexual harassment is rarely an isolated incident. Usually, it is a pattern of offensive or unwelcome behaviour that takes place over a period of time. In many instances, sexual harassment involves a supervisor or colleague using power to demand sexual favours—from coercing a subordinate to perform sexually in order to guarantee her or his job to making sex a prerequisite for securing a promotion, a higher salary, or extra time off. Sexual harassment may also include demeaning or offensive communication in the form of emails containing sexually explicit messages and jokes, inappropriate comments made directly to a co-worker, or postings of sexual images in staff rooms.

Research reports that many victims of sexual harassment experience "decreased work performance, anxiety, depression, self-blame, anger, feelings of helplessness, fear of further or escalating harassment, and fear of reporting the incident."[26] Although most workers say that they would immediately address or report harassment, research reveals that, when confronted with the situation, many people feel uncomfortable and fail to report the behaviour.[27]

Most organizations take allegations of sexual harassment very seriously and have established policies against sexual harassment as well as grievance procedures for reporting such behaviour.

Both the Canadian Human Rights Act and the Canada Labour Code protect employees from harassment related to work. Provincial human rights laws also prohibit harassment, and the Criminal Code protects people from physical or sexual assault.[28]

Bill 168, an Act to amend the Occupational Health and Safety Act with respect to violence and harassment in the workplace and other matters, came into effect June 15, 2010. Workplaces in Ontario are now required to have the necessary policies, programs, measures, and procedures in place.[29]

COMMUNICATION

Exercise

To learn more about Ontario's Bill 168 watch this YouTube video.
www.youtube.com/watch?v=s2rboi5Dop8

COMMUNICATION&CULTURE

NotarYES/Shutterstock

DIFFERING VIEWS ON SEXUAL HARASSMENT

Identifying sexual harassment is complicated by the fact that men and women often have different perceptions of similar behaviour. Thus, women may view telling a sexually explicit joke in the office as harassment, whereas men may see it as harmless. Both men and women, however, judge overt behaviour, such as demands for sexual favours, as harassment.

How would you answer this question: Have any of the following incidents happened to you or someone you know in the workplace?

1. Unwanted and deliberate touching, leaning over, cornering, or pinching
2. Unwanted sexually suggestive looks or comments

3. Unwanted letters, telephone calls, or materials of a sexual nature
4. Unwanted pressure for dates
5. Unwanted sexual teasing, jokes, remarks, or questions

Now ask yourself this question: Are any of these incidents examples of sexual harassment? No one should have to tolerate a sexually hostile work environment.[30]

Exercise

This clip from the TV show *The Big Bang Theory* illustrates that what one person perceives as harassment, another may view as helpful suggestions. Regardless of perception, harassment is against the law in Ontario.

www.youtube.com/watch?v=RUIAiYBeLc0

... the typical Canadian will change *careers* approximately **7** times.[34]

Workplace Friendships

Many co-worker relationships are personal as well as professional. Mixing personal and professional relationships, however, can be difficult: You want your friend to like you, but you also need co-workers, superiors, and subordinates to respect you; you want approval from your friend, but you also must make objective decisions in the workplace; you hope for professional success but not at the expense of your friends' advancement.

In *Organizational Communication*, communication scholar Daniel Modaff and his colleagues recommend that you seek your most important relationships outside the workplace and that, if you do have a friend relationship at work, you should be prepared to manage the consequences.[31] Telling a best friend that he has not met expectations on a work team can be difficult and even impossible if you want to preserve the friendship. At the same time, letting a friend get away with less-than-excellent work can destroy the morale of a group and put your reputation and leadership at risk.

Leaving a Job

While the Government of Canada does not keep statistics on the number of lifetime careers an average person holds, it is thought to be around seven.[32] There are many reasons for leaving a job or changing careers. Whatever your reason, always try to depart on as good terms as possible and handle your resignation or exit with professionalism and courtesy. Just as you want to make a good first impression when interviewing and beginning a new job, it is equally important to leave a positive impression when departing from or ending a job.

Even when a resignation is the result of dissatisfaction with the job or a poor relationship with a boss or co-workers, leaving on good terms is important. After you resign, a supervisor or human resources manager may request an **exit interview**. Organizations gather information in exit interviews to develop strategies for retaining other employees and to improve the workplace for those who remain. Because you don't know how the information will be used or whether it will be treated confidentially, remain calm and communicate a positive attitude. Focus on issues, not people. An "exit interview is not the time to burn bridges. Most industries are small, and bad behaviour is not something you want people remembering about you."[33]

Sometimes, leaving a job is not a decision you make by choice. As a stressful event, job loss ranks right up there with death in the family, divorce, and serious illness. Job loss can have a profound effect on your emotional well-being. Typically, most people experience a resulting cycle of denial, anger, frustration, and eventually adaptation.[35] If you lose your job, and your anxiety seems out of control, go back to the section on communication apprehension in Chapter 2. The relaxation strategies recommended there—cognitive restructuring, visualization, and systematic desensitization—can help you build confidence and reduce stress.

STRAINS[36]

on FRIENDSHIPS

- Equal status in a friendship may be compromised by inequality at work.
- The need to withhold confidential work information may clash with the need for openness in a friendship.
- Collaboration may be impossible when one friend has more decision-making power at work.
- The friendship may be damaged by negative feedback given at work.
- Public expressions of friendship may need to be minimized in the workplace.

on PROFESSIONAL RELATIONSHIPS

- A friendship may make it difficult to manage unequal levels of power at work.
- It may be difficult to handle sensitive work information with discretion.
- Personal knowledge and feelings about a friend may compromise objectivity at work.
- A friend may be held to a higher performance standard at work.
- Socializing may adversely affect productivity and the quality of performance at work.

professional communication challenges

LEAVING YOUR JOB
Best Practices[37]

- Follow company policies and procedures when resigning.
- Inform your immediate supervisor of your plans first.
- Resign in person but also write a brief resignation letter.
- Give the appropriate advance notice.
- Phrase feedback and explanations positively.

CHECKLIST for Coping with Job Loss[38]

BE PROACTIVE

☐ Did you discuss the details of any unemployment benefits (e.g., severance, health insurance, life insurance) with a human resources officer?

☐ Did you honestly and objectively assess the reasons why you lost or left your job?

KNOW THY SELF

☐ Have you asked yourself whether you want to stay in the same field?

☐ Is it, perhaps, time for a career change?

☐ Is there a skill you need to learn to become a more skilful employee?

USE YOUR COMMUNICATION SKILLS

☐ Have you networked with family members, friends, and colleagues to connect with potential employers?

☐ Have you consulted employment agencies, checked the classifieds, and surfed the Internet for available jobs?

☐ Do you know the dos and don'ts of effective job interviewing?

CRAFT A PERSUASIVE MESSAGE

☐ Does your résumé highlight your marketable skills?

☐ Does your résumé reflect your knowledge of economic and industry trends?

☐ Does your cover letter express how ready, willing, and able you are to give 100 percent to a new position?

9.3
Workplace and Job Interviews

What are the most effective ways to prepare for, participate in, and follow up after workplace and job interviews?

When you hear the phrase "job interview," what comes to mind? Most people think of a job interview as one of the last steps in the job application process. However, interviews do not end once you get a job.

Workplace Interviews

You will encounter several types of interviews in the workplace, including selection interviews, appraisal interviews, information-gathering interviews, disciplinary interviews, and exit interviews. The table on p. 166 identifies

the purpose and function of workplace interviews. Each type of interview has a unique purpose and process.

In the world of work, an **interview** is an interpersonal interaction between two parties in which at least one party has a predetermined purpose and uses questions and answers to share information, solve a problem, or influence the other.[39]

Although a traditional job interview (a form of selection interview) can be a stressful communication situation, a good interview can land you the job

of your dreams. Unfortunately, a poor interview can result in a major disappointment and the loss of a promising career opportunity.

In the following section, we focus on the communication skills needed to prepare for, participate in, and follow up on a job interview.

Before the Job Interview

In *What Color Is Your Parachute?*, the best-selling guidebook for career changers and job seekers, Richard Bolles recounts the story of an interview between an IBM recruiter and a college senior. The recruiter asked the student, "What does IBM stand for?" The student didn't know and thus ended the interview.[40] As with any important communication situation, a successful job interview requires careful preparation. In a survey of the most common job interview mistakes, senior executives identified three major errors, all of which related to poor interview preparation: (1) having little or no knowledge of the company, (2) being unprepared to discuss skills and experiences, and (3) being unprepared to discuss career plans and goals.[41] Before going to an interview, make sure you research the organization, assess your own strengths and weaknesses, and practise interviewing.

Research the Organization Learn as much as you can about the organization. As a first step, do a thorough search of the organization's website. A good website will tell you a great deal about the organization's mission, products and services, and achievements. If the website includes information about key employees, research the person or persons you will meet at the interview. You also may find news stories about the company or organization on other websites.

Expect that other good candidates will be researching the website, and go one step further. Contact the company or organization directly and request documents that they make available to the public, such as brochures, catalogues, newsletters, and annual reports. If you know current or former employees, ask them about the organization. The more you know, the easier it is to explain how you can make a positive contribution. Research may also uncover reasons you don't want to work for that organization, ranging from a company's policy on unions or political issues to its health benefits or pension options.

Assess Your Strengths and Weaknesses Ron, a 26-year-old man with some sales experience, was preparing to interview for a sales position at a midsized company. He found a story on the Internet reporting that the company was considering restructuring its product pricing. Although the job description did not mention needing experience in this area, Ron decided to make a point of saying that his marketing co-op placement involved reevaluating product pricing. Using the information he unearthed about the organization helped Ron demonstrate why he was the best candidate for the position.

Be prepared to explain your weaknesses as well as your strengths. Plan how to address unexplained gaps of time on your résumé, several jobs in a short period of time, or the lack of a skill specifically mentioned in the job description. The time to develop an acceptable answer to such reasonable concerns is not in the middle of an interview. For example, Sharon quit her graphic design job when her first child was born and was a stay-at-home mother for seven years. When she decided to re-enter the workplace, she knew she would have to address concerns about being up to date in her field. After careful consideration, she developed an answer that focused on refresher courses that she had taken during the past two years as well as the volunteer design work she had done for community groups. She also suggested that her design "eye" had matured and grown more sophisticated than it was when she was a younger artist. Whatever your perceived weakness might be, don't assume that the interviewer hasn't noticed it on the application or résumé. Instead, be ready with a thoughtful response.

The saying that you never get a *second* chance to make a first impression is especially true in job interviews.

Practise Interviewing During a job interview, you have a limited amount of time to make a good impression in a fairly stressful communication situation. Practising with a mock interview *before* the real thing will make a difference. Create a list of interview questions you might be asked (see the list of common questions on page 168).

Because the interview will probably take place in a meeting room or office, sit at your desk or a table and practise your answers out loud and confidently. After you are comfortable with your responses, ask a few friends or family members to interview you. They can give

Patricia Marks/Shutterstock

In terms of specific communication skills, how is this television interview similar to or different from other types of workplace interviews?

you feedback on the quality of your answers and may suggest some additional questions to consider.

During the Job Interview

An interview is a golden opportunity for both you and the interviewer. The interviewer wants to learn more about you, and you need to learn about the job and the organization while creating a positive impression. The extent to which you accomplish these goals depends on how well you respond to questions and present yourself.

Most interviews use one or more of the five standard types of questions listed. Regardless of the type of question, you must know how to formulate an appropriate response for every question asked of you. Consider, for example, how the following answers to two commonly asked interview questions illustrate the differences between an effective and an inappropriate response.

Question 1: Why did you leave your last job?

Inappropriate Response: My boss and I just didn't get along. She expected me to do work that was really her responsibility. They didn't pay me enough to do my job and someone else's. When I complained, nobody did anything about it.

Analysis: While honest, this is not a very effective or flattering response. Interviewers often ask questions like these to determine whether you had problems with a former employer and whether you will be just as troublesome in a new job. In this example, the interviewer could conclude that the applicant doesn't work well with others, resists doing required work, complains a lot, and evaluates work only in terms of a paycheque. A better approach is to focus on why a new job would offer more desirable opportunities and better match your values and goals. A job interview is not the time or place to vent frustrations about a former boss.

Question 2: What, in your opinion, is your greatest job-related weakness?

Effective Response: My natural tendency is to focus on one thing at a time until it's completed. However, most of my jobs have required me to manage several projects at once. I've had to learn how to juggle a variety of tasks, particularly when things get

Types of Workplace Interviews	Purpose	Process
Selection interview	To evaluate and choose a candidate for a job or promotion	Potential employer assesses whether a job candidate's knowledge, maturity, personality, attitude, communication skills, and work record match the job.
Appraisal interview	To evaluate an employee's job performance	Employer/employee assesses an employee's work record, identifies training needs, and provides motivation and self-reflection through constructive feedback.
Information-gathering interview	To obtain facts, opinions, data, feelings, attitudes, and reactions	Employer and employee analyze important issues and try to solve identified problems.
Disciplinary interview	To identify, discuss, and/or correct problematic behaviours	Employer assesses why problems are occurring and how/if the employee can change behaviour and resolve the problem.
Exit interview	To learn why an employee is leaving and what factors contributed to that decision	Employer provides closure for the departing employee and identifies ways to improve retention and employee satisfaction and retention.

hectic. A couple of years ago I started using a project management software system to track projects and keep things organized. This has helped me shift attention back and forth among projects without losing track of priorities and deadlines.

Analysis: This answer is effective and strategic. When answering a question about a weakness, figure out how to acknowledge it while simultaneously demonstrating how you learned to deal with or overcome it. As a result, you transform the weakness into an example of your problem-solving abilities. But, don't exaggerate. When asked about your weakness, don't say, "I work too hard." We all do that. Working hard is usually considered a strength.

In addition to preparing to answer questions, be prepared to ask some questions. Many interviewers assess your knowledge, interest, and communication

Identify what you can bring to the job that will promote the organization's goals.

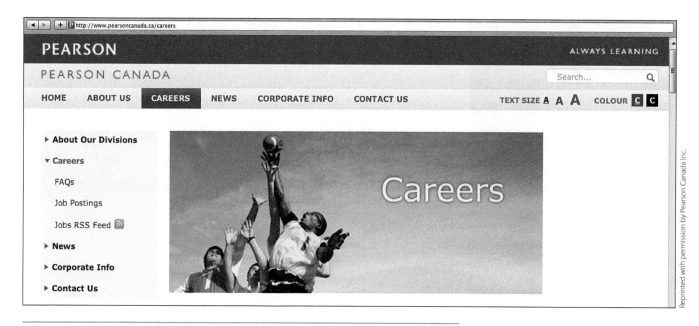

In addition to telling you about an organization's mission, products, services, and achievements, a website gives you a feel for the company's organizational culture and career opportunities.

> **Never hesitate to ask for clarification before giving a response.**

skills based on the kinds of questions you ask. Use this opportunity to enhance your credibility and to learn more about the job, the organization, and its employees.

Interviews help employers decide whether you are the right person for a job, not just from your answers but also from the way you speak and be-

have during the interview. Remember that you are being observed from the moment you arrive until the time you leave the building. In fact, it's not unusual for an interviewer to ask receptionists or secretaries for their impressions of you.

In a survey conducted by Northwestern University, 153 companies

ETHICAL COMMUNICATION

Never Lie During a Job Interview

Approximately 20 to 45 percent of applicants lie on a résumé or in a job interview.[42] Another study reports that 11 percent of applicants do not tell the truth about why they left a previous job, and 9 percent lie about their education and responsibilities in previous jobs.[43] Not only is lying to a prospective employer unethical, but it can backfire and have serious personal consequences.

Most organizations have become much more rigorous when screening applicants. Private detective Fay Faron explains that many organizations conduct extensive background checks to avoid a lawsuit and ensure the safety of customers.[44] Count on being carefully screened, having your references checked, and being investigated for a criminal background. Furthermore, if your lie is discovered, your application will be rejected or, if you're already hired, you will be fired. A survey conducted by an executive search firm

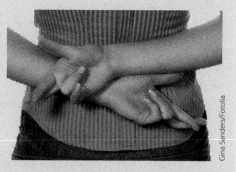

revealed that 95 percent of employers would reject applicants who lied about a college degree and that 80 percent would not hire someone who falsified previous job titles.[45]

Your goal is more than getting a job, it is getting a job that is right for you.[46] If you have to falsify your credentials or work experience, you are not qualified for the job. Moreover, the consequences of lying can be long lasting. If your lie is discovered, it can ruin your reputation for years to come.

Strategies for ENHANCING YOUR FIRST IMPRESSION DURING AN INTERVIEW

- Arrive a few minutes early.
- Wear appropriate business attire.
- Make sure clothes, hair, and nails are clean and appropriate.
- Listen attentively.
- Answer questions using correct grammar and appropriate language.
- Smile and use direct eye contact.
- Maintain a posture that appears relaxed but not too informal.
- Try to appear calm and confident; avoid fidgeting.
- End the interview on a positive note.

when it is your turn to speak or answer a question in an interview, try "not to speak any longer than two minutes at a time if you want to make the best impression."[48] Generally, it's better to leave interviewers hungry for more information about you rather than to overwhelm them with information.

Closed-ended question	Requires only a short answer, such as *yes* or *no*.
Open-ended question	Requires or encourages a more detailed answer.
Hypothetical question	Describes a set of circumstances and asks how you would respond.
Leading question	Suggests or implies the response the questioner wants to hear.
Probing question	Follows up another question, encouraging more depth or detail.

were asked why they rejected job applicants.[47] Of the 50 reasons identified; almost half were related to lack of communication skills and failure to create a positive impression. One of the most common mistakes made by applicants is talking too much. If you talk *too* much, you may bore your listeners or may appear insensitive to the time limits of an interview. According to Richard Bolles,

STANDARD Interview Questions and Examples[49]

Closed-ended question → Are you able to work on weekends?

Open-ended question → What do you view as the most significant challenges facing this industry over the next few years?

Hypothetical question → How would you handle an employee who does good work but, even after being warned, continues to arrive late?

Leading question → Do you think the ability to work well in a group is just as important as the ability to perform routine technical tasks?

Probing question → Could you explain what you mean by a "difficult client"?

COMMON Interview Questions[50]

1. Briefly, tell me about yourself.
2. What do you hope to be doing five years from now?
3. Where do you hope to be in ten years?
4. In terms of this job, what is your greatest strength?
5. What, in your opinion, is your greatest weakness?
6. What motivates you to work hard and do your best?
7. How well do you deal with pressure? Give an example.
8. What are the two or three characteristics you are seeking in a job?
9. Describe a major problem you encountered in a previous job. How did you deal with it?
10. What kind of relationship should be established between a supervisor and subordinates?
11. Why did you choose to pursue this particular career?
12. Why did you leave your last job(s)?
13. How can you contribute to our company?
14. How do you evaluate or determine success?
15. Given the fact that we have other applicants, why should we hire you?

mybaitshop/Fotolia

Questions **TO ASK**
During an Interview[51]

- Can you tell me more about the specific, everyday responsibilities of this position?

- What, in your opinion, are the major challenges facing the organization?

- What is the most important characteristic you are looking for in an employee for this position?

- How would you describe the culture of your organization?

- How will success be measured for this position?

- What other people or departments will I be working with?

Common Interview **MISTAKES TO AVOID**[52]

- Unprofessional appearance
- Aggressive or arrogant manner
- Poor grammar and vocal expression
- Lack of interest or enthusiasm
- Lack of confidence
- Evasiveness and tendency to make excuses
- Lack of discretion

- Immaturity
- Poor manners
- Tendency to criticize past employers
- Lack of direct eye contact
- Weak or limp handshake
- Late to the interview
- Vague responses to questions

Sean De Burca/Shutterstock

STOP & THINK

How Would You Handle Inappropriate Questions?

Federal and provincial laws prohibit discrimination in hiring. Generally, an interview should not include a discussion of race or ethnicity, gender, marital status, religion, sexual orientation, or disabilities. The best approach to answering inappropriate questions depends on the situation, what information you feel comfortable revealing, and your personal communication style. Consider the following questions; which, in your mind, are inappropriate during a job interview? Why?

_____ What does your husband or wife do?
_____ Do you plan to have children?
_____ How many more years do you plan to work before retiring?
_____ Which religious holidays will you take off from work?
_____ Do you have any disabilities?
_____ What country are your parents or grandparents from?

Answers: All of the above questions are inappropriate for a job interview.[53]

You have the right to refuse to answer a question you believe is inappropriate, but before you assume it is inappropriate, assess the purpose of the question. Once you've assessed the intent and decide you will respond, be as tactful as possible so as not to embarrass the interviewer and redirect the interview to a discussion of your qualifications. For example, "Do you have children?" may reflect the interviewer's concern that a busy parent won't work the number of hours necessary to demonstrate a full commitment to the job. An appropriate response might be, "If you're asking whether I can balance a demanding job with family obligations, I have always effectively done so in the past."

Furthermore, don't assume that the interviewer intends to discriminate. For instance, a hiring manager who asks whether you plan to have children may simply want to talk about the company's excellent maternity and child care benefits or brag about his or her own child. These types of questions are often asked out of simple curiosity or an effort to engage in conversation.

workplace and job interviews

After the Job Interview

Immediately after an interview, send a note thanking the interviewer for her or his time and consideration. The note should briefly refer to issues discussed in the interview and emphasize that you can perform the job and help the organization meet its goals. A brief but well-written letter (or, if appropriate, an email or text message) reinforces that you have a professional approach to and enthusiasm for the job.

Although it's natural to wonder how well you did during the interview, you may never learn how the interviewer evaluated you and your responses. An analytical self-evaluation may be more useful (see the Communication Assessment: Evaluating Your Job Interview Performance on p. 171).

Keep in mind that you can make an excellent impression during an interview and still not be hired because you may have been one of several outstanding candidates. Regardless of whether you are selected or not, view each interview as an opportunity to practice your skills.

COMMUNICATION

Exercise

Choose a partner and practise asking and answering the questions found in this chapter. The more you practise these skills, the more confident you will become in the job interview situation.

In this video clip from YouTube, the interviewer asks real questions of someone interviewing for an entry level position, and after each question is asked, there is a pause of time, allowing you to answer.

www.youtube.com/watch?v=2zKsBfsrxrs

Evaluating Your Job Interview Performance

Use this instrument to evaluate the performance of the woman shown in this YouTube video interviewing for a position: **www.youtube.com/watch?v=5QOR3GPb7hk**. Using criteria based on the seven key elements of communication discussed in Chapter 1, rate the interviewee with the following scores:

E = excellent; G = good; A = average; W = weak; P = Poor or N/A = not applicable.

Job Interview Competencies	E	G	A	W	P	N/A
Self: Interviewee was well prepared and confident.						
Others: Interviewee listened effectively and adapted to the interviewer or interviewers.						
Purpose: Interviewee could explain how hiring her would promote her professional goals as well as the organization's mission.						
Context: Interviewee adapted to the logistics and psychosocial climate of the interview.						
Content: Interviewee included ideas and information relevant to and needed in the job or assignment; asked good questions; knew a great deal about the organization.						
Structure: Interviewee organized the content of her answers in a clear and professional way. Interviewee asked questions at appropriate points in the interview.						
Expression: Interviewee used verbal and nonverbal behaviour appropriately and effectively. Interviewee was dressed appropriately and professionally.						
Overall Assessment:						

Additional Assessment Questions:

1. Which questions did the interviewee answer best? What made her answers effective?

2. Which questions were the most difficult? Are these questions likely to be asked in future interviews? How could she answer such questions more effectively in the future?

3. Did she miss opportunities to emphasize particular strengths? How might she have incorporated those into her other answers?

4. What additional questions should she have asked?

5. What should she do differently in a future job interview?

communication assessment

9.1
The Nature of Professional Relationships

How can you improve your professional relationships?

- Superiors request work, supervise projects, and assess a subordinate's performance; subordinates provide information about themselves and co-workers as well as information about the progress of work, what needs to be done, and how to do it.

- Satisfying co-worker relationships are characterized by individual excellence, interdependence, investment, information, integration, and integrity.

- Customers have three basic communication needs: to feel welcome, to have enough good information to make a decision, and to be treated with respect.

- When dealing with someone's difficult behaviour at work, identify specific successes and failures, listen actively, explain the consequences of the behaviour, call on the person's strengths, and mutually agree and follow up on an action plan.

9.2
Professional Communication Challenges

How should you deal with office rumours and gossip, working with friends, and leaving a job?

- Although rumours and gossip serve several social functions in an organization, self-serving rumours and malicious gossip can embarrass others, damage your credibility, waste time, and create a hostile and distrustful work environment.

- Sexual harassment is characterized by unwanted sexual advances, inappropriate verbal or physical conduct of a sexual nature, or a hostile, or offensive work environment.

- Working with a close friend at work can put strains on the friendship and the professional relationship.

- Leaving a job—either voluntarily or involuntarily—requires communication strategies that leave a good impression with your former employer and create an equally good impression with your new or potential employer.

9.3
Workplace and Job Interviews

What are the most effective ways to prepare for, participate in, and follow up after workplace and job interviews?

- Workplace interviews serve several purposes and come in many forms such as selection, appraisal, information-gathering, disciplinary, and exit interviews.

- Before going to a job interview, research the organization, assess your own strengths and weaknesses, and practice answering probable questions.

- During an interview, answer questions directly and concisely while presenting yourself and your skills positively.

- In addition to sending a follow-up note to the interviewer after an interview, assess your own performance and how you can do better in future interviews.

Monkey Business/Fotolia

TEST YOUR KNOWLEDGE

9.1 How can you improve your professional relationships?

1 According to a Canadian study in this chapter, the number of Canadians who are happy in their employment is _____ .
- a. one in five
- b. one in three
- c. two in four
- d. two in three

2 In a superior–subordinate relationship at work, effective subordinates provide all of the following to their boss or manager except _____.
- a. information about themselves and co-workers
- b. information on the progress of work
- c. information on what needs to be done
- d. information about how to do the work more effectively
- e. subordinates usually provide all of the above types of information

3 According to organizational culture theory, the practise of giving colleagues nicknames is an example of a _____ behaviour.
- a. ritual
- b. impersonal
- c. communication
- d. celebratory
- e. personal

9.2 How should you deal with office rumours and gossip, working with friends, and leaving a job?

4 Whereas a rumour is an unverified story or statement about the facts of a situation, gossip
- a. is a type of rumour that focuses on the private and personal interactions of other people.
- b. focuses on the scandalous affairs of other people.
- c. is more social in nature.
- d. is usually more personal and derogatory in nature.
- e. All of the above are characteristics of gossip.

5 Each of the following behaviours is an example of sexual harassment except _____.
- a. a supervisor demands sexual favours from a subordinate as a guarantee of keeping a job
- b. a supervisor demands sexual favours from a subordinate in order to earn a promotion
- c. a colleague passes around sexually explicit images and jokes via email
- d. a co-worker makes sexually demeaning comments about another co-worker
- e. All of the above are examples of sexual harassment.

9.3 What are the most effective ways to prepare for, participate in, and follow up after workplace and job interviews?

6 Which type of interview is conducted for the purpose of evaluating an employee's job performance?
- a. selection interview
- b. appraisal interview
- c. information-gathering interview
- d. disciplinary interview
- e. exit interview

7 "What are the most significant challenges facing this industry in the current economic climate?" is what type of interview question?
- a. closed-ended question
- b. leading question
- c. probing question
- d. open-ended question
- e. hypothetical question

8 Which of the following questions is technically inappropriate and illegal during a job interview?
- a. Do you plan to have children?
- b. Have you ever sought treatment for physical or mental disabilities?
- c. What country are your parents or ancestors from?
- d. Which religious holidays will you take off from work?
- e. All of the above are inappropriate and illegal questions.

9 Before ending an interview, interviewers often ask if you have additional questions. Which of the following questions would be an appropriate response?
- a. Do you have any disabilities?
- b. Will I be permitted to take off three very important holidays celebrated by my religion?
- c. What position does this company take on the abortion issue?
- d. How will my success be measured for this position?
- e. Will I be working with a culturally diverse group of people?

10 During an interview you will most likely be asked _____.
- a. closed questions
- b. hypothetical questions
- c. leading questions
- d. probing questions
- e. b, c, and d are correct.

Answers found on page 330.

Key Terms

Co-worker relationship	**Interview**	**Probing question**
Customer relationship	**Leading question**	**Rumour**
Exit interview	**Organizational culture theory**	**Sexual harassment**
Gossip	**Organizational subculture**	**Superior–subordinate relationships**
Hypothetical question		

Working in **GROUPS**

The music group Three Days Grace was formed in Norwood, Ontario, in 1992 but under a different name, Groundswell.[1] They were able to make some great music from 1992 to 1995, but like many bands, they experienced difficulty and broke up when two members left the group. The remaining members reformed in 1997 under their current name.[2] New members joined the group, and vocalist Adam Gontier dealt with drug addiction and recovery. During the span of their careers, the band has had contracts with several production companies, releasing hit albums in 2003, 2006, 2008, 2009, and 2012. In January 2013, Gontier decided to leave the band, noting that he was sober, but that after 20 years singing in a group, it was time for a personal change.[3] Matt Walst, brother of bassist Brad Walst, took over lead singer duties.[4] In this chapter, we look at the nature of groups: how they form and the communication challenges they face as they develop, deal with conflict, and hopefully become productive.

and ASK YOURSELF ...

THINK About ...

The Challenges of Working in Groups

What are the pros and cons of working in groups?

All of us work in groups. We work in groups at school and on the job; with family members, friends, and colleagues; and in diverse locations, from sports fields and battlefields to courtrooms and classrooms. Whereas individual achievement was once the measure of personal success, success in today's complex world depends on the ability to work in groups. Researchers Steve Kozlowski and Daniel Ilgen describe our profound dependence on groups:

> Teams of people working together for a common cause touch all of our lives. From everyday activities like air travel, fire fighting, and running the United Way drive to amazing feats of human accomplishments like climbing Mt. Everest and reaching for the stars,

teams are at the centre of how work gets done in modern times.[5]

The Nature of Group Communication

Working in groups may be one of the most important skills you learn in college. The Ontario Skills Passport describes the ability to work in groups as an essential employability skill.[6] Verbal communication (see Chapter 5) and the ability to make decisions and solve conflict (see Chapter 11) are also highly valued employability skills. The ability to work successfully in groups is grounded in the ability to understand how groups develop and function.

> **❝I look for people [who] are** good team people **over anything else. I can teach the technical. ❞**
> —Business executive[7]

Group Size The phrase "two's company; three's a crowd" recognizes that an interaction between two people is quite different from a three-person discussion. The ideal size for a problem-solving group is five to seven members. To avoid ties in decision making, it is usually better to have an odd number of members instead of an even number. Groups larger than seven tend to divide into subgroups;

talkative members may dominate or drown out quiet members.

Interaction and Interdependence Next time you're in a group, observe the ways members behave toward one another. A group member raises a controversial issue. In response, everyone starts talking at the same time. Later, the group listens intently to a member explain an important concept or describe a possible solution to a problem. When tensions arise, a funny comment may ease the strain. Members celebrate as they conclude their meeting or finalize a course of action. What you have just observed is group *interaction*—a necessity for effective group communication in both face-to-face and virtual meetings.

Group members are *interdependent*—that is, the actions of an individual group member affect every other member. For example, if a member fails to provide needed background information, the group as a whole will suffer when it attempts to make an important decision or solve a significant problem.

Common Goal Group members come together for a reason: a collective purpose or goal that defines and unifies

Marzky Ragsac Jr/Fotolia

Members of Canada's 2012 Olympic men's rowing team depended on one another to achieve a common goal—if they couldn't row as a team, they would not be able to come back from last place in qualifying. They did and placed second![8]

Sean Kilpatrick/THE CANADIAN PRESS

Without a common goal, groups wonder: Why are we meeting? Why should we care or work hard?

Gino Santa Maria/Fotolia

Working in groups often leads to friendships, enhanced learning, and member satisfaction.

the group. A classic study by Carl Larson and Frank LaFasto concludes, "in every case, without exception, where an effectively functioning team was identified, it was described . . . as having a clear understanding of its objective."[9]

While some groups have the freedom to develop their own goals, other groups are assigned a goal. For example, a gathering of neighbours may meet to discuss ways of reducing crime in the neighbourhood. Students may form a study group to prepare for an upcoming exam. On the other hand, a marketing instructor may assign a semester-long project to a group of students to research, develop and present a marketing campaign. A manufacturing company may assemble a group of employees from various departments and ask them to develop recommendations for safer storage of hazardous chemicals. Whatever the circumstances, effective groups work to accomplish a common goal.

Advantages and Disadvantages of Working in Groups

If you're like most people, you have had to sit through some long and boring meetings. You may have lost patience (or your temper) in a group that couldn't accomplish a simple task you could have done better and more quickly by yourself. In the long run, however, the advantages of working in groups usually outweigh the potential disadvantages.

Advantages In *The Wisdom of Teams*, Jon Katzenbach and Douglas Smith note that groups "outperform individuals acting alone . . . especially when performance requires multiple skills, judgments, and experiences."[10] In general, the "approaches and outcomes of cooperating groups are not just better than those of the average group member, but are better than even the group's best problem solver functioning alone." Furthermore, the lone problem solver can't match the diversity of knowledge and perspectives of a group.[11]

Many of us also belong to and work in groups because we can make friends, socialize, and feel part of a successful team. Working in groups can enhance

the challenges of working in groups

177

learning when members share information, stimulate critical thinking, challenge assumptions, and establish high standards of achievement.

Disadvantages Working in groups requires time, energy, and resources. For example, when 3M Corporation researchers calculated the hourly wages and overhead costs of workplace meetings, they concluded that meetings cost the company $78.8 million annually.[13] In addition to financial costs, there is also the potential for conflict among members.

As much as we may want everyone in a group to cooperate and work hard, the behaviour of some members may create problems. They may talk too much, arrive late for meetings, and argue aggressively. However, these same members may also be excellent researchers, effective critical thinkers, and good friends.

Types of Groups

Groups are as diverse as the people in them and the goals they seek. Yet there are common characteristics that can be used to separate groups into several categories. These categories range from the most personal and informal types of groups to more professional and formal types. You can identify each type of group by noting its purpose (why the group meets) and by its membership (who is in the group).

The first six types of groups described in the figure below serve your personal needs and interests. In Chapter 8 we examined the importance of effective communication with family members and friends—the people who belong to family and social groups. Self-help, learning, service, and civic groups you join by choice because they offer support and encouragement, help you gain knowledge, and assist others. There are two other types of groups—work groups and public groups—that serve the diverse interests of organizations and public audiences. Understanding your role in these types of groups requires more detailed information about their various forms, functions, and goals.

Work Groups Labour crews, sales staff, faculty, management groups, and research teams are all **work groups**—groups that are responsible for making decisions, solving problems, implementing projects, or performing routine duties in an organization. Committees and work teams are both types of work groups. **Committees** (social committees, budget committees, and awards committees) are created by a larger group or by a person in a position of authority to take on specific tasks. **Work teams** are usually given full responsibility and resources for their projects. Unlike committees, work teams are relatively permanent. They don't take time *from* work to meet—they unite *to* work.

Public Groups Panel discussions, symposiums, forums, and governance groups are types of **public groups** that discuss issues in front of or for the benefit of the public. Their meetings usually occur in unrestricted public settings in front of public audiences. During a **panel discussion**, several people interact about a common topic to educate, influence, or entertain an audience. In a **symposium**, group members present short, uninterrupted presentations on different aspects of a topic for the benefit of an audience. Very often, a panel or symposium is followed by a **forum**, which provides an opportunity for audience members to comment or ask questions. A strong moderator is needed in a forum to make sure that all audience

TYPES OF GROUP

	PURPOSE	MEMBERSHIP
Primary	To provide members with affection, support, and a sense of belonging	Family members, best friends
Social	To share common interests in a friendly setting or participate in social activities	Athletic team members, hobbyists, sorority and fraternity members
Self-Help	To support and encourage members who want or need help with personal problems	Therapy group members, participants in programs such as Weight Watchers and Alcoholics Anonymous
Learning	To help members gain knowledge and develop skills	Classmates, book group members, participants in a ceramic workshop
Service	To assist worthy causes that help other people outside the group	Members of Me to We, Police Athletic League, charity groups, Facebook groups
Civic	To support worthy causes that help people within the group or community	Members of a PTA, labour unions, veterans' groups, neighbourhood associations
Work	To achieve specific goals on behalf of a business or organization	Committee members, employees, task force members, management teams
Public	To discuss important issues in front of or for the benefit of the public	Participants in public panel discussions, symposiums, forums, governance groups

Monkey Business Images/Shutterstock

Mauricio Valenzuela/Xinhua/Zuma ZUMA Press/Newscom

Tyler Olson/Fotolia

Sam Spiro/Fotolia

VIRTUAL TEAM MEMBER **RESPONSIBILITIES**

When conducting or participating in a virtual team meeting, every group member should assume the following responsibilities:

- Prepare for the meeting by reading the background material and becoming familiar with the technology
- Speak out during the meeting (or respond using the available media)
- Listen to and consider others' ideas
- Make suggestions and decisions
- Follow up on meeting actions[14]

goodluz/Fotolia

members have an equal opportunity to speak and that the meeting is orderly and civil. **Governance groups** such as provincial legislatures, city and county councils, and governing boards of public agencies and educational institutions make policy decisions in public settings.

Virtual Groups In addition to face-to-face meetings with others, technology has made it possible to work in virtual groups. A **virtual group** relies on tools such as email, audioconferencing, videoconferencing, and Web conferencing to communicate across time, distance, and organizational boundaries. Unfortunately, when some members participate in virtual groups, they mistakenly believe it will be easier than meeting face-to-face. As a result, they underestimate the time needed to prepare, coordinate, and collaborate.[15] Members may also think they can "hide" during remote conferences. Although you may not be in the same room or even on the same continent as the other members of a virtual group, you are just as personally responsible for being fully prepared to contribute to the group's work.

OnlineCollege.org published an article outlining 10 steps to online group success. The author, Melissa Venable, asked her students for suggestions to help other online teams in college; the students' responses are shown in the box below.[16]

iQoncept/Fotolia

Good teams are more than friendships.

Ten Student Suggestions for Virtual Groups in College[17]

1. Make sure everyone has a voice. It is important to ask and listen to each group members' concerns and ideas.
2. Meet online in chat rooms, Facebook, and Google groups often and divide the work to be done early in the process.
3. Assign individual group roles and responsibilities. (See section 10.5 in this chapter.)
4. Choose helpful online tools to make meeting and sharing of ideas easier. Examples include Google drive, Skype or Facetime, and wikis.
5. Let everyone know when there is a problem.
6. Be proactive, show initiative, and communicate often and clearly.
7. Virtual groups need leaders too. (See section 10.5 in this chapter.)
8. Plan a schedule of meetings, dates, and times, and due dates for work to be completed.
9. Pool your resources and work with group members' strengths and skills.
10. Be flexible and remember to be reasonable with expectations.

10.2
Balancing Individual and Group Goals

How can you balance individual and group needs in groups?

As groups form and develop, effective members learn how to balance individual and group goals. In the best of groups, your personal goals support the group's common goal. This balancing act, however, requires an understanding of two potential roadblocks to success: primary tension and hidden agendas.

Primary Tension

Group communication scholar Ernest G. Bormann describes **primary tension** as the social unease and inhibitions that accompany the getting-acquainted period in a new group.[18] Because most new group members want to create a good first impression, they tend to be overly polite with one another.

In most groups, primary tension decreases as members feel more comfortable with one another. But if a group is bogged down in primary tension, you can and should intervene by talking about it and discussing how to break the cycle. Urge members to stick to the group's agenda and express opinions about relevant issues. When your group meets, be positive, energetic, patient, open-minded, and well prepared.

Characteristics of PRIMARY TENSION

- Members rarely interrupt one another.
- Long, awkward pauses often come between comments.
- Members are soft-spoken and very polite.
- Members avoid expressing strong opinions and emotions.

Hidden Agendas

Many (if not most) of us have personal goals we want to achieve in a group. As long as our personal goals support the group's goal, all is well. A **hidden agenda**, however, occurs when a member's private goals conflict with the group's goals. Hidden agendas represent what people *really* want rather than what they *say* they want. When hidden agendas become more important than a group's public agenda or goal, the result can be group frustration, unresolved conflicts, and failure.

Even when a group recognizes the existence of hidden agendas, some of them cannot and should not be shared because they may create an atmosphere of distrust. For instance, not many people would want to deal with the following revelation during a group discussion: "The reason I don't want to be here is that I don't want to work with Kenneth, who is unreliable and incompetent."

Group Membership

Sometimes we get to choose the groups we wish to work with, and other times we are assigned groups. How we form groups when given the choice is very important to individual success as well as the group's success. Several scholars who have spent time studying group membership have identified three contributing factors that come into play when students or employees choose their own groups: homophily, competence, and familiarity.[19] **Homophily** is a preference to be with others who share your values, attitudes, and even personal characteristics. This preference is often carried forward to joining or forming groups either for academic or personal reasons.[20] Homophily can inspire feelings of trust and comfort, so it makes sense that many of us choose our groups through this lens. However, it is important to remember that academic groups are not solely about having only like-minded members or social experiences. Groups and teams form with a specific task or goal and will require a variety of skills and viewpoints if they are to achieve optimum success.[21] **Competence**, when considering group or team memberships, refers to the necessary skills, knowledge, and abilities to contribute to the group work and to achieve the goal of successful completion. Familiarity, while having aspects of homophily, also includes the known attributes of group members.[22] **Familiarity** reduces anxiety, and if the group work is successfully completed, members are more likely to re-form for subsequent projects at work or in school. Social interactions, group roles, and the "forming" stage of Tuckman's group development model (see p. 181) have already taken place, letting the group perhaps focus more quickly on the tasks of the assigned work.

> Dealing with hidden agendas means knowing that some of them can and should be confronted, whereas others cannot and should not be shared.

COMMUNICATION

Exercise

Choose one of the scenarios below and in pairs carefully consider each person's rights, ethical practice and homophily, competence, and familiarity when answering the following questions: Will this person make a good team member? Why? Why not? What other information is needed to make an appropriate decision?

1. Eric is dyslexic and uses the support services at the college to assist him with reading and writing. Students are asked to form into groups to conduct an experiment in the lab. Eric has lots of friends, but often finds that even his friends do not seem to want to choose him as a group member and he assumes that it is because he is dyslexic.

2. Jamaal is in the media and advertising program at college and is in a group that is jointly reviewing a film. He feels that some of the views of his group are racially prejudiced—but he is the only one to feel this way. He speaks up and insists that all views be included in the report.

3. In your accounting class, you are instructed to create groups of four to six to complete a semester-long project. There will be one group mark given, and Reesa approaches you assuming she will be working with you again in this class. The problem is that in your English class, your group received only a "C" grade, and the feedback is that the section of the group work for which Reesa was responsible was not satisfactory.

FACTS **THINK** ABOUT THEORY
TEST IDEA PLAN
EXPERIMENT
METHOD
KNOWLEDGE

Tuckman's Group Development Model

Most groups experience recognizable milestones. A "newborn" group behaves differently from an "adult" group that has worked together for a long time. In 1965, Bruce Tuckman, an educational psychologist, identified four discrete stages in the life cycle of groups: forming, storming, norming, and performing.[23] Since Tuckman introduced his **group development model**, more than 100 theoretical models have described how a group moves through several "passages" during its lifetime.[24] Tuckman's original four stages are, however, considered one of the most comprehensive models relevant to *all* types of groups.[25]

Stage 2: **STORMING**

During the **storming stage**, groups become more argumentative and emotional as they discuss important issues and vie for leadership. Some groups are tempted to suppress this stage in an effort to avoid conflict. However, conflict can help members develop relationships, decide who's in charge and who can be trusted, and clarify the group's common goal.

"Communication becomes more open and task oriented" as "members solidify positive working relationships with each other."[26]

Stage 4: **PERFORMING**

During the **performing stage**, members focus their energy on working harmoniously to achieve group goals. Roles and responsibilities change according to group needs. Decisions are reached, problems are solved, and ideas are implemented. When the performing stage is going well, members are highly energized, loyal to one another, and willing to accept every challenge that arises.

Tuckman's group development theory helps explain why and how groups and their members behave at different stages in their development. Understanding the natural development of a group can help explain, predict, and improve group productivity and member satisfaction.

Stage 1: **FORMING**

During the **forming stage**, group members may be more worried about themselves ("Will I be accepted and liked?") than about the group as a whole. Understandably, members are hesitant to express strong opinions or assert their personal needs during this phase until they know more about how other members think and feel about the task and about one another. Although little gets done during this stage, members need time to become acquainted with one another and define group goals.

Stage 3: **NORMING**

During the **norming stage**, members define roles and establish norms. The group begins to work harmoniously as a cohesive team and makes decisions about the best ways to achieve a common goal. At this point group members feel more comfortable with one another and are willing to disagree and express their opinions.

Like people, groups move through stages as they develop and mature.

Sociologists Rodney Napier and Matti Gershenfeld suggest that discussing hidden agendas during the early stages of group development can counteract their disruptive power.[27] Initial discussion could include some of the following questions:

• What are the group's goals?
• Do any members have any personal concerns or goals that differ from these?
• What outcomes do members expect?

Unrecognized and unresolved hidden agendas can permeate and infect *all* stages of group development.

Balancing Conflict and Cohesion

How can you balance conflict and cohesiveness in groups?

Conflict is valuable in groups because it forces us to analyse our opinions and decisions. As groups develop and begin discussing important issues, members may become more argumentative and emotional. Many groups are tempted to discourage or avoid conflict. When conflict is accepted as normal and beneficial, it helps establish a climate in which members feel free to disagree with one another.[28] At the same time, groups also benefit from **cohesion**—the mutual attraction that holds the members of a group together.

> Effective groups learn to balance conflict and cohesion as they interact to achieve a common goal.

Secondary Tension

When a group moves from the polite interactions of the forming stage to the storming stage, confident members begin to compete with one another. They openly disagree on substantive issues. It is still too early in the group's existence to predict the outcome of such competition. At this point, a different kind of tension may emerge. **Secondary tension** describes the frustrations and personality conflicts experienced by group members as they compete for social acceptance, status, and achievement.[29] Regardless of the causes, a group cannot hope to achieve its goals if secondary tension is not managed effectively.

If you sense that your group cannot resolve its secondary tension, it is time to intervene. One strategy is to joke about the tension. The resulting laughter can ease individual and group stress. Another option is to work outside the group setting to discuss any personal difficulties and anxieties with individual group members.

Ian Wedgewood/Pearson

Characteristics of SECONDARY TENSION

■ Energy and alertness levels are high.
■ The group is noisy and dynamic; members are loud and emphatic.
■ Several members may speak at the same time.
■ Members sit up, lean forward, and squirm in their seats.

Most groups experience some primary and secondary tension. A little bit of tension can motivate a group toward action and increase a group's sensitivity to feedback. As Donald Ellis and Aubrey Fisher point out, "The successful and socially healthy group is not characterized by an absence of social tension, but by successful management of social tension."[30]

Group Cohesion

Group cohesion can be expressed as "All for one and one for all!" Cohesive groups are united and committed to a common goal, have high levels of interaction, and enjoy a supportive communication climate. Their members also share a sense of teamwork and pride in the group, want to conform to group expectations, and are willing to use creative approaches to achieve the group's goals.[31]

Cohesive group members feel responsible for and take pride in their own work as well as the work of other members.

Cohesive groups are happier and get more done, and members use the terms *we* and *our* instead of *I* and *my*. Members of a cohesive group treat one another with respect, showing concern for members' personal needs, and appreciating the value of member diversity.

Cohesive groups create an encouraging climate that rewards quality contributions. Many groups use celebration dinners, letters of appreciation, certificates, and gifts to reward individual effort and initiative, although even a simple compliment

can make a group member feel appreciated. And, rather than take personal and individual credit for success, members of a cohesive group emphasize the group's accomplishments.

10.4
Balancing Conformity and Nonconformity
How can you balance conformity and nonconformity in groups?

During the norming stage of group development, members define their roles and determine how the group will do its work. Effective groups learn to balance a commitment to group practices, rules, and standards (conformity) with a willingness to differ and change (nonconformity).

Group Norms

Communication scholar Patricia Andrews defines **norms** as "sets of expectations held by group members concerning what kinds of behaviour or opinions are acceptable or unacceptable, good or bad, right or wrong, appropriate or inappropriate."[32] Group norms express the values of a group, help the group to function smoothly, define appropriate and inappropriate behaviour, and facilitate group success.[33] Norms are the group's rules of behaviour; they determine how members dress, speak, listen, and work. For example, one group may discourage interruptions, whereas another group may view interruptions and overlapping conversations as acceptable forms of interaction. Without norms, a group lacks agreed-on ways to organize and perform a task.

Group norms can have positive or negative effects on member behaviour and group success. For example, if your group's norms place a premium on pleasant and peaceful discussions, members may be reluctant to voice disagreement or share bad news. If group norms permit members to arrive late and leave early, you

may not have enough members to do the job. Norms that don't support your group's goals can prevent the group from succeeding. When this is the case, you are perfectly within your rights (in fact, it may be your duty) to engage in nonconforming behaviour. **Constructive nonconformity** occurs when a member resists a norm while still working to promote the group goal.

> "I know we always have our annual retreat at a golf resort, but many of our new staff members

Group norms function only to the extent that members conform to them.

don't play golf and may feel out of place or bored."

There are times when constructive nonconformity is needed and valued. Movies, television shows, and books champion the holdout juror,

Peter Mccabe/Canadian Press Images

How does this parade of Royal Military College of Canada graduates demonstrate the importance and value of group norms?

balancing conformity and nonconformity

183

the stubbornly honest politician, and the principled but disobedient soldier or crew member. Sometimes there is so much pressure for group members to conform that they need a nonconformist to shake up the process, to provide critical feedback, and to create doubt about what had been a group-sanctioned but poor decision. Nonconformity can serve a group well if it prevents members from ignoring important information or making poor decisions.

Constructive nonconformity contributes to effective group decisions and more creative solutions because it allows members to voice serious and well-justified objections without fear of personal criticism or exclusion for taking a different position. In contrast, **destructive nonconformity** occurs when a member resists conformity without regard for the best interests of the group and its goal, such as by showing up late to attract attention or interrupting others to exert power.

When members do not conform to norms, a group may have to discuss the value of a particular norm and then

Effective groups appreciate constructive nonconformity.

billdayone/Shutterstock

choose to change, clarify, or continue to accept it. At the very least, nonconforming behaviour helps members recognize and understand the norms of the group. For instance, if a member is confronted for leaving early, other members learn it is not acceptable to leave before a meeting is adjourned.

STOP&THINK

Can You Name Your Norms?

The left-hand column in the following table describes several types of group norms. In the middle column, list the related group norms in your classroom. In the right column, list the related group norms in a current or former workplace. Examine all these norms with a critical eye. Do they help the group achieve its common goal? If not, are you willing to challenge these norms for the good of the group?

Types of Group Norms	Classroom	Workplace
Verbal (e.g., formal, casual, jargon, profanity)		
Nonverbal (e.g., formal or informal attire, seating arrangements, activity level, appropriate touching, eye contact)		
Interactional (e.g., use of first or last names, nicknames, speaking turns, listening behaviour, unruly behaviour)		
Content (e.g., discussions are: serious, work-related, social, intimate, humorous)		
Status (e.g., who makes decisions, who has influence, is disagreement allowed)		
Rewards (e.g., how success is determined, how achievement is rewarded)		

10.5
Balancing Task and Maintenance Roles

How can you balance task and maintenance roles in groups?

Group members assume different roles depending on the nature of the group, its membership, and its goal. A **group role** is a pattern of behaviours associated with an expected function within a particular group context. For example, when someone asks, "Who will get the information we need for our next meeting?" all eyes turn to Zhu because researching and sharing information are tasks he performs well. If a disagreement between two group members becomes heated, the group may look to Alicia for help because she has a talent for resolving conflicts and mediating differences.

Every group member brings unique talents, preferences, and perspectives to a group.

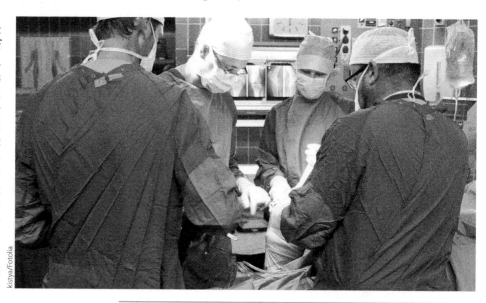

kistya/Fotolia

What task roles are critical to the success of a surgical team? Is there an appropriate place for maintenance roles in this group?

GROUP **TASK** ROLES[34]

ROLE	DESCRIPTION	EXAMPLE
INITIATOR/ CONTRIBUTOR	Proposes ideas; provides direction; gets the group started	"Let's begin by considering the client's point of view."
INFORMATION SEEKER	Asks for relevant information; requests explanations; points out information gaps	"How can we decide on a policy without knowing more about the cost and the legal requirements?"
INFORMATION GIVER	Researches, organizes, and presents relevant information	"I checked with human resources and they said . . ."
OPINION SEEKER	Asks for opinions; tests for agreement and disagreement	"Lyle, what do you think? Will it work?"
OPINION GIVER	States personal belief; shares feelings; offers analysis and arguments	"I don't agree that he's guilty. He may be annoying, but that doesn't constitute harassment."
CLARIFIER/ SUMMARIZER	Explains ideas and their consequences; reduces confusion; summarizes	"We've been trying to analyse this problem for two hours. Here's what I think we've agreed on."
EVALUATOR/ CRITIC	Assesses the value of ideas and arguments; diagnoses problems	"These figures don't consider monthly operating costs."
ENERGIZER	Motivates members; creates enthusiasm, and, if needed, a sense of urgency	"This is incredible! We've come up with a unique and workable solution to the problem."
PROCEDURAL TECHNICIAN	Helps prepare meetings; makes room arrangements; provides materials and equipment	"Before our next meeting, let me know if you will need a flip chart again."
RECORDER/ SECRETARY	Keeps accurate written records of group recommendations and decisions	"Maggie, please repeat the two deadline dates so I can get them into the minutes."

balancing task and maintenance roles

Group Task and Maintenance Roles

Group member roles are divided into two functional categories: task roles and maintenance roles. Group **task roles** focus on behaviours that help manage the task and complete the job. When members assume task roles, they provide useful information, ask important questions, analyze problems, and help the group stay organized. Group **maintenance roles** affect whether group members get along with one another while pursuing a common goal. Members who assume maintenance roles help to create a supportive and inclusive communication climate, resolve conflicts, and encourage members or acknowledge good work.

In addition to assuming roles on your own, ask the group to determine whether important roles are missing. For example, if members are becoming frustrated because one or two people are doing all the talking, you might suggest that someone serve as a gatekeeper. If the group has trouble tracking its progress, suggest that someone take on the role of recorder/secretary. In highly effective groups, all the task and maintenance roles are available to mobilize a group toward achieving its common goal.

Self-Centred Roles

Sometimes group members assume **self-centred roles** in which they put their own goals ahead of the group's goal and other member needs. Self-centred roles can disrupt the work of a group, adversely affect member relationships, and prevent the group from achieving its goals.

Three strategies can help you and your groups deal with self-centred members: accept, confront, or even exclude the troublesome member. Acceptance is not the same as approval. A group may allow disruptive behaviour

Common Self-Centred Roles: [36]

- **Aggressor.** Puts down other members, is sarcastic and critical, takes credit for someone else's work or ideas
- **Blocker.** Stands in the way of progress, presents uncompromising positions, uses delay tactics to derail an idea or proposal
- **Dominator.** Prevents others from participating, interrupts others, tries to manipulate others
- **Recognition Seeker.** Boasts about personal accomplishments, tries to be the centre of attention, pouts if not getting enough attention
- **Clown.** Injects inappropriate humour, seems more interested in goofing off than working, distracts the group from its task
- **Deserter.** Withdraws from the group, appears "above it all" and annoyed or bored with the discussion, stops contributing
- **Confessor.** Shares very personal feelings and problems, uses the group for emotional support in ways that inappropriately distract members from the group's task

GROUP **MAINTENANCE** ROLES [35]

ROLE	DESCRIPTION	EXAMPLE
ENCOURAGER/ SUPPORTER	Praises and encourages group members; listens empathically	"Thanks for taking all that time to find the information we needed."
HARMONIZER	Helps resolve conflicts; mediates differences; encourages teamwork and group harmony	"I know we're becoming edgy, but we're almost done. Let's focus on the task, not our frustrations."
COMPROMISER	Offers suggestions that minimize differences; helps the group reach consensus	"Maybe we can improve the old system rather than adopting a brand-new way of doing it."
TENSION RELEASER	Uses friendly humour to alleviate tensions, tempers, and stress	"Can Karen and I arm-wrestle to decide who gets the assignment?"
GATEKEEPER	Monitors and regulates the flow of communication; encourages productive participation	"I think we've heard from everyone except Michelle, who has strong feelings about this issue."
STANDARD MONITOR	Reminds group of norms and rules; tests ideas against group-established standards	"We all agreed we'd start at 10 A.M. Now we sit around waiting for latecomers until 10:30."
OBSERVER/ INTERPRETER	Monitors and interprets feelings and nonverbal communication; paraphrases member comments	"Maybe we're not really disagreeing. I think we're in agreement that ..."
FOLLOWER	Supports the group and its members; willingly accepts others' ideas and assignments	"That's fine with me. Just tell me when it's due."

to continue when it's not detrimental to the group's ultimate success or when the member's positive contributions far outweigh the inconvenience or annoyance of putting up with the negative behaviour. For example, a "clown" may be disruptive on occasion but may also be the group's best report writer or a valued harmonizer.

When it becomes impossible to accept or ignore self-centred behaviour, the group should take action. For instance, members can confront a member by making it clear that the group will progress despite that person's nonproductive behaviour. "Ron, I think we fully understand your strong objections, but ultimately this is a group decision." In a moment of extreme frustration, one member may say what everyone is thinking—"Lisa, please let me finish my sentence!" Although such an outburst may make everyone uncomfortable, it can put a stop to disruptive behaviour.

When all else fails, a group may ask disruptive members to leave the group and bar them from meetings; this is a humiliating experience that all but the most stubborn members would prefer to avoid.

Know Thy SELF

Do You Disrupt Group Work?

Disruptive group behaviour comes in all varieties. Do any of the following types describe the way you communicate in groups?[37] For each item, indicate how frequently you behave like the description: (1) usually, (2) often, (3) sometimes, (4) rarely, or (5) never.

—— **1.** *The Put-Downer.* Do you assume that members are wrong until they're proven right? Do you make negative remarks such as "That will never work," "Been there, done it, forget it," or "I don't like it" before the group has had time to discuss the issue in detail?

—— **2.** *The Interrupter.* Do you start talking before others are finished? Do you interrupt because you're impatient or annoyed?

—— **3.** *The Nonverbal Negative Naysayer.* Do you disagree nonverbally in a dramatic or disruptive manner? Do you frown or scowl, shake your head, roll your eyes, squirm in your seat, audibly sigh or groan, or madly scribble notes after someone has said something?

—— **4.** *The Laggard.* Are you late to meetings? Do you ask or demand to be told what happened before you arrived? Are you usually late in completing assigned tasks?

—— **5.** *The Chronic Talkaholic.* Talkaholics are compulsive communicators who have great difficulty (and often little desire for) being quiet in groups. Chronic talkaholics talk so much that they disrupt the group and annoy or anger other members. Do you ever talk when you know it would be much smarter to keep quiet? Do other group members often tell you that you talk too much?[37]

Jupiterimages/Photos.com/Getty Images/Thinkstock

10.6

Developing Group Leadership

What are the characteristics of a successful group leader?

If you enter the word *leadership* into any major online bookseller's search engine, you will find thousands of books. And if you review these offerings, you'll see that highly respected scholars and well-regarded business leaders write most of them. Some unusual titles demonstrate the range of leadership books. Here are just a few:

Popular Trade Books on Leadership

- *Leadership Secrets of Hillary Clinton*
- *Made in Canada Leadership*
- *Me to We, Marc and Craig Kielburger*

- *Jesus on Leadership*
- *Leadership Secrets of Attila the Hun*
- *The Leadership Secrets of Santa Claus*

Before you chuckle too much over *The Leadership Secrets of Santa Claus*, consider how you could translate some of his "secrets" into useful leadership tips: choose your reindeer wisely, make a list and check it twice, listen to the elves, find out who's naughty and nice, and be good for goodness' sake.[38]

Leadership is the ability to make strategic decisions and use communication to mobilize group members toward achieving a common goal.

Even though just about everyone recognizes the importance of leadership, it is not always easy to practise effectively. One review of leadership studies estimates that leadership incompetence is "as high as 60 to 75 percent—and that our hiring practices are so flawed that more than 50 percent of leaders hired by organizations are doomed to fail."[39]

In his book on leadership, Antony Bell describes communication as the mortar or glue that connects all leadership competencies. The abilities to think and act while remaining self-aware and self-disciplined are critical building blocks to leadership competency, but it takes communication to bind these blocks together.[40]

Three Approaches to Leadership

Leadership is a quality that defies precise measurement. However, three theories can help you understand your own and others' approaches to leadership: trait theory, styles theory, and situational theory.

Trait Theory Based on the belief that leaders are born, not made, the **trait theory of leadership** identifies specific characteristics associated with leadership. Most of us can come up with a list of desirable leadership traits: intelligence, confidence, enthusiasm, organizational talent, and good listening skills. The weakness of trait theory is that it doesn't account for the fact that many effective leaders possess only a few of these traits. Just because you have most of these traits does not mean that you will be a great leader. At the same time, great leaders have emerged who have very few of these traits. For example, Harriet Tubman, an illiterate slave, did little talking but led hundreds of people from bondage in the American South to freedom in the North.

Styles Theory The **styles theory of leadership** examines a collection of specific behaviours that constitute three distinct leadership styles: autocratic, democratic, and laissez-faire. **Autocratic leaders** try to control the direction and outcome of a discussion, make many of the group's decisions, give orders, expect followers to obey orders, focus on achieving the group's task, and take credit for successful results. An autocratic style is often appropriate during a serious crisis when there may not be time to discuss issues or consider the wishes of all members. In an emergency, the group may want its leader to take total responsibility. However, too much control can lower group morale and sacrifice long-term productivity.

A **democratic leader** promotes the social equality and task interests of group members. This type of leader shares decision making with the group, helps the group plan a course of action, focuses on the group's morale as well as on the task, and gives the entire group credit for success. In groups with democratic leadership, members are often more satisfied with the group experience, more loyal to the leader, and more productive in the long run.

Laissez-faire is a French phrase that means, "to let people do as they choose." A **laissez-faire leader** lets the group take charge of all decisions and actions. Such a leader may be a perfect match for mature and highly productive groups because a laid-back leadership style can generate a climate in which communication is encouraged and rewarded. Unfortunately, some laissez-faire leaders do little or nothing to help a group when it needs decisive leadership.

Situational Leadership Theory Rather than describing traits or styles, **situational leadership theory** seeks an ideal fit between leaders and leadership roles.[41] The situational approach explains how leaders can become more effective by analyzing themselves, their group, and the context.

Situational theory identifies two leadership styles: task motivated and relationship motivated. **Task-motivated leaders** want to get the job done. They gain satisfaction from completing a task even if it results in bad feelings between the leader and group members. As a result, task-motivated leaders are often criticized for being too focused on the job and overlooking group morale. **Relationship-motivated leaders** gain satisfaction from working well with other people even if the cost is failing to complete a task. Not surprisingly, they are sometimes criticized for paying too much attention to how members feel and for tolerating disruptive behaviour.

> **Without leadership,** a group may be nothing more than a collection of individuals lacking the coordination and will to achieve a goal.

maigi/Fotolia

Three Theoretical
APPROACHES to Leadership

1 TRAIT THEORY ▶ You Have It or You Don't

2 STYLES THEORY ▶ Are Democracies Always Best?

3 SITUATIONAL THEORY ▶ Matching Leaders and Jobs

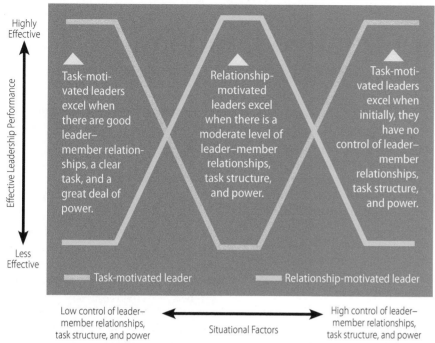

Relationship between leadership style and situational factors

Highly Effective

Effective Leadership Performance

Task-motivated leaders excel when there are good leader–member relationships, a clear task, and a great deal of power.

Relationship-motivated leaders excel when there is a moderate level of leader–member relationships, task structure, and power.

Task-motivated leaders excel when initially, they have no control of leader–member relationships, task structure, and power.

Less Effective

━━ Task-motivated leader   ━━ Relationship-motivated leader

Low control of leader–member relationships, task structure, and power

Situational Factors

High control of leader–member relationships, task structure, and power

structure can range from disorganized and chaotic to highly organized and rule driven. Are the goals and task clear? The third situational factor is the amount of power and control the leader possesses.

The figure to the left shows that task-motivated leaders perform best in extremes, such as when the situation requires high levels of leader control or when it is almost out of control. They excel when there are good or poor leader–member relationships, a clear or unclear task, and a great deal of or no power. Relationship-motivated leaders do well when in the middle ground where there is a mix of conditions, such as a semi-structured task or a group of interested but not eager followers.

Situational theory requires you to match your leadership style to the situation in terms of three important dimensions: leader–member relations, task structure, and power. **Leader–member relations** can be positive, neutral, or negative. Are group members friendly and loyal to the leader and the rest of the group? Are they cooperative and supportive? **Task**

COMMUNICATION

Exercise

Watch this YouTube video about leadership.

www.youtube.com/watch?v=_8YYbYAXcXk

In small groups, discuss the similarities between diversity of leadership and choosing group members to work on projects.

COMMUNICATION IN *ACTION*

How to Become a Leader

The path to a leadership position can be as easy as being in the right place at the right time or being the only person willing to take on a difficult job.[42] Although there is no foolproof method, there are ways to improve your chances of becoming a group's leader.

- *Talk early and often (and listen).* The person who speaks first and most often is more likely to emerge as the group's leader.[43] How frequently you talk is even more important than what you say. The quality of your contributions becomes more significant *after* you become a leader.

- *Know more (and share it).* Leaders often are seen as experts. A potential leader can often explain ideas and information more clearly than other group members, and therefore be perceived as knowing more. While groups need well-informed leaders, they do not need know-it-alls who see their own comments as most important; effective leaders value everyone's contributions.

- *Offer your opinion (and welcome disagreement).* Groups appreciate someone who offers valuable ideas and informed opinions. However, this is not the same as having your ideas accepted without question. If you are unwilling to compromise or listen to alternatives, the group may be unwilling to follow you. Effective leaders welcome constructive disagreement and discourage hostile confrontations.

The strategies for becoming a leader are *not* necessarily the same strategies for successful leadership.

After you become a leader, you may find it necessary to listen more than talk, welcome and reward better-informed members, and strongly criticize the opinions of others. Your focus should shift from *becoming* the leader to *serving* the group you lead.

developing group leadership

10.7

The 5-M Model of Effective Leadership

Which communication strategies and skills characterize effective leadership?

The **5-M Model of Effective Leadership**[©44] is an integrated model of leadership effectiveness that emphasizes specific communication strategies and skills and identifies five interdependent leadership functions: modelling, motivating, managing, making decisions, and mentoring.

Model Leadership Behaviour

Model leaders project an image of confidence, competence, and trustworthiness. Model leaders publicly champion the group and its goals rather than their personal accomplishments and ego needs. They speak and listen effectively, behave consistently and assertively, confront problems head-on, and work to find solutions.

Motivate Members

Motivating others is a critical task for leaders. Effective leaders guide, develop, support, defend, and inspire group members. They develop relationships that meet the personal needs and expectations of followers. Motivational strategies include supporting and rewarding deserving members, helping members solve interpersonal problems, and adapting tasks and assignments to member abilities and expectations. Most important of all, motivating leaders give members the authority to make judgments about doing the group's work.

Mike Krzyzewski (Coach K), the highly successful men's basketball coach at Duke University, believes that motivating team members is the key to his success. "As a coach, leader, and teacher, my primary task is motivation. How do I get a group motivated, not only to be their individual best but also to become better as a team?"[45]

Manage Group Processes

From the perspective of group survival, managing group processes may be the most important function of leadership.[46] If a group is disorganized, lacks sufficient information to solve problems, or is unable to make important decisions when necessary, the group cannot be effective. Effective leaders are well organized and fully prepared for all group meetings and work sessions. They adapt to member strengths and weaknesses and help solve task-related and procedural problems. They also know when to monitor and intervene to improve group performance.

Make Decisions

An effective leader is willing and able to make appropriate, timely, and responsible decisions. When you assume or are appointed to a leadership role, you should accept the fact that some of your decisions may be unpopular, and some may even turn out to be wrong. But you still have to make them. It's often better for a group leader to make a bad decision than no decision at all, "for if you are seen as chronically indecisive, people won't let you lead them."[47]

In "Building the 21st Century Leader," Carol Tice reviews the evolution of corporate leadership, claiming that today's leaders must be able to do *both*—collaborate with others *and* be decisive.[48]

Several strategies can help a leader make decisions that help a group achieve its goal. First, make sure everyone has and shares the information needed to make a quality decision. If appropriate, discuss your pending decision and solicit feedback from members. Listen to members' opinions, arguments, and suggestions *before* making a decision. When you make a decision, explain your reasons for doing so and communicate your decision to everyone.

Effective leaders intervene and tell members what to do when a group lacks the confidence, willingness, or ability to make decisions. However, when group members are confident, willing, and skilled, a leader can usually turn full responsibility over to the group and focus on helping members implement the group's decision.

Model leadership behaviour
Pope John Paul II

Motivate members
Jack Layton

Manage group processes
Information and Privacy Commissioner
Dr. Ann Cavoukian

Make decisions
Stephen Harper

Mentor members
Michaelle Jean

Darryl Dyck/THE CANADIAN PRESS

ZUMA Press, Inc/Alamy

Chris Wattie/Reuters

Sean Kilpatrick/THE CANADIAN PRESS

CHAPTER 10 | working in groups

Mentor Members

Good leaders are very busy people, particularly if they model leadership, motivate members, manage group process, and make decisions. Even so, great leaders find the time and energy to mentor others. They know that good mentoring does more than teach someone how to do a job—it also motivates that person to set high standards, seek advice when needed, and develop the skills characteristic of an excellent leader. In his book *Great Leadership*, Anthony Bell urges would-be leaders to find a mentor because a "good mentor will challenge you to ask (and answer) the tough questions."[49]

The following strategies can help a leader decide when and how to mentor group members:

1. *Be ready and willing to mentor every group member.* Although you cannot be a full-time mentor for everyone, you should be open to requests for advice. Eventually, you may develop a close relationship with a few mentees (the people being mentored) who share your vision.

2. *Encourage and invite others to lead.* Look for situations in which group members can assume leadership responsibilities. Ask them to chair a meeting, take full responsibility for a group project, or implement a group's decision. And make sure they know you're there as a resource.

3. *Inspire optimism.* When problems or setbacks occur, do not blame the group or its members. Instead, convert the situation into a teachable moment and help members to accept personal responsibility for a problem and its consequences.[50]

4. Effective mentors create appropriate balance and boundaries. They know when to intervene and when to back off. A mentor is neither a psychiatric counsellor nor a group member's best friend. At some point, even the best mentors must let their mentees succeed or fail on their own.

COMMUNICATION&CULTURE

DIVERSITY AND LEADERSHIP

In the early studies of leadership, there was an unwritten but additional prerequisite for becoming a leader: be a man. Despite the achievements of exceptional female leaders, some people still question the ability of women to serve in leadership positions.

A summary of the research on leadership and gender concludes that "women are still less likely to be preselected as leaders, and the same leadership behaviour is often evaluated more positively when attributed to a male than a female."[51]

Developing a leadership style is a challenge for most young managers but particularly for young women. If their behaviour is similar to that of male leaders, they are perceived as unfeminine, but if they act "like a lady," they are viewed as weak or ineffective. One professional woman described this dilemma as follows:

I was thrilled when my boss evaluated me as "articulate, hard-working, mature in her judgment, and a skilful diplomat." What disturbed me were some of the evaluation comments from those I supervise or work with as colleagues. Although they had a lot of good things to say, a few of them described me as "pushy," "brusque," "impatient," "disregards social niceties," and "hard driving." What am I supposed to do? My boss thinks I'm energetic and creative while other people see the same behaviour as pushy and aggressive.

Cultural differences also affect whether members become and succeed as leaders. For example, individualistic Western cultures (United States, Canada, Great Britain) assume that members are motivated by personal growth and achievement. However, a collectivist member might desire a close relationship with the leader and other group members rather than personal gain or growth. The same member may act out of loyalty to the leader and the group rather than for personal achievement or material gain.[52]

10.1
The Challenges of Working in Groups
What are the pros and cons of working in groups?

- Group communication refers to the interaction of three or more interdependent people working to achieve a common goal.
- In general, the advantages of working in groups far outweigh the disadvantages.
- Groups differ in terms of whether they are meeting personal goals, work goals, or public goals.
- Bruce Tuckman's Group Development stages include forming, storming, norming, and performing.

10.2
Balancing Individual and Group Goals
How can you balance individual and group needs in groups?

- During the forming stage of group development, most groups experience primary tension, the social unease and inhibitions that accompany the getting-acquainted period in a new group.
- Hidden agendas occur when a member's private goals conflict with the group's goals.

10.3
Balancing Conflict and Cohesion
How can you balance conflict and cohesiveness in groups?

- During the storming stage of group development, groups must resolve secondary tensions and personality conflicts in order to achieve cohesion.
- Cohesive groups share a sense of teamwork and pride.

10.4
Balancing Conformity and Nonconformity
How can you balance conformity and nonconformity in groups?

- Whereas constructive nonconformity is appropriate and helps a group achieve its goal, destructive nonconformity has no regard for the best interests of the group and its goal.

10.5
Balancing Task and Maintenance Roles
How can you balance task and maintenance roles in groups?

- Group task roles help a group achieve its goals. Group maintenance roles affect how group members get along.
- Self-centred roles adversely affect task and social goals.

10.6
Developing Group Leadership
What are the characteristics of a successful group leader?

- Leadership is the ability to make strategic decisions and use communication to mobilize group members toward achieving a common goal.

- The trait theory of leadership identifies individual leadership characteristics.
- The styles theory of leadership examines autocratic, democratic, and laissez-faire leadership.
- Situational leadership theory seeks an ideal fit between a leader's style and the leadership situation.

10.7
The 5-M Model of Effective Leadership©
Which communication strategies and skills characterize effective leadership?

- The 5-M Model of Effective Leadership identifies five critical leadership tasks: (1) model leadership behaviour, (2) motivate members, (3) manage group processes, (4) make decisions, and (5) mentor members.
- People become leaders by talking more, knowing more, and offering their opinions.
- Female and nonmajority group members are less likely to be preselected as leaders and are often evaluated less positively than are male leaders.

Gino Santa Maria/Fotolia

TEST YOUR KNOWLEDGE

10.1 What are the pros and cons of working in groups?

1 The ideal size for a problem-solving group is —— members.
   a. 2–4
   b. 3–5
   c. 5–7
   d. 7–12
   e. 12–15

2 Which of the following best describes a forum?
   a. Several people interact about a common topic in front of an audience.
   b. Group members present short, uninterrupted presentations on different aspects of a topic for the benefit of an audience.
   c. Audience members comment or ask questions to a speaker or group of speakers.
   d. Elected officials and governing boards of public agencies conduct their meetings in public.
   e. None of the above is an example of a forum.

10.2 How can you balance individual and group needs in groups?

3 Which is the correct order for Tuckman's group development stages?
   a. forming, storming, norming, performing
   b. storming, forming, performing, norming
   c. forming, norming, storming, performing
   d. norming, forming, performing, storming
   e. performing, norming, storming, forming

10.3 How can you balance conflict and cohesiveness in groups?

4 Which of the following is the best depiction of secondary tension in groups?
   a. The group resolves conflicts and establishes norms.
   b. The frustrations and conflicts experienced by group members as they compete for status, acceptance, and achievement.
   c. The social unease and inhibitions that accompany the getting-acquainted period in a new group.

   d. The social unease and inhibitions that accompany the process of competing for status, acceptance, and achievement in groups.
   e. The process during which group decisions are reached, problems are solved, and plans are implemented.

10.4 How can you balance conformity and nonconformity in groups?

5 Which answer best completes the following statement: Nonconformity ——
   a. will always undermine group performance.
   b. can improve group performance.
   c. occurs only when stubborn members are present.
   d. occurs under poor leadership.
   e. occurs only in the storming stage.

10.5 How can you balance task and maintenance roles in groups?

6 Which of the following represents a group task role?
   a. tension releaser
   b. compromiser
   c. gatekeeper
   d. encourager/supporter
   e. clarifier/summarizer

7 Which of the following represents a self-centred group role?
   a. evaluator/critic
   b. opinion giver
   c. gatekeeper
   d. confessor
   e. follower

10.6 What are the characteristics of a successful group leader?

8 Which leadership theory or model can be summarized as "either you have it or you don't"?
   a. trait theory
   b. styles theory
   c. situational theory
   d. The 5-M Model of Effective Leadership
   e. the styles and situational theories

9 According to situational leadership theory, which style of leadership is most appropriate when a leader has poor leader–member relations, a highly organized task, and little or no power or control?
   a. a laissez-faire leader
   b. a task-motivated leader
   c. a democratic leader
   d. a relationship-motivated leader
   e. an autocratic leader

10.7 Which communication strategies and skills characterize effective leadership?

10 Which of the following strategies is most likely to help you *become* a leader?
   a. Talk early.
   b. Talk often.
   c. Know more.
   d. Offer your opinion.
   e. all of the above

Answers found on page 330.

Key Terms

Autocratic leader	Group role	Self-centred role
Cohesion	Hidden agenda	Situational leadership
Committee	Homophily	theory
Competence	Laissez-faire leader	Storming stage
Constructive	Leader–member	Styles theory of
nonconformity	Relationships	leadership
Democratic leader	Leadership	Symposium
Destructive	Maintenance role	Task-motivated leader
nonconformity	Norming stage	Task role
5-M Model of Effective	Norms	Task structure
Leadership	Panel discussion	Trait theory of
Familiarity	Performing stage	leadership
Forming stage	Primary tension	Virtual group
Forum	Public group	Work group
Governance group	Relationship-motivated	Work team
Group Development	leader	
Model	Secondary tension	

Group DECISION MAKING, PROBLEM SOLVING, AND CONFLICT

The classic 1957 film *12 Angry Men* is a story about decision making and problem solving.[1] Twelve jurors (all male, mostly middle aged, white, and generally of middle-class status) must reach a verdict in a seemingly open-and-shut murder trial. The film examines how the jurors' deep-seated prejudices, flawed judgments, cultural differences, ignorance, and fears taint their decision-making abilities, cause them to ignore the real issues in the case, and potentially lead them to a miscarriage of justice. Fortunately, one brave dissenting juror votes "not guilty" because of his reasonable doubt. Persistently and persuasively, he compels the other men to slowly reconsider and review the shaky case.[2]

In all likelihood, you have been or will be called for jury duty. Like the characters in *12 Angry Men*, you will have to make a decision—guilty or not guilty, liable or not liable, severe or light sentence. The fairness of that decision will rely, in large part, on how well jury members communicate with one another and how well they employ critical thinking skills. Clearly, there is a world of difference between making any decision and making a good decision.[3]

United Artists/Album/Newscom

11.1

Prerequisites for Group Decision Making and Problem Solving

What prerequisites help groups make good decisions and solve problems?

You make hundreds of decisions every day. You decide when to get up in the morning, what to wear, when to leave for class or work, and with whom to spend your leisure time. Many factors influence how you make these decisions—your culture, age, family, education, social status, and religion, as well as your dreams, fears, beliefs, values, interpersonal needs, and personal preferences.[4] Now take five people, put them in a room, and ask them to make a *group* decision. As difficult as it can be to make personal decisions, the challenge is multiplied many times over in groups.

Fortunately and in large part because of the many differences among members, effective groups have the potential to make excellent decisions because more minds are at work on the problem. As we noted in Chapter 10, groups have the potential to accomplish more and perform better than individuals working alone. So, while the road may be paved with conflict and challenges, group decision-making and problem solving can be more satisfying, creative, and effective.

Although the terms *decision making* and *problem solving* are often used interchangeably, their meanings differ. **Decision making** refers to making a judgment, reaching a conclusion, or making up your mind. In a group setting, decision making results in a position, opinion, judgment, or action. For example, hiring committees, juries, and families decide which applicant is best, whether the accused is guilty, and whom they should invite to the wedding, respectively. Management expert Peter Drucker put it simply: "A decision is a judgment. It is a choice between alternatives."[5]

As difficult as it can be to make personal decisions, the challenge is multiplied many times over in groups.

Most groups make decisions, but not all groups solve problems. **Problem solving** is a complex *process* in which groups make *multiple* decisions as they analyze a problem and develop a plan for solving the problem or reducing its harmful effects. For instance, if student enrolment has significantly declined, a college faces a serious problem that must be analyzed and dealt with if the institution hopes to survive. Fortunately, decision-making and problem solving strategies can help a group "make up its mind" and resolve a problem.

Conflict is often associated with quarrelling, fighting, anger, and hostility. Although these elements can be present, conflict does not have to involve negative emotions, and may be helpful in the problem-solving and decision-making process.

However, before a group takes on such challenges, three prerequisites should be in place: a clear goal, quality content, and structured procedures.

A Clear Goal

The first and most important task for all groups is to make sure that everyone understands and supports the group's goal. One strategy to achieve this is to word the goal as a question. In Chapter

4, we discussed the importance of critical thinking and how identifying claims of fact, conjecture, value, and policy helps you decide whether you should accept, reject, or suspend judgment about an idea, belief, or proposal. Groups face the same challenge when framing a discussion question.

A group may ask four types of questions to achieve its goal. **Questions of fact** investigate the truth, reliability, and cause of something using the best information available. **Questions of conjecture** examine the possibility of something happening in the future using valid facts and expert opinions to reach the most probable conclusion. **Questions of value** consider the worth or significance of something, and **questions of policy** investigate a course of action for implementing a plan.

Group members understand that the answers to each type of question will shape the discussions that take place. For example, a work group may be asked to find timesaving ways to process an order or contact a customer. A research group may be asked to test the durability of a new product.

Quality Content

Well-informed groups are more likely to make good decisions. The amount and accuracy of information available to a group are critical factors in predicting its success.

The key to becoming a well-informed group lies in the ability of members to collect, share, and analyze the information needed to achieve the group's goal. When a group lacks relevant and valid information, effective decision making and problem solving become difficult, even impossible. During an initial meeting, a group should discuss how to become better informed.

QUESTION TYPES **TO ACHIEVE GROUP GOALS**

QUESTION OF FACT	QUESTION OF CONJECTURE	QUESTION OF VALUE	QUESTION OF POLICY
Are the charts ready for printing?	What topic do you think will be best for our group next semester?	Which is more important, adding the pictures or increasing the content of our presentation?	What should be done about work not completed in time?

COMMUNICATION IN *ACTION*

Can You Identify the Question Type?

Each of the following examples represents a question members might address while trying to make a group decision. Identify the type of question (fact, conjecture, value, or policy).

1. What causes global warming?
2. Are community colleges a better place than a prestigious university to begin higher education?
3. Will company sales increase next quarter?
4. Which candidate should we support for president of the student government association?

GROUP RESEARCH STRATEGIES

- Assess the group's current knowledge.
- Identify areas needing research.
- Assign research responsibilities.
- Set research deadlines.
- Determine how to share information effectively.

"Tribe" members on *Survivor* solve conflict and make strategic group decisions in order to win a team "challenge."

Structured Procedures

Groups need clear procedures that specify how they will make decisions and solve problems. Group communication scholar Marshall Scott Poole claims that structured procedures are "the heart of group work [and] the most powerful tools we have to improve the conduct of meetings."[6]

There are, however, many different kinds of procedures, including complex, theory-based problem-solving models designed to tackle the overall problem as well as decision-making methods designed for interim tasks such as idea generation and solution implementation. The next few sections of this chapter describe how various procedures can and should be used to improve group decision making and problem solving.

11.2

Effective Group Decision Making

What are the advantages and disadvantages of various decision-making methods?

All groups make decisions. Some decisions are simple and easy; others are complex and consequential. Regardless of the issue, effective groups look for the best way to reach a decision, one that considers the group's common goal and the characteristics and preferences of its members.

Decision-Making Methods

Although there are many ways to make decisions, certain methods work best for groups. Groups can let the majority have its way by voting, strive to reach consensus, or leave the final decision to a person in a position of authority. Each approach has its strengths, and

an appropriate approach should be selected to match the needs and purpose of the group and its task.

Voting When a quick decision is needed, there is nothing more efficient and decisive than voting. Sometimes, though, voting may not be the best way to make important decisions.

FACTS **THINK** ABOUT THEORY

Groupthink

In his book *Group Genius,* Keith Sawyer retells a story about a group of 12 heavy smokers who signed up for a stop-smoking group at a local health clinic. One heavy smoker revealed that he had stopped smoking right after joining the group. His comment infuriated the other 11 members. They ganged up on him so fiercely that at the beginning of the next meeting, he announced that he'd gone back to smoking two packs a day. The entire group cheered. "Keep in mind," writes Sawyer, "that the whole point of the group was to reduce smoking!"[7]

What happened in the stop-smoking group is not unusual. Although conforming to group norms and promoting group cohesiveness benefit groups in many ways, too much of either is a bad thing. They can result in a phenomenon that Yale University psychologist Irving Janis identified as **groupthink**—the deterioration of group effectiveness as a consequence of in-group pressure.[8] It is "a mode of thinking that people engage in when they are deeply involved in a cohesive in-group, when the members' striving for unanimity overrides their motivation to realistically appraise alternative courses of action."[9]

> Groupthink stifles the free flow of information, suppresses constructive disagreement, and erects nearly impenetrable barriers to effective decision making and problem solving.

Janis's groupthink theory focuses on patterns of behaviour in policy-making fiascos, such as decision errors during the Korean and Vietnam wars, the tragic *Challenger* space shuttle disaster, and the decision to invade Iraq in 2003, to name a few.

Groupthink tends to occur when one or more of three preconditions or causes are present in a group:

- The group is highly cohesive. Members overestimate their competence and perceptions of rightness. In order to maintain cohesiveness, the group may discourage disagreement in order to achieve total consensus.

- Structural flaws in the group process can "inhibit the flow of information and promote carelessness in the application of decision-making procedures."[10] For example, a leader or member may have too much influence, or the group's procedures may limit access to outside or contrary information.

- The situation is volatile. When a group must make a high-stakes decision, stress levels are high. Members may rush to make a decision that turns out to be flawed, and they may shut out other reasonable options.

Fortunately, there are ways to minimize the potential for groupthink. Every member should assume the role of critical evaluator and should ask questions, offer reasons for their positions, express disagreement, and evaluate one another's ideas.

Consider inviting an expert to your meeting and encourage constructive criticism. If nothing else, the group should discuss the potential negative consequences of any decision or action. Finally, before finalizing a decision, give members a second chance to express any lingering doubts.

Effective groups avoid groupthink by spending time and energy working through differences without sacrificing group cohesiveness in pursuit of responsible decisions. As an added and positive consequence, taking such "steps to minimize groupthink can turn a dysfunctional group into a highly competent one."[11]

How Can Groupthink Show Up in Groups?

- Group discounts others and makes excuses for their ideas/actions
- Group is overconfident in their position
- Group may ignore ethical and moral consequences
- Group believes that outsiders are not smart enough to affect them
- Group members are pressured to agree to positions and ideas
- Group members actually believe that everyone in the group agrees on ideas or positions
- Group members filter information containing opposing views

COMMUNICATION

Exercise

For a humorous example of groupthink, watch this YouTube video.

www.youtube.com/watch?v=TS7P-eo-COo

VOTING WORKS BEST WHEN . . .

- a group is pressed for time.
- the issue is not highly controversial.
- a group is too large to use any other decision-making method.
- there is no other way to break a deadlock.
- a group's constitution or rules require voting to make decisions.

When a group votes, some win, but others lose.

A **majority vote** requires that more than half the members vote in favor of a proposal. However, if a group is making a major decision, there may not be enough support if only 51 percent of the members vote in favor of

the project because the 49 percent who lose may resent working on a project they dislike. To avoid such problems, some groups opt for a two-thirds vote rather than majority rule. In a **two-thirds vote**, at least twice as many group members vote for a proposal as against it.

When a group votes, some members win, but others lose.

Consensus Because voting has built-in disadvantages, many groups rely on consensus to make decisions. **Consensus** is reached when "all members have a part in shaping and that all find at least minimally acceptable as a means of accomplishing some mutual goals."[12] Consensus does not work for all

groups. Imagine how difficult it would be to achieve genuine consensus among pro-life and pro-choice or pro–gun control and anti–gun control group members. If your group seeks consensus when making decisions, follow the guidelines below.

Before choosing consensus as a decision-making method, make sure that group members trust one another and expect honesty, directness, and candour. Avoid rushing to achieve consensus—make sure that everyone's opinion is heard. Finally, be cautious of a dominant leader or member who may make true consensus impossible. Sociologists Rodney Napier and Matti Gershenfeld put it this way: "A group that wants to use a consensual approach to decision making must be willing to develop the skills and discipline to take the time necessary to make it work. Without these, the group becomes highly vulnerable to domination or intimidation by a few and to psychological game playing by individuals unwilling to 'let go.'"[13]

Authority Rule Sometimes a single person or someone outside the group makes the final decision. When **authority rule** is used, groups may be asked to gather information for and recommend decisions to another person or larger group. For example, an association's nominating committee considers potential candidates and recommends a slate of officers to the association. Or a hiring committee screens dozens of job applicants and submits a top-three list to the person or persons making the hiring decision.

If a leader or outside authority ignores or reverses group recommendations, members may become demoralized, resentful, and unproductive on future assignments. Even within a group, a strong leader or authority figure may use a group and its members to give the appearance of collaborative decision making. The group becomes a "rubber stamp" and surrenders its will to authority rule. Group scholars Randy Hirokawa and Roger Pace warn that "influential members [can] convince the group to accept invalid facts and assumptions, introduce poor ideas and suggestions, lead the group to misinterpret information presented to them, or lead the

Guidelines for ACHIEVING GROUP CONSENSUS

DO THIS:

- Listen carefully to and respect other members' points of view.
- Try to be logical rather than emotional.
- If there is a deadlock, work to find the next best alternative that is acceptable to all.
- Make sure that members not only agree but also will be committed to the final decision.
- Get everyone involved in the discussion.
- Welcome all opinions.

DON'T DO THIS:

- Don't be stubborn and argue only for your own position.
- Don't change your mind just to avoid conflict or reach a quick decision.
- Don't give in, especially if you have a crucial piece of information to share.
- Don't agree to a decision or solution you can't possibly support.
- Don't use "easy" or arbitrary ways to reach a solution such as flipping a coin, letting the majority rule, or trading one decision for another.

Is There Consensus About Consensus?

Many believe a group *must* reach consensus on *all* decisions. The problem of false consensus is possible in every decision-making group. **False consensus** occurs when members reluctantly give in to group pressures (like groupthink) or an external authority. Rather than achieving consensus, the group agrees to a decision masquerading as consensus.[14]

In addition, the all-or-nothing approach to consensus "gives each member veto power over the progress of the whole group." In order to avoid impasse, members may "give up and give in" or seek a flawed compromise. This is much like the "illusion of unanimity" symptom of groupthink; members work hard to achieve total agreement even though the outcome may be a flawed decision. When this

happens, the group will fall short of success as "it mindlessly pursues 100% agreement."[15]

In *The Discipline of Teams*, John Katzenbach and Douglas Smith observe that members who pursue complete consensus often act as though disagreement and conflict are bad for the group. Nothing, they claim, could be further from the reality of effective group performance. "Without disagreement, teams rarely generate the best, most creative solutions to the challenges at hand. They compromise . . . rather than developing a solution that incorporates the best of two or more opposing views. . . . The challenge for teams is to learn from disagreement and find energy in constructive conflict, not get ruined by it."[16]

The limited time and format of the television show *Top Chef Masters* requires judges to reach consensus— even if it's false consensus.

One powerful but misguided member can be responsible for the poor quality of a group's decision.

group off on tangents and irrelevant discussion."[17]

Decision-Making Styles

The Myer-Briggs Type Indicator scales describe two traits—thinking and feeling—that focus on how we make decisions. Thinkers are task-oriented members who prefer to use logic in making decisions. Feelers, on the other hand, are people-oriented members who want everyone to get along, even if it means spending more time on a task or giving in to some members to avoid interpersonal problems. Each type of decision making impacts a group's choice of decision-making methods and their outcomes.

In "Decision Making Style: The Development of a New Measure," Suzanne Scott and Reginald Bruce describe five decision-making styles, each of which has the potential to improve or impair member interaction and group outcomes.[18]

Rational decision makers carefully weigh information and options before making a decision. They claim, "I've carefully considered all the issues," and make decisions systematically using logical reasoning to justify their final

ETHICAL COMMUNICATION

Ethical Group Decision Making

Regardless of how contentious the discussion or controversial an issue, group members should always apply ethical standards to decision making.[19]

1. **Research.** Group members are well informed and use what they know honestly.
   - Do not distort, suppress, or make up information.
   - Reveal the sources of information so others can evaluate them.

2. **Common Good.** Ethical group members are committed to achieving the group goal rather than winning a personal argument.
   - Consider the interests of those affected by group decisions.
   - Promote the group's goal ahead of personal goals.

3. **Reasoning.** Ethical group members avoid presenting faulty arguments; they build valid arguments and recognize fallacies.
   - Do not misrepresent the views of others.
   - Use sound critical thinking supported by evidence.
   - Avoid making fallacious arguments.

4. **The Social Code.** Group members promote an open, supportive, and group centred climate for discussion.
   - Treat other group members as equals.
   - Do not insult or attack the character of group members.
   - Respect established group norms.

Isabella Vosmikova/Bravo/NBCU Photo Bank/Getty Images

decisions. This type of person must be careful not to analyze a problem for so long that she or he never makes a decision. **Intuitive decision makers**, on the other hand, make decisions based on instincts, feelings, or hunches. They tend to say, "It just feels like the right thing to do." They may not always be able to explain the reasons for their decisions but know that their decisions "feel" right.

Dependent decision makers solicit the advice and opinions of others before making a decision: "If you think it's okay, then I'll do it." They feel uncomfortable making decisions that others disapprove of or oppose. They may even make a decision they aren't happy with just to please others. **Avoidant decision makers** feel uncomfortable making decisions. As a result, they may not think about a problem at all or will make a final decision at the very last minute: "I just can't deal with this right now." **Spontaneous decision makers** tend to be impulsive and make quick decisions on the spur of the moment: "Let's do it now and worry about the consequences later." As a result, they often make decisions they later regret.

Now consider what would happen if you had a group where half the members were rational decision makers and the other half were intuitive decision makers. Or what would happen if the group included *only* dependent or avoidant decision makers? Different decision-making styles can disrupt a group, but having only one type also has its pitfalls. The key is learning to recognize and adapt to different decision-making styles while pursuing a common goal.

Know Thy SELF

What Is Your Decision-Making Style?[20]

Indicate the degree to which you agree or disagree with each of the statements below by circling the appropriate number: (1) strongly disagree, (2) disagree, (3) undecided (neither agree nor disagree), (4) agree, or (5) strongly agree. There are no right or wrong answers; answer as honestly as you can. Think carefully before choosing option 3 (undecided)—it may suggest you cannot make decisions.

1. When I have to make an important decision, I usually seek the opinions of others.	1	2	3	4	5
2. I tend to put off decisions on issues that make me uncomfortable.	1	2	3	4	5
3. I make decisions in a logical and systematic way.	1	2	3	4	5
4. When making a decision, I usually trust feelings or gut instincts.	1	2	3	4	5
5. When making a decision, I generally consider the advantages and disadvantages of many alternatives.	1	2	3	4	5
6. I often avoid making important decisions until I absolutely have to.	1	2	3	4	5
7. I often make impulsive decisions.	1	2	3	4	5
8. When making a decision, I rely on my instincts.	1	2	3	4	5
9. It is easier for me to make important decisions when I know others approve or support them.	1	2	3	4	5
10. I make decisions very quickly.	1	2	3	4	5

Scoring: To determine your score for each type of decision making, add the total of your responses to specific items as indicated below. Your higher scores identify your preferred decision-making styles.

Answers to items 3 and 5 = _____ (rational decision maker)
Answers to items 4 and 8 = _____ (intuitive decision maker)
Answers to items 1 and 9 = _____ (dependent decision maker)
Answers to items 2 and 6 = _____ (avoidant decision maker)
Answers to items 7 and 10 = _____ (spontaneous decision maker)

11.3
Resolving Interpersonal Conflict
What communication strategies and skills help resolve interpersonal conflicts?

All healthy relationships, no matter how important or well managed, involve interpersonal conflict. Conflict is often associated with quarrelling, fighting, anger, and hostility. Although these elements can be present, conflict does not have to involve negative emotions. We define **conflict** as the disagreement that occurs in relationships when differences are expressed.

Many people avoid conflict because they do not understand the differences between destructive and constructive conflict. **Destructive conflict** is the result of behaviours that create hostility or prevent problem solving. Constant complaining, personal insults, conflict avoidance, and loud arguments or threats all contribute to destructive conflict.[21] This kind of conflict has the potential to permanently harm an individual or group relationship.

In contrast, **constructive conflict** occurs when you express disagreement in a way that respects others' perspectives and promotes problem solving. Kenneth Cloke and Joan Goldsmith of the Center for Dispute Resolution explain that all of us have a choice about how to deal with conflict. We can treat conflict as dialectic experiences "that imprison us or lead us on a journey, as a battle that embitters us or as an opportunity for learning. Our choices between these contrasting attitudes and approaches will shape the way the conflict unfolds."[22]

Conflict Styles

When you are involved in conflict, do you jump into the fray or run the other way? Do you marshal your forces and play to win, or do you work with everyone to find a mutually agreeable solution? Psychologists Kenneth Thomas and Ralph Kilmann claim that we use one or two of five conflict styles in most situations: avoidance, accommodation, competition, compromise, and collaboration.[23]

DESTRUCTIVE CONFLICT

- **Attacks others**
- **Insults others**
- **Defensive**
- **Inflexible**
- **Competitive**
- **Avoids or aggravates conflict**

CONSTRUCTIVE CONFLICT

- **Focuses on issues**
- **Respects others**
- **Supportive**
- **Flexible**
- **Cooperative**
- **Committed to conflict management**

Constructive and Destructive Conflict[22]

These five styles represent the extent to which you focus on achieving personal needs or mutual needs. People who are motivated to fulfill their own needs tend to choose more competitive approaches, whereas collaborative people are more concerned with achieving mutual goals. Figure 11.1 illustrates the relationship of each conflict style to an individual's motivation.[24]

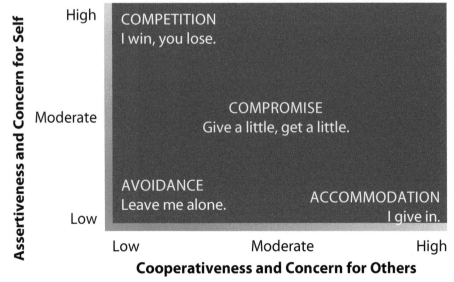

Figure 11.1 Conflict Styles

Constructive Conflict in Everyday Life

A couple passionately disagree, but are not hostile toward each other.

Friends disagree about something, but are not threatening or insulting one another.

Avoidance If you are unable or unwilling to stand up for your own needs or the needs of others, you may rely on the **avoidance conflict style**. People who use this style often change the subject, sidestep a controversial issue, or deny that a conflict exists. Avoiding conflict can be counterproductive because you fail to address a problem and can increase tension in a relationship.

Ignoring or avoiding conflict does not make it go away.

However, in some circumstances, avoiding conflict is an appropriate response. Consider avoiding conflict when the issue is not important to you, when you need time to collect your thoughts or control your emotions, when the consequences of confrontation are too risky, or when the chances of resolution are unlikely.

Accommodation Do you give in to others during a conflict at the expense of meeting your own needs? If so, you use the **accommodating conflict style**. You may believe that giving in to others preserves peace and harmony, but frequently dealing with conflict by accommodating others may make you less influential in personal or professional relationships.

On the other hand, when the issue is very important to the other person but not very important to you, an accommodating conflict style may be appropriate and effective. Accommodation is also appropriate when it is more important to preserve harmony in a relationship than to resolve a particular issue, when realize you are wrong, or if you have changed your mind.

Competition If you are more concerned with fulfilling your own needs than with meeting the needs of others, you are using a **competitive conflict style**. Quite simply, you want to win because you believe that your ideas are better than anyone else's. When used inappropriately, the competitive style may result in hostility, ridicule, and personal attacks against others. Approaching conflict competitively tends to reduce people to winners or losers.

In certain situations, however, the competitive approach may be the most appropriate style. Approach conflict competitively when you have strong beliefs about an important issue or when immediate action is needed in an urgent situation. The competitive approach is particularly appropriate when the consequences of a bad decision may be harmful, unethical, or illegal.

Compromise The **compromising conflict style** is a "middle-ground" approach that involves conceding some goals to achieve others. Many people believe that compromise is an effective and fair method of resolving problems because, in theory, everyone loses and wins equally. However, if you are dissatisfied with the outcome or believe it is unfair, you may not do much to implement the solution or course of action.

The compromise approach should be used when you are unable to reach a unanimous decision or resolve a problem. Consider compromising when other methods of conflict resolution are not effective, when you have reached an impasse, or if there is not enough time to explore more creative options.

Collaboration The **collaborative conflict style** searches for new solutions that will achieve both your goals and the goals of others. Also referred to as a *problem-solving* or *win-win approach*, the collaborative conflict style permits debate about ideas and allows the parties to collaborate for creative solutions that are satisfactory to everyone.

There are two potential drawbacks to the collaborative approach. First, collaboration requires a lot of time and energy, and some issues may not be important enough to justify the extra time and effort. Second, in order for collaboration to be successful, everyone—even the avoiders and accommodators—must fully participate in the process. Collaboration works best when both parties welcome new and creative ideas and are committed to the resulting decision.

Exercise

Identify the conflict style in the following scenarios and provide a reason for your choice.

1. Nicole and Danya have been assigned to research the resources available for their group's assignment. They have very different ideas about how to research and the amount of time each is willing to put into the task. They each identify that they can feel the tension rising between them and decide to sit down and just figure out what each will be responsible for and when they will meet again to pool their resources.

2. Rick has a very strong opinion about almost any topic and he is very vocal in his team, always saying what is on his mind. In the group's last meeting they decided to make a decision this week regarding the choice of topic for their year-end presentation. Eva's choice is childhood poverty, Dana's is access to quality service, Eric's is absent fathers, but Rick states that he has the winner, the best idea. Rick's idea is sustaining funding. Rick argues that the other topics are too easy, but the group doesn't readily agree. Rick reminds the others that he is the one with the access to city hall. Rick demands they vote on the best idea. The rest of the group exchange glances, and they vote. Rick reads the votes.... Sustaining funding wins: three yeses for his choice. Rick smiles knowing he is the winner.

3. Some of your group is really upset that they have more work because some of the group can no longer complete the assigned tasks. All members of the group are anxious and are feeling that they can't assume the work of the others. Instead of letting the anxiety rise between group members, they decide to sit down and restructure the work. This means that tasks assigned will change, some will do a little more, some will do different work, and the group will still be able to work together to be successful.

4. Ezra, Bill, Shelley, and Selena are meeting to discuss how to organize their presentation. They have been considering the idea of a video or PowerPoint presentation, and early in the discussion Bill offered that he would be able to put together a great video with the material they already had gathered. Shelley and Selena didn't want to be in the video and said they absolutely wanted the PowerPoint presentation. Ezra offered the idea of taking a vote. Bill said "never mind it's ok, we can do the PowerPoint."

5. Sara is new to the class and has just joined a study group with three other classmates: Dave, Ben, and Rashida. The group has been meeting every Thursday for the semester, at 4:00 in the cafeteria to review their notes and make sure they understand the content. Sara tells the group that she would rather meet on Wednesdays. Ben and Dave don't have any objections; Rashida meets with friends on Wednesdays, but she doesn't want Sara to be upset or to think that she isn't friendly, so she agrees to the change of day.

Conflict Resolution Strategies

Effective communicators are flexible and use a variety of approaches to resolving conflict. In this section we present two conflict resolution strategies: the A-E-I-O-U model and the six-step model.

The **A-E-I-O-U Model of Conflict Resolution** If you want to resolve a conflict, you should try to understand the attitudes, beliefs, and values of those involved in that conflict. The **A-E-I-O-U model of conflict resolution** focuses on communicating personal concerns and suggesting alternative actions to resolve a conflict.[25]

The **Six-Step Model of Conflict Resolution** The **six-step model of conflict resolution** offers a series of steps to help you move a conflict toward successful resolution. The six steps illustrated in the figure on the facing page are neither simple nor easy. They do, however, tell you "what to do and what not to do when confronting someone" in a conflict situation.[26]

AEIOU Model of Conflict Resolution

A ssume the other person means well and wants to resolve the conflict. "I know that both of us want to do a good job and complete this project on time."

E xpress your feelings. "I'm frustrated when you ask me to spend time working on a less important project."

I dentify what you would like to happen. "I want to share the responsibility *and* the work with you."

O utcomes you expect should be made clear. "If both of us don't make a commitment to working on this full time, we won't do a good job or get it done on time."

U nderstanding on a mutual basis is achieved. "Could we divide up the tasks and set deadlines for completion or bring in another person to help us?"

The Six-Step Model of Conflict Resolution

Step	Task	Strategies
1 Preparation	Identify the problem, issues, and causes of the conflict.	Analyze the conflict by asking yourself: Who is involved? What happened? Where, when, and why did the conflict occur? **Example:** Ask yourself: "Why and how did things go wrong?"
2 Initiation	Tell the person: "We need to talk."	Ask the other person to meet and talk about the problem. Provide some information about the subject. **Example:** "Can we get together for lunch and talk about the late report?"
3 Confrontation	Talk to the other person about the conflict and the need to resolve it.	Express your feelings constructively and describe, specifically, what you see as a solution. **Example:** "I want you to come to the family reunion with us."
4 Consideration	Consider the other person's point of view.	Listen, empathize, paraphrase, and respond with understanding. **Example:** "I didn't realize your mother was sick when I asked you to stay late."
5 Resolution	Come to a mutual understanding and reach an agreement.	Specify the outcome that both parties accept. **Example:** "Okay. I'll make sure I call you if they make me stay later than 6 P.M."
6 Reevaluation	Follow up on the solution.	Set a date for seeing whether the solution is working as hoped. **Example:** "Let's meet for lunch in two weeks to see if this is working as we hope it will."

STOP&THINK

Should You Apologize?

An apology can go a long way toward diffusing tension and hostility and opening the door to constructive conflict resolution and solving problems Many people find it difficult to say the words "I'm sorry." A sincere and well-timed apology can earn the respect of others and help build trusting relationships. Consider the following guidelines for making an effective apology: [27]

• Take responsibility for your actions with "I" statements. "I paid the bills late."

• Clearly identify the behaviour that was wrong. "I made a major commitment without talking to you about it first."

• Acknowledge how the other person might feel. "I understand that you are probably annoyed with me."

When you say you are sorry, you take responsibility for your behaviour and actions.

• Acknowledge that you could have acted differently. "I should have asked if you wanted to work together on this project."

• Express regret. "I'm upset with myself for not thinking ahead."

• Follow through on any promises to correct the situation. "I'll send an email message today acknowledging that your name should have been included on the report."

• Request, but don't demand, forgiveness. "I value our relationship and hope that you will forgive me."

COMMUNICATION

Exercise

This YouTube video clip discuss the power of an authentic apology in the business world.

www.youtube.com/watch?v=nplinUox428

11.4
Effective Group Meetings
How can you plan and conduct an effective group meeting?

Although there are several problem-solving methods, there is no "best" model or magic formula that ensures effective problem solving. However, as groups gain experience and succeed as problem solvers, they learn that some procedures work better than others and that some need modification to suit group needs. Here we present three problem-solving methods: Brainstorming, the decreasing options technique (DOT), and the standard agenda.

Brainstorming

In 1953, Alex Osborn introduced the concept of brainstorming in *Applied Imagination*.[28] **Brainstorming**, a fairly simple and popular method, is used for generating as many ideas as possible in a short period of time. It assumes that postponing the evaluation of ideas improves the quality of participants' input. It also assumes that the quantity of ideas breeds quality, based on the notion that creative ideas will come only after we have gotten the obvious suggestions out.[29] More than 70 percent of businesspeople claim that brainstorming is used in their organizations.[30] Unfortunately, many groups fail to use brainstorming effectively.

Brainstorming is a great way to tackle open-ended, unclear, or broad problems. If you're looking for lots of ideas, it is a very useful technique. But if you need a formal plan of action or you have a critical problem to solve that requires a single "right" answer, you may be better off trying another method.

There are several sure-fire ways to derail a productive brainstorming session.[31] If, for example, leaders or dominant members speak first and at length, they may influence and limit the direction and content of subsequent input and ideas. In an effort to be more democratic, some brainstorming groups require members to speak in turn. However, this approach prevents a group from building momentum and will probably result in fewer ideas. Finally, members who try to write down all of the group's ideas may end up being so focused on note taking that they rarely contribute ideas. It is better to have one person record all the ideas contributed by the group members.

Monkey Business/Fotolia

Brainstorming Guidelines[32]

Sharpen the focus	• Start with a clear question or statement of the problem. • Give members a few minutes to think about possible ideas before brainstorming begins.
Display ideas for all to see	• Assign someone to write down the group's ideas. • Post the ideas where everyone can see them.
Number the ideas	• Numbering can motivate a group: for example, "Let's try to list 20 or 30 ideas." • Numbering makes it easier to jump back and forth among ideas.
Encourage creativity	• Announce that wild and crazy ideas are welcome. • Announce that quantity is more important than quality.
Emphasize input, prohibit put-downs	• Keep the ideas coming. • Evaluate ideas only *after* brainstorming session is over.
Build and jump	• Build on, modify, or combine ideas offered by others to create new ideas.

WHEN NOT TO BRAINSTORM

- **In a crisis.** If the group needs to make decisions quickly or follow a leader's directions.

- **To repair.** If the group knows what went wrong and how to fix it, organize a repair team.

- **For planning.** If the group knows exactly what it has to do to reach its goal, hold a planning session to map out details.

Although many groups use brainstorming, their success depends on the nature of the group and the characteristics of its members. If a group is self-conscious and sensitive to implied criticism, brainstorming can fail. However, if a group is comfortable with such a freewheeling process, brainstorming can enhance creativity and produce numerous ideas and suggestions.

Decreasing Options Technique

The **decreasing options technique (DOT)** helps groups reduce and refine a large number of suggestions and ideas into a manageable set of options.[33] This technique can be used to assist small and large groups facing a variety of decision-making tasks, such as creating an ethics credo for a professional association and drafting a vision statement for a college. The DOT method works best when a group needs to sort through a multitude of ideas and options.

Generate Individual Ideas At the beginning of the DOT process, the group members generate ideas or suggestions related to a specific topic. Ideas can be single words or full-sentence suggestions. For example, when creating a professional association's ethics credo, participants contributed words such as *honesty*, *respect*, and *truth*.[34]

Post Ideas for All to See Each idea should be written on a separate sheet of thick paper in large, easy-to-read letters—only one idea per page. These pages are posted on the walls of the group's meeting room for all to see and consider. Postings should be displayed only after all members have finished writing their ideas on separate sheets of paper.

Sort Ideas Not surprisingly, many group members will contribute similar or overlapping ideas. When this happens, sort the ideas and post similar ideas close to one another. For example, when facilitating the development of a college's vision statement, phrases such as *academic excellence*, *quality education*, and *high-quality instruction* were posted near one another. After everyone is comfortable with how the postings are sorted, give

The Decreasing Options Technique (DOT)
✔ **Generate Ideas**   ✔ **Sort Ideas**
✔ **Post Ideas**   ✔ **Prioritize Ideas**

a title to each grouping of ideas. In the vision statement session, for instance, the term *quality education* was used as an umbrella phrase for nearly a dozen similar concepts.

Prioritize Ideas At this point, individual members decide which of the displayed ideas are most important: Which words *best* reflect the vision we have for our college? Which concepts *must* be included in our association's ethics credo?

In order to prioritize ideas efficiently, every member receives a limited number of coloured sticker dots. They use their stickers to "dot" the most important ideas or options. In our example, each member of the vision statement group was given 10 dots and asked to "dot" the most important concepts from among the 25 phrases posted on the walls. After everyone has finished walking around the room and posting dots, the most important ideas are usually very apparent. Some ideas will be covered with dots, others will be speckled with only three or four, and some will remain blank. After a brief review of the outcome, the group can eliminate some ideas, decide whether marginal ideas should be included, and end up with a limited and manageable number of options to consider and discuss.

Advantages of the DOT Method When a group generates dozens of ideas, valuable meeting time can be consumed by discussing every idea, regardless of its merit or relevance. The DOT method reduces the quantity of ideas to a manageable number.

Although the examples described focus on face-to-face interaction, the DOT strategy also works very well in virtual settings. A virtual group can follow the same steps by using email or networked software designed for interactive group work.

When to Use the DOT METHOD

- When the group is so large that open discussion of individual ideas is unworkable.

- When a significant number of competing ideas are generated that must be evaluated.

- When members want equal opportunities for input.

- When dominant members do not exert too much influence.

- When there is not enough time to discuss multiple or controversial ideas.

The Standard Agenda

The founding father of problem-solving procedures is philosopher and educator John Dewey. In 1910, Dewey wrote a book titled *How We Think* in which he described a set of practical steps that a rational person should follow when solving a problem.[35] These guidelines have come to be known as Dewey's *reflective thinking process*.

Dewey's step-by-step guidelines have been adapted for group problem solving. They begin with a focus on the problem itself and then move to a systematic consideration of possible solutions. In this chapter, we offer one version of this process: the **standard agenda** involves clarifying the task at hand, understanding and analyzing the problem, assessing possible solutions, and implementing the decision or plan.[36]

Task Clarification: Make Sure That Everyone Understands the Group's Assignment The primary purpose of a group's first meeting is to determine what the group wants or needs to accomplish so that everyone is working to achieve a common goal. During this phase, group members should ask questions about their roles and responsibilities in the problem-solving process.

Problem Identification: Avoid Sending the Group in the Wrong Direction Once a group understands and supports a common goal, members should focus on understanding the problem and developing a set of key questions. Identifying questions of fact, value, conjecture, and/or policy can help focus and aim the group in the right direction.

Fact-Finding and Analysis: Ask Questions of Fact and Value The following questions require research and critical thinking about the facts, causes, and seriousness of a problem, as well as an analysis of the barriers that prevent a solution:

- What are the facts of the situation?
- What additional information or expert opinion do we need?
- How serious or widespread is the problem?
- What are the causes of the problem?
- What prevents or inhibits us from solving the problem?

Although carefully evaluating facts and opinions is critical to effective problem solving, groups must also avoid analysis paralysis.

Analysis paralysis occurs when groups are so focused on analyzing a problem that they fail to make a decision.[37] "Chances are you've been in [situations where] good ideas have been presented, but by the time enough people consider and reconsider the situation, it seems more complex, or not as great an idea as you originally thought. Or, in most cases, a conclusion about how to act is never reached."[38]

Rather than spending too much time arguing about the issue or giving up on finding the correct answer, a group may have to move on and begin its search for solutions.

Solution Criteria and Limitations: Set Standards for an Ideal Resolution Solution criteria are standards that should be met for an ideal resolution of a problem. A group can establish criteria by asking questions such as: Is the solution reasonable and realistic? Is it affordable? Do we have the staff, resources, and time to implement it? The development of solution criteria should also include an understanding of solution limitations, which may be financial, institutional, practical, political, and legal in scope.

Solution Suggestions: Consider Multiple Solutions Without Judgment At this point in a group's deliberations, some solutions are probably obvious. Even so, the group should suggest or engage in brainstorming to identify as many solutions as possible without criticizing them. Having spent time analyzing the problem and establishing solution criteria, members should be able to offer numerous solutions.

Solution Evaluation and Selection: Discuss the Pros and Cons of Each

Suggestion During this phase, a group should return to the solution criteria and use them to evaluate the strengths and weaknesses of each suggested solution. This stage of the standard agenda may be the most difficult and controversial. Discussion may become heated, and disagreements may grow fierce. If, however, the group has been conscientious in analyzing the problem and establishing criteria for solutions, some solutions will be rejected quickly, whereas others will swiftly rise to the top of the list.

Solution Implementation: Decide on a Plan of Action Having made a difficult decision, a group faces one more challenge: How should the decision be implemented? For all the time a group spends trying to solve a problem, it may take even more time organizing the task of implementing the solution. Brilliant solutions can fail if no one takes responsibility or has the authority to implement a group's decision.

Whether you are a student meeting for course assignments or an employee in the workforce, most of us do not enjoy meetings. The *Business Management Daily* reports that "too many meetings" is the second biggest employee complaint, with "too much work" being the first.[39] However, when meetings are well planned and conducted, they build strong alliances and confer a sense of control. Members are more motivated to implement group ideas and actions when they have a real voice in the decision-making process.[40]

Before looking at how to plan and conduct a meeting, we should specify what we mean by the word. A random gathering of people in one place does not constitute a meeting. Rather, a **meeting** is a scheduled gathering of

The Seven Basic Steps in the Standard Agenda

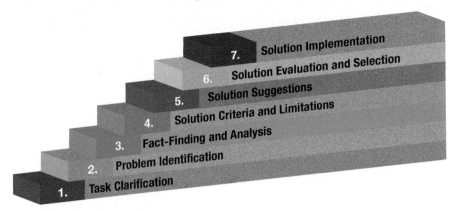

7. Solution Implementation
6. Solution Evaluation and Selection
5. Solution Suggestions
4. Solution Criteria and Limitations
3. Fact-Finding and Analysis
2. Problem Identification
1. Task Clarification

COMMUNICATION&CULTURE

MOTIVATING CULTURALLY DIVERSE GROUP MEMBERS

In Chapter 3, we described five cultural dimensions, each of which has implications for motivating group members to fully participate in group decision making and problem solving.

- *Individualism–collectivism.* Individualistic members may need praise and seek public recognition for their personal contributions. Collectivistic members may be embarrassed by public praise and prefer being honoured as a member of an outstanding group.

Andres Rodriguez/Fotolia

- *High power distance–low power distance.* Members from high-power-distance cultures value recognition by a leader and take pride in following instructions accurately and efficiently. Members from low-power-distance cultures prefer compliments from other group members and enjoy working in a collaborative environment.

- *Masculine–feminine.* Members—both male and female—who hold masculine values are motivated by competition, opportunities for leadership, and tasks that require assertive behaviour. Members with more feminine values may be extremely effective and supportive of group goals but have difficulty achieving a respected voice or influence in the group. Such members are motivated by taking on group maintenance roles, such as encourager/supporter, harmonizer, or compromiser.

- *High context–low context.* Group members from high-context cultures do not need to *hear* someone praise their work—they are highly skilled at detecting admiration and approval because they are more sensitive to nonverbal cues. Members from low-context cultures often complain that they never receive acknowledgment when, in fact, other members respect them and value their contributions. Low-context members need to hear words of praise and receive tangible rewards.

- *Monochronic–polychronic.* Members from monochronic cultures are motivated in groups that concentrate their energies on a specific task and meeting deadlines. Members from polychronic cultures often find the single-mindedness of monochronic members stifling rather than motivating. The opportunity to work on multiple tasks with flexible deadlines can motivate polychronic members to work more effectively.

---

group members for a structured discussion guided by a designated chairperson. The leader designated as a meeting's chairperson has a tremendous amount of influence over and responsibility for its success.

Planning the Meeting

Proper planning largely determines the success or failure of a meeting. To assist you in planning meetings, ask and answer the five W questions (see the feature on p. 210): Why are we meeting? Who should attend? When should we meet? Where should we meet? and What materials do we need?

Preparing the Agenda

The most important item to prepare and distribute to a group prior to a meeting is an **agenda**, an outline

that puts the meeting topics in the order in which they will be discussed.

> An agenda ... is a road map for the discussion that helps a group focus on its task and goal.

While this may seem unnecessary for groups working together on assignments, it can prevent conflict and wasting time. A well-prepared agenda serves many purposes. First and foremost, the agenda is an organizational tool—a road map for the discussion that helps a group focus on its task and goal.

In *Meetings: Do's, Don'ts, and Donuts,* Sharon Lippincott uses a simile to explain why a well-planned agenda is essential for conducting effective meetings:

> Starting a meeting without an agenda is like setting out on a journey over unfamiliar roads with no map and only a general idea of the route to your destination. You may get there, but only after lengthy detours. A good agenda defines the destination of the meeting, draws a map of the most direct route, and provides checkpoints along the way.[41]

When used properly, an agenda identifies what participants should expect and prepare for in a meeting. After a meeting, the agenda can be used to assess a meeting's success by

209

5 W's of Planning a Meeting

Gabriel Blaj/Fotolia

Why Are We Meeting? The most important step in planning a meeting is defining its purpose and setting clear goals. Merely asking what a meeting is about only identifies the topic of discussion: "employer-provided day care." Asking why this topic is being discussed will lead you to the purpose: "to determine whether our employer-provided day care system needs to be expanded." Groups should be able to achieve their purpose by the end of a single meeting. However, if this is not possible, the purpose statement should be revised to focus on a more specific outcome. In many cases, a series of meetings is needed to achieve group goals.

Who Should Attend? Most group membership is predetermined. However, if a task requires input only from certain people, you should select only those participants who can make a significant contribution. Invite participants with special expertise, different opinions and approaches, and the power to implement decisions.

When Should We Meet? Seek input and decide on the best day and time for the meeting, as well as when a meeting should begin and end. Schedule the meeting when the most essential and productive members are free.

Where Should We Meet? Choose a location that is appropriate for the purpose and size of the meeting. Do your best to find a comfortable setting, making sure that the meeting room is free of distractions such as ringing phones and noisy conversations. An attractive and quiet meeting location will help your group stay motivated and focused.

What Materials Do We Need? The most important item to prepare and distribute to the group is the meeting's agenda. You may also need to distribute reports or other reading material for review before the meeting. Distribute all materials far enough in advance of the meeting so that everyone has time to prepare. In addition, make sure that supplies and equipment such as pens, paper, or computers and screens are available.

---

determining the extent to which all items were addressed.

The following guidelines for agenda preparation can help to improve meeting productivity:

- Note the amount of time it should take to complete a discussion item or action. This lets the group see the relative importance of the item and help to manage the time available for discussion.

- Identify how the group will deal with each item. Will the group share information, discuss an issue, and/or make a decision? Consider putting the phrases *For Information*, *For Discussion*, and *For Decision* next to appropriate agenda items.

- Include the names of members responsible for reporting information on a particular item or facilitating a portion of the discussion. Such assignments remind members to prepare for participation.

> Careful planning can prevent at least 20 minutes of wasted time for each hour of a group's meeting.[42]

After selecting the agenda items, carefully consider the order for discussing each topic. When a group must discuss several topics during a single meeting, put them in an order that will maximize productivity and group satisfaction:

- Begin the meeting with simple business items and easy-to-discuss issues.

- Use the middle portion of the meeting for important or difficult items.

- Use the last third of the meeting for easy discussion items that do not require difficult decisions.

Taking Minutes

Most business and professional meetings require or benefit from a record of group progress and decision making. Responsible group leaders assign the important task of taking **minutes**—the written record of a group's discussion and activities—to a recorder, secretary, or a volunteer. The minutes cover discussion issues and decisions for those who attend the meeting and provide a way to communicate with those who do not attend. Most important, minutes help prevent disagreement about what was said or decided in a meeting and what tasks individual members agreed to or were assigned to do.

Well-prepared minutes are brief and accurate. They are not a word-for-word

Information to Include While Taking Minutes

✔ Name of the group.

✔ Date and place of the meeting.

✔ Names of those attending and absent.

✔ Name of the person chairing the meeting.

✔ Exact time the meeting was called to order and adjourned.

✔ Name of the person preparing the minutes.

✔ Summary of the group's discussion and decisions, using agenda items as headings.

✔ Specific action items or tasks that individual members have been assigned to do after the meeting.

record of everything that members say. Instead, they summarize arguments, key ideas, actions, and votes. Immediately after a meeting, minutes should be prepared for distribution to group members. The longer the delay, the more difficult it will be for members to recall the details of the meeting and the individual task assignments made at the meeting.

Chairing a Meeting

The responsibilities of planning a meeting, preparing an agenda, and making sure that accurate and useful minutes are recorded belong to the person with the title of *chair*. The person who chairs a meeting may be the group leader, a designated facilitator, or a group member who usually assumes that role.

The 3M Meeting Management Team describes the critical role of the chair as "a delicate balancing act" in which chairpersons must:

> ...influence the group's thinking—not dictate it. They must encourage participation but discourage domination of the discussion by any single member. They must welcome ideas but also question them, challenge them, and insist on evidence to back them up. They must control the meeting but take care not to over control it.[43]

Guidelines for CHAIRING A MEETING

- Begin on time. Discourage chronic or inconsiderate late arrivals.

- Create a positive climate. Establish ground rules for member behaviour.

- Delegate someone to take the minutes.

- Follow the agenda. Keep the group on track and aware of its progress.

- Ensure that all views are heard. Intervene when members ramble or discuss irrelevant topics. Summarize ideas and suggestions.

- Provide closure and stop on time.[44]

COMMUNICATION ASSESSMENT

Group Problem-Solving Competencies

Listed below are 10 important competencies of group problem solving. For each competency, write an example of a situation that illustrates the competency in action. Each example should demonstrate clearly your understanding of the competency.

1. *Clarifies the task.* Helps clarify the group's overall goal as well as member roles and responsibilities.
2. *Identifies the problem.* Helps the group define the nature of the problem and the group's responsibilities.
3. *Analyzes the issues.* Identifies and analyzes several of the issues that arise from the problem. Contributes relevant and valid information.
4. *Establishes solution criteria.* Suggests criteria for assessing the workability, effectiveness, and value of a solution.
5. *Generates solutions.* Identifies possible solutions that meet the solution criteria.
6. *Evaluates solutions.* Evaluates the potential solutions.
7. *Plans solution implementation.* Helps the group develop a workable implementation plan that includes necessary resources.
8. *Maintains task focus.* Stays on task and follows the agreed-on agenda. If responsible for taking or distributing minutes, makes sure the minutes are accurate.
9. *Maintains supportive climate.* Collaborates with and appropriately supports other group members.
10. *Facilitates interaction.* Communicates appropriately, manages interaction, and encourages others to participate.

11.1
Prerequisites for Group Decision Making and Problem Solving

What prerequisites help groups make good decisions and solve problems?

- Whereas *decision making* refers to the passing of judgment or making up your mind, *problem solving* is a complex process in which groups make multiple decisions while trying to solve a problem.

- Groups should take steps to prevent groupthink, which results in the deterioration of group effectiveness as a consequence of in-group pressure.

- The first and most important task for all groups is to make sure that all members understand and support the group's common goal. Group members should determine whether they are trying to answer a question of fact, conjecture, value, or policy.

- In addition to being well-informed, groups need clear procedures that specify how they will make decisions and solve problems.

11.2
Effective Group Decision Making

What are the advantages and disadvantages of various decision-making methods?

- Although voting is the easiest way to make a group decision, some members win while others lose when a vote is taken.

- Consensus requires that all members agree to support a decision. Groups should look for and prevent false consensus.

- Authority rule occurs when a single person or someone outside the group makes the final decision.

- Different decision-making styles—rational, intuitive, dependent, avoidant, and spontaneous—have the potential to improve or impair group decision making.

11.3
Resolving Interpersonal Conflicts

What communication strategies and skills help resolve interpersonal conflicts?

- Conflict can be constructive or destructive depending on your intentions and how well you communicate.

- There are five conflict styles: avoidance, accommodation, competition, compromise, and collaboration.

- The A-E-I-O-U model and the six-step model can help you resolve conflicts.

11.4
Effective Group Meetings

How can you plan and conduct an effective group meeting?

- Brainstorming works well when members are comfortable with the rules.

- The decreasing options technique (DOT) helps groups reduce and refine a large number of suggestions or ideas into a manageable set of options.

- The standard agenda divides problem solving into a series of ordered steps.

- An agenda—the outline of items to be discussed and the tasks to be accomplished at a meeting—should be prepared and delivered to all group members in advance of a meeting.

Monkey Business/Fotolia

TEST YOUR KNOWLEDGE ─────────

11.1 What prerequisites help groups make good decisions and solve problems?

1 Which of the following groups is *primarily* responsible for solving a problem?

a. a jury

b. a hiring committee

c. a department's social committee

d. a toxic waste disaster team

e. None of the above is a problem-solving group.

2 Which of the following symptoms of groupthink is expressed by a member who says, "Let's not worry about how the other departments feel about this—they're so dumb they don't even know there's a problem"?

a. invulnerability

b. stereotyping others

c. rationalization

d. mindguarding

e. illusion of unanimity

11.2 What are the advantages and disadvantages of various decision-making methods?

3 All of the following answers are guidelines for achieving consensus except which one?

a. Use stress-free ways of achieving consensus, such as flipping a coin or letting the majority make the decision.

b. Try to be logical rather than highly emotional.

c. Welcome differences of opinion.

d. Listen carefully to and respect other members' points of view even if they are very different from your point of view.

e. Get everyone involved in the discussion.

4 Which ethical responsibility are you assuming in a group if you treat other group members as equals and give everyone, including those who disagree, the opportunity to respond to an issue?

a. the research responsibility

b. the common good responsibility

c. the social code responsibility

d. the moral responsibility

e. the reasoning responsibility

11.3 What communication strategies and skills help resolve interpersonal conflict?

5 In which of the following conflict styles do people respond by giving in to others at the expense of meeting their own needs?

a. avoidance

b. accommodation

c. competition

d. compromise

e. collaboration

6 Which word does the *I* in the A-E-I-O-U model of conflict resolution stand for?

a. ignore

b. intimidate

c. identify

d. intuitive

e. initiation

7 Which step in the six-step method of conflict resolution requires you to listen empathically, use paraphrases, and respond with understanding?

a. preparation

b. consideration

c. confrontation

d. reevaluation

e. resolution

11.4 How can you plan and conduct an effective group meeting?

8 Use the decreasing options technique (DOT) when

a. the group is small and can discuss individual ideas openly.

b. the group must confront and discuss two competing ideas.

c. the group wants to prevent a dominant member from sharing ideas.

d. the group does not want to discuss controversial ideas.

e. ensuring equal opportunities for input by all members is important.

9 If your group is using the standard agenda model to discuss a question (What is the best way to reduce domestic violence in our community?), in which agenda steps would you ask the following questions: "What are the causes of domestic violence?" and "How widespread and serious is the problem?"

a. task clarification

b. problem identification

c. fact-finding and analysis

d. solution suggestions

e. solution evaluation and selection

10 Before calling a meeting, ask all of the following questions except which one?

a. Why are we meeting?

b. Who should attend?

c. When and where should we meet?

d. What materials do we need?

e. Who will implement decisions?

Answers found on page 330.

Key Terms

Accommodating conflict style	Conflict	Minutes
A-E-I-O-U model of conflict resolution	Consensus	Problem solving
	Constructive conflict	Questions of conjecture
Agenda	Decision making	Questions of fact
Analysis paralysis	Decreasing options technique (DOT)	Questions of policy
Authority rule		Questions of value
Avoidance conflict style	Dependent decision maker	Rational decision maker
Avoidant decision maker	Destructive conflict	Six-step model of conflict resolution
Brainstorming	False consensus	
Collaborative conflict style	Groupthink	Spontaneous decision maker
Competitive conflict style	Intuitive decision maker	Standard agenda
Compromising conflict style	Majority vote	Two-thirds vote
	Meeting	

Michael Jung/Fotolia

Communicating in a Digital World

What do you do first each day when you wake up? Do you (a) get dressed, (b) turn on the television, (c) get something to eat, or (d) check your smartphone for messages? If you answered (d), you are not alone.

A recent survey conducted in Canada by Wind, a cell-phone company, was interested in finding out just how important smartphones are to the average Canadian. The results showed that Canadians love their technology-rich smartphones: 40 percent of Canadians would give up their video games, 28 percent would give up drinking alcohol, and 23 percent would give up drinking coffee in order to keep their phone technology.[1]

Today communication happens faster and more dynamically than ever before, and every generation is involved, including baby boomers, and generations X, Y, and Z. The abundance of technology options not only affects how we communicate a message, but also when, where, why, and with whom that message is communicated.

The Nature of Digital Communication

How does digital communication affect the way we communicate?

Digital communication uses the **interactive communication model** explained in Chapter 1, and builds upon it to expand the role of channels in the communication process. In today's work environment, Canadian employers expect as part of an employee's interpersonal communication skills an ability to communicate through a variety of media.[2]

Beginning in the 1960s, Canadian communications theorist Marshall McLuhan explored the potential of the media to affect our lives and how we communicate with each other.[3] McLuhan coined two phrases that now seem prophetic. "**The medium is the message**" refers to the idea that the user's experience of an act of communication differs greatly depending on the medium being used.[4] If you think about the how an individual's experience would differ greatly between sending (or receiving) a telegraph message, putting a letter in the post, and writing multiple texts to friends nowadays, you can see how McLuhan's phrase has become so apt over time. Our lives are shaped by the dominant modes of communication.

McLuhan's second renowned phrase, "**global village**," appeared in *Understanding Media: The Extensions of Man* (1964) to describe how he believed that new electronic communication technology would allow for the immediate transfer of information throughout the world. Many believe that what McLuhan was describing anticipated the impact of the Internet on our world today.[5]

Moving Beyond Tasks

Initially many of us used the **Internet** to complete tasks. It was a luxury to send an **email** or to complete some banking online. But as the Internet grew, so did our creativity, and before long a whole new world of possibilities opened up. Initially an invention to make our lives easier through the completion of daily tasks, the Internet became a new social and interactive way to communicate with others.

> Initially an invention to make our lives easier ... the Internet became a new social and interactive way to communicate with others.

In November 2012, the *Huffington Post Canada* reported on a study conducted by Pew Research Centre showing a marked growth in the use of social media, from 55 percent of respondents in 2006 to 80 percent in 2011. These findings seem to be supported, at least anecdotally, by Carleton University professor Eileen Saunders, who when asking her students found that they preferred communicating with each other in the following order: 1. **texting**, 2. by phone, 3. face to face.[6]

Technology Becomes the Medium

When technology becomes the medium for communication, it causes changes to the communication process. Technological choices change the **channel of communication** from a face-to-face exchange of ideas to a channel that includes a variety of structures as noted in the **transactional communication model** (see Chapter 1).

The wide variety of tools used to create and send messages has the potential to change the receiver's interpretation of the message. The receiver can also now adjust the style, **context**, and language of the message before sending it again, thereby becoming the new creator of

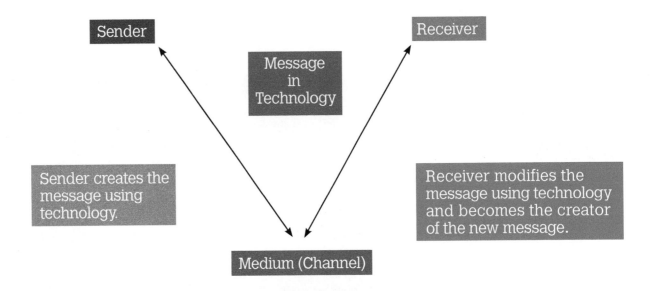

Sender

Receiver

Message in Technology

Sender creates the message using technology.

Receiver modifies the message using technology and becomes the creator of the new message.

Medium (Channel)

Exercise

After watching the student panel on Interpersonal Communication in a Digital World at the website below, answer this question posed on the site: In the midst of a digital society, has interpersonal communication been compromised?

www.jou.ufl.edu/news/2010/11/23/interpersonal-communication-in-a-digitalworld

the message. **Perception**, **values**, and **culture** will influence the original creator, the actual message, and the receiver in the communication process.

The Importance of Social Media in Communication

If you look up the term "**social media**" online, you will find many definitions. The definition in the *Merriam-Webster Dictionary* is the basis for our discussion: "forms of electronic communication (as Web sites for social networking and microblogging) through which users create online communities to share information, ideas, personal messages, and other content (as videos)."[7] It is widely accepted that the term "social media" was developed in 2004 in order to identify the new and fast-paced ways in which participants were using the Internet to communicate with each other.[8]

Canadians are among the most prolific users of social media. Social media is part of an online structure that provides opportunities for individuals, groups, or organizations to easily interact with others online. **Social networks** often include user profiles, commenting opportunities, and the ability to invite or exclude others. They provide an opportunity to meet with others online, share hobbies, make friendships, and even find life partners. Social media can be part of an organization's social structure (company blogs) or used for personal socializing only (car enthusiasts, online groups).

Choosing your channel to communicate in the online world is complicated. You must know your audience, understand the purpose of your message, and choose the appropriate language, style, and tone. Because you do not have the ability to read body language or **nonverbal messages** in most online media, there are some inherent risks in using social media to communicate with others. Over time, however, a shift has happened creating more opportunities for the individual consumer to control the messages they communicate with others using technology.

In Canada the use of Twitter has seen an increase of 27 percent in one year, and Toronto seems to have a growing appetite for instant communication with others.[9]

Exercise

This Ted Talk discusses the power of the Internet and its impact on how we live our lives.

www.ted.com/talks/chris_anderson_how_web_video_powers_global_innovation.html

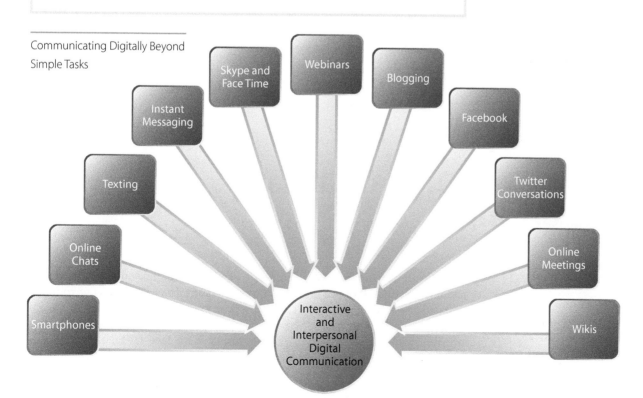

Communicating Digitally Beyond Simple Tasks

Social Networking

Social networking in Canada overall grew 3 percent in the last year, with Pinterest growing significantly in the category.[10]

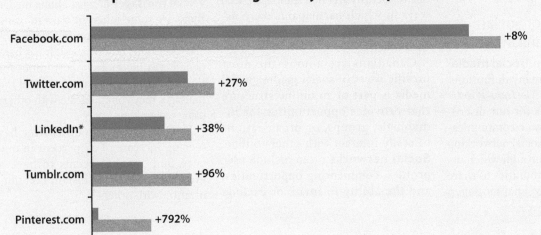

Total Unique Visitors

■ Monthly Q4 Avg. 2011   ■ Monthly Q4 Avg. 2012

Social Networking	23,216
	23,921

Top 5 Social Networking Sites by Total Unique Visitors

Facebook.com	+8%
Twitter.com	+27%
LinkedIn*	+38%
Tumblr.com	+96%
Pinterest.com	+792%

COMMUNICATION

Exercise

If you have a Facebook account, log in and answer these questions:

How many "friends" or contacts do you have on Facebook or your phone?

How many of these people do you consider in your inner circle and do you communicate with them regularly? How many do you communicate with exclusively on Facebook?

12.2

Understanding Digital Citizens and Citizenship

What are the rights and responsibilities associated with digital communication?

Digital Natives and Digital Immigrants

Marc Prensky, an acclaimed speaker and the author of *All Things Digital*, coined the term **"digital native"** to describe the generation of young adults who have always had access to the Internet and all of the digital tools and gadgets available.[11]

Digital natives approach communication with others very differently and expect to be able to use technology in all aspects of their lives. Their exploration of new media and technology is intuitive. Even young toddlers now approach their interactions and attempts to communicate with others using both face-to-face interactions and technology to connect with others in their world.

Children using Skype to keep in contact with grandparents

Are You Sharing Too Much?

While some of us are using Twitter for research, work groups, or to follow breaking news, many of us are tweeting personal information about our days and our lives. It is important to begin to think about how much sharing is too much.

Online providers can barely keep up as they scramble to fix security breaches that allow users to see other people's supposedly private information and personal chats. The problem of private information becoming public is not just the online provider's fault. Researchers in a study published in the *Journal of General Internal Medicine* looked up more than 800 medical students by name on Facebook. Although only 6 percent revealed their home address, "students were looser with lifestyle information including sexual orientation, relationship status, and political opinions and positions." Only 37 percent had made their Facebook entries private. Some profiles included photos of medical students engaged in excessive or hazardous drinking behaviours. Others shared sexist and racist comments.[13] How would you feel seeing postings of your emergency room doctor or hospital intern bragging about binge drinking or writing sexist or racist statements?

Now transform the above examples into questions about *your* posting. If you answer *yes* to any of these questions, you should consider changing your posting habits and Web messages:

- Do you post your home address and/or phone number?
- Do you post photos in which you're engaging in foolish, excessive, hazardous, or illegal behaviour?
- Do you post comments that could be interpreted as offensive, racist, sexist, or exceptionally bizarre?

Facial Expressions in CYBERSPACE

:)	Happiness, sarcasm, joking
:P	Sticking out your tongue
;)	Wink
:(	Unhappy or sad
:o	Surprise
:D	Laughing
XD	Hysterical laughter
:S	Indecision or disappointment
:3	coy/cutesy/self-conscious smile

So, if you were not born in the digital age, how are you identified? Marc Prensky describes these digital users as **digital immigrants.** Prensky goes on to explain that, as with immigrants who come to a new country, there is a learning curve. Digital immigrants need to learn how to navigate in this "new world." Digital immigrants often complain that they don't like communicating using technology due to the lack of nonverbal cues that can help to give messages meaning. Especially when new to the digital communication process, they find it difficult to interpret messages effectively.[12] This lack of mutual understanding of a message can interrupt the communication cycle by providing another layer of noise to the message, as described in Chapter 1.

Know Thy SELF

How Much Online Sharing Is Too Much?

"We are constantly Googling, Facebooking, and searching Blogger.com and other sites for applicants," says an admissions officer at the University of Connecticut.[14] Many Canadian colleges and universities do the same—as do businesses, corporations, and professional associations. The next time you are about to update your status or post a picture, here are a few questions to ask yourself:

- Would you want a college dean, a potential or current employer, or your mother to see everything you post online?
- Would you share the same information with them face-to-face?
- Does the personal information you share have a legitimate purpose, or is it unnecessary to your message?

Fortunately, the practice of over-sharing has begun to lessen on many social networking sites. Participants are becoming more cautious about what they disclose. Even more interesting, a study by the Pew Internet Project found that "people in their twenties exert more control over their digital reputation than older adults do, more vigorously deleting unwanted posts and limiting information about themselves."[15]

Always remember that regardless of whether you are interacting face-to-face or via cyberspace, *you* are responsible for deciding what to share about yourself with others.

Understanding digital citizenship and the responsibilities of each digital citizen will create opportunities for digital communication skill development.

> **❝Canada continues to lead the world in online engagement.❞**[16]

In our increasingly connected world, the ability to communicate within channels using a wide variety of media will become more important.

Digital Citizenship

Digital citizenship is typically defined as the norms of behaviour with respect to the use of technology. ITSE (the International Society for Technology in Education) developed the following rubric of nine elements that serve to guide the behaviours within digital citizenship.[17]

NINE **ESSENTIAL** ELEMENTS AND STRATEGIES TO GUIDE DIGITAL CITIZENS' BEHAVIOUR

ELEMENT	DESCRIPTION	STRATEGIES
1. ETIQUETTE	Electronic standards of conduct or procedure	Follow the rules and policies set by your school, agency, employer, or digital site.
2. COMMUNICATION	Electronic exchange of information	Model good use of electronic communication.
3. EDUCATION	Process of teaching and learning about technology and its use.	Learn information literacy skills to identify, access, apply, synthesize, and create new information.
4. ACCESS	Full electronic participation in society	Advocate for worldwide access regardless of ability, culture, or geography, both in language and structure.
5. COMMERCE	Electronic buying and selling of goods	Learn how to use and be effective consumers of products and services on the World Wide Web.
6. RESPONSIBILITY	Electronic responsibility for actions and deeds	Develop a code of ethics (personal or professional) to specify conduct on the Internet as a digital citizen.
7. RIGHTS	Freedoms extended to everyone in the digital world	Understand that when creating or publishing anything digitally, you have the same copyright protection as any other content creators.
8. SAFETY	Physical well-being in a digital technology world	Be aware of risks regarding physical strain, eye strain, and Internet addiction issues.
9. SECURITY (SELF-PROTECTION)	Electronic precautions to guarantee safety. Includes protecting all of us from outside influences that would do us physical harm.	Engage in online safety training. Be aware of spyware. Share personal information carefully.

COMMUNICATION

Exercise

1. Use this link to view a short video about digital citizenship:

   http://youtu.be/fdexijfxfd8

2. After viewing the video clip, review the "Nine Essential Elements and Strategies to Guide Citizens' Behaviour" chart and discuss in small groups how easy or difficult it is to adapt the strategies in your daily online life.

Etiquette for Cellphone Conversations and Texting

Cellphone etiquette has been the subject of countless newspaper and magazine articles—and for good reason. There is almost nothing as annoying and even embarrassing as being forced to listen in on someone else's cellphone conversation.[18]

To avoid embarrassing yourself and annoying others nearby, follow a few simple rules when talking on a cellphone or texting in public:[19]

- Do not make or take personal calls or send texts during business meetings, family celebrations, or class sessions.

- Maintain at least a 3 metre distance from others when talking on the phone.

- Avoid cellphone conversations in enclosed public spaces, such as elevators, waiting rooms, or buses and trains.

- Avoid cellphone conversations and texting in public places. Side talk or disregarding others is considered bad manners in places such as libraries, museums, theatres, restaurants, and houses of worship.

- Control the volume of your voice. Tilt your chin downward so that you are speaking toward the floor. That way, your voice won't carry as far.

- Do not have cellphone conversations or send texts when you are engaged in other tasks. Driving, eating, or shopping requires your full attention.

- Do not talk on the phone or text someone while engaged in a face-to-face conversation or interaction with another person.

Scott Griessel/Fotolia

- Take advantage of your phone's features, such as vibrate mode and voicemail. When you step into your workplace or a classroom, put your cellphone on silent and let your calls roll to your voicemail.

12.3

Ethics and Digital Communication
Why are ethics so important in the online world?

There is a temptation to behave differently in the online digital world than you would in real-life, face-to-face situations. Looking directly into someone's eyes and lying, stealing a paper from your friend's notebook, or copying answers from the person sitting next to you in class are actions that, for many, seem much worse than downloading a song illegally or quoting from someone else's work online.

Ethical Communication and Canadian Law

The laws that govern Canadians when we are offline are the same laws that are in place when we are online.[20] In 2013, the Canadian federal government is trying to have legislation passed that would further protect online users while keeping the freedom of ideas flowing and flourishing.[21] Canada continues to promote child and family safety on the Internet through education and tools that protect families in an ethical manner—without interfering with individuals' personal freedoms and their right to express ideas.

Having well-crafted government policies about the ethical practices

COMMUNICATION

Exercise

To Learn More . . .

1. Read this Canadian article about workplace and digital ethics:

   www.canadianbusiness.com/blogs-and-comment/ethics-law-and-social-media-in-the-workplace/

2. Watch this webinar about Workplace Digital Ethics at Ryerson University:

   https://ryecast.ryerson.ca/12/watch/2522.aspx

3. Visit the Privacy and Cyber Crime Institute of Canada at

   www.ryerson.ca/tedrogersschool/privacy/

ethics and digital communication

221

digital citizens need to engage in while online is an important first step toward creating a safe environment for all users.

Digital Code of Ethics

Richard Mason (1986) discussed **four dimensions of ethical communication**, and during the 2011 Information Systems Educators Conference, attendees suggested that his concept would be useful in developing a **digital code of ethics**.[22] The four dimensions that Mason described are privacy issues, accuracy issues, property issues, and accessibility issues (see the box below). [23]

Internet safety and ethical conduct will continue to evolve as the Internet evolves and its uses change and grow. As the twenty-first century moves forward, it will be necessary to evaluate and re-evaluate policies, codes of ethics, and laws that govern the World Wide Web.

12.4

Online Communication Tools
How do we connect, create, and collaborate online?

Connecting through a variety of channels, with a variety of creative tools, in **collaboration** with others is central to becoming a skilful communicator. How we choose to connect, create, and collaborate with others will be influenced by our own preferences, values, and beliefs. In this section, we will explore just a few of the many options for communicating found on the Internet.

We can create new material, synthesize presentations, add audio, video, and make it available worldwide or for just a few participants. Having these tools available can be overwhelming for some, while for others it presents an exciting challenge.

Exploring Some Popular Social Media Tools

The "Social Media Landscape" graphic includes some of the tools available in social media that foster interaction among users. Such tools allow communicators using the Internet to explore and create meaningful messages using the tool best suited for the content. Online communication tools range from casual gaming apps; to more creative tools for expressing ideas, perspectives, and factual content; to platforms that provide access to just a few people or to a worldwide audience.

As we have discussed throughout this text, communication is a sophisticated, complicated process. Digital communication is part of our daily lives, whether we describe ourselves as digital native, or digital immigrant. As in face-to-face communication or written communication, we are ethically responsible for our digital messages and their content. How we choose to send our messages is open to many possibilities when we consider the variety of tools available.

It is difficult to limit digital social media tools to one category of function. Many of the tools are multidimensional and can be used at different times to create, share, or collaborate. This flexibility suits them to the digital world and allows opportunities for users to make individual choices that match their needs and their abilities.

Collaborating, Presenting, Meeting, Curating, and Sharing

Collaboration Tools There are also instances when you are part of a group or team and a meeting is difficult to arrange, due to either distance or time constraints. Using digital tools to set up a virtual meeting can provide opportunities for several group members to contribute to the overall project or presentation. This type of interpersonal communication opens up possibilities to include perspectives from a variety of people who might otherwise be excluded from the process. Two of the most popular and useful tools for collaboration are Google Docs and Evernote. Each of these are accessible from the Internet and have the ability to store information that can be viewed by others who have been invited to the website.

Presentation Tools For many, PowerPoint (Microsoft), and Keynote (Apple) have been the go-to presentation tools in all levels of school and in business. Both of these tools have the ability to add interactive components such as audio voice over and inclusion of video and URL links. They are also easily embedded into social media platforms such as YouTube and into webpages. Now we have the ability to create more interactive presentations that encourage creativity, and blending of the other dynamic tools available to us now in our digital world. Prezi is a web-based tool that is free to use and enables users to create exciting multi-dimensional presentations. In Prezi collaboration happens online, which allows people in different locations to contribute to the creation of the presentation.

Meeting Tools The practice of meeting online, whether with classmates or business associates,

Meeting Skills in the Virtual World

- Email an agenda and information prior to the virtual meeting.
- Ensure that all participants have and can navigate the chosen software for the meeting.
- Ensure that all presentation materials are working and that audio as well as visual components can be accessed.
- Set a goal for each meeting and be aware and respectful of participants' time. Begin and end on time.
- Acknowledge and encourage participation in discussion.
- Follow up with an email summarizing main points and assigned tasks.

Exercise

Explore this site to learn more about how to shape your digital presence online.

www.2learn.ca/ydp

The Social Media Landscape

Rudie/Fotolia

Exercise

Explore Google Docs and Evernote

www.google.com/google-d-s/intl/en/tour1.html

http://evernote.com

1. How can these sites be useful tools for academic assignments or projects?
2. How could business benefit from the type of collaboration these tools foster?

Apops/Fotolia

online communication tools

Virtual meetings and other collaborative tools can provide numerous benefits for both the employer and the employee. Depending on the company or organization, one or more of these tools may already be in use. As college students' lives become more complex, virtual team meetings and group work help them to complete, share, and finalize their assignments. Looking at the pie chart, which of these do you or could you use to be successful? Do, or should, these aspects of virtual meetings and collaboration have equal importance as the pie chart indicates, or would you alter the percentages? Might the percentages change depending on the type of work being done and the location of the employees?

- Reducing travel time and costs
- Reaching a wider audience
- Improving the spectator experience
- Encouraging online participation
- Conveying a professional image of the organization or group

Exercise

To learn more about the benefits of Prezi vs PowerPoint visit

http://ltlatnd.wordpress.com/2011/03/22/comparison-chart-powerpoint-and-prezi/

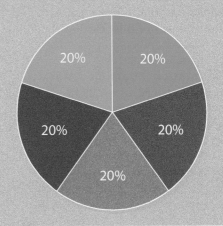

Zakokor/Fotolia

continues to grow, especially in Asia Pacific and North America. A 2013 survey by Carson Wagonlit Travel (CWT) found that up to 50 percent of managers surveyed believe that technology combined with face-to-face meetings will be part of their company strategies. As the business world adapts to the demands of clients and employees, the opportunities to blend traditional with cutting-edge communication technology becomes an opportunity for many employers.[26]

One easy to use program to meet online is www.skype.com, which has grown from a social purpose only to be an important tool for both business and academic meetings.

Curating and Sharing Tools
Pinterest is an image-based social network that continues to grow globally. Curators of ideas, images, and information simply pin their interests on a virtual bulletin board. It is also a web-based tool that allows for sharing with friends and colleagues, creating private collections, and the ability to export information to PDF files.

Twitter can be used to curate and to follow news, people, and ideas that are relevant to your academic, business, or personal interests. URLs can be shared, allowing the Twitter follower to visit websites, articles, and video directly from the Twitter platform.

In Chapter 1, we discussed some of the issues that have developed around the use of Twitter, and explored the growth of this social media service. When used with some guidelines and some understanding, Twitter can be a remarkably powerful tool for communicating, advocating, collaborating and sharing ideas and information.

Exercise

To learn more about Pinterest, watch this short YouTube video.

http://youtu.be/nDbufMXjo2w

What do you see as the possibilities for this tool?

Twitter is an example of a social media tool that is multi-functional in a variety of contexts. Once thought of only as a social tool to share personal bits of information or to follow famous people's daily lives, it is now recognized as an opportunity to create discussion, share ideas, curate, and present information through weblinks. In the "Understanding Tweeting" box, some guidelines and suggestions are presented to further your exploration of Twitter and tweeting.

UNDERSTANDING **TWEETING**

■ BEGINNING TO TWEET[27]

- Choose a username.
- Create your profile.
- Choose an avatar or upload a photo.
- Choose your **privacy settings**.
- Decide who to follow.
- Decide who can follow your tweets.
- Begin to tweet.

Tweet

Pixxart Photography/Fotolia

■ QUALITY TWEETS[28]

Is the message informative?

- Does it answer a question posed?
- Does it pose a follow up question, to continue the conversation?
- Are the links provided working, useful, and ethical?
- Is the tweet free of bias, prejudice, and racism?

- Is it grammatically correct?
- Is the tweet free of spelling errors?

■ WHAT'S A HASHTAG?

Hashtags (Signified by the number symbol: #) are used within Twitter to create categories of online conversations in order to target specific groups of people (a college class or interest group). You can search topics by using the hashtag symbol in your tweet.

COMMUNICATION

Exercise

Create an account on Twitter and find a # of interest to follow, or create a # as a class to have an online Twitter conversation.

https://support.twitter.com/articles/215585-twitter-101-how-should-i-get-started-using-twitter

Are You a Digital Native or a Digital Immigrant?[29]

After answering these questions, look back at section 12.2 to reflect upon your responses.

1. How many days out of the week do you use digital communication (instant messages, social media sites, emails, text messages, etc.) to communicate with others?

   a. 0
   b. 1–2
   c. 3–4
   d. 5–6
   e. 7

2. Please fill in the blank: When making plans with friends or family, I most often _____.

   a. call
   b. text message
   c. email
   d. write on his/her Facebook wall
   e. stop by his/her home or office

3. Please fill in the blank: The Internet enables me to communicate _____ with others.

   a. more
   b. less
   c. the same amount

4. Please fill in the blank: When using the Internet, I spend most of my time _____.

   a. speaking to others
   b. surfing the Internet for enjoyment
   c. researching and learning new information
   d. shopping
   e. paying bills/managing accounts

5. Please fill in the blank: When trying to keep in touch with friends or family, I most often _____.

   a. call
   b. text message
   c. email
   d. write on his/her Facebook wall
   e. stop by his/her home or office

6. When speaking to others online or through text messages there are misunderstandings between what I am saying and what I really mean.

   a. never
   b. rarely
   c. sometimes
   d. often
   e. always
   f. I don't know.

7. True or False: I have met a friend or a significant other via the Internet.

8. Please fill in the blank: I speak more openly and more freely when I communicate with others via _____.

   a. Internet
   b. text messages
   c. phone
   d. face-to-face interaction.
   e. I speak with the same amount of disclosure either way.

9. Please fill in the blank: I believe my generation uses the Internet to communicate _____ members of Generation Y (ages 15–30).

   a. more than
   b. less than
   c. the same amount as

10. True or False: In the past month I have not understood the tone (whether it was a joke, serious statement, sarcastic statement) of someone I was communicating with via computerized channels.

11. True or False: In the past year, digital communication (Instant messages, social media, emails, text messages, etc.) has allowed me to reach out to an old friend.

12. What do you believe is the major advantage of email?

   a. increased convenience
   b. increase of privacy
   c. more control
   d. immediacy
   e. absence of face-to-face interaction

13. What do you believe is the major disadvantage of email?

   a. lack of privacy
   b. absence of face-to-face interaction
   c. impersonal nature
   d. permanence
   e. possibility of being ignored

14. What is your ideal mode of communicating with friends? _____

12.1

The Nature of Digital Communication
How does digital communication affect the way we communicate?

- In today's work environment, Canadian employers expect as part of an employee's interpersonal communication skills an ability to communicate through a variety of media.

- Canadian communications theorist Marshall McLuhan's coined the phrases "the medium is the message" and "global village" in the 1960s to describe the variety of technologies used to send and receive messages around the world, communication technologies that McLuhan prophesied would make the globe more like a small village.

- Canadians are among the most prolific users of social media.

12.2

Understanding Digital Citizens and Citizenship
What are the rights and responsibilities associated with digital communication?

- Marc Prensky, an acclaimed speaker and the author of *All Things Digital*, coined the term "digital native" to describe the generation of young adults who have always had access to access to the Internet and all of the digital tools and gadgets available.

- Digital immigrants often complain that they don't like communicating with technology due to the lack of nonverbal cues that can help to give messages meaning.

- Many of us are tweeting personal information about our days and our lives. It is important to consider if you are sharing too much.

- Digital citizenship is typically defined as the norms of behaviour with respect to the use of technology.

- ITSE (the International Society for Technology in Education) developed a rubric of nine elements that serve to guide the behaviours included in digital citizenship.

12.3

Ethics and Digital Communication
Why are ethics so important in the online world?

- The laws that govern Canadians when we are offline are the same laws that are in place when we are online.

- In 2013, the Canadian federal government is trying to have legislation passed that would further protect online users.

- The four dimensions of ethical communication that Mason described are privacy issues, accuracy issues, property issues, and accessibility issues.

12.4

The Use of Online Communication Tools
How do we connect, create, and collaborate online?

- Connecting through a variety of channels, with a variety of creative tools, in collaboration with others is central to becoming a skilful communicator.

- Twitter can be a remarkably powerful tool for communicating, advocating, collaborating, and sharing ideas and information.

- Online communication tools range from casual gaming; to more creative tools for expressing ideas, perspectives, and factual content; to platforms that provide the access to just a few people or to a worldwide audience.

- The practice of meeting online, whether with classmates or business associates, continues to grow, especially in Asia Pacific and North America.

- Two of the most popular and useful tools for collaboration are Google Docs and Evernote.

Apops/Fotolia

TEST YOUR KNOWLEDGE

12.1 How does digital communication affect the way we communicate?

1 Channels of communication are important to consider when using technology to communicate with others and are affected by
   a. face-to face communication.
   b. style.
   c. context.
   d. language.

2 Social media is _____ used to create online communities, in order to share ideas, personal messages, and content.
   a. new communication
   b. face-to-face communication
   c. electronic communication
   d. the preferred method of communication

12.2 What are the rights and responsibilities associated with digital communication?

3 Digital natives expect to use _____ in all aspects of their lives.
   a. social media
   b. technology
   c. smartphones
   d. computers

4 Digital immigrants find that the lack of _____ makes digital communication more difficult to understand.
   a. words
   b. images
   c. verbal messages
   d. nonverbal messages

5 ITSE (International Society for Technology in Education) has developed a rubric of _____ elements that help to guide your behaviour online.
   a. six
   b. four
   c. seven
   d. nine
   e. three

12.3 Why are ethics so important in the online world?

6 Part of a safe online environment for everyone includes
   a. knowing who you are communicating with online.
   b. not sharing too much personal information.
   c. developing ethical practices and policies.
   d. a, b, and c are correct.
   e. b and c are correct.

7 Richard Mason's work includes _____ dimensions of ethical communication and these can be useful in developing _____.
   a. three; digital policies
   b. three; a digital code of ethics
   c. four; digital policies
   d. four; a digital code of ethics

12.4 How do we connect, create, and collaborate online?

8 Virtual meetings create opportunities for participants to _____, even though they may not be physically together.
   a. share responsibilities
   b. share knowledge
   c. collaborate
   d. compete
   e. a, b, and c are correct.

9 In order to begin tweeting, you need
   a. a profile.
   b. a username.
   c. privacy settings.
   d. all of the above

10 When you compose a tweet, you should ask yourself the following question(s).
   a. Is it informative?
   b. Is it funny and does it include a photo?
   c. Is it free of bias, prejudice, and racism?
   d. a and b are correct.
   e. a and c are correct.

Answers found on page 330.

Key Terms

Channels of communication	**Four dimensions of ethical communication**	**Nonverbal messages**
Collaboration		**Perception**
Context	**Global village**	**Privacy settings**
Culture	**Hashtag**	**Social media**
Digital citizenship	**Interactive communication model**	**Social networks**
Digital code of ethics		**Texting**
Digital communication	**Internet**	**Transactional communication model**
Digital immigrant	**The medium is the message**	
Digital native		**Values**
Email		

CREATING CAPTIVATING
PRESENTATIONS

Having a great idea is only the first step of several when preparing a presentation. Some readers may look at this photo of the Canadian Juno Award-winning rap artist Shad K and wonder, "What does he have to do with presentations?"[1] But if you pause for a moment, and consider what goes into his rap artistry, you quickly realize that rapping performances require planning, organization, and words that are meant to inform or persuade while engaging the audience. Shad also has excellent communication skills, speaking both French and English fluently, and earning a business degree from Wilfrid Laurier and a master's degree in liberal studies from Simon Fraser.[2] In this chapter, we will look more deeply into how you can inform, persuade, and engage your audience of choice, whether as Canada's next songwriter, in class presentations, or at work.

David Mbiyu/Demotix/Corbis

13.1
Beginning with the Plan
What should you consider when beginning the planning process?

Effective presentations have enormous power. They can delight us, inspire us, and even make us cry. You do not have to be famous or known for your eloquence to be a great speaker. What matters is that you have a compelling message worth sharing with others. What *also* matters is that you know *how* to share that message.

> Without a purpose, it is difficult to decide what to say, what materials to include, and how to deliver your presentation.

Martin McDermott, author of *Speak with Courage*, writes, "A successful speech is not a matter of luck; it's a matter of preparation." He then describes watching *unprepared* students deliver speeches in classes. "It's like watching a deer in the headlights of an oncoming tractor trailer . . . in slow motion. Both speakers and audience feel gruelling pain." To prevent such torment, he offers three important pieces of advice: "prepare, prepare, prepare."[3]

When discussing the wide variety of speaking opportunities and occasions, we use the phrase **presentation speaking** to describe the process of using verbal and nonverbal messages to generate meaning with audience members. Presentation speaking encompasses oral reports, informal talks, and business briefings in private settings as well as public speeches to small and large audiences. Regardless of its purpose, audience, or place, if you know how to effectively plan and deliver a strong presentation, you are more likely to be noticed, believed, respected, and remembered.

Several years ago, we conducted two national surveys—one administered to working professionals and the other to students enrolled in public speaking courses in a variety of colleges and universities.[4] We asked respondents to identify the *most* important skills for effective presentations. For the most part, student results were similar to those of the working professional respondents (see below), with two exceptions, which we'll discuss later in this and subsequent chapters.[5] Knowing how to prepare a presentation is the first step in mastering the top-ranked speaking skills the survey respondents identified. Effective preparation can also reduce your anxiety and increase your likelihood of delivering a successful speech.

Presentation Goals

Having a clear purpose does not guarantee you will achieve it. But without a purpose, it is difficult to decide what to say, what materials to include, and how to deliver your presentation. Begin your search for a purpose by deciding whether you want to inform, persuade, entertain, inspire, or combine all four of these goals.

Narrow Your Topic

Make sure that you appropriately narrow or modify your topic to achieve

TOP-RANKED SPEAKING SKILLS[6]

WORKING PROFESSIONALS		COLLEGE STUDENTS
Keeping your audience interested	**1**	Keeping your audience interested
Beginning and ending your presentation	**2**	Organizing your presentation
Organizing your presentation	**3**	Deciding what to say; choosing a topic or approach to your presentation
Selecting ideas and information for your presentation	**4**	Using your voice effectively
Deciding what to say; choosing a topic or an approach	**5**	Selecting ideas and information for your presentation
Understanding and adapting to your audience	**6**	Determining the purpose of your presentation
Determining the purpose of your presentation	**7**	Overcoming/reducing nervousness/stage fright
Choosing appropriate and effective words	**8**	Understanding and adapting to your audience
Enhancing your credibility	**9**	Beginning and ending your presentation
Using your voice effectively	**10**	Choosing appropriate and effective words

Characteristics of an EFFECTIVE PURPOSE STATEMENT

	EFFECTIVE	NOT EFFECTIVE
SPECIFIC Narrows a topic to content appropriate for your purpose and audience.	I want my audience to understand how to use the government's new food group recommendations as a diet guide.	The benefits of good health.
ACHIEVABLE Purpose can be achieved in the given time limit.	There are two preferred treatments for mental depression.	Be able to identify all the the causes, symptoms, treatments, and preventions of mental depression.
RELEVANT Topic is related to specific audience needs and interests.	Next time you witness an accident, you'll know what to do.	Next time you encounter an exotic Australian tree toad, you'll appreciate its morphology.

your purpose and adapt to listeners' needs and interests. Select the most important and interesting ideas and information for your presentation rather than telling your audience everything you know about a topic.

Although *you* may be an expert on your topic, your audience may be hearing about it for the first time. Don't bury them under mounds of information. Ask yourself, "If I only have time to tell them one thing about my topic, what would it be?" Chances are that conveying a single important idea is enough to achieve your purpose.

Develop a Purpose Statement

When you know *why* you are speaking (your purpose) and *what* you are speaking about (your topic), develop a clear **purpose statement** that identifies the purpose and main ideas of your presentation. It is not enough to say, "My purpose is to tell my audience about my job as a phone solicitor." This statement is too general and probably an impossible goal to achieve in a time-limited presentation. Instead, your purpose statement must convey the specific focus of your presentation, such as "I want my audience to recognize two common strategies used by effective phone solicitors to overcome listener objections."

A purpose statement guides how you research, create, organize, and present your message.

A purpose statement is similar to a writer's thesis statement, which identifies the main idea you want to communicate to your reader.

Know Your Audience

Audience analysis refers to the ability to understand, respect, and adapt to audience members before and during a presentation. Knowing your audience means asking questions about audience members' characteristics, attitudes, values, backgrounds, and needs as well as what they may and may not know about your topic. The answers to these questions will help you understand your audience and help you to decide what to include in your presentation.

Who Are They? Gather as much general **demographic information** (information about audience characteristics such as age, gender, marital status, race, religion, place of residence, ethnicity, occupation, education, and income) as you can about the people who will be watching and listening to you. If the audience is composed of a particular group or is meeting for a special reason, gather more specific demographic information as well. (See the figure on the next page.)

Avoid "one-size-fits-all" conclusions about audience members based on visible or obvious characteristics, such as age, race, gender, occupation, nationality, or religion.

Adapt to Your Audience

Everything you learn about your audience tells you something about how to prepare and deliver your presentation. Depending on the amount of audience research and analysis you do, you can adapt your presentation to your audience as you prepare it. In other cases, you may use audience feedback to modify your presentation as you speak.

Prepresentation Adaptation After researching and analysing information about your audience's characteristics and attitudes, go back to your purpose statement and apply what you've learned. Carefully considering what you now know about your audience can help you modify your preliminary purpose into one that better suits them.

Midpresentation Adaptation No matter how well you prepare for an audience, you must expect for the unexpected. What if audience members seem restless or hostile? How can you adjust? What if you must shorten your 20-minute presentation to 10 minutes to accommodate another speaker?

Adapting to your audience *during* a presentation requires you to do three things at once: deliver your presentation, correctly interpret audience feedback as you speak, and successfully modify your message. Interpreting audience responses involves looking at your audience members, reading their nonverbal signals, and sensing their moods. If audience feedback suggests that you're not getting through, don't be afraid to stop and ask comprehension questions such as, "Would you like more detail on this point before I go on to the next one?"

Think about adjusting your presentation in the same way you adjust your conversation with a friend. If your friend looks confused, you might ask what's unclear. If your friend interrupts with a question, you probably will answer it or ask if you can finish your thought before answering. If your friend tells you that he has a pressing appointment, you are likely to shorten what you have to say. The same adaptations work just as well when speaking to an audience.

Adapt to Cultural Differences

Respecting and adapting to a diverse audience begins with understanding the nature and characteristics of various cultures. Two of the cultural dimensions we examined in Chapter 3 are especially critical for presentations: power distance and individualism/collectivism.

Power Distance As we indicated in Chapter 3, *power distance* refers to varying levels of equality and status among the members of a culture. In Canada, a low-power-distance culture, authority figures often play down status differences.

If most of your audience members are from a low-power-distance culture, you can encourage them to challenge authority and make independent decisions. However, if many audience members come from high-power-distance culture *and* if you also

AUDIENCE DEMOGRAPHICS

GENERAL

Age	Cultural background	Place of residence	Education
Race	Marital status	Income level	Parental status
Occupation	Religion	Gender	Disabilities

SPECIFIC

Political affiliations	Professional memberships
Employment positions	Career goals
Military experience	Individual and group achievements

What do you know about your audience?

Know Thy SELF

Do You Honour the Audience's Bill of Rights?

In his book *Say It with Presentations*, Gene Zelazny proposes an Audience's Bill of Rights.[7] Here we present a modified version of Zelazny's rights. Review each of the audience's rights listed in the left-hand column. In the right-hand column, describe a speaking strategy you can use to ensure this right.

Audience Rights	Speaker Strategies
1. The right to receive value for the time you spend attending a presentation.	I can _____
2. The right to be spoken to with respect for your experience, intelligence, knowledge, and culture; the right to ask questions and expect answers.	I can _____
3. The right to know what the speaker wants you to do or think as a result of a presentation.	I can _____
4. The right to have a presentation start and stop on time and to know, in advance, how much time it will take.	I can _____
5. The right to know the speaker's position, the rationale for that position, and the evidence that supports the position; the right to have complex charts explained.	I can _____
6. The right to know where the speaker is going and how the presentation will progress.	I can _____
7. The right to hear and see a speaker from anywhere in a room; the right to be able to read every word on every visual no matter where you sit.	I can _____

COMMUNICATION&CULTURE

ADAPT TO NON-NATIVE SPEAKERS OF ENGLISH

Have you studied a foreign language in school? If so, what happens when you listen to a native speaker of that language? Do you understand every word? Probably not. Such an experience can be difficult and frustrating. Imagine what it must be like for a non-native speaker of English to understand a presentation in English. The following guidelines are derived from general intercultural research and from observations of international audiences, both at home and abroad.[8]

Steve Russell/ZUMA Press/Newscom

- *Speak slowly and clearly*. Many non-native speakers of English need more time because they translate your words into their own language as you speak. But don't shout at them; they are not hearing impaired.
- *Use visual aids*. Most non-native speakers of English are better readers than listeners. Use slides or provide handouts for important information. Give the audience time to read and take notes.

Rudie/Fotolia

- *Be more formal*. In general, use a more formal style and dress professionally when speaking to international audiences.
- *Adapt to contextual perspectives*. If you are addressing an audience from a high-context culture (see Chapter 3), be less direct. Let them draw their own conclusions. Give them time to get to know and trust you.
- *Avoid humour and clichés*. Humour rarely translates into another language and can backfire if misunderstood. Avoid clichés—overused expressions familiar to a particular culture—or obscure idioms. Will a non-native speaker of English understand "Cool as a cucumber" or "Shop 'til you drop"?

---

command authority and influence, you can tell them exactly what you want them to do—and expect compliance.

Individualism and Collectivism When speaking to individualistic audiences (e.g., listeners from Canada, the United States, and Great Britain), you can appeal to their sense of adventure, their desire to achieve personal goals, and their defence of individual rights. When speaking to a collectivist audience (e.g., listeners from most Asian and Latin American countries), you may want to demonstrate how a particular course of action will benefit their company, family, or community.

Speaker Credibility

The more credible you are in the eyes of your audience, the more likely it is that you will achieve the purpose of your presentation. If your audience rates you as highly credible, they may excuse poor delivery. They are so ready to believe you that the presentation doesn't have to be perfect.[9]

Researchers identify three major components of **speaker credibility** that have a strong impact on the believability of a speaker: **character**, **competence**, and **charisma**.[10] The speaker credibility chart on the next page summarizes the distinct characteristics that personify each of these three components.

The **more credible** you are in the eyes of your audience, the more likely it is that you will achieve the purpose of your presentation.

COMPONENTS OF SPEAKER CREDIBILITY

Character	Competence	Charisma
Honest	Experienced	Active
Kind	Well prepared	Enthusiastic
Friendly	Qualified	Energetic
Fair	Up to date	Confident
Respectful	Informed	Stimulating
Caring	Intelligent	Dynamic

Aristotle's Ethos

Aristotle's concept of ethos evolved into what we now call *speaker credibility.*

The concept of speaker credibility is more than 2,000 years old. Aristotle's *Rhetoric*, written during the late fourth century B.C., established many of the public-speaking strategies we use today. His definition of **rhetoric** as the ability to discover "in the particular case what are the available means of persuasion"[11] focuses on strategies for selecting the most appropriate persuasive arguments for a particular audience in a particular circumstance. His division of proof into logical arguments (*logos*), emotional arguments (*pathos*), and arguments based on speaker credibility (*ethos*) remains a basic model for teaching the principles of persuasive speaking.

Here we focus on Aristotle's **ethos**, a Greek word meaning *character.* "The character [ethos] of the speaker is a cause of persuasion when the *speech* is so uttered as to make him worthy of belief . . . His character [ethos] is the most potent of all the means to persuasion."[12]

We want to emphasize that a speaker's ethos varies with audiences and varies over time. "That is to say, a speaker may have a positive ethos with one set of listeners and a negative ethos with another; a speaker who is highly regarded at one time may be considered a has-been ten years later."[13]

Aristotle confines his discussion of ethos to what a speaker does *during* a speech because what people think of a speaker *before* a speech is not related to the three modes of persuasion.[14] Later in our discussion of speaker credibility, we examine the ways in which an audience's previous knowledge and beliefs about a speaker affect ethos or, as it's now called, speaker credibility.

ETHICAL COMMUNICATION

The Perils of Plagiarism

Any discussion of speaker ethics must address the perils of plagiarism. The word **plagiarism** comes from the Latin, *plagium*, which means, "kidnapping." Simply put, if you include a quotation or idea from another source and pretend it's your idea and words, you are plagiarizing. Some speakers believe that plagiarism rules don't apply to them.

When you plagiarize, you are stealing or kidnapping something that belongs to someone else.

Others think they can get away with it. Still others plagiarize without knowing they are doing it. Ignorance, however, is no excuse.

Although most speakers don't intend to kidnap or steal another person's work, plagiarism occurs more frequently than it should, often with serious consequences. Students have failed classes, been expelled from programs and schools, or been denied degrees when caught plagiarizing in college. In the publishing business, other writers who claim that their ideas and words

were plagiarized have sued authors. The careers of well-respected scientists, politicians, university officials, and civic leaders have been tarnished and even ruined by acts of plagiarism.

For many students and speakers, the Web has become the primary source for plagiarism. In an article in *Prism*, a publication of the American Society of Engineering Education, author Julie Ryan describes the problem of Web plagiarism:

A few words typed into a Web search engine can lead a student to hundreds, sometimes thousands, of relevant documents, making it easy to "cut and paste" a few paragraphs from here and a few more from there until the student has an entire paper-length collection. Or a student can find a research paper published in one of the hundreds of new journals that have gone online over the past few years, copy the entire text, turn it into a new document, and then offer it up as original work without having to type anything but a cover page. Even recycling efforts and ghost writers have gone global with Web sites offering professionally or student-written research papers for sale, some even with a money-back guarantee against detection. [15]

PLAGIARISM IS NOT JUST UNETHICAL; IT IS ILLEGAL.

We extend Julie Ryan's examples to visual resources too. Given how easy it is to find good photographs, graphics, and PowerPoint slides on the Web, plagiarists may download someone else's visual and treat it as if it were their original work. Fortunately, the Web also provides instructors with the same access to information so they can check the originality of the material submitted by students. With time and a good search engine, many would-be plagiarizers have been caught *and* appropriately punished.

The key to avoiding plagiarism and its consequences is identifying the sources of your information in your presentation. Changing a few words of someone else's work is not enough to avoid plagiarism. Some of our students have told us that plagiarism occurs *only* if they use an entire article or someone else's written presentation. Some also believe that it's okay to "borrow" a few phrases or someone else's idea. We quickly tell them that this behaviour is plagiarism—no matter how small the amount you are stealing, it is still stealing. If they're not your original ideas, and most of the words are not yours, you are ethically obligated to tell your audience who wrote or said them and where they came from.

The following guidelines can help you avoid plagiarism:

- If you include an identifiable phrase or an idea that appears in someone else's work, always acknowledge and document your source.
- Do not use someone else's sequence of ideas and organization without acknowledging and citing the similarities in structure.
- Tell an audience exactly when you are citing someone else's exact words or ideas in your presentation. It is plagiarism even when the words are spoken!
- Never buy or use someone else's speech or writing and claim it as your own work.

Remember that ethical speakers are liked and respected by their audiences because they are honest, fair, caring, informed, and justifiably confident. Do not use what you know about the audience, the occasion, the setting, or the time limits to take unfair advantage of the audience or to achieve unethical goals. Make sure that both you and the audience benefit from your purpose. Always check that your content and your sources of information are truthful and qualified. Furthermore, if you present an argument, acknowledge both sides.

COMMUNICATION

Exercise

Examine your academic institution's policies about plagiarism. Can you identify the consequences for committing an act of plagiarism?

Researching Content and Organizing Your Presentation

What strategies should you use to research and organize the content of a presentation?

Content and organization work together in any presentation. It is important to see them as intertwined, creating a strong presentation. The **content** of your presentation consists of the ideas, information, and opinions you include in your message. Even if you are an expert or have a unique background or life experience related to your topic, good research can help you support, verify, and reinforce the content of your message. Michael Kepper, a marketing communication specialist, compares the need for organizing a presentation's content with the needs of a human body:

> A speech without structure is like a human body without a skeleton. Having structure won't make the speech a great one, but lacking structure will surely kill all the inspired thoughts . . . because listeners are too busy trying to find out where they are to pay attention.[16]

Gathering Supporting Material

Supporting material comes in many different forms from many different sources: definitions in dictionaries, background and historical information in encyclopaedia, facts and figures online and in almanacs, true-life stories in magazines and on personal websites, and editorial opinions in newspapers, newsletters, and online sources. The best presenters use a mix of supporting material; they don't rely on just one type. Why? Different types of material have different strengths and weaknesses. Most audiences find an unending list of statistics boring. A speaker who tells story after story frustrates listeners if there's no clear reason for telling the stories.

> *Different types of information give a presentation added life and vitality.*

Facts A **fact** is a verifiable observation, experience, or event known to be true. For example, the statement "*The King's Speech* won the 2011 Academy Award for Best Picture" is a fact, but the statement "I think *The Social Network* should have won" is not a fact—it is an opinion. Facts can be personal ("I went to the 2012 Grey Cup ") or the official record of an event (" The Toronto Argos won the 2012 Grey Cup").

Regardless of their purpose, most presentations are supported by facts, which serve to remind, illustrate, demonstrate, and clarify.

Statistics **Statistics** is a branch of mathematics concerned with collecting, summarizing, analysing, and interpreting numerical data. Statistics are used for many purposes— from describing the characteristics of a specific population to predicting events ranging from economic trends to football games.

Although audiences often equate statistics with facts, statistics are factual only if they are collected and analyzed fairly.

Testimony **Testimony** refers to statements or opinions that someone has spoken or written. You can support a presentation with testimony from books, speeches, plays, magazine articles, radio or television, courtrooms, interviews, or webpages. Here is an excerpt from a student presentation:

> In her book *Mommy, I'm Scared*, Professor Joanne Cantor writes: "From my 15 years of research on mass media and children's fear, I am convinced that TV programs and movies are the number-one preventable cause of nightmares and anxiety in children."

The believability of testimony depends on the credibility of the speaker or writer.

Definitions **Definitions** explain or clarify the meaning of a word, phrase, or concept. A definition can explain what *you* mean in a word or be as detailed as an encyclopaedia definition. In the following example, in a presentation explaining the differences between jazz and the blues, a speaker used two types of definitions:

> The technical definition of the blues is a vocal and instrumental music style that uses a three-line stanza and, typically, a 12-measure form in which expressive inflections—blues notes—are combined with uniquely African American tonal qualities. Or according to an old bluesman's definition: The blues ain't nothin' but the facts of life.

> Use definitions if your presentation includes words or phrases that your audience may not know or may misunderstand.

Descriptions **Descriptions** create mental images for your listeners. They provide more details than definitions by offering causes, effects, historical background information, and characteristics.

Analogies **Analogies** compare two things in order to highlight some point of similarity. Analogies are a useful way of describing a complex process or relating a new concept to something that the audience understands well. For example you might use an analogy of a computer to explain how our brain processes memories.

Examples An **example** refers to a specific case or instance. Examples make a large or abstract idea concrete and understandable; they can be facts, brief descriptions, or detailed stories. When someone says, "Give me an example," it's natural to reply with an illustration or instance that explains your idea. When asked for examples of individualistic cultures, you might list Canada, the United States, and

Library of Congress Prints and Photographs Division [LC-DIG-ppmsca-09571]

A speech on female blues singers from the 1920s is strengthened by specific examples. Playing a song by Bessie Smith (shown here) can make a good speech even better.

> Audiences often remember a good story **even when they can't remember much else about a presentation.**

Great Britain. Or, if you were making a presentation on female blues singers from the 1920s, you might name Ma Rainey, Bessie Smith, Victoria Spivey, and Alberta Hunter.[17]

Stories Real stories about real people in the real world can arouse attention, create an appropriate mood, and reinforce important ideas. **Stories** are accounts or reports about something that happened.

For example, a successful attorney with an incapacitating physical disability due to a car accident might use her brief, personal story to emphasize the importance of hope, hard work, and determination.

Documenting Your Sources

Documentation is citing the sources of your supporting material. You should document all supporting material (including information from Internet sources and interviews) in writing and then orally in your presentation.

Unlike writers, speakers rarely display complete footnotes during a presentation. Of course, they don't recite every detail such as the publisher, publisher's city, and page number of a citation. In speaking situations, citations must be oral. Your spoken citation—sometimes called an **oral footnote**—should include enough information to allow an interested listener to find the original sources you're citing. Generally, it's a good idea to provide the name of

> Documentation enhances your credibility as a speaker while assuring listeners of the validity of your content.

the person (or people) whose work you are citing, to say a word or two about that person's credentials, and to mention the source of the information. If you want the audience to have permanent access to the information you use, provide a handout listing your references with complete citations. Failing to document your oral sources is plagiarism and is punishable under the same policy.

Evaluating Your Supporting Material

Many speakers rely on researched information to support their claims and enhance their credibility. It is important that you evaluate every piece of supporting material before you use it. Make sure your information is **valid**—that the ideas, information, and opinions you include are well founded, justified, and accurate. The questions described in the sections that follow will help you test the validity of your supporting material.

Is the Information Recent? Always note the date of the information you want to use. When was the information collected? When was it published? In this age of rapidly changing

COMMUNICATION IN *ACTION*

Evaluating Internet Information

Criteria #1: Source Credibility

1. Is the author's or sponsor's identity and qualifications evident?
2. Have you checked other websites or sources to determine whether the author's or sponsor's credentials are legitimate and/or reflect a particular bias?
3. Does the author or sponsor provide a contact email or address/phone number?

Criteria #2: Accuracy

1. Are the sources of factual information clearly listed so that you can verify them in another source?
2. Are there statements indicating where data from charts and graphs were gathered?
3. Is the information free of grammatical, spelling, and typographical errors that would indicate a lack of quality control?

Criteria #3: Objectivity

1. Is information represented as fact, or is it a mask for advertising and biased opinions?

2. Is the sponsor's point of view expressed clearly with well-supported arguments?
3. If the site is not objective, does it account for opposing points of view?

Criteria #4: Currency

1. When was the information produced or updated?
2. Is the material recent enough to be accurate and relevant?
3. Are there any indications that the material is kept up to date?

LINEAR VERSUS SPIRAL THINKING

Low-context cultures like the United States tend to use a linear style of thinking when developing a message—moving from facts, evidence, and proof to drawing logical conclusions. Other cultures use a more spiral style of thinking when developing a message—moving from dramatic supporting material to subtle conclusions. For example, members of many Arab and African cultures use detailed metaphors, similes, stories, and parables to reinforce or dramatize a point. The final message may be quite subtle or even elusive. It's up to the audience to draw the intended conclusion.[18]

Because this textbook is primarily written for Canadian speakers and audiences, we focus on a more linear thinking style in which speakers use clear supporting material to back up their claims and outlines to map the content of their messages. When speaking to an audience that prefers a more spiral style of thinking, consider ways to use supporting material more dramatically and to present your conclusions in a less direct style.

information, your information can become old news in a matter of hours. For current events or scientific breakthroughs, use magazines, journals, newspaper articles, or reliable Web sources. Look for the date indicating when the page was written or revised. If a website makes it difficult to locate this information, this may be a sign that the site is not credible and reliable.

Is the Information Consistent? Check whether the information you want to use reports facts and findings similar to information on the same subject from other reputable sources. Does the information make sense based on what you know about the topic? For example, if most doctors and medical experts agree that penicillin will *not* cure a common viral cold, why believe an obscure source that recommends it as a treatment?

Are the Statistics Valid? Good statistics can be informative, dramatic, and convincing. But statistics also can mislead, distort, and confuse. Make sure your statistics are well founded, justified, and accurate. Closely consider whether the statistics are believable and whether the researcher who collected and analyzed the data is a well-respected expert. Confirm who is reporting the statistics as well—is it the researcher or a reporter?

The Importance of Organization

Organization refers to the way you arrange the content of your presentation into a clear and appropriate format. Organization helps you focus on the purpose of your presentation while deciding what to include and how to maximize the impact of your message.

As an audience member, you know that organization matters. It is difficult to understand and remember the words of a speaker who rambles and doesn't connect ideas. In fact, you may never want to hear that speaker again.

> Research confirms that audiences react positively to well-organized presentations and negatively to poorly organized ones.[19]

Identifying Your Central Idea

The **central idea** is a sentence that summarizes the key points of your presentation. Your central idea provides a brief preview of the organizational pattern you will follow to achieve your purpose.

The following example illustrates how topic area, purpose, and central idea are different but closely linked to one another:

Topic area   Traveling abroad
Purpose   To prepare travellers for a trip abroad
Central idea   Before visiting a foreign country, research the culture and the places you will visit, make sure you have the required travel documents, and get any immunizations and medicines you might need.

Determining Your Key Points

Begin organizing your presentation by determining your key points. **Key points** represent the most important issues or the main ideas you want your audience to understand and remember about your message.

Look for a pattern or natural groups of ideas and information as the basis for key points. Depending on your purpose and topic area, this can be an easy task or a daunting puzzle. Inexperienced speakers often feel overwhelmed by what seems to be mountains of unrelated facts and figures. Don't give up!

Before creating an outline, consider using two other techniques to identify your key points and build a preliminary structure for your message: mind mapping and the Speech Framer.

Determining the key points of your presentation is like fitting together the pieces of a puzzle—if one point doesn't fit or follow, the rest may not work.

Gunnar Pippel/Shutterstock

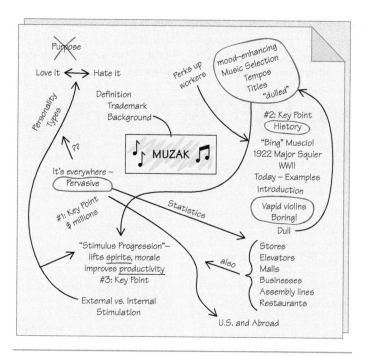

This mind map for a speech about Muzak demonstrates one method of determining key points and establishing relationships among ideas.

Mind Mapping **Mind mapping** encourages the free flow of ideas and lets you define relationships among those ideas. It harnesses the potential of your whole brain while it's in a highly creative mode of thought to generate ideas.[20] For instance, the mind map above was created to explore the ever-present background music commonly heard in stores, elevators, and offices. The mind map is a hodgepodge of words, phrases, lists, circles, and arrows. Certainly it contains more concepts than should be included in a single presentation. After completing such a mind map, you can label circled ideas as key points and put them in a logical order.

Mind maps allow you to see your ideas without superimposing a predetermined organizational pattern on them. They also let you postpone the need to arrange your ideas in a pattern until you collect enough information to organize the content. Use mind mapping when you have lots of ideas and information but are having trouble deciding how to select and arrange the materials for a presentation.

The Speech Framer The **Speech Framer** is a visual model for organizing presentation content that provides a place for every component of a presentation while encouraging experimentation and creativity.[21]

The Speech Framer lets you experiment with a variety of organizational formats. For example, if you have four key points, you merely add a column to the frame. If you think you have three key points but find that you don't have good supporting material for the second key point, you might consider deleting that point. If you only have three types of supporting material for one key point and two for the others, that's okay—just make sure all the supporting material is strong. If you notice that several pieces of supporting material apply to two key points, you can combine them into a new key point. And if you must have five or more key points, use only one or two pieces of supporting material for each point to control the length of your presentation.

In addition to helping you organize the content of your presentation, you can use the single-page Speech Framer as your speaking notes. It allows you to see the presentation laid out entirely before you practice or deliver it.

Outlining a Presentation

Outlines—just like presentations and speakers—come in many shapes and forms. Here we look at one type of outline and how it can help you organize the content of a presentation.

Preliminary Outlines Outlines begin in a preliminary form with a few basic building blocks. You can use a **preliminary outline** to put the major pieces of almost any presentation in order, modifying it on the basis of the number of key points and the types and amount of supporting material. Aim for at least two pieces of supporting material under each key point—facts, statistics, testimony, definitions, descriptions, analogies, examples, or stories.

Preliminary
OUTLINE FORMAT

Topic Area

I Introduction

  A Purpose/topic
  B Central idea
  C Brief preview of key points
    1 Key point #1
    2 Key point #2
    3 Key point #3

II Body of the presentation

  A Key point #1
    1 Supporting material
    2 Supporting material
  B Key point #2
    1 Supporting material
    2 Supporting material
  C Key point #3
    1 Supporting material
    2 Supporting material

III Conclusion

Strategies for **ORDERING KEY POINTS**[22]

■ **STRENGTH AND FAMILIARITY.** Place your strongest points first and last and your weakest or least familiar idea in the middle position so that you start and end with strength.

■ **AUDIENCE NEEDS.** If your audience needs current information, satisfy that need early. Background information can come later. If you are speaking about a controversial topic, begin with a point that focuses on the background of an issue or on the reasons for a change.

■ **LOGISTICS.** If you're one of a series of presenters, you may end up with less time to speak than was originally scheduled. Plan your presentation so that the strongest key points come first in case you need to cut your presentation short.

After you identify the key points that will support your central idea and after you choose an organizational pattern to structure your message, determine which key points go first, second, or last. In many cases, the organizational pattern you choose dictates the order. For example, if you use time arrangement, the first step in a procedure comes first. If your format does not dictate the order of key points, place your best ideas in strategic positions.

THE SPEECH FRAMER: ASLEEP AT THE WHEEL

Introduction: Story about my best friend's death in a car accident.

Central Idea: Falling asleep accounts for 100,000 car accidents and 1,500 deaths every year. Everyone knows about the dangers of drunk driving, but very few of us know about the dangers of sleep deprivation—and what to do about it.

Key Points	#1 Why we need sleep. Transition: What happens when you don't get enough sleep?	#2 Sleep deprivation affects your health, well-being, and safety. Transition: So how can you ease your tired body and mind?	#3 Three steps can help you get a good night's sleep.
Support	Would you drive home from class drunk? 14 hrs w/o sleep = .1 blood alcohol level Very long day = .05 blood alcohol level	Lack of sleep affects your attitude and mood (results of study)	1 Decide how much sleep is right for you: a Keep a sleep log. b Most people need 8 or more hours a night.
Support	Circadian clock controls sleep & also regulates hormones, heart rate, body temperature, etc.	Lack of sleep affects your health. Most important sleep is between 7th and 8th hour of sleep.	2 Create a comfy sleep environment. a Don't sleep on a full or empty stomach. b Cut back on fluids. c No alcohol or caffeine before sleep.
Support	Things that rob you of sleep: 24-hour stores; Internet; television; studying; homework	Symptoms: • Crave naps or doze off? • Hit snooze button a lot? • Hard to solve problems? • Feel groggy, lethargic?	3 Don't take your troubles to bed. a Can't sleep, get up. b Soothing music. c Read.

Conclusion: Summarize the Three Key Points. Final line: There is so much in life to enjoy. Sleep longer, live longer.

Preliminary Outline: Asleep at THE WHEEL

Brief Outline

I Introduction: Story of Best Friend's Death in Car Accident

II Central idea: Stay Longer, Drive Safer, Live Longer

III Key Points

  A Importance and Need for Sleep
    1 Lack of sleep = alcohol-impaired effects
    2 Things that rob our sleep: media, work hours, study and homework, etc.
    3 Circadian clock regulates body functions

  B Sleep Deprivation
    1 Influences attitudes and moods
    2 Symptoms of sleep deprivation: dozing, groggy, flawed thinking, etc.

  C How to Get a Good Night's Sleep
    1 Decide how much sleep you need
    2 Create a comfy sleep environment
    3 Don't take trouble to bed

IV Conclusion: Recognize the symptoms; alter your habits. Sleep Longer, Live Longer

Arto/Fotolia

Jessmine/Fotolia

Know Thy SELF

How Creative Are You?

If you want your presentation to be interesting and memorable, think creatively about its structure. Lee Towe, president of Innovators International, defines creativity as consisting of two parts: creative thinking and creative output. [23] *Creative output* consists of connecting and combining previously unrelated elements. For example, the circles and arrows you draw on a mind map allow you to combine ideas from various places on the page.

For example, Patricia Phillips, a customer service expert, used excerpts from popular songs to begin each major section of her training seminar in a creative way: "I Can't Get No Satisfaction" by the Rolling Stones, "Help" by the Beatles, "Respect" by Aretha Franklin, and "Don't You Come Back No More" by Ray Charles.

Creativity, however, runs some risks. Some audience members may be unfamiliar with the songs chosen by a speaker. Or, the audience may have expected or wanted a more technical presentation. **If you want to use creative patterns, make sure your audience will understand and appreciate your creativity.**

COMMUNICATION

Exercise

In three minutes, list all of the uses you can imagine for a balloon. When the time is up, rate the creativity of your answers using these criteria:

Quantity: Did you come up with more than 24 ideas?

Variety: Did you come up with at least 5 categories of answers? For example birthdays and proms both use balloons as decorations (one category).

Uniqueness: Did you have unusual items on your list? Very creative people will be able to move beyond the category of decorations to more unusual ideas. [24]

13.3

Beginning and Ending Your Presentation

What strategies will help you begin and end your presentation effectively?

Introductions capitalize on the power of first impressions. First impressions can create a positive, lasting impression and pave the way for a highly successful presentation. A weak beginning gives audience members a reason to tune out or remember you as a poor speaker. Effective introductions give your audience time to adjust, to block out distractions, and to focus attention on you and your message.

There are many strategies for beginning a presentation effectively. Having a clear goal for your introduction will help you to effectively engage the audience and keep them involved.

The Primacy and Recency Effects

As predicted by Hermann Ebbinghaus, a German psychologist who spearheaded the research on memory and recall, the parts of a presentation audiences most remember are the beginning and the end. Ebbinghaus, who is best known for his discovery of the *forgetting curve* and the *learning curve*, also discovered the *serial position effect*, which explains that "for information learned in a sequence, recall is better for items at the beginning (**primacy effect**) and the end (**recency effect**) than for items in the middle of the sequence." [25]

TIPS FOR STARTING STRONG

- PLAN THE BEGINNING AT THE END. Don't plan your introduction until you have developed the content of your presentation.

- DON'T APOLOGIZE. Don't use your introduction to offer excuses or apologize for poor preparation, weak delivery, or nervousness.

- AVOID BEGINNING WITH "MY SPEECH IS ABOUT . . ." Boring beginnings do not capture audience attention or enhance a speaker's credibility. Be original and creative.

GOALS OF THE INTRODUCTION

Focus Audience Attention and Interest
Gain audience attention by using compelling supporting material, involving them actively, and speaking expressively.

Connect to Your Audience
Find a way to connect your message to audience interests, attitudes, beliefs, and values.

Put You in Your Presentation
Link your expertise, experiences, and personal enthusiasm to your topic or purpose. Personalize your message.

Set the Emotional Tone
Make sure the introduction sets an appropriate emotional tone that matches its purpose. Use appropriate language, delivery styles, and supporting material.

Preview the Message
Give your audience a sneak preview about the subject. State your central idea and *briefly* list the key points you will cover.

Interestingly, the primacy and recency effects link up with what we know about listening and memory. We are more likely to recall the last thing we hear because the information is still in our short-term memory. In contrast, we are likely to remember the first thing we hear because the information has had time to become part of our long-term memory. The poorest recall of information is in the middle of a sequence "because the information is no longer in short-term memory and has not yet been placed in long-term memory."[26]

Originally, the primacy and recency effects evolved from studies of what people remember after hearing a list of words or numbers. Today, it has been applied to studying how first and last impressions affect how we react to and feel about other people. It also has found its way into the study of presentations, specifically to emphasize the critical importance of a presentation's introduction and conclusion.

Concluding Your Presentation

Just as audiences remember things that are presented first (the primacy effect), they also remember information that comes last (recency effect). Your final words have a powerful and lasting effect on your audience members and determine how they think and feel about you and your presentation.[27]

Like the introduction, a conclusion establishes a relationship among you, your topic, and your audience.

TIPS FOR ENDING STRONG

Make Sure the Mood and Style Are Consistent
Don't tack on an irrelevant or inappropriate ending.

Have Realistic Expectations
Most audience members will not act when called on unless the request is carefully worded, reasonable, and possible.

Don't end by demanding something from your audience unless you are reasonably sure you can get it.

Knowing that you have a well-prepared and strong ending for your presentation can calm your nerves and inspire your audience. The most effective endings match the mood and style of the presentation, and make realistic assumptions about the audience.

Some methods of concluding your presentation reinforce your message; others strengthen the audience's final impression of you. Use any of the following approaches separately or in combination: summarize, quote someone, tell a story, use poetic language, call for action, or refer to the beginning.

GOALS OF THE CONCLUSION

Be Memorable
Give the audience a reason to remember you and your presentation. Show how your message affected you and how it affects them.

Be Clear
Repeat the one thing you want your audience to remember at the end of your presentation.

Be Brief
The announced ending of a presentation should never go beyond one or two minutes.

13.4

Inform Me!
What is informative speaking and how can you do it successfully?

Informative speaking is the most common type of presentation. Students use informative speaking to present oral reports, to share research with classmates, and to explain group projects. Beyond the classroom, business executives use informative presentations to orient new employees, to present company reports, and to explain new policies.

The primary purpose of an **informative presentation** is to instruct, enlighten, explain, describe, clarify, correct, remind, and/or demonstrate. Informative presentations can present new information, explain complex concepts and processes, and clarify and correct misunderstood information. You will be asked to prepare and deliver informative presentations throughout your lifetime and career, so learning how to do it well can give you a competitive edge.[28]

Sometimes it's difficult to determine where an informative presentation ends and a persuasive presentation begins. Most informative presentations contain an element of persuasion. For example, an informative presentation explaining the causes of global warming may convince an audience that the problem is serious and requires stricter controls on air pollution. Even demonstrating how to sew on a button properly can persuade some listeners to change the way they've been doing it for years. It may also persuade someone to do it himself or herself rather than giving it to mom or paying to have it done at the cleaner. Your purpose signifies the difference between informative and persuasive presentations. When you ask listeners to change their opinions or behaviour, your presentation becomes persuasive.

Involve the Audience

One of the most powerful ways to keep audience members alert and interested during your informative presentation is to ask them to participate actively in your presentation. When audience members are encouraged to speak, raise their hands, write, or interact with one another, they become involved in the speechmaking process. You can involve the audience by using several strategies: ask questions, encourage interaction, do an exercise, ask for volunteers, and invite feedback.

Ask Questions Involve audience members by asking questions, posing riddles, or soliciting reactions during or at the end of your presentation. Even if your listeners do little more than nod their heads in response, they will be involved in your presentation. Audience members will be more alert and interested if they know that they will be quizzed or questioned during or after a presentation.

Encourage Interaction Something as simple as asking audience members to shake hands with one another or to introduce themselves to the people sitting on either side of them generates more audience attention and interest. If you are addressing a professional or business audience, ask them to exchange business cards. If you're addressing young college students, ask them to tell each other their majors or career aspirations.

Do an Exercise Simple games or complex training exercises can involve audience members in your presentation and with one another. Bookstores sell training manuals describing ways to involve groups in games and exercises. Interrupting a presentation for a group exercise gives the audience and the speaker a break during which they can interact in a different but equally effective way.

Ask for Volunteers If you ask for volunteers from the audience, someone will usually offer to participate. Volunteers can help you demonstrate how to perform a skill or how to use

---

COMMUNICATION IN *ACTION*

Focus on What's Valuable to Your Audience

Just because *you* love banjo music, bowling, or bidding on eBay doesn't mean audience members share your enthusiasm. How, then, do you give them a reason to listen? The answer is: Include a value step in your introduction to capture their attention. A **value step** explains how the information can enhance their success and personal well being. While this step may not be necessary in all informative presentations, it can motivate a disinterested audience to listen to you.

> If there's a good reason for you to make a presentation, there should be a good reason for your audience to listen.

When looking for a value step, ask yourself whether your presentation will benefit your audience in any of the following ways:

- *Socially.* Will your presentation help listeners interact with others, become more popular, or throw a great party?

- *Physically.* Will your presentation offer advice about improving physical health, treating common ailments, or losing weight?

- *Psychologically.* Will your presentation help audience members feel better about themselves or help them cope with common psychological problems?

- *Intellectually.* Will your presentation explain intriguing and novel discoveries in science? Will you satisfy listeners' intellectual curiosity?

- *Financially.* Will your presentation help audience members make, save, or invest money wisely?

- *Professionally.* Will your presentation help audience members succeed and prosper in a career or profession?

a piece of equipment. Some can even be persuaded to participate in a funny exercise or game. Most audiences love to watch a volunteer in action.

Invite Feedback Invite questions and comments from your audience. If audience members seem reluctant to participate, don't badger or embarrass them. If no one responds, continue your presentation. It takes a skilful presenter to encourage and respond to feedback without losing track of a prepared presentation. The more you speak, the easier and more useful feedback is.

Strategies That Inform

In her book *Theory of Informatory and Explanatory Communication* Katherine Rowan explains how to make strategic decisions about the content and structure of an informative presentation. Her two-part theory focuses on the differences between informatory and explanatory communication. **Informatory communication** seeks to create or increase audience awareness about a topic by presenting the latest information—much like news reporting. **Explanatory communication** seeks to enhance or deepen an audience's understanding about a topic so that listeners can understand, interpret, and evaluate complex ideas and information. Good explanatory presentations answer such questions as "Why?" or "What does that mean?"[29]

Not surprisingly, different types of informative messages have different purposes and require different communication strategies. Rowan offers one set of strategies for informatory communication. Explanatory communication is divided into three different types of explanatory functions, as shown in the Classifications of Informative Communication graphic below.

Report New Information

Reporting new information is what most journalists do when they answer *who, what, where, when, why,* and *how* questions. New information is published in newspapers, popular magazines, and online.

You face two challenges when reporting new information. First, when information is new to an audience, it must be presented clearly and in a well-organized manner. Second, you may need to give audience members a reason to listen, learn, and remember. Rowan recommends four strategies for reporting new information as shown below.

Informatory strategies work best when reporting new, uncomplicated information about objects, people, procedures, and events. Keep in mind, however, that an object, person, procedure, or event is not a purpose statement or central idea, so you need to develop one, as the example on fire ants shows (see p. 247).

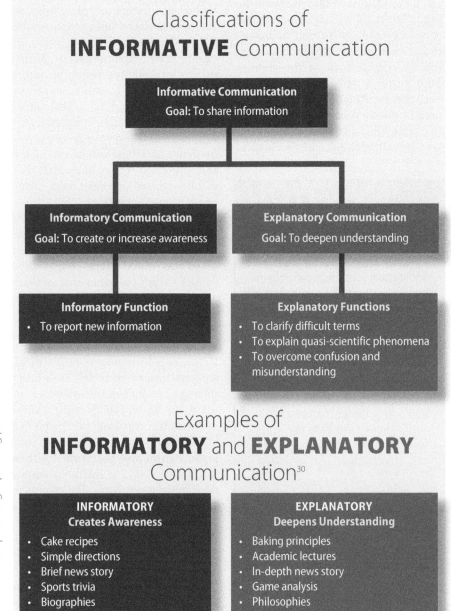

Classifications of
INFORMATIVE Communication

Informative Communication
Goal: To share information

Informatory Communication
Goal: To create or increase awareness

Explanatory Communication
Goal: To deepen understanding

Informatory Function
• To report new information

Explanatory Functions
• To clarify difficult terms
• To explain quasi-scientific phenomena
• To overcome confusion and misunderstanding

Examples of
INFORMATORY and **EXPLANATORY**
Communication[30]

INFORMATORY
Creates Awareness
• Cake recipes
• Simple directions
• Brief news story
• Sports trivia
• Biographies

EXPLANATORY
Deepens Understanding
• Baking principles
• Academic lectures
• In-depth news story
• Game analysis
• Philosophies

Strategies for REPORTING NEW INFORMATION

■ Include a value step in the introduction.

■ Use a clear, organizational pattern.

■ Use a variety of supporting materials.

■ Relate the information to audience interests and needs.

Informatory presentations often describe simple procedures that focus on how to do something. When informing an audience about a procedure or how something works, consider

Topic area Fire ants

Purpose To familiarize audience members with the external anatomy of a fire ant

Central idea A tour of the fire ant's external anatomy will help you understand why these ants are so hard to exterminate.

Value step In addition to inflicting painful and sometimes deadly stings, fire ants can eat up your garden, damage your home, and harm your pets and local wildlife.

Organization Space arrangement—a visual tour of the fire ant's external anatomy

Key points
A. Integument (exoskeleton)
B. Head and its components
C. Thorax
D. Abdomen

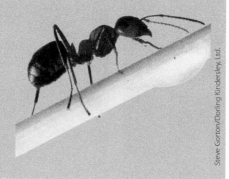

Steve Gorton/Dorling Kindersley, Ltd.

or doing a magic trick. Obvious organizational patterns for such presentations include topical, time, and space arrangement, often along with effective visual aids.

When informing about an event such as the race to the moon or a national campaign, remember that the *purpose* of your presentation will determine how you will talk about that event—regardless of the date, size, or significance of the event.

Strategies for CLARIFYING DIFFICULT TERMS

■ Define the term's essential features.

■ Use various and typical examples.

■ Contrast examples and non-examples.

■ Quiz the audience.

demonstrating the process. Through a series of well-ordered steps, **demonstration speeches** show an audience how to do something and/or how to understand how something works. These presentations can range from signing for the deaf or washing clothes properly to making guacamole

13.5
Persuade Me!

What is the goal of a persuasive presentation and how can you achieve it?

Every generation—from traditionalists and baby boomers to Generations X, Y, and Z—has had its fads and product loyalties. And every one of these generations has been exposed to carefully targeted persuasion. Today, however, there are more sources sending more persuasive messages more often through more types of media. Persuasive messages bombard us from the time we wake up until the moment we end each day. Sometimes persuasion is obvious—a sales call, a political campaign speech, or a television commercial. At other times it's subtler—a sermon, an investment newsletter, a product sample in the mail.[31]

Businesses use persuasion to sell products. Colleges use persuasion to recruit students and faculty. Children persuade parents to let them stay up late or to buy the newest toy.

And speakers use persuasion in everyday presentations and in major public speeches.

Persuasion seeks to change audience opinions (what they think) or behaviour (what they do). Your purpose determines whether you will speak to inform or to persuade. Whereas informative presentations *tell* audiences something by *giving* them information or explanations, **persuasive presentations** *ask* for something *from* audiences—their agreement or a change in their opinions or behaviour.

Persuading Others

If you want to change audience members' opinions or behaviour, you need to understand why they resist change. Why don't people vote for the first candidate who asks for their support? Why don't we run out and

buy every cereal a sports star recommends? Why don't workers quit their job if they dislike their boss? All these questions have good answers—and that's the problem. Most audience members know why they *won't* vote, buy, quit, or do any of the things you ask them to do. It's up to you to determine what the reasons are and address them.

Classifying Audience Attitudes

The more you know about audience members and their attitudes, the more effectively you can adapt your message to them. For example, an audience of homeowners may strongly agree that their property taxes are too high, but a group of local college students may support more taxes for higher education. Review what you

PERSUASION CHANGES
OPINIONS AND BEHAVIOUR

- Your family is more important than your job.

- Japan makes the best automobiles.

- Vegetarian diets are good for your body and good for the planet.

- Eat dinner with your family at least five times a week.

- Buy a Japanese-made car.

- Stop eating meat.

Yuri Arcurs/Shutterstock

Andrea Skjold/Shutterstock

PERSUASIVE PRESENTATIONS *ask* for something *from* audience members—their agreement or a change in their opinions or behavior.

know about your audience's demographic characteristics and attitudes. Then place your audience along a continuum such as the one shown below that measures the extent to which *most* members will agree or disagree with you. When you understand where audience members stand, you can begin the process of adapting your message to the people you want to persuade.

Persuading Audience Members Who Agree with You

When audience members already agree with you, you don't have to *change* their way of thinking. Rather, your goal is to strengthen their attitudes and encourage behavioural change.

When audience members agree with you, consider giving them an **inoculation**. According to social

psychologist William McGuire, protecting **audience attitudes** from counter persuasion by the "other side" is like inoculating the body against disease.[32] You can build up audience resistance by exposing flaws in the arguments of the opposition *and* showing your audience how to refute them. This strategy creates a more enduring change in attitudes or behaviour.

CONTINUUM OF AUDIENCE ATTITUDES

| Strongly agree with me | Agree | Undecided | Disagree | Strongly disagree with me |

Persuading Indecisive Audience Members

Some audience members may not have an opinion about your topic because they are uninformed, unconcerned, or undecided. Knowing which type of persuasive strategy to apply in each case depends on audience members' reasons for indecision. In the following example, a college student begins her presentation on the importance of voting by getting the attention of the undecided students and giving them a reason to care.

How many of you applied for some form of financial aid for college? [More than half the class raised their hands.] How many of you got the full amount you applied for or needed? [Less than one-fourth of the class raised their hands.] I have some bad news for you. Financial aid may be even more difficult to get in the future. But the good news is that there's something you can do about it.

In the real world of persuasive speaking, you are likely to face audiences with some members who agree

Apple keeps its devoted fans all over the globe happy by preaching to the faithful and, as a result, keeps them coming back for the newest versions and upgrades.

Thesimplify/Fotolia

with your message, others who don't, and still others who are indecisive. In such cases, you can focus on just one group—the largest, most influential, or easiest to persuade—or appeal to all three types of audiences by providing new information from highly respected sources.

Toulmin Model of an Argument

Some people think of an *argument* as a dispute or hostile confrontation between two people. In this textbook however, we define an **argument** as a claim supported by evidence and reasoning either for or against that claim.

To help understand the essential structure of an argument, we turn to the **Toulmin model of an argument**, which was developed by Stephen Toulmin, a British philosopher. Toulmin's model maintains that a complete argument requires three essential components: a claim, evidence, and a warrant. In many speaking situations, three supplementary components—backing for the warrant, reservations, and qualifiers—are also necessary.[33] Regardless of whether you are putting together an argument for a speech or you are an audience member listening to a speaker make an argument, you should think critically about all of Toulmin's components to determine whether the argument is worthy of belief.

Claim, Evidence, and Warrant. A **claim** is the conclusion of an argument or the overall position you advocate in a presentation. Claims answer the question, *What is the argument trying to prove?* Stating a claim, however, is not an argument—it is only the starting point. "Where an argument starts is far less important than where it finishes because the logic and evidence in between [are] crucial."[34]

In a complete argument, you support and prove the claim you advocate by providing relevant evidence. **Evidence** answers the question, *How do you know that?* A sound argument relies on strong evidence, which can range from statistics and multiple examples to the advice of experts and generally accepted audience beliefs.

Without the support of good evidence, your audience may be reluctant to accept your claims.

For example, if you claim that keeping a food-intake diary is the best way to monitor a diet, you might share the

persuade me!

249

Can You Find Common Ground?

Below are two controversial topics often chosen by students for class presentations that are often unsuccessful in achieving their purpose. Complete each sentence by stating an issue on which a speaker and audience might find **common ground**. For example, "Free speech advocates and anti-pornography groups would *probably* agree that . . . pornography should not be available to young children." Note that the word *probably* is written in italics. Audience members at extreme ends of any position or belief may not make exceptions and may not be willing to stand on common ground with you.

1. Pro–capital punishment and anti–capital punishment groups would *probably* agree that

   _____

   _____

2. People who are for and against gay marriages would *probably* agree that

   _____

   _____

> If you find common ground, your audience is more likely to listen to you when you move into less friendly territory.

results of a study conducted at a major medical school, which concluded that food-intake diaries produce the best results. Alternatively, you might tell stories about how your attempts to lose weight failed until you spent two months keeping a food-intake diary. You might even distribute examples of food-intake diaries to the audience to show them how easy it is to surpass a 30-gram fat allowance during a "day of dieting."

The **warrant** explains why the evidence is relevant and why it supports the claim. For example, the warrant might say that the author of the article on food-intake diaries is one of the country's leading nutrition experts. Rather than asking, *How do you know that?* the warrant asks, *How did you get there? What gives you the right to draw that conclusion?* In their book *The Well-Crafted Argument*, Fred White and Simone Billings write that "compelling warrants are just as vital to the force of an argument as compelling evidence because they reinforce they validity and trustworthiness of both the claim and evidence."[35] The "Basic T" of the

---

FACTS **THINK** ABOUT THEORY
TEST IDEA PLAN EXPERIMENT METHOD KNOWLEDGE

Psychological Reactance Theory

Psychologist Jack W. Brehm explains why telling an audience what *not* to do can produce the exact opposite reaction. His **psychological reactance theory** suggests that when you perceive a threat to your freedom to believe or behave as you wish, you may go out of your way to *do* the forbidden behaviour or rebel against the prohibiting authority.[36]

Children react this way all the time. You tell them, "Don't snack before

dinner!" or "Don't hit your brother!" or "Stop texting, now!" so they hide their snacks, sneak in a few punches, and spend more time texting. Consider this interesting fact: Although legally designated "coffee shops" in Amsterdam sell marijuana, only about 15 percent of Dutch people older than 12 years have ever used marijuana.[37]

> If you tell an audience "Do this" or "Don't believe that," you may run into strong resistance.

If you believe that your audience may react negatively to your advice or directions, use the following strategies to reduce the likelihood of a reactance response:

- Avoid strong, direct commands such as "don't," "stop," and "you *must*."
- Avoid extreme statements depicting terrible consequences such as "You will die," or "You will fail," or "You will be punished."
- Avoid finger pointing—literally and figuratively. Don't single out specific audience members for condemnation or harsh criticism.
- Advocate a middle ground that preserves audience members' freedom and dignity while moving them toward attitude or behaviour change.
- Use strategies appropriate for audience members who disagree with you.
- Respect your audience's perspectives, needs, and lifestyles.

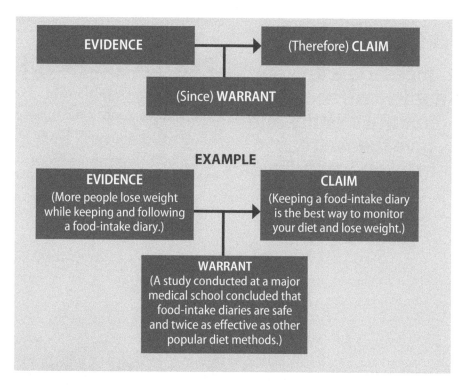

Figure 13.1 The Basic "T" of the Toulmin Model of Argument

Toulmin Model represents the three components—claim, evidence, and warrant—of an argument.

Choosing Persuasive Claims

A good way to start building a persuasive argument is by listing all the possible **claims** you could use—all the reasons why the audience should agree with you. For example, a student speaker planning a presentation on hunting as a means of controlling the growing deer population listed several reasons:

The enormous deer population . . .
. . . is starving and dying of disease.
. . . is eating up crops, gardens, and forest seedlings.
. . . is carrying deer ticks that cause Lyme disease in people.
. . . is causing an increase in the number of highway accidents.
. . . is consuming the food needed by other forest animals.

Although there were many arguments for advocating hunting to reduce the deer population, the speaker had to choose the arguments that, based on his analysis of the audience, were most likely persuade his audience in the amount of time he was scheduled to speak.

Choosing Persuasive Proof

Like lawyers before a jury, persuasive speakers must prove their case.

Lawyers decide what evidence to use when in court, but it's up to the jury or judge to determine whether the evidence is valid and persuasive. When trying to persuade an audience, your success depends on the quality and validity of your **proof**, the arguments and evidence you use to support and strengthen a persuasive claim. Because audiences and persuasive situations differ, so should your proof.[38]

In *Rhetoric*, Aristotle identifies three major types of proof: *logos* (message logic), *pathos* (audience emotions), and *ethos* (the personal nature of the speaker). To that list we add a fourth type of proof—*mythos* (social and cultural values often expressed through narratives).

Logos: Logical Proof Arguments that rely on reasoning and analysis are using **logos** or logical proof. Logical proof relies on an audience's ability to think critically and arrive at a justified conclusion or decision.

Pathos: Emotional Proof Pathos is aimed at deep-seated, emotional feelings about justice, generosity, courage, forgiveness, and wisdom. Many television commercials succeed because they understand the power of emotional proof.[39]

> **Most commercials succeed because they understand the power of emotional proof.**

Ethos: Personal Proof Ethos (speaker credibility) has three major dimensions: competence, character, and charisma. Each of these dimensions can serve as a form of personal proof in a persuasive presentation. To demonstrate that you are a competent speaker of good character, deliver your presentation

Know Thy SELF

Do Fear Appeals Scare You?

Richard Perloff offers the following conclusions about using fear appeals to successfully persuade others:

- **Scare the heck out of listeners.** Describe the dangers in graphic details. Don't beat around the bush.
- **Discuss solutions as well as problems**. Offer them hope. Once you've scared audience members, tell them how to prevent the problem and avoid the danger.
- **Emphasize the costs of not taking action as well as the benefits of taking action.** In other words, you must "get 'em well" after you "get them sick."
- **Make sure that what scares you also scares your audience.** Consider the values and needs of your audience when considering what frightens them.[40]

Now consider the conditions listed below and assess whether fear appeals affect or have affected your attitudes, opinions, and behaviour about each:

1. Your choice of locks or a security system to protect your home
2. Your decision to own a handgun for protection
3. Your willingness to travel abroad
4. Your decision to stop smoking or drinking
5. Your decision to use hand sanitizer and take vitamins and medicines to inhibit viral infections

Jenny Matthews/Alamy

A persuasive speech can motivate audience members to take actions such as joining the CARE Action Network to help women in Afghanistan.

MYTHOS can connect your message with your audience's social and cultural identity, and give them a reason to listen carefully to your ideas.⁴²

with conviction. Audiences are more likely to be persuaded when a speaker seems committed to the cause. Ethos is a powerful form of proof—but you have to *earn* it from your audience if you expect it to help you achieve your persuasive purpose

Mythos: Narrative Proof During the second half of the twentieth century, *mythos*, or narrative proof, emerged as a fourth and significant form of persuasive proof. According to communication scholars Michael and Suzanne Osborn, **mythos** is a form of proof that addresses the values, faith, and feelings that make up our social character and is most often expressed in traditional stories, sayings, and symbols.⁴¹

Junial Enterprises/Shutterstock

COMMUNICATION IN *ACTION*

Watch Out for Heuristics

Heuristics help explain our susceptibility to claims that rely on questionable evidence and warrants. **Heuristics** are cognitive thinking shortcuts we use in decision making because they are correct often enough to be useful. Unfortunately, unethical persuaders sometimes use them to win agreement from their audiences even though their arguments are flawed.⁴³

When audience members are not very interested or motivated to listen or when they are not thinking critically,

they are more likely to believe arguments that lack valid evidence or that offer evidence unrelated to a speaker's claim. The following brief list includes common heuristics we see and hear in everyday life:

- The quality of an item correlates with its price.

- We should believe likable people.

- The behaviour of others is a good guide as to how *we* should behave.

- Confident speakers know what they are talking about.

- Something that is scarce is also valuable.

- Longer messages are strong messages; vivid examples are strong evidence.

Successful salespeople often use heuristics. They appear confident, likable, and trustworthy. They also give you multiple reasons for purchasing expensive, high-quality, limited-edition products that are very popular with discerning customers. When you hear a message that is loaded with heuristics, be cautious. Analyse the arguments carefully before you succumb to their persuasive power.

13.6

Engage Me!

How can you actively engage your audience?

Many of our students ask, "How can I make sure I'm not boring?" Novice speakers often *assume* they're not interesting; they can't imagine why an audience would want to listen to them. Or they have heard lots of boring presentations and fear they are doomed to the same fate. Rarely is either assumption true. Fortunately, three strategies can help keep your audience interested: tell stories, use humour, and involve your audience.

Tell Stories

Throughout history, storytellers have acted as the keepers of tradition and held honoured places in their societies.[44] All of us respond to stories, whether they are depicted in prehistoric cave paintings, portrayed in a film, or read to us.[45]

Stories are accounts of real or imagined events. They can be success stories, personal stories, humorous stories, and even startling stories. Members of the clergy use parables, or stories with a lesson or moral, to apply religious teachings to everyday life.

Joanna Slan, author of *Using Stories and Humor*, claims that the ability to tell stories separates great presenters from mediocre ones.[46] Audiences remember stories because they have the power to captivate, educate, and create lasting images. Stories evoke emotional responses; they communicate the shared experiences of all people.

> Stories evoke emotional responses; they communicate the shared experiences of all people.

Storytelling also benefits speakers. If you're anxious, it can reduce your nervousness. Stories are easy to remember and usually easy to tell, particularly when they relate to events that you experienced personally.

Where to Find Stories Stories are everywhere, from your favourite children's book to your local news. To find the "right" story for your presentation, consider three rich sources: you, your audience, and other people.

You are a living, breathing collection of stories. The origin of your name, for example, might produce a fascinating narrative. Personal incidents or events that changed your life can lead to a good story. Or consider your family's roots, a place that holds significant meaning for you, your successes or failures, and your values.[47]

Your *audience* is also a rich source of stories. Tap into their interests, beliefs,

STORYTELLING
Best Practices

- **Use a simple story line.** Long stories with complex themes are hard to follow and difficult to tell. If you can't summarize your story in less than 25 words, don't tell it.[48]

- **Limit the number of characters.** Unless you're an accomplished actor or storyteller, limit the number of characters in your story. If your story has more than three or four characters, look for another story.

- **Connect to the audience.** Make sure that your story is appropriate for your audience.

- **Exaggerate effectively.** You can exaggerate both content and delivery when telling a story. Exaggeration makes a story more vivid and helps you highlight its message. The tone of your voice, the sweep of your gestures, and your facial expression add a layer of meaning and emphasis to your story.

- **Practise.** Practise telling your story to others—your friends, colleagues, or family members. Practise until you can tell a planned story without notes.

and values. If your audience is deeply religious, you may share a story about a neighbour who gave up her worldly goods to work on a mission. If your audience loves sports, you may share a story about your own triumphs or trials as an athlete. If your audience is culturally diverse, you may share a story about how you, a friend, or colleagues succeeded in bridging cultural differences.

Finally, stories about *other people* can help you connect with your audience. Think about people you know or people you have read about. Consider interviewing friends or family to uncover relevant stories about their life and knowledge. If you are going to tell a story about someone you know, make sure you have that person's permission. Don't embarrass a good friend or colleague by divulging a private story.

Use Humour

Humour in a presentation can capture an audience's attention and help them remember your presentation. Audience members tend to remember humorous speakers positively, even when they are not enthusiastic about the speaker's message. Humour can generate audience respect for the speaker,

7 Tips for USING HUMOUR in a Presentation[49]

1. Focus your humour on the message.
2. Make sure the humour suits you.
3. Practise, practise, practise.
4. Avoid offensive humour such as talking about body functions.
5. Don't tease anyone in your audience.
6. Avoid ethnic or religious humour, unless you are making fun of yourself in an inoffensive way.
7. Limit your funny content.

COMMUNICATION

Exercise

"The Art of Purposeful Storytelling"
https://www.youtube.com/watch?v=8-KtR4vM4eg

After viewing this video clip, and reviewing the content in this section, create your own story to tell based on something you are passionate about. Remember, you should be able to summarize the story in 25 words.

STORY-BUILDING CHART[50]

	STORY-BUILDING GUIDELINES	STORY EXAMPLE
TITLE OF THE STORY	Title of the Story	The Three Little Pigs[51]
BACKGROUND INFORMATION	• Where and when does the story take place? What's going on? • Did anything important happen before the story began? • Provide an initial buildup to the story. • Use concrete details. • Create a vivid image of the time, place, and occasion of the story.	Once upon a time, three little pigs set off to seek their fortune. . . .
CHARACTER DEVELOPMENT	• Who is in the story? • What are their backgrounds? • What do they look and sound like? • How do you want the audience to feel about them? • Bring them to life with colorful and captivating words.	Each little pig built a home. One was made of straw and one was made of sticks. The most industrious pig built a house of bricks. . . .
ACTION OR CONFLICT	• What is happening? • What did you or a character see, hear, feel, smell, or taste? • How are the characters reacting to what's happening? • Let the action build as you tell the story.	Soon, a wolf came along. He blew down the houses made of straw and sticks, but both pigs ran to the house of bricks. At the house of bricks the wolf said, "Little pig, little pig, let me come in." All three pigs said, "No, no, not by the hair of our chinny chin chin." So the wolf huffed and puffed but could not blow the house in. . . .
HIGH POINT OR CLIMAX	• What's the culminating event or significant moment in the story? • What's the turning point in the action? • All action should lead to a discovery, decision, or outcome. • Show the audience how the character has grown or has responded to a situation or problem.	The wolf was very angry. "I'm going to climb down your chimney and eat all of you up," he laughed, "including your chinny chin chins.". . .
PUNCH LINE	• What's the punch line? • Is there a sentence or phrase that communicates the climax of the story? • The punch line pulls the other five elements together. • If you leave out the punch line, the story won't make any sense.	When the pigs heard the wolf on the roof, they hung a pot of boiling water in the fireplace over a blazing fire. . . .
CONCLUSION OR RESOLUTION	• How is the situation resolved? • How do the characters respond to the climax? • Make sure that you don't leave the audience wondering about the fate of a character. • In some cases, a story doesn't need a conclusion—the punch line may conclude it for you.	When the wolf jumped down the chimney, he landed in the pot of boiling water. The pigs quickly put the cover on it, boiled up the wolf, and ate him for dinner. And the three little pigs lived happily ever after.
THE CENTRAL POINT OF THE STORY	The Central Point of the Story	The time and energy you use to prepare for trouble will make you safe to live happily ever after.

hold listeners' attention, and help an audience remember your main points.

Typically, the best source of humour is *you*. **Self-effacing humour**—directing humour at yourself—is usually much more effective than funny stories you've made up or borrowed from a book. But be careful that you don't poke too much fun at yourself. If you begin to look foolish or less than competent, you will damage your credibility.

Involve the Audience

One of the most powerful ways to keep audience members alert and interested is to ask them to participate actively in your presentation. When audience members are encouraged to speak, raise their hands, write, or interact with one another, they become involved in the speechmaking process. You can involve the audience by using several strategies: ask questions, encourage interaction, do an exercise, ask for volunteers, and invite feedback.

Ask Questions Involve audience members by asking questions, posing riddles, or soliciting reactions during or at the end of your presentation. Even if your listeners do little more than nod their heads in response, they will be involved in your presentation. Audience members will be more alert and interested if they know that they

FACTS
TEST
IDEA PLAN
EXPERIMENT
METHOD
KNOWLEDGE

THINK ABOUT THEORY

Narrative Theory

Walter R. Fisher, a respected communication scholar, studies the nature of **narratives**, a term that encompasses the process, art, and techniques of **storytelling**. Fisher sees storytelling as an essential aspect of being human. We experience life "as an ongoing narrative, as conflict, characters, beginnings, middles, and ends."[52] Good stories, he claims, have two essential qualities: probability and fidelity.[53]

Story probability refers to the formal features of a story, such as the consistency of characters and actions, and whether the elements of a story "hang together" and make sense. Would it, for example, seem right if Harry Potter double-crossed his best friends and teachers (unless, of course, he was under some diabolical spell)? Stories that make sense have a clear and coherent structure—one event leads logically to another. When trying to assess a story's probability, ask yourself the following questions:

- **Does the story make sense?** Can you follow the events as they unfold?

- **Do the characters behave in a consistent manner?** Do you wonder "Why did he do that?" or "How could she do that given everything else she's said and done?"

- **Is the plot plausible?** Do you find yourself saying "That just couldn't happen?"

Story fidelity refers to the apparent truthfulness of a story. Whereas story probability investigates the formal storytelling rules related to plot and characters, story fidelity focuses on the story's relationships to the audience's values and knowledge.[54] According to Walter Fisher, when you evaluate a story's fidelity, you try to determine whether the audience's experience rings true "with the stories they know to be true in their lives."[55] To assess the fidelity of a story, ask the following questions:

- **Do the facts and incidents in the story seem realistic?**

- **Does the story reflect your personal values, beliefs, and experiences?**

---

will be quizzed or questioned during or after a presentation.

Encourage Interaction Something as simple as asking audience members to shake hands with one another or to introduce themselves to the people sitting on either side of them generates more audience attention and interest. If you are addressing a professional or business audience, ask them to exchange business cards. If you're addressing young college students, ask them to tell each other their majors or career aspirations.

Do an Exercise Simple games or complex training exercises can involve audience members in your presentation and with one another. Bookstores sell training manuals describing ways to involve groups in games and exercises. Interrupting a presentation for a group exercise gives the audience and the speaker a break during which they can interact in a different but equally effective way.

Ask for Volunteers If you ask for volunteers from the audience, someone will usually offer to participate. Volunteers can help you demonstrate how to perform a skill or how to use a piece of equipment. Some can even

When audience members are encouraged to speak, raise their hands, write, or interact with one another, they become involved in the speechmaking process.

Chris Ryan/OJO Images/Getty Images

What do the raised hands in this photo reveal about the way the speaker has involved the audience in his presentation?

engage me!

be persuaded to participate in a funny exercise or game. Most audiences love to watch a volunteer in action.

Invite Feedback Invite questions and comments from your audience. If audience members seem reluctant to participate, don't badger or embarrass them. If no one responds, continue your presentation. It takes a skilful presenter to encourage and respond to feedback without losing track of a prepared presentation. The more you speak, the easier and more useful feedback is.

Exercise

This chapter has looked at elements to consider when preparing and delivering a presentation. This Ted Talk from 2012, "Nancy Duarte: The Secret Structure of Great Talks," presents Duarte's ideas about some of the great presentations of our time.

www.ted.com/talks/nancy_duarte_the_secret_structure_of_great_talks .html

After viewing the Ted Talk, discuss in small groups how you can borrow from the great presenters to create engaging presentations.

COMMUNICATION **ASSESSMENT**

What's Your Preparation Plan?

Before you determine the content and structure of your message or practice your delivery, make sure you have considered the following checklist designed to help determine whether you are ready to take the next steps in preparing your presentation.

Purpose and Topic

_____ 1. I know my purpose will inform, persuade, entertain, and/or inspire.

_____ 2. I have developed a specific, achievable, and relevant purpose statement.

_____ 3. My topic area reflects my interests, values, and/or knowledge.

Audience Analysis

_____ 1. I have researched, analyzed, and planned ways of adapting to audience characteristics, knowledge, and interests.

_____ 2. I have researched, analyzed, and planned ways of adapting to audience attitudes.

_____ 3. I have researched, analyzed, and planned ways of adapting to cultural differences in my audience.

Speaker Credibility

_____ 1. I have assessed my potential credibility by identifying my strengths, talents, achievements, and positive character traits.

_____ 2. I will demonstrate my competence and good character.

_____ 3. I have made ethical decisions about myself, others, purpose, context, content, structure, and expression.

Context

_____ 1. I have researched, analyzed, and planned ways of adapting to the logistics of the presentation (audience size, facilities, equipment, time).

_____ 2. I have researched, analyzed, and planned ways of adapting to the psychosocial context and occasion.

_____ 3. I have researched, analyzed, and planned ways of adapting to the cultural context.

Preparation Notes

Ways to Improve My Preparation

_____
_____
_____
_____
_____
_____
_____
_____
_____
_____
_____
_____
_____
_____
_____
_____
_____
_____
_____
_____
_____
_____
_____
_____
_____
_____
_____
_____
_____
_____
_____
_____
_____
_____
_____

13.1

Beginning with the Plan

What should you consider when beginning the planning process?

- Determining the purpose of a presentation helps you decide what your audience to know, think, feel or do.

- Decide whether you want to inform, persuade, entertain, inspire, or a combination of all four goals in your presentation.

- Develop a specific, achievable, and relevant purpose statement to guide your presentation and narrow your topic appropriately.

- Make sure your sources are identified, credible, and unbiased for both written and spoken elements

13.2

Researching Content and Organizing Your Presentation

What strategies should you use to research and organize the content of a presentation?

- Identify your central idea and your key points. Make sure the key points reflect your central idea and goal.

- Supporting material comes in many different forms from many different sources: definitions in dictionaries, background and historical information in encyclopaedias, facts and figures online and in almanacs, true-life stories in magazines and on personal websites, and editorial opinions in newspapers, newsletters, and online sources.

13.3

Beginning and Ending Your Presentation

What strategies will help you begin and end a presentation effectively?

- The primacy effect explains our tendency to recall the introduction of a presentation better than the middle.

- Presentation introductions should attempt to focus attention and interest, connect the audience, enhance your credibility, set the emotional tone, and preview the message.

- The recency effect explains our tendency to recall the conclusions of a presentation.

- Methods of concluding a presentation include summarizing, quoting someone, telling a story, calling for action, and referring back to your beginning.

- Your conclusion will be stronger if you make realistic expectations about audience reactions.

13.4

Inform Me!

What is informative speaking and how can you do it successfully?

- An effective informative presentation can instruct, inspire, explain, describe, clarify, correct, remind, and/or demonstrate.

- The dividing line between informing and persuading is the speaker's purpose.

- When speaking to inform, include a value step that explains why the information is valuable to audience members and how it can enhance their success or well-being.

- In order to tell stories that captivate and educate your audience, look for good sources of stories, structure the story effectively, check the story

for fidelity and probability, and use effective storytelling skills.

13.5

Persuade Me!

What is the goal of a persuasive presentation and how can you achieve it?

- Persuasion seeks to change audience members' opinions (what they think) or behaviour (what they do).

- Persuasive presentations ask for their agreement or a change in their opinions or behaviour.

- Psychological reactance theory explains why telling an audience what *not* to do can produce the exact opposite reaction.

13.6

Engage Me!

How can you actively engage the audience?

- Stories and storytelling strategies engage audiences because they can connect with the speaker.

- Well-placed humorous anecdotes can engage your audience, providing an authentic connection between the speaker and the audience.

- Actively engage your audience with direct interactions: ask questions, request volunteers, provide the audience with feedback.

Junial Enterprises/Shutterstock

TEST YOUR KNOWLEDGE

13.1 What should you consider when beginning the planning process?

1 Which type of presentation seeks to instruct, enlighten, explain, describe, and/or demonstrate?

a. informative presentation

b. persuasive presentation

c. entertainment presentation

d. inspirational presentation

e. manuscript presentation

2 A student is presenting information about the importance of literacy. The student has documented sources for a handout given to participants. During the presentation, the student refers to some of the statistical information **not** found on the handout but does not reference the authors of the statistics.

a. The student has documented all the necessary information.

b. Plagiarism rules do not apply to spoken words.

c. It is necessary to state the sources for all spoken words that are not your own; therefore, the student has plagiarized.

d. Plagiarism only applies to written documents.

13.2 What strategies should you use to research and organize the content of a presentation?

3 Which of the following answers constitutes the best example of a central idea for a presentation on the different meanings of facial expressions in other cultures?

a. Facial expressions differ across cultures.

b. The meaning of some facial expressions differs from culture to culture.

c. Facial expressions for fear, sadness, and disgust are the same across cultures.

d. Although many facial expressions are the same in different cultures—such as smiling—other facial expressions differ.

e. Americans and native Japanese often misinterpret facial expressions depicting fear, sadness, and disgust.

4 What kind of supporting material is used in the following excerpt from a student's presentation? *Indigenous artist Henry Bud's work is representative of the elders in his community. It depicts life as a member of the Iroquois nation.*

a. fact

b. statistics

c. testimony

d. description

e. story

13.3 What strategies will help you begin and end a presentation effectively?

5 The primacy effect explains why _____.

a. an effective introduction is so important to the beginning of a presentation.

b. an effective conclusion is so important to the end of the presentation.

c. transitions are so important in the middle of a presentation.

d. presentations should end with a "bang".

e. a presentation's key points should be determined before looking for supporting material.

13.4 What is informative speaking and how can you do it successfully?

6 If you ask yourself, "Will my presentation explain intriguing and novel discoveries in science?" when searching for a value step, which audience benefit are you trying to achieve?

a. social benefit

b. psychological benefit

c. physical benefit

d. intellectual benefit

e. professional benefit

7 When clarifying a difficult term in an informative presentation, which of the following strategies should you exploit?

a. Use analogies and metaphors.

b. Use various examples.

c. Use presentation aids.

d. Explain theories.

e. Quiz the audience.

13.5 What is the goal of a persuasive presentation and how can you achieve it?

8 Given that persuasion seeks to change audience opinions and/or behaviour, which of the following examples represents an appeal to audience opinion?

a. Eat dinner with your family at least five times a week.

b. Vegetarian diets are good for you and the planet.

c. Buy a gas-electric hybrid car.

d. Vote!

e. Choose a college that matches your interests, personality, and needs.

9 What kind of audience should you try to find common ground?

a. an audience that agrees with you

b. an audience that disagrees with you

c. an audience that is uninformed

d. an audience that is unconcerned

e. an audience that is undecided

13.6 How can you actively engage your audience?

10 What introductory technique did Dalton McGuinty use when he began his resignation speech in October, 2012 with these words?: *Sixteen years ago, when I was elected leader of our party, the Ontario Liberals had won exactly one election in fifty years. We couldn't do anything to help families because we couldn't win an election. That's changed. We've won three elections in a row. But more important is what those election wins have allowed us to do.*

a. Refer to a current place or occasion.

b. Refer to a well-known incident or event.

c. Use a metaphor.

d. Quote someone.

e. Address the audience needs.

Answers found on p. 330.

Key Terms

Analogies	**Explanatory**	**Primacy effect**
Argument	**communication**	**Proof**
Audience analysis	**Fact**	**Psychological reactance**
Audience	**Heuristics**	**theory**
attitudes	**Informative presentation**	**Purpose statement**
Central idea	**Informatory**	**Recency effect**
Character	**communication**	**Rhetoric**
Charisma	**Inoculation**	**Self-effacing humour**
Claim	**Key points**	**Speaker credibility**
Competence	**Logos**	**Speech Framer**
Content	**Mind mapping**	**Statistics**
Definitions	**Mythos**	**Stories**
Demographic	**Narratives**	**Story fidelity**
information	**Oral footnote**	**Story probability**
Demonstration	**Organization**	**Supporting material**
speeches	**Pathos**	**Testimony**
Description	**Persuasion**	**Toulmin model of an**
Documentation	**Persuasive presentation**	**argument**
Ethos	**Plagiarism**	**Valid**
Evidence	**Preliminary outline**	**Value step**
Example	**Presentation speaking**	**Warrant**

LANGUAGE and **DELIVERY**

At the 2010 Winter Olympics, Canadian poet Shane Koyczan burst onto the world stage with his moving poem about Canada, "We Are More."[1] His poems are usually hard hitting, with carefully chosen words that evoke strong emotional responses. In his stories and poems, Shane uses language in performances and unique presentation styles to distinguish his messages from all others on the Internet, on college and university campuses, or in print. As a young boy, Koyczan was bullied, and his latest work, "To This Day," is a moving testament to the effects of bullying and the importance of inspiring change.[2]

In this chapter, we focus on two performance components of presentation speaking: language and delivery.

Presenting involves more than the words you choose; it also includes the tone, volume, and style of your message. Understanding the power of presentation will help you to be a strong and effective communicator.

Ryan Remiorz/The Canadian Press

COMMUNICATION

Exercise

View and listen to "We Are More," Shane Koyczan's Olympic poem on YouTube:

http://www.youtube.com/watch?v=zsq68qRexFc

An audio-only version can be heard at

http://houseofparlance.com/VisitingHours/wearemore.html

1. Which presentation of Koyczan's poem do you find more effective? Why?
2. How important do you think the visuals are to help the listener to fully understand the message?

The CORE Language Styles

How do you choose appropriate language for a presentation?

Carefully chosen words can add power and authority to a presentation and transform good speeches into great ones. Your speaking style can add a distinct flavour, emotional excitement, and brilliant clarity.

Speaking style refers to how you use vocabulary, sentence structure and length, grammar and syntax, and rhetorical devices to express a message.[3] In this section, we describe four **CORE speaking styles:** clear style, oral style, rhetorical style, and eloquent style. Your task is to decide which style or styles suit you, your purpose, your audience, the setting and occasion of your presentation, and your message.

The four CORE speaking styles are often most effective when used in combination. Once you become capable and comfortable using the clear and oral styles, you are on "firm ground" to use the rhetorical and eloquent styles to persuade and inspire your audience. While you may use all four styles, we recognize that some speakers are more comfortable using only the clear and oral styles whiles others prefer the added intensity of the rhetorical and eloquent styles. Depending on your purpose, audience, setting, and occasion, use the styles that best match you and your messages.

Clear Style

Clarity always comes first. If you aren't clear, your audience won't understand you or your message. The **clear style** uses short, simple, and direct words and phrases as well as active verbs, concrete words, and plain language.

Oral Style

In Chapter 5, "Verbal Communication," we emphasize the importance of using oral language when interacting with others. Recall the features of the **oral style:** short, familiar words; shorter, simpler, and even incomplete sentences; and more personal pronouns and informal colloquial expressions.

> When using an oral style, say what you mean by speaking the way you talk, **not the way you write.**

Rhetorical Style

The **rhetorical style** uses language designed to influence, persuade, and/or inspire. Vivid and powerful words enhance the intensity of a persuasive presentation. **Language intensity** refers to the degree to which your language deviates from bland, neutral terms.[4] For example, instead of using a word like *nice*, try *delightful* or *captivating*. *Disaster* is a much more intense word than *mistake*. A *vile* meal sounds much worse than a *bad* meal.

The rhetorical style often relies on **rhetorical devices,** word strategies designed to enhance a presentation's impact and persuasiveness. Two rhetorical devices work particularly well in presentations: repetition and metaphors.

Repetition Because your listeners can't rewind and immediately rehear what you've just said, use repetition to highlight the sounds, words, ideas, and phrases you want your audience to remember. Repetition can be as simple as beginning a series of words (or words placed closely together) with the same sound. This type of repetition is called **alliteration.** A fun example from childhood occurs when the Tin Man in Wizard of Oz asks for a heart, "Step forward, Tin Man. You dare to come to me for a heart, do you? You clinking, clanking, clattering collection of caliginous junk. . . ."

Repetition can be extended to a word, a phrase, or an entire sentence.

The **CORE** Speaking Styles

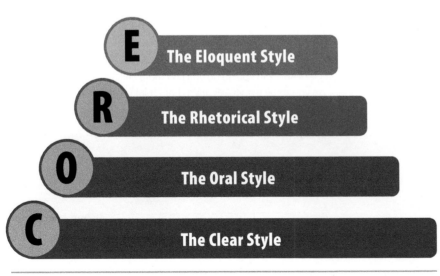

The CORE speaking styles build on a foundation that uses the clear and oral styles as firm ground for enlisting the rhetorical and eloquent speaking styles.

Dr. Martin Luther King, Jr., used the phrase "I have a dream" nine times in his famous 1963 speech in Washington, D.C. He used "let freedom ring" 10 times. Repetition can drive home an idea and provoke action. Audience members anticipate and remember repeated phrases.

Metaphors Metaphors and their cousins—similes and analogies—are powerful rhetorical devices. Shakespeare's famous line "All the world's a stage" is a classic metaphor. The world is not a theatrical stage, but we do assume many roles during a lifetime. Author Isabel Allende's colourful description of art is another potent metaphor: "*Art is a rebellious child, a wild animal that will not be tamed.*" Metaphors leave it to the audience to get the point for themselves.[5]

Many linguists claim that metaphors are the most powerful figures of speech. Some researchers believe that metaphors are windows into the workings of the human mind.[6]

Eloquent Style

The **eloquent style** uses poetic and expressive language in a way that makes thoughts and feelings clear, inspiring, *and* memorable. Eloquent language does not have to be flowery or grand; it can use an oral style, personal pronouns, and repetition or metaphors.

In *Eloquence in an Electronic Age: The Transformation of Political Speechmaking*, Kathleen Jamieson notes that eloquent speakers comfortably disclose personal experiences and feelings. Rather than explaining the lessons of the past or creating a public sense of ethics, today's most eloquent speakers often call on their own past or their own sense of ethics to inspire an audience.[7] Consider the ideas expressed by Frank O'Dea, co-founder of the Second Cup chain of coffee stores, in his speeches about homelessness and hope, in which he describes how both of these experiences—hope and homelessness—have shaped his life. He chooses words carefully, drawing the audience into his speech, asking each of us to make a difference.[8]

The Canadian Press

POETIC LANGUAGE has the remarkable ability to capture profound ideas and feelings in a few simple words.

COMMUNICATION

Exercise

To listen to Frank O'Dea's story in his own words, visit this YouTube link.

www.youtube.com/watch?v=fX7ya8UoLLE

How does Frank O'Dea use experiences and feelings to create an inspiring and memorable presentation?

14.2

Modes of Delivery

How do you choose an appropriate delivery style for a presentation?

The term **delivery** describes the ways in which you use your voice, body, and presentation aids to express your presentation's message. You should begin planning how to deliver your presentation by deciding which delivery mode to use: impromptu, extemporaneous, manuscript, memorized, or a combination of forms. But,

ADVANTAGES AND DISADVANTAGES
OF IMPROMPTU DELIVERY

ADVANTAGES

- Natural and conversational speaking style
- Maximum eye contact
- Freedom of movement
- Easier to adjust to audience feedback
- Demonstrates speaker's knowledge and skill

DISADVANTAGES

- Limited time to make basic decisions about purpose, audience adaptation, content, and organization
- Speaker anxiety can be high
- Speaker may be at a "loss for words"
- Delivery may be awkward and ineffective
- Difficult to gauge speaking time
- Limited or no supporting material
- Speaker may have nothing to say on such short notice

before you do, decide which of these modes best suits your purpose.

Impromptu

Impromptu speaking occurs when you speak without advanced preparation or practice. For example, you may be called on in class or at work to answer a question or share an opinion. You may be inspired to get up and speak on an important issue at a public meeting. Even in those instances when you don't have a lot of time to prepare, you can quickly think of a purpose and a way to organize and adapt your message to the audience.

Extemporaneous

Extemporaneous speaking is the most common form of delivery and occurs when you use an outline or a set of notes to guide you through a well-prepared presentation. Your notes can be a few words on a card or a detailed, full-sentence outline. Classroom lectures, business briefings, and courtroom arguments are usually delivered extemporaneously.

COMMUNICATION

Exercise

In small groups of three or four students, practise impromptu speaking.

To practise this skill, choose one of the topics listed below.

You will have only five minutes to prepare, and you will not have the opportunity to research.

Important reminders:

1. Think of a purpose for your chosen topic.

2. Organize your thoughts.

3. Consider your audience (class members).

Provide feedback to each group member after his or her impromptu speech.

1. Was the purpose clearly defined?

2. Did the speech flow and have a beginning, middle, and end?

3. Did the speaker make eye contact?

4. Did the speaker adjust tone and word choice for the audience?

Topics:

(1) How can you be wise but not smart? (2) Explain how to change a tire. (3) Tell us about a life-changing moment you have experienced. (4) Convince the group that college is a waste of time.

DISADVANTAGES	ADVANTAGES
• Speaker anxiety can increase for content not covered by notes • Language may not be well chosen or eloquent • Can be difficult to estimate speaking time	• More preparation time than impromptu delivery • Seems spontaneous but is actually well prepared • Speaker can monitor and adapt to audience feedback • Allows more eye contact and audience interaction than manuscript delivery • Audiences typically respond positively to extemporaneous delivery • Speaker can choose concise language for central idea and key points • With practice, it becomes the most powerful form of delivery

WavebreakmediaMicro/Fotolia

Extemporaneous speaking is easiest for beginners to do well and the method preferred by professionals. No other form of delivery gives you as much freedom and flexibility with preplanned material. A well-practised extemporaneous presentation seems spontaneous and has an ease to it that makes the audience and speaker feel comfortable.

Manuscript

Manuscript speaking involves writing your presentation in advance and reading it out loud. For very nervous speakers, a manuscript may *seem* like a lifesaving document, keeping them afloat when they feel as though they're drowning. However, manuscript speeches are difficult to deliver for all but the most skilled speakers, and we strongly discourage speakers from using manuscript delivery. When, however, an occasion is a major public event after which your words will be published word for word, you may have no choice but to use a manuscript for at least part of your presentation. And if an occasion is highly emotional—such as delivering a eulogy—you may need the support of a manuscript.

Using a manuscript allows you to choose each word carefully. You can plan and practise every detail. It also ensures that your presentation will fit within your allotted speaking time.

If you must use a manuscript, focus on maintaining an oral style when you write your speech: *Write as though you are speaking.*

Memorized

Memorized speaking requires a speaker to deliver a presentation from recall with very few or no notes. A memorized presentation offers one major advantage and one major disadvantage. The major advantage is physical freedom. You can gesture freely and look at your audience 100 percent of the time. The disadvantage, however, outweighs any and all advantages. If you forget the words you memorized, it is more difficult to recover your thoughts without creating an awkward moment for both you and your audience.

Rarely do speakers memorize an entire presentation. However, there's nothing wrong with memorizing your introduction or a few key sections as long as you have your notes to fall back on.

Mix and Match Modes of Delivery

Learning to mix and match modes of delivery appropriately lets you select the method that works best for you and your purpose. An impromptu speaker may recite a memorized statistic or a rehearsed argument in the same way that a politician responds to

ADVANTAGES	DISADVANTAGES
• Speaker can pay careful attention to all the basic principles of effective speaking • Speaker can choose concise and eloquent language • Speaker anxiety may be eased by having a "script" • Speaker can rehearse the same presentation over and over • Ensures accurate reporting of presentation content • Speaker can stay within time limit	• Delivery can be dull • Difficult to maintain sufficient eye contact • Gestures and movement are limited • Language can be too formal, lacking oral style • Difficult to modify or adapt to the audience or situation

Blend Images/Hill Street Studios/Sarah Golonka/Getty Images

ADVANTAGES AND DISADVANTAGES OF MEMORIZED DELIVERY

ADVANTAGES	DISADVANTAGES
• Incorporates the preparation advantages of manuscript delivery and the delivery advantages of impromptu speaking • Maximizes eye contact and freedom of movement	• Requires extensive time to memorize • Disaster awaits if memory fails • Can sound stilted and insincere • Very difficult to modify or adapt to the audience or situation • Lacks a sense of spontaneity unless expertly delivered

press questions. An extemporaneous speaker may read a lengthy quotation or a series of statistics and then deliver a memorized ending.

Speaking Notes

Effective speakers use their notes efficiently. Even when your presentation is impromptu, you may use a few quick words jotted down just before you speak. Speaking notes may appear on index cards and outlines or as a manuscript.

Index Cards and Outlines A single card can be used for each component of your presentation; for example, you can use one card for the introduction, another card for each key point, and one card for your conclusion. Record key words rather than complete sentences; use only one side of each index card. To help you organize your presentation and rearrange key points at the last minute, number each of the cards. If you have too many notes for a few index cards, use an outline on a full sheet of paper.

Manuscript When preparing a speech manuscript, double space each page and use a 14- to 16-point font size. Use only the top two-thirds of the page to avoid having to bend your head to see the bottom of each page and lose eye contact with your audience or constrict your windpipe. Set wide margins so that you have space on the page to add any last-minute changes. Remember to number each page so that you can keep everything in order and do not staple your pages together. Instead, place your manuscript to one side of the lectern and slide the pages to the other side when it's time to go on to the next page.

14.3

Confident Delivery

How can you reduce presentation anxiety?

We often ask students to complete the sentence "Giving a speech makes me feel. . . ." Their responses range from feelings of empowerment to total terror.

Are You More Nervous Than Most People?

When we ask students about their presentation speaking goals, they tell us that they want to "gain confidence," "overcome anxiety," "stop being nervous," "get rid of the jitters," and "calm down." No other answer comes close in terms of frequency. Most of these students also believe they are more nervous than other speakers are.

Successful presenters know two very important facts about speaking anxiety: They know that it's very common and that it's usually invisible. As speakers— experienced or otherwise—we all

Lorelyn Medina/Fotolia

Will the Audience Know I'm Nervous?

Many speakers fear that audience members know they're anxious. Although there are some signs of nervousness that an audience can see or hear, most signs are invisible. Use the following table to make a list of your own symptoms of speaking anxiety or symptoms you have seen or heard in others. In the left-hand column, list symptoms the audience *can* see or hear. In the right-hand column, list symptoms the audience *cannot* see or hear. An example is provided for each type of symptom.

Here's the good news: In most cases, speaking anxiety is invisible. Audiences cannot see a pounding heart, an upset stomach, cold hands, or worried thoughts. They do not notice small changes in your vocal quality or remember occasional mistakes. Although you may feel as though your legs are quivering and quaking uncontrollably, the audience will rarely see any movement.

Most speakers who describe themselves as being nervous appear confident and calm to their audiences. Even experienced communication instructors, when asked about how anxious a speaker is, seldom accurately estimate the speaker's anxiety.[9] Now recheck the symptoms you believe the audience *can* see or hear in the chart you just filled out. In all probability, you will want to move some of those symptoms to the list of symptoms that listeners *cannot* see or hear.

Symptoms the audience *can* see or hear	Symptoms the audience *cannot* see or hear
Example: Shaking hands	*Example:* Upset stomach
1.	1.
2.	2.
3.	3.
4.	4.
5.	5.

share many of the same worried thoughts, physical discomforts, and psychological anxieties. This means that most audience members understand your feelings, don't want to trade places with you, and may even admire your courage for being up there.

If you still believe that you are more nervous than anyone else is, make an appointment with your instructor to discuss your concerns. Many colleges and departments offer special assistance to students who feel disabled by their level of fear and anxiety associated with speaking to others.

Will Reading About Speaking Anxiety Make You *More* Nervous?

You may think that the more you learn about speaking anxiety, the more nervous you'll become. Just the opposite is true: The more accurate information and sound advice you read about speaking anxiety, the more likely you are to build confidence. In his study on reading about public speaking apprehension, Michael Motley had one group of college students read a booklet that discussed the nature and causes of, as well as strategies for minimizing, speaking anxiety. A second group viewed relaxation tapes, read an excerpt from a popular self-help book on reducing fears, or received no treatment at all. The greatest decrease in speaking anxiety occurred in the group that read the booklet on speaking anxiety.[10] Similarly, reading this textbook can help you understand why you become anxious when you have to make a presentation and help calm your fears, expose you to techniques for dealing with those fears, and increase your speaking confidence.

> Despite most people's worst fears, audiences are usually kind to speakers. They are willing to forgive and forget an honest mistake.

COMMUNICATION

Exercise

Visit the website of Toastmasters, an international organization dedicated to helping members hone their speaking and leadership skills:

www.toastmasters.org

Explore the online free resources and discover the connection between confident delivery of your message and personal and professional success.

confident delivery

14.4
Vocal Delivery
What are the components of effective vocal delivery?

Developing an effective speaking voice requires the same time and effort that you would devote to mastering any skill. You can't become an accomplished carpenter, pianist, swimmer, writer, or speaker overnight. Because only a few lucky speakers are born with beautiful voices, the majority of us must work at sounding clear and expressive. Fortunately, there are ways to improve the characteristics and quality of your voice. Begin by focusing on the basics: breathing, volume, rate, pitch, fluency, articulation, and pronunciation.

Breathing

Effective breath control enables you to speak more loudly, say more in a single breath, and reduce the likelihood of vocal problems such as harshness or breathiness. Thus, the first step in learning how to breathe for presentation speaking is to note the differences between the shallow, unconscious breathing you do all the time and the deeper breathing that produces strong, sustained sound quality. Many speech coaches recommend practising deep, abdominal breathing.

Volume

Volume measures the loudness level of your voice. The key to producing adequate volume is adapting to the size of the audience and the dimensions of the room in which you will be speaking. If there are only five people in an audience and they are sitting close to you, speak at a normal, everyday volume. If there are 50 people in your audience, you need more energy and force to support your voice. When your audience exceeds 50, you may be more comfortable with a microphone. However, a strong speaking voice can project to an audience of a thousand people without electronic amplification. Professional actors and classical singers do it all the time.

Practise your presentation in a room about the same size as the one in which you will be speaking, or, at least, imagine speaking in such a room. Ask a friend to sit in a far corner and report back on your volume and clarity. Also note that a room full of people absorbs sound; you will have to turn up your volume another notch when your audience is present. Speakers who cannot be heard are a common problem. It's very rare, though, for a speaker to be too loud.

Rate

Your speaking **rate** refers to the number of words you say per minute (wpm). Generally, a rate less than 125 wpm is too slow, 125 to 145 wpm is acceptable, 145 to 180 wpm is better, and 180 wpm or more exceeds the speed limit. But these guidelines are not carved in stone. Your preferred rate depends on you, the nature and mood of your message, and your audience. If you are explaining a highly technical process or expressing personal sorrow, your rate may slow to 125 wpm. On the other hand, if you are telling an exciting, amusing, or infuriating story, your rate may hit 200 wpm. For maximum effectiveness, speakers vary their rate.

> Remember that audiences can listen faster than you talk, so it's better to keep the pace up than speak at a crawl.

Listeners perceive presenters who speak quickly *and* clearly as energized, motivated, and interested. Given the choice, we'd rather be accused of speaking too quickly than run the risk of boring an audience. Too slow a rate may suggests that you are unsure of yourself or, even worse, that you are not knowledgeable about your topic.

Pitch

Pitch is how high or low your voice sounds—just like the notes on a musical scale. Anatomy determines pitch (most men speak at a lower pitch than women and children). Your **optimum pitch** is the pitch at which you speak most easily and expressively. If you speak at your optimum pitch, you will not tire as easily; your voice will sound stronger and will be less likely to fade at the end of sentences. It will also be less likely to sound harsh, hoarse, or breathy.

Think of your optimum pitch as "neutral" and use it as your baseline, then increase the expressiveness of your voice through **inflection**—the changing pitch within a syllable, word, or group of words. Your voice will sound monotone without the use of inflection. A slight change, however, even just a fraction, can change the entire meaning of a sentence or the quality of your voice:

I was born in North Bay. (You, on the other hand, were born in Ottawa.)

I *was* born in North Bay. (No doubt about it!)

I was *born* in North Bay. (So I know my way around.)

I was born in *North Bay*. (Not in St. Catharines.)

Fluency

When you speak with **fluency,** you speak smoothly without tripping over words or pausing at awkward moments. The more you practise your presentation, the more fluent you will become. Practice will alert you to words, phrases, and sentences that may look good in your notes but sound awkward or choppy when spoken. You'll also discover words that you have trouble pronouncing or notice **filler phrases**—*you know,*

Gay activist, politician, and founder of milkfoundation.org, Harvey Milk was well known for his dynamic speeches, often delivered without the aid of a microphone.

uh, um, okay, and *like*—that can break up your fluency and annoy your audience. There is nothing wrong with an occasional filler phrase, particularly when you're speaking informally or impromptu. What you want to avoid is excessive use. Try recording your practice sessions and listening for filler phrases as you play back the recording. To break the filler-phrase habit, slow down and listen to the words you use. To break the habit, you must work on it all the time, not just when you are speaking in front of an audience.

COMMUNICATION IN *ACTION*

Master the Microphone

If your speaking situation requires a microphone, make the most out of this technology. Unless a sound technician is monitoring the presentation, your microphone will be preset for one volume. If you speak with too much volume, it may sound as though you are shouting at your audience. If you speak too softly, the microphone may not pick up everything you have to say. The trick is to go against your instincts. If you want to project a soft tone, speak closer to the microphone and lower your volume. If you want to be more forceful, speak farther away from the microphone and project your voice.

Most important, familiarize yourself with the specific microphone and system you will be using. For example, when placed on a lapel, a microphone faces outward rather than upward. As a result, it receives and sends a less direct sound than a handheld microphone.[11] Tips to follow for all microphones:

- Test the microphone ahead of time.
- Determine whether the microphone is sophisticated enough to capture your voice from several angles and distances or whether you will need to keep your mouth close to it.
- Place the microphone about 5 to 10 inches from your mouth. If you are using a handheld microphone, hold it below your mouth at chin level.
- Focus on your audience, not the microphone. Stay near the mic but don't tap it, lean over it, keep readjusting it, or make the p-p-p-p-p "motorboat sounds" as a test.

Experienced speakers make the adjustments they need during the first few seconds that they hear their own voices projected through an amplification system.

- Keep in mind that a microphone will do more than amplify your voice; it will also amplify other sounds—coughing, clearing your throat, shuffling papers, or tapping a pen.
- If your microphone is well adjusted, simply speak in a natural, conversational voice.

vocal delivery

Articulation

A strong, well-paced, optimally pitched voice that is also fluent and expressive may not be enough to ensure the successful delivery of a presentation. Proper **articulation**—clearly making the sounds in the words of a language—is just as important as your volume, rate, pitch, and fluency. Poor articulation is often described as sloppy speech, poor diction, or mumbling. Fortunately, you can improve and practise your articulation by speaking more slowly, speaking with a bit more volume, and opening your mouth wider when you speak.

Certain sounds account for most articulation problems: combined words, "-ing" endings, and final consonants. Many speakers combine words—"what's the matter" becomes "watsumata." Some speakers shorten the "ing" sound to an "in" sound: "sayin" instead of "saying." The final consonants that get left off most often are the ones that pop out of your mouth. Because these consonants—*p, b, t, d, k,* and *g*—cannot be hummed like an "m" or hissed like an "s," it's easy to lose them at the end of a word. Usually you can hear the difference between "Rome" and "rose," but poor articulation can make it difficult to hear the difference between "hit" and "hid" or "tap" and "tab." In the professional world, poor articulation can quickly give the impression that you are not as knowledgeable as one of your peers. The way you speak can be very important in any given situation.

Pronunciation

Proper **pronunciation** involves putting all the correct sounds of a word in the correct order with the correct stress. In a presentation-speaking situation, poor pronunciation can result in misunderstanding and embarrassment. For example, we once heard a speaker undermine her credibility in a talk about effective communication when she repeatedly said the word "pro*noun*ciation" instead of "pro*nun*ciation."

Pronunciations can and do change. According to most dictionaries, the word *often* should be pronounced "awfen," but many people now put the "t" sound in the middle and pronounce it the way it's spelled. The word *a* should be pronounced "uh," not rhymed with *hay*, but many people now use both versions. Even the word *the* is often mispronounced. When *the* appears before the sound of a consonant as in "the dog" or "the paper," it should be pronounced "thuh." When *the* comes before the sound of a vowel as in "the alligator" or "the article," it should be pronounced "thee." These guidelines can make English an even more difficult language to master for those for whom English is not their first language.

COMMUNICATION&CULTURE

ADAPT YOUR GESTURES TO CULTURAL DIFFERENCES

All over the world, people "talk" with their hands. The meanings of gestures, however, may be quite different in different cultures and cultural contexts—both domestic and international. Everett Rogers and Thomas Steinfatt share a story about a U.S. professor teaching at Bangkok University in Thailand. The professor frequently put his hands in his pockets or held them behind his back while lecturing to his class. At the end of the semester, his polite Thai students gently informed him that he should hold his hands in front of himself. They had been embarrassed and distracted when he broke the cultural norm of keeping your hands visible when communicating.[12]

Most of our hand gestures are culturally determined. One of the best examples is a gesture in which you touch the tips of your thumb to index finger to form a circle. In Canada, this gesture usually means that everything is "A-okay." The same gesture, however, can be a sign for the sex act in some Latin American nations. To the French, the sign may indicate that someone is a "zero," and to people in Malta, it is an invitation to have homosexual sex.[13]

In most speaking situations—both inside and outside Canada—certain gestures can trigger negative responses from an audience. Pointing or wagging the index finger at your audience, for example, may be seen as rude and offensive because it is associated with parental scolding. Instead of pointing your index finger at your audience, try gesturing with an open hand—fingers together, palm and inner wrist turned slightly toward the audience, and forearm slightly bent and extended at about a 45-degree angle to the side (not aimed directly *at* the audience).[14]

Physical Delivery

What are the components of effective physical delivery?

The key to effective physical delivery is naturalness. However, being natural doesn't mean "letting it all hang out." Rather, it means being so well prepared and well practised that your presentation is an authentic reflection of you.

Your delivery tells an audience a great deal about who you are and how much you care about reaching them.

After all, if you don't look at your audience, why should they look at you?

Audience members jump to conclusions about speakers based on first impressions of appearance and behaviour. The way you stand, move, gesture, and make eye contact has a significant impact on your presentation.

Eye Contact

Eye contact, establishing and maintaining direct, visual links with individual audience members, may be the most important component of effective physical delivery. Generally, the more eye contact you have with your audience, the better. Try to maintain eye contact during *most* of your presentation. If you are using detailed notes or a manuscript, use a technique called *eye scan*. **Eye scan** involves glancing at a specific section of your notes or manuscript and then looking up at your audience to speak. Begin by placing your thumb and index finger on one side of the page to frame the section of the notes you are using. Then, as you approach the end of a phrase or sentence within that section, glance down again and

visually grasp the next phrase to be spoken. This allows you to maintain maximum eye contact without losing your place.

Eye contact does more than ensure that you are looking in the direction of your audience. It also helps you to initiate and control communication, enhance your credibility, and interpret valuable audience feedback.

Strategies for MAINTAINING EYE CONTACT

- Talk to your audience members and look at them the same way you would talk and look at a friend, co-worker, or customer

- Move your gaze around the room, occasionally settle on someone, and establish direct eye contact

- Don't move your eyes in a rigid pattern; try to establish eye contact with as many individual people as you can

---

Control Have you ever noticed a teacher "catch the eye" of a student or "give the eye" to an inattentive student? When you establish initial eye contact with your audience, you indicate that you are ready to begin speaking and that they should get ready to listen. Lack of eye contact communicates a message, too: It says that you don't care to connect with your audience.

Credibility Direct eye contact says, "I'm talking to *you*; I want *you* to hear this." In Western cultures, such directness positively affects your credibility.[15] It says, "I'm of good character (I care enough to share this important message with you)," "I'm competent (I know this subject

so well I can leave my notes and look at you)," and "I'm charismatic (I want to energize and connect with everyone in this room)."

Feedback Eye contact is the best way to gauge audience feedback during a presentation. At first, looking audience members in the eye may distract you. Some people smile, others may look bored or confused, and some may be looking around the room or passing notes to their friends. With this going on in the audience, it's easy to become sidetracked. However, these different responses are also the very reason you must establish and maintain eye contact. Speakers who don't look directly at audience members rarely have a clue about why their presentations succeed or fail.

Facial Expression

Your face reflects your attitudes and emotional states, provides nonverbal feedback, and, next to the words you speak, is the primary source of information about you.[16]

Despite the importance of facial expressions, they are difficult to control. Most of us tend to display a particular style of facial expression. Some people show little expression—they have a stoic, poker face most of the time. Others are as open as a book—you have little doubt about how they feel. It's very difficult to change a "poker face" into an "open book" or vice versa. A nervous speaker may be too distracted to smile, too frightened to stop smiling, or too giddy to register displeasure or anger when appropriate.

Audiences will direct their eyes at your face; so unless your topic is very solemn or serious, try to smile. A smile shows your listeners that you are comfortable and eager to share your ideas and information. Audience members are more likely to smile if you smile. However, if you do not feel comfortable smiling, don't force it. Let your face communicate your feelings; let your face do what comes naturally. If you speak honestly and sincerely, your facial expression will be appropriate and effective.

Gestures

As Chapter 6, "Nonverbal Communication," explains, a gesture is a body movement that conveys or reinforces a thought or an emotion. Most gestures are made with your hands and arms, but shrugging a shoulder, bending a knee, and tapping a foot are gestures, too. Gestures can clarify and support your words, relieve nervous tension, and arouse audience attention.

Repetitive movements such as constantly pushing up your eyeglasses, tapping on a lectern, or jingling change or keys in your pocket can distract and eventually annoy an audience. One of the best ways to eliminate unwanted gestures is to video yourself during a practice session and then review the video to see how you can improve. Once you see how often you fidget, you'll work even harder to correct your behaviour.

Your face . . .

Kazoka303030/Fotolia

Olenny/Shutterstock

Jason Stitt/Shutterstock

. . . is the primary source of information about you.

— Mark Knapp and Judith Hall

Posture and Movement

Posture and movement involve how you stand and move and whether your movements add or detract from your presentation. If you stand comfortably and confidently, you will radiate alertness and control. If you stoop or look unsure on your feet, you will communicate anxiety or disinterest. Try to stand straight but not rigid. Your feet should be about a foot apart. If you stand tall, lean forward, and keep your chin up, you will open your airway and help make your voice clear and your volume appropriate.

Your posture communicates.

In general, a purposeful movement can attract attention, channel nervous energy, or support and emphasize a

---

STOP&THINK

What Should You Do with Your Hands?

We hear this question all the time, and our answer is always the same: Do what you normally do with your hands. If you gesture a lot in conversations with other people, keep doing what comes naturally. If you rarely gesture, don't try to invent new and unnatural hand movements.

Effective gestures are a natural outgrowth of what you feel and what you have to say. If you start thinking about your gestures, you are likely to appear awkward and unnatural. Rather than thinking about your hands, think about your audience and your message. In all likelihood, your gestures will join forces with your emotions in a spontaneous mixture of verbal and nonverbal communication.

WavebreakmediaMicro/Fotolia

point you are making. Movement allows for short pauses during which you can collect your thoughts or give the audience time to ponder what you have said.

If your presentation is formal or your audience large, you will probably have a lectern. Learn how to take advantage of a lectern without allowing it to act as a barrier. First, don't lean over your lectern. It may look as though you and the lectern are about to come crashing down into the audience. Second, avoid hitting the lectern or tapping it with a pen or pointer while you speak. Given that a microphone is often attached to the lectern, the tapping can become a deafening noise.

Lecterns provide a place to put your notes, a spot to focus audience attention, and even an electrical outlet for a light and microphone. When possible *and* appropriate, come out from behind the lectern and speak at its side. In this way, you can remain close to your notes but also get closer to the audience.

Bst2012/Fotolia

14.6
Presentation Aids

What guidelines should you follow when designing and displaying presentation aids?

We use the term **presentation aids** to refer to the many supplementary resources—most often visual—for presenting and highlighting key ideas and supporting material.

Remember that you and your presentation come first. Prepare visuals only after deciding what you want to say and what you want audience members to understand and remember.

> **Choose and prepare visuals only after deciding what you want to say.**

Functions and Types of Presentation Aids

Presentation aids are more than pretty pictures or a set of colourful computer graphics. They serve specific functions, namely, to attract audience attention and to enhance the comprehension of ideas through clarification and reinforcement. Presentation aids can also save you time and help audiences remember your message.

There are as many different types of presentation aids as there are people to imagine them. The key to selecting an appropriate type requires a thoughtful answer to the following question: Which type of aid will help you achieve your purpose?

Choosing the Media

Selecting the right media is one of the first challenges you face when preparing presentation aids. Consider your purpose, the audience, the setting, and the logistics of the situation. You may want to do a multimedia presentation, but the place where you're scheduled to speak cannot be darkened or the facility doesn't have the equipment you need. Writing detailed notes on a board or flip chart for an audience of hundreds will frustrate listeners in the back rows.

A predesigned flip chart with one- or two-word messages in huge lettering on each page would work in front of an audience of 300 people, whereas a PowerPoint slide with too much data or a Prezi tool that moves too quickly would not.

Using Design Principles

Even with the best intentions, equipment, and cutting-edge software, presentation aids can fail to have an impact. They can be dull, distracting, and difficult to follow. Regardless of what type of supporting materials or in which medium you choose to display them, the basic visual design principles shown above can help you create aids that inform and please the eye without distracting or detracting from your presentation.

Keep the basic design principles in mind but remember not to be too rigid. Although these rules are based on sound principles, they are often misunderstood or followed blindly.

STRATEGIES FOR USING PRESENTATION AIDS

- **Begin with you, not your visual.** Establish rapport with your audience before you start using presentation aids.

- **Touch, turn, talk.** Touch your aid (or refer to it with your hand or a pointer), turn to your audience, then talk.

- **Pick the right time to display your aids.** Display aids for at least the length of time it takes an average reader to read them twice. When you're finished talking about a presentation aid, remove it.

- **Be prepared to do without.** Can you deliver your presentation without your presentation aids? It's always a good idea to have a "plan B" in case something goes wrong.

- **Practise before you present.** Rehearse as you would in an actual presentation. Don't sit at your computer mouthing the words as you scroll through your visuals.

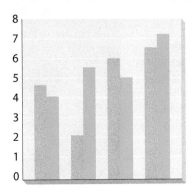

Graphs show *how much* by demonstrating comparisons. They can illustrate trends and show increases or decreases by using bars or lines to represent countable things.

Maps show *where* by translating data into spatial patterns. Maps give directions; compare locations, or link statistical data to population characteristics.

Media	Small Audience (50 or fewer)	Medium Audience (50–150)	Large Audience (150 or more)
Chalk/white board	✓		
Flip chart	✓		
Handheld object	✓	✓	
Overhead transparencies	✓	✓	✓
Presentation software slides	✓	✓	✓
Videotapes/DVDs	✓	✓	✓
Multimedia	✓	✓	✓

Tables *summarize and compare* data. When graphs aren't detailed enough and descriptions require too many words, tables are an effective alternative for showing numeric values. Tables also summarize and compare key features.

Anatomy of the Human Heart

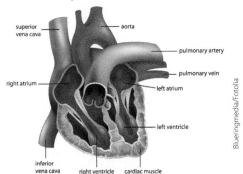

Blueringmedia/Fotolia

Diagrams and illustrations show *how things work*. They take many forms: flowcharts, organizational diagrams, timelines, floor plans, and even enlargements of physical objects so that you can see the inside of an engine, a heart, or a flower.

Group Advantages	Group Disadvantages
• Groups generally accomplish more and perform better than individuals working alone. • Groups provide members with an opportunity to socialize and create a sense of belonging. • Collaborative group work promotes learning.	• Group work requires a lot of time, energy, and resources. • Conflict among group members can be frustrating and difficult to resolve. • Working with members who are unprepared, unwilling to work, or have difficult personalities can be aggravating.

Text charts *list ideas or key phrases*, often under a title or headline. They depict goals, functions, formats, recommendations, and guidelines. Items listed on a text chart may be numbered, bulleted, or set apart on separate lines. These may be better suited to small groups or as handouts.

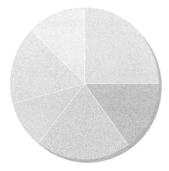

Pie charts show *how much* by identifying proportions in relation to a whole. Each wedge of the pie usually represents a percentage. Most audiences comprehend pie charts quickly and easily.

Note: Several technology-based presentation aids are discussed in Chapter 12, "Communicating in a Digital World."

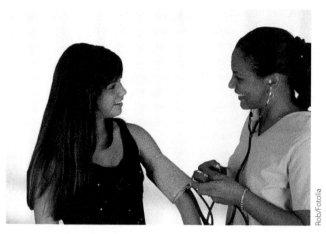

Objects are *physical examples* of items commonly used in a job. These are often used in training sessions.

Photographs *portray reality*—a real face or place is easily recognized and can capture emotions.

Physical demonstrations *illustrate or demonstrate* techniques or skills.

Handouts include references, copy of speaker notes, and additional resources. Handouts should be *used sparingly*.

COMMUNICATION

Exercise

To see a list of websites offering visual images in the public domain, visit

http://guides.library.utoronto.ca/content.php?pid=261020&sid=2155173

Handling Presentation Aids

After you invest time, effort, and significant resources to plan and prepare presentation aids, make sure you handle your aids smoothly and professionally by following several general rules of thumb: Don't turn your back to the audience or stand in front of your screen or flip chart while speaking. Decide when to introduce your aids, how long to leave them up, and when to remove them. Even if you have numerous presentation aids to display, always start and end your presentation by making direct

DESIGN PRINCIPLES FOR PRESENTATION AIDS

Preview and Highlight	Presentation aids should preview your key points and highlight important facts and features.
Headline Your Visuals	Clear headlines reduce the risk that readers will misunderstand your message.
Exercise Restraint	Avoid using too many graphics, fonts, colours, and other visual elements and effects.
Choose Readable Type and Suitable Colours	Don't use more than two different fonts, a font size smaller than 24 points, or illegible colours.
Use Appropriate Graphics	Make sure your graphics are essential and support your purpose.

and personal contact with your audience. (For more instruction on how to design presentations aids effectively—including a special focus on computer-generated slides—see "Effective Presentation Aids" at www.thethinkspot.com.)

> **Remember that presentation aids are not the presentation; they are only there to assist you. You and your message should always come first.**

ETHICAL COMMUNICATION

Plagiarism Plagues Presentation Aids

When the creation of visuals or audio is a person's livelihood, the uncompensated use of such works raises ethical questions about applying federal copyright laws.

To respond to this concern, companies such as Microsoft have developed online banks of clip art, clip video, and clip audio for fair use. For instance, Microsoft's Design Gallery Live site offers more than 250,000 graphics. In Canada, 50 years after the death of the author, most works enter the public domain and are free to use. However, while a work may be in the public domain, a specific edition or image of the work may remain under copyright.[17] If you purchase a graphics package, you have the right to make copies of the images and use them in your presentations.

If, however, you use a photo scanned from a photographer's portfolio, an audio clip copied from a CD, or a graph downloaded from the Internet without giving these works proper attribution, you are plagiarizing.

COMMUNICATION

Exercise

View this presentation by Steve Jobs, founder and former CEO of Apple:

www.youtube.com/watch?v=zU7BRvejni4

1. Discuss in pairs or small groups which, if any, presentation aids Jobs uses in his speech.
2. How are the ideas presented in 14.3, 14.4, and 14.5 evident in Jobs's speech?
3. Evaluate this presentation on a scale of 1 to 10—1 = poor, 10 = excellent—and explain the reasons why you have made this choice.

14.7
Practising Your Presentation
Why is practice essential for effective presentations?

In *Present Like a Pro*, Cyndi Maxey and Kevin E. O'Connor describe a study of the National Speakers Association's nearly 4,000 professional members who were asked for their top tips for a successful speech. *Practice* received more than 35 percent of the vote, making it first in importance.[18]

Effective practice sessions require more than repeating your presentation over and over again. Practice lets you know whether there are words you have trouble pronouncing or sentences that are too long to say in one breath. In addition, you may discover when you practise that what you thought was a 10-minute talk takes 30 minutes to deliver. Practising with presentation aids is critical, as anyone can tell you who has seen the embarrassing results that befall speakers who don't have their visuals in order. Practising is the only way to make sure that you sound and look good in a presentation.

Practice can take many forms. It can be as simple as closing your door and rehearsing your presentation in private or as complex as an onstage, videotaped dress rehearsal in front of a volunteer audience.

At the same time, don't get carried away with excessive practising. Too much practice can make you sound canned, a term used to describe speakers who have practised so much or given the same speech so many times that they no longer sound spontaneous, sincere, or natural. Our advice: Keep practising until you feel satisfied. Then, practise with the goal of improving the fine points of your presentation. Practise until you feel confident. Then, stop.

As you practise and deliver a presentation, remember that there are very few "must do" rules for effective speaking. Although this book is filled with good advice, successful speakers adapt that advice to their purpose, their audience, and the situation. Is it sometimes all right to put your hands in your pockets while speaking? Yes. Is it acceptable, in some situations, to sit down rather than to stand when speaking? Sure. Will the audience protest if you occasionally say "um" or "uh"? Nope.

> ## To put it another way, "give your speech *before* you give it."[19]

Delivery and practice "rules" are guidelines, not regulations. Sometimes breaking a commonly accepted rule can make your presentation more interesting and memorable. Smart speakers use rules when they improve their presentations and dismiss them when they get in the way. For example, if everyone around you is using dozens of complex PowerPoint slides, consider using just a few or even none. If your audience seems resigned to sitting in silence as they listen, sprinkle your speech with a few questions. If there is one cardinal rule in presenting, it's this: Rules only work when they help you achieve your purpose.

Know Thy SELF

Do You Practise Your Presentations?

Be honest. Do you devote significant time to practising a presentation before you deliver it? Take a few seconds to answer the following questions:

1. Do you practise your entire presentation several different times rather than devoting one long single session to the process?

2. Do you divide each practice session into manageable, bite-sized chunks?

3. Do you practise in at least three complete run-through sessions?

4. Do you make changes to your notes or presentation as you practise?

5. Do you practise using an audio or video recorder, or do you ask someone to listen to you?

6. Do you believe that practice helps you gain confidence?

While this may seem unnecessary, presenters who take the time to be comfortable and confident with their presentation materials enjoy more success.

Practise Your Presentation DOS & DON'TS

- **Do not memorize your presentation.** Not only do such presentations sound memorized, but you run the risk of forgetting. If you want to memorize a few key portions of a presentation, practise those sections so they sound natural.

- **Practise wherever and whenever you can.** If you have a long commute to work or school, turn off the radio and practise portions of your presentation out loud. Practise while you exercise, while you shower, when there's no one around to interrupt or distract you.

- **Time your practice session and understand that your actual presentation will take longer.** So if you are scheduled for a 10-minute speech, make sure it only takes 8 minutes in a practice session.

- **If possible audio record and video your presentation practice sessions.** Completing this step will let you see the gestures that might be distracting, or hear "ums" or "ehs" you are not aware of when you speak.

- **Practise in front of a friend or a small volunteer audience.** Listen carefully to their comments and decide which ones can help you improve your presentation.

- **Practise your entire presentation at several different times rather than devoting one long session to the process.**

- **Schedule brief 5- to 10-minute sessions of small segments.** "If you divide your practice time into manageable, bite-sized chunks, you'll find yourself practising more often and building confidence for each segment."[20]

- **Schedule at least three—but no more than five—complete run-through sessions.** If you rehearse too much, you may sound dull or bored.

Chad McDermott/Shutterstock

Pojoslaw/Shutterstock

What Message Are You Giving Your Audience?

For each of the competencies listed, choose the best response based on your current view of your speaking skills.

COMPETENCIES	YES	NO	DON'T KNOW
Body Awareness			
Confident			
Relaxed			
Stiff/awkward			
Hunched posture			
Uninterested posture			
Assertive			
Facial Expressions			
Friendly			
Natural			
Matches words spoken			
Frozen/artificial			
Making Eye Contact with Audience			
Scan full audience			
Contact with specific audience members			
Focus stays too long in one area			
Hand Gestures			
Appear natural			
Match the content of your speech or presentation			
Too big /distracting			
Enhances the presentation by adding emphasis			

14.1
The CORE Language Styles

How do you choose appropriate language for a presentation?

- Choose an appropriate language style from among the CORE speaking styles: **c**lear style; **o**ral style, **r**hetorical style, and **e**loquent style.
- The clear style uses short, simple, and direct words.
- The oral style employs familiar words, short sentences, personal pronouns, and colloquial expressions.
- The rhetorical style features vivid and powerful language.
- The eloquent style includes poetic and persuasive language in inspiring and memorable ways.

14.2
Modes of Delivery

How do you choose an appropriate delivery style for a presentation?

- Impromptu speaking occurs without advance preparation or practice.
- Extemporaneous speaking involves using an outline or a set of notes.
- Manuscript speaking involves reading a written presentation out loud.
- Memorized speaking is delivering a presentation without notes.

14.3
Confident Delivery

How can you reduce presentation anxiety?

- Although all speakers experience speaking anxiety, it is usually invisible. Audiences cannot see or hear your fear.

- When you read accurate information about speaking anxiety, you build confidence rather than increase your fear.
- To relax and reduce speaking anxiety, know your audience, focus on your message, and be well prepared.

14.4
Vocal Delivery

What are the components of effective vocal delivery?

- Effective breath control enables you to speak more loudly and say more in a single breath.
- Adapt your volume to the size of the audience and the dimensions of the room.
- Your speaking rate depends on your speaking style, the nature of your message, and your audience.
- Optimum pitch is the pitch at which you speak most easily and expressively.
- Frequent use of filler phrases can annoy your audience.
- Articulation involves clearly making the sounds in words; pronunciation refers to whether you say a word correctly.

14.5
Physical Delivery

What are the components of effective physical delivery?

- Direct effective eye contact helps you control communication, enhance your credibility, and interpret audience feedback.
- Speak naturally to ensure that your facial expressions and gestures support your message.
- Speakers who stand and move confidently radiate alertness and control.

14.6
Presentation Aids

What guideline should you follow when designing and displaying presentation aids?

- Choose media and presentation aids appropriate for your purpose, context, audience, and content.
- Five basic design principles for creating presentations aids include (1) preview and highlight, (2) headline your visuals, (3) exercise restraint, (4) choose readable type and suitable colours, and (5) use appropriate graphics.
- When handling presentation aids, focus on your audience (not the aids or yourself), begin with you, not your aids, and be prepared to do without your aids.

14.7
Practising Your Presentation

Why is practice essential for effective presentations?

- Practising ensures that you sound and look good.
- Practise your entire presentation several different times by dividing each practice session into bite-sized chunks.

TEST YOUR KNOWLEDGE

14.1 How do you choose appropriate language for a presentation?

1 In a speech about his life and homelessness Second Cup co-founder Frank O'Dea declared, "I'm interested in leaving the message that although people are homeless, if you had seen me when I was 26 would you have thought that it was possible that that person could make a difference? There are people on the streets here who will make a difference—we need to help them." Which speaking style was Mr. O'Dea using here?

    a. clear style

    b. oral style

    c. rhetorical style

    d. eloquent style

    e. academic style

2 When you are presenting technical or complicated material, it is often recommended to use the _____ style of speaking.

    a. clear style

    b. oral style

    c. rhetorical style

    d. eloquent style

    e. academic style

14.2 How do you choose an appropriate delivery style for a presentation?

3 Which is the most common mode of presentation delivery?

    a. impromptu

    b. extemporaneous

    c. manuscript

    d. memorized

    e. none of the above

14.3 How can you reduce presentation anxiety?

4 Which of the following statements is *NOT* a myth about speaking anxiety?

    a. Reading about speaking anxiety will make you more nervous.

    b. Speaking anxiety is usually invisible to audience members.

    c. All of the above are myths about public speaking.

14.4 What are the components of effective vocal delivery?

5 What, in general, is the most effective rate of delivery?

    a. 100–125 words per minute

    b. 125–145 words per minute

    c. 145–180 words per minute

    d. 180–200 words per minute

    e. 200–250 words per minute

14.5 What are the components of effective physical delivery?

6 Which component of physical delivery is the most important for a successful presentation?

    a. eye contact

    b. facial expression

    c. gestures

    d. posture

    e. movement

14.6 What guideline should you follow when designing and displaying presentation aids?

7 When delivering a presentation that includes presentation aids, it is important to remember all but which one of the following?

    a. Presentation aids are supposed to add variety and clarity to your ideas.

    b. The relationship with your audience is important in all presentations.

    c. The success of your presentation relies solely on your presentation aids.

    d. You should be able to continue with your presentation, even if your presentation aids are not available.

8 Which presentation aid design principle advises speakers to avoid using too many graphics, fonts, colours, and other visual elements and effects?

    a. Use appropriate graphics.

    b. Headline your visuals.

    c. Exercise restraint.

    d. Select appropriate media.

    e. Preview and highlight.

9 Which presentation aid design principle advises speakers to avoid more than two different fonts on a slide as well as font sizes smaller than 24 points?

    a. Preview and highlight.

    b. Exercise restraint.

    c. Choose readable type and suitable colours.

    d. Use appropriate graphics.

    e. Headline your visuals.

14.7 Why is practice essential for effective presentations?

10 All of the following recommendations for practising a presentation can help improve your delivery and confidence when speaking except _____.

    a. practising until you have memorized your presentation

    b. practising several times

    c. practising using a voice or video recorder

    d. practising in front of someone and asking for feedback

    e. practising by dividing each session into manageable, bite-sized chunks

Answers found on page 330.

Key Terms

Alliteration	**Eye scan**	**Oral style**
Articulation	**Filler phrases**	**Pitch**
Clear style	**Fluency**	**Presentation aids**
CORE speaking styles	**Impromptu speaking**	**Pronunciation**
Delivery	**Inflection**	**Rate**
Eloquent style	**Language intensity**	**Rhetorical devices**
Extemporaneous speaking	**Manuscript speaking**	**Rhetorical style**
	Memorized speaking	**Speaking style**
Eye contact	**Optimum pitch**	**Volume**

glossary

A

Abdicrat   A type of leader who emerges when control needs are unmet. The abdicrat wants control but is reluctant to pursue it and therefore is often submissive.

Abstract word   Word that refers to ideas or concepts that cannot be observed or touched and often require interpretation.

Accenting nonverbal behaviour   Nonverbal behaviour that emphasizes important elements in a message by highlighting its focus or emotional content.

Accommodating conflict style   A conflict style in which you give in to others for the purpose of preserving peace and harmony.

Active voice   A sentence in which the subject performs the action. Example: *Erin read the book.*

A-E-I-O-U Model of Conflict Resolution   A model of conflict resolution that focuses on communicating personal concerns and suggesting alternative actions.

Adaptors   Habitual gestures that help manage and express emotions.

Affection need   The need to feel liked by others.

Agenda   An outline that puts meeting topics in the order in which they will be discussed.

Aggression   Behaviour in which communicators put their personal needs first and demand compliance of others, often at the expense of someone else's needs and rights.

Alliteration   A type of repetition in which a series of words with the same sound are placed together or very near one another.

Analogy   Comparison of two things in order to highlight a point of similarity.

Analysis paralysis   A crippling situation where group members are so focused on analyzing a situation that they fail to make a decision.

Appeal to authority   A fallacy of argument in which the opinion of a supposed expert who has no relevant experience on the issues being discussed is solicited.

Appeal to popularity   A fallacy of argument in which an action is deemed acceptable or excusable because many people are doing it.

Appeal to tradition   A fallacy of argument in which a certain course of action is recommended because it has always been done that way in the past.

Argument   A claim supported by evidence and reasons for accepting the claim.

Articulation   The process of clearly making the sounds in the words of a language.

Assertiveness   The willingness and ability to stand up for your own needs and rights while also respecting the needs and rights of others.

Attacking the person   A fallacy of argument in which irrelevant or untrue attacks are made against a person rather than the substance of that person's argument.

Audience analysis   The process of understanding, respecting, and adapting to audience members before and during a presentation.

Audience attitudes   The degree or extent to which the audience agrees or disagrees with the speaker.

Authority rule   A decision making method in which the leader or an authority outside the group makes the final decision.

Autocrat/Autocratic Leader   A type of leader who emerges when control needs are unmet. The autocrat wants control but tries to take over or dominate others by criticizing members and forcing decisions on them. An autocratic leader tries to control the direction and outcome of a discussion, makes many of the group's decisions, gives orders, expects people to obey orders, and takes credit for successful results.

Avoidance conflict style   A conflict style in which people change the subject, sidestep a controversial issue, or deny that a conflict exists because they are unable or unwilling to stand up for their own needs or the needs of others.

Avoidant decision maker   A person who is uncomfortable making decisions, may not think about a problem at all, or who makes a decision at the last minute.

B

Basic terms   General words that come to mind when you see an object, such as *car* or *cat*.

Beliefs   Opinions and convictions that are held as truths

Brainstorming   A simple and popular problem solving method in which group members generate as many ideas as possible in a short period of time.

Bypassing   A form of miscommunication that occurs when people "miss each other with their meanings."

C

Cathartic   A term used to describe the act of expressing or experiencing the deep emotions often associated with events in an individual's life.

Central idea   A sentence that summarizes the key points of a presentation.

Channels   The various physical and electronic media through which we express messages.

Channels of communication   The methods by which communication moves between the sender and receiver of messages.

Character   A component of speaker credibility that focuses on the speaker's perceived honesty and goodwill.

Charisma A component of speaker credibility that focuses on the speaker's levels of energy, enthusiasm, vigor, and commitment.

Claim The conclusion of an argument or the overall position advocated in a presentation or discussion.

Claims of Conjecture Statements that something will or will not happen in the future.

Claims of Fact Statements that can be proved true or false.

Claims of Policy Statements that recommend a course of action or solution to a problem.

Claims of Value Statements that assert the worth of something—good or bad, right or wrong, best, average, or worst.

Clear style A speaking style that features short, simple, and direct words and phrases as well as active verbs, concrete words, and plain language.

Closed-ended question A question that requires only a short and direct response and can generally be answered with a yes or no.

Closure principle Filling in missing elements to form a more complete impression of an object, person, or event.

Co-cultures A group of people who coexist within the mainstream society yet remain connected to one another through their cultural heritage.

Code switching The process of modifying the use of verbal and nonverbal communication in different contexts.

Cognitive interpretation The use of intelligence (cognitive abilities) to analyze ideas, situations, or events.

Cognitive restructuring A method for reducing communication anxiety by replacing negative, irrational thoughts with more realistic, positive self-talk.

Cohesion The mutual attraction that holds the members of a group together.

Collaboration Working with others to achieve a common goal.

Collaborative conflict style An approach to conflict resolution in which people search for new solutions that will achieve both personal goals and the goals of others.

Collectivism A cultural dimension that emphasizes the views, needs, and goals of the group rather than focusing on the individual.

Committee A group created by a larger group or by a person in a position of authority to take on specific tasks.

Common ground A place where you and your audience can stand without disagreement, often in terms of shared beliefs, values, attitudes, or opinions.

Communication The process of using verbal and non-verbal messages to generate meaning within and across various contexts, cultures, and channels.

Communication accommodation theory A theory that claims that when we believe others have more power or have desirable characteristics, we may adopt their accepted speech behaviours and norms.

Communication apprehension An individual's level of fear or anxiety associated with real or anticipated communication with another person or persons.

Communication models Illustrations that simplify and present the basic elements and complex interaction patterns in the communication process.

Competence A component of speaker credibility that focuses on the speaker's perceived expertise and abilities.

Competitive conflict style A conflict style in which people are more concerned with fulfilling their own needs than with meeting the needs of others.

Complementary nonverbal behaviour Nonverbal behaviour that is consistent with the verbal message being expressed at the same time.

Compromising conflict style A "middle-ground" approach to conflict resolution that involves conceding some goals to achieve others.

Concrete word Words that refer to specific things you can perceive with your senses—smell, taste, touch, sight, or hearing.

Conflict A disagreement that occurs in relationships when differences are expressed.

Connotation The emotional responses or personal thoughts connected to the meaning of a word.

Consensus A group agreement, which all members have a part in shaping and that all find at least minimally acceptable as a means of accomplishing mutual goals.

Constructive conflict A conflict style in which people express disagreement in a way that respects others' perspectives and promotes problem solving.

Constructive nonconformity A situation that occurs when someone resists a group norm while still working to promote the group goal.

Content The ideas, information, and opinions included in a message.

Context The circumstances and settings in which communication takes place.

Contradictory nonverbal behaviour Nonverbal behaviour that conflicts with the meaning of spoken words.

Control need The need to feel influential, competent, and confident.

Conversation An interaction, often informal, in which a person exchanges speaking and listening roles with another person.

CORE speaking styles Four basic speaking styles—Clear Style, Oral Style, Rhetorical Style, and Eloquent Style—used to express a message.

Co-worker relationship A relationship characterized by interactions among people who have little or no official authority over one another but who must work together to accomplish the goals of an organization.

Critical thinking The thought process you use to analyze what you read, see, or hear to arrive at a justified conclusion or decision.

Culture A learned set of shared interpretations about beliefs, values, norms, and social practices that affect the behaviours of a relatively large group of people.

Cultural diversity The variety of human cultures in a specific region, or in the world as a whole.

Customer relationship Professional interactions between someone communicating on behalf of an organization and an individual who is external to the organization.

D

Decision making   The process of making a judgment, reaching a conclusion, or making up your mind.

Decoding   The decision-making process used to interpret, evaluate, and respond to the meaning of verbal and nonverbal messages.

Decreasing Options Technique (DOT)   A problem-solving method which helps groups reduce and refine a large number of suggestions or ideas into a manageable set of options.

Defensive behaviours   Behaviours that reflect our instinct to protect ourselves when we are being physically or verbally attacked by someone.

Definition   A statement that explains or clarifies the meaning of a word, phrase, or concept.

Deintensification   The process of displaying facial expressions that reduce or downplay emotional displays in an effort to accommodate others.

Delivery   The various ways in which you use your voice, body, and presentation aids to express a message.

Democratic leader   A leader who promotes the social equality and task interests of group members.

Demographic information   Information about audience characteristics such as age, gender, marital status, race, religion, place of residence, ethnicity, occupation, education, and income.

Demonstration speeches   Speeches that show an audience how to do something and/or how something works.

Denotation   The specific and objective dictionary-based meaning of a word.

Dependent decision maker   A person who solicits the advice and opinions of others before making a decision.

DESC script   A four-step assertiveness process (describe, express, specify, consequences) that provides an appropriate way of addressing another person's objectionable behaviour.

Description   An explanation that creates a mental image in the minds of listeners by providing details about causes, effects, historical background information, and characteristics.

Destructive conflict   The result of behaviours such as constant complaining, personal insults, conflict avoidance, and aggressive arguments that create hostility or prevent problem solving.

Destructive nonconformity   A situation that occurs when a group member resists conformity without regard for the best interests of the group and its goal, such as by showing up late to attract attention or interrupting others to exert power.

Digital citizenship   Norms and behaviours for the appropriate use of technology.

Digital code of ethics   A standard to guide the use of digital technology.

Digital communication   Electronic communication sent with the aid of digital technology.

Digital immigrant   A person born before the existence of digital technology, who is learning to use it later in life.

Digital native   A person born after the existence of digital technology, who has grown up using it throughout his or her life.

Discrimination   Behaviour that expresses and manifests prejudice.

Documentation   The practice of citing the sources of supporting material in writing or orally in a presentation.

E

Eloquent style   A speaking style that features poetic and expressive language used in a way that makes thoughts and feelings clear, inspiring, and memorable.

Email   Electronic mail; messages sent digitally to communicate with others.

Emblems   Gestures that express the same meaning as a word in a particular group or culture.

Emoticons   Typographical characters such as :-) or :-(that serve as substitutes for expressing emotions verbally.

Emotion   The feeling you have when reacting to a situation; it is often accompanied by physical changes.

Emotional intelligence   The capacity for recognizing our own feelings and those of others, for motivating ourselves, and for managing emotions in ourselves and in our relationships.

Empathic listening   The ability to understand and identify with someone's situation, feelings, or motives when you hear what they say.

Encoding   The decision-making process you use to create and send messages that generate meaning.

Ethics   Agreed-on standards of right and wrong.

Ethnocentrism   The mistaken belief that your culture is a superior culture with special rights and privileges that are or should be denied to others.

Ethos (personal proof)   A Greek word for speaker credibility that refers to the perceived character, competence, and charisma of a speaker; also a form of persuasive proof.

Etuaptmumk   The Mi'kmaw word for "two-eyed seeing." Refers to learning to see from one eye with the strengths of indigenous/Aboriginal knowledge and ways of knowing, and from the other eye with the strengths of Western knowledge and ways of knowing . . . and learning to use both these eyes together, for the benefit of all.

Euphemism   A bland, mild, vague, or unobjectionable word or phrase that substitutes for indecent, harsh, offensive, or hurtful words.

Evidence   The component of the Toulmin model of argument that answers the question, how do you know that? Evidence can range from facts, statistics, and multiple examples to the advice of experts and generally accepted audience beliefs.

Example   A word or phrase that refers to a specific case or instance in order to make large or abstract ideas concrete and understandable.

Exemplification   An impression management strategy that entails offering yourself as a good example or a model of noteworthy behaviour.

Exclusionary language   Words that reinforce stereotypes, belittle other people, or exclude others from understanding an in-group's message.

Exit interview   An interview conducted after an employee resigns in order to learn why the employee is leaving and what factors contributed to the decision to leave.

Expectancy violation theory   A theory that explains how your expectations about nonverbal behaviour significantly affect how you interact with others and how you interpret the meaning of nonverbal messages.

Explanatory communication   Communication that seeks to enhance or deepen an audience's understanding about a topic so listeners can understand, interpret, and evaluate complex ideas and information.

Extemporaneous speaking   The most common form of delivery, which occurs when you use an outline as a guide for delivering a prepared presentation.

External noise   Physical elements in the environment that interfere with effective communication.

Eye contact   The practice of establishing and maintaining direct, visual links with individual audience members.

Eye scan   The practice of glancing at a specific section of your speaking notes or manuscript and then looking at your audience.

F

Fact   A verifiable observation, experience, or event known to be true.

Fallacy   An error in thinking that leads to false and invalid claims and has the potential to mislead or deceive others.

False consensus   A state of agreement in a group when members reluctantly give in to group pressures or an external authority in order to make a decision masquerading as consensus.

Familiarity   A feeling of understanding created by close relationships and intimacy.

Faulty cause   A fallacy of argument that claims a particular situation or event is the cause of another event before ruling out other possible causes.

Feedback   Any verbal or nonverbal response you can see or hear from others.

Feminine societies   Societies in which gender roles overlap; both men and women are expected to be modest, tender, and concerned with the quality of life.

Figure–ground principle   A perception principle that explains why people focus on certain features (the figure) while deemphasizing less relevant background stimuli (the ground).

Filler phrases   Frequently overused and usually unnecessary words, phrases, or sounds such as *you know*, *uh*, *um*, *okay*, and *like* that break up a speaker's fluency and that can also annoy listeners.

5-M Model of Effective Leadership   An integrated model of leadership effectiveness that emphasizes specific communication skills and identifies five interdependent leadership functions: modeling, motivating, managing, making decisions, and mentoring.

Fluency   The ability to speak smoothly without tripping over words.

Forming stage   A group development stage in which group members are becoming acquainted with each other and may be more worried about themselves ("Will I be accepted and liked?") than about the group as a whole.

Forum   An opportunity for audience members to comment or ask questions after a public discussion or presentation.

Four dimensions of ethical communication   A rubric developed by Richard Mason in 1986; the four dimensions are privacy, accuracy, property, and accessibility as they relate to communication messages.

Fundamental interpersonal relationship orientation (FIRO) theory   A theory that asserts that people interact with others to satisfy their own needs for inclusion, control, and affection.

G

Gesture   A body movement that communicates an idea or emotion.

Gibbs' reflective cycle   One of the most popular models for reflection, named after Graham Gibbs, professor at the University of Oxford. This model consists of six steps for reflection: description of what occurred, feelings about what occurred, evaluation of what occurred, analysis of why it occurred, conclusion, and action plan.

Global village   A term used to describe the effect of digital communication technology on all societies—the reduction of the world to one "village."

Gobbledygook   The result of using many words in place of one or using a multi syllable word where a single-syllable word would suffice.

Gossip   A type of rumour that focuses on the private, personal, or even scandalous affairs of other.

Governance group   An elected or appointed group that makes public policy decisions in public settings.

Group communication   The interaction of three or more interdependent people who interact for the purpose of achieving a common goal.

Group development model   A model that identifies four discrete stages in the life cycle of groups—forming, storming, norming, and performing.

Group role   A pattern of behaviours associated with an expected function within a particular group context.

Groupthink   The deterioration of group effectiveness as a consequence of in-group pressure.

H

Hashtag   A symbol (#) that enables Twitter users to track a topic. A hashtag provides a simple way for people to search for tweets that have a common topic. For example, if you wanted to search for information about public speaking, you could enter #public speaking and only the tweets specifically related to that topic would appear.

Hasty generalization   A fallacy argument that claims something is true based on too little evidence or too few experiences.

Hearing   The ability to make clear, aural distinctions among the sounds and words in a language.

Heuristics   Cognitive thinking shortcuts we use in decision making because they are correct often enough to be useful.

Hidden agenda   Occurs when a member's private goals conflict with the group's goals.

High power distance   A cultural dimension in which people accept differences in power as normal.

High-context culture   A cultural dimension in which very little meaning is expressed through words.

Homophily   The tendency to create bonds with people who are similar in culture, beliefs, and opinions.

Hypothetical question A question that describes a set of circumstances and asks how you would respond to those circumstances.

I

I language Taking responsibility for one's own feelings and actions by using the word *I* rather than *you* or *they*.

Illustrators Gestures used with a verbal message that would lack meaning without the words.

Immediacy The degree to which a person seems approachable or likable.

Impression management The strategies people use to shape and control the way other people see them.

Impromptu speaking The practice of speaking without advanced preparation or practice.

Inclusion need The need to belong, to be involved, and to be accepted.

Individualism A cultural dimension that emphasizes the values of independence, personal achievement, and individual uniqueness.

Inference A conclusion based on claims of fact.

Inflection The changing pitch within a syllable, word, or group of words during a presentation that makes speech expressive.

Informative presentation A presentation designed to instruct, enlighten, explain, describe, clarify, correct, remind, and/or demonstrate.

Informatory communication Communication that seeks to create or increase audience awareness about a topic by presenting the latest information.

Ingratiation The most common impression management strategy; the goal of integration is to be liked by others. Ingratiation skills include giving compliments, doing another person a favour, and comforting someone.

Inoculation The act of causing or influencing beliefs.

Intensification The process of exaggerating facial expressions in an effort to meet other people's needs or to express strong feelings.

Interactional context Refers to whether the interaction is between two people, among group members, or between a presenter and an audience.

Interactive communication model This model includes the concepts of noise and feedback to show that communication is not an unobstructed one-way street.

Intercultural dimension An aspect of a culture that can be measured relative to other cultures.

Internal noise Thoughts, feelings, and attitudes that interfere with your ability to communicate and understand a message as it was intended.

Internet A global system of interconnected computer networks used to share information throughout the world.

Interpersonal communication Communication that occurs when a limited number of people, usually two, interact for the purpose of sharing information, accomplishing a specific goal, or maintaining a relationship.

Interview An interpersonal interaction between two parties in which at least one party has a predetermined purpose and uses questions and answers to share information, solve a problem, or influence the other.

Intimacy The feeling or state of knowing someone deeply in physical, psychological, emotional, intellectual, and/or collaborative ways because that person is significant in your life.

Intimate distance One of four spatial zones or distances, intimate distance is usually 0 to 18 inches and is associated with love, comfort, protection, and increased physical contact.

Intimidation An impression management strategy, the goal of which is to provoke fear.

Intuitive decision maker A person who makes decisions based on instincts, feelings, or hunches.

J

Jargon The specialized or technical language of a profession or homogeneous group that allows members to communicate with each other clearly, efficiently, and quickly.

Johari Window A model for understanding the connections between willingness to self-disclose and receptivity to feedback.

K

Key points Points that represent the most important issues or main ideas in the message.

L

Laissez-faire leader A leader who lets the group take charge of all decisions and actions.

Language A system of arbitrary signs and symbols used to communicate thoughts and feelings.

Language intensity The degree to which one's language deviates from bland, neutral terms.

Leader–member relations A situational leadership factor that assesses how well a leader gets along with group members and whether the group is cooperative and supportive.

Leadership The ability to make strategic decisions and use communication to mobilize group members toward achieving a common goal.

Leading question A question that suggests or implies the response the questioner wants to hear.

Leakage cues Unintentional nonverbal behaviour that may reveal deceptive communication.

Leet Also known as *eleet* or *leetspeak*, a way of communicating online that uses an alternative alphabet to create words.

Linear communication model The earliest type of communication model that addresses communication that functions in only one direction: a source creates a message and sends it through a channel to reach a receiver.

Listening The process of receiving, constructing meaning from, and responding to a spoken and/or nonverbal message.

Listening to evaluate The ability to analyze and make judgments about the validity of someone's spoken and nonverbal messages.

Listening to hear The ability to make clear, aural distinctions among the sounds and words in a language.

Listening to interpret The ability to empathize with another person's feelings without judging the message.

Listening to remember   The ability to store, retain, and recall information you have heard.

Listening to respond   The ability to respond in a way that indicates you fully understand someone's meaning.

Listening to understand   The ability to accurately grasp the meaning of someone's spoken and nonverbal messages.

Logistical context   The physical characteristics of a particular communication situation—focuses on a specific time, place, setting, and occasion.

Logos (logical proof)   A Greek word for a form of proof that relies on reasoning and analysis and an audience's ability to think critically and arrive at a justified conclusion or decision.

Low power distance   A cultural dimension in which power distinctions are minimized: supervisors work with subordinates; professors work with students; elected officials work with constituents.

Low-context culture   A cultural dimension in which meaning is expressed primarily through language; low-context speakers talk more, speak directly, and may fail to notice or correctly interpret nonverbal messages.

M

Maintenance role   A member role that positively affects how group members get along with one another while pursuing a common goal.

Majority vote   A vote in which more than half the members of the group vote in favour of a proposal.

Manuscript speaking   A form of delivery in which a speaker writes a presentation in advance and reads it out loud.

Marker   The placement of an object to establish nonverbal "ownership" of an area or space.

Masculine societies   Societies in which men are supposed to be assertive, tough, and focused on material success, whereas women are supposed to be more modest, tender, and concerned with the quality of life.

Masking   The process of changing your facial expressions to conceal true emotions by displaying expressions considered more appropriate in a particular situation.

Mass communication   Forms of mediated communication that occur between a person and large, often unknown audiences; radio, television, film, publications, and computer-based media are all forms of mass communication.

Media richness theory   A theory that examines how the qualities of different media affect communication and helps explain why your physical presence makes a significant difference in communication situations.

Mediated context   Any form of communication in which something (usually technology) exists between communicators; telephone, email.

"The medium is the message."   A phrase coined by communications theorist Marshall McLuhan, meaning that the form of a message (print, visual, etc.) determines how the message will be perceived.

Meeting   A scheduled gathering of group members for a structured discussion guided by a designated chairperson.

Memorized speaking   The practice of delivering a presentation from recall with very few or no notes.

Messages   Verbal and nonverbal contents that generate meaning.

Metamessage   A message about a message.

Mind mapping   An organizing technique that uses a hodgepodge of words, phrases, lists, circles, and arrows in order to encourage the free flow of ideas and help define the relationships among ideas.

Mindfulness   The ability to be fully aware of the present moment without making hasty judgments.

Mindlessness   A state that occurs when people allow rigid categories and false distinctions to become habits of thought and behaviour.

Minutes   The written record of a group's discussion and activities.

Mixed message   A contradiction between the verbal and nonverbal meanings of a message.

Mnemonic   A memory aid based on similarities in the beginning letters of words, acronyms, or rhyme.

Monochronic time   A cultural dimension (also referred to as M-time) in which people emphasize promptness and schedule events as separate items—one thing at a time.

Motivation   The desire to work toward goals or change behaviour.

Muted group theory   A theory, which claims that powerful, wealthy groups at the top of a society determine and control who will communicate and be listened to.

Mythos (narrative proof)   A Greek word for persuasive proof that addresses the values, faith, and feelings that make up our social character and is most often expressed in traditional stories, sayings, and symbols.

N

Narratives   The process, art, and techniques of storytelling.

Netlingo   A variety of language forms used in Internet communication.

Netspeak   Typographic strategies used to achieve a sociable, oral, and interactive communication style on the Internet.

Neutralization   The process of controlling your facial expressions in order to eliminate all displays of emotions.

Noise   Internal and external obstacles that can prevent a message from reaching its receivers as intended.

Nonverbal communication   Message components other than words that generate meaning; nonverbal communication encompasses physical appearance, body movement, facial expressions, touch, vocal characteristics, and the communication context.

Nonverbal messages   Messages conveyed through body language, gestures, and facial expressions.

Nonverbal reactions   Reactions to situations, experiences, or events that are portrayed through body language, facial expressions, and gestures.

Norming stage   A group development stage in which members define their roles, establish norms, and determine how the group will do its work.

Norms   Sets of expectations held by group members concerning what kinds of behaviour or opinions are acceptable or unacceptable.

O

Open-ended question   A question that encourages specific or detailed responses.

Optimum pitch   The pitch at which you speak most easily and expressively.

Oral footnote   A spoken citation that includes enough information for listeners to find the original sources.

Oral style   The use of short, familiar words when presenting to an audience.

Organization   The way you arrange the content of your presentation into a clear and appropriate format.

Organizational culture theory   A theory which describes the ways in which shared symbols, beliefs, values, and norms affect the behaviour of people working in and with an organization.

Organizational subculture   A group of people who engage in behaviours and share values that are, in part, different from that of the larger organizational culture.

Other oriented   People who are effective self-monitors and who give serious, undivided attention to, feel genuine concern for, and focus on the needs of other communicators.

P

Panel discussion   A type of public discussion in which several people interact about a common topic to educate, influence, or entertain an audience.

Paraphrasing   The ability to restate what people say in a way that indicates you understand them.

Passive aggressive   Behaviour that appears to accommodate another person's needs, but actually represents subtle aggressive behaviour.

Passive voice   A sentence in which the subject receives the action. Example: *The book was read by Erin.*

Passivity   Behaviour characterized by giving in to others at the expense of your own needs in order to avoid conflict and disagreement.

Pathos (emotional proof)   A Greek word for a form of persuasive proof that appeals to deep-seated feelings and emotions.

Perception   The process we use to select, organize, and interpret sensory stimuli in the world around us.

Perception checking   A method for testing the accuracy of your perceptual interpretations.

Performing stage   A group development stage in which members focus their energy on working harmoniously to achieve group goals.

Personal distance   One of four spatial zones or distances, personal distance is 18 inches to 4 feet.

Personal integrity   Behaving in ways that are consistent with your values and beliefs while also understanding and respecting others.

Personal relationship   A relationship characterized by a high level of emotional connection and commitment.

Person-centred message   A message that reflects the degree to which a helper validates a distressed person's feelings and encourages the person to talk about the upsetting event.

Persuasion   Messages that seek to change audience members' opinions (what they think) or behaviour (what they do).

Persuasive presentation   A presentation designed to change or influence audience members' opinions and/or behaviour.

Physiological response   An automatic, instinctive, unlearned reaction to a stimulus—a reflexive reaction.

Pitch   How high or low your voice sounds in terms of the notes on a musical scale.

Plagiarism   Using a quotation or idea from another source and passing it as your own.

Polychronic time   A cultural dimension, also referred to as P-time, in which schedules are not as important and are frequently broken; P-time people are often late and are easily distracted and tolerant of interruptions.

Power distance   A cultural dimension in which there is a large physical and psychological gap between those who have power and those who do not.

Prejudices   Positive or negative attitudes about an individual or cultural group based on little or no direct experience with that person or group.

Preliminary outline   A first-draft outline that puts the major pieces of a presentation in a clear and logical order.

Presentation aids   Supplementary aids—most often visual—used for presenting and highlighting key ideas and supporting material.

Presentation speaking   The process of using verbal and nonverbal messages to generate meaning with audience members.

Presentational communication   Communication that occurs between speakers and their audience members.

Primacy effect   Our tendency to recall the first item in a sequence; the reason why audiences often recall a presentation's introduction.

Primary emotion   First emotional response to a stimulus—instinctive and automatic.

Primary tension   The social unease and inhibitions that accompany the getting-acquainted period in a new group.

Privacy settings   Decisions made about the level of privacy an individual wishes on a variety of websites.

Probing question   A question used to follow up another question or a response by encouraging clarification and elaboration.

Problem solving   A complex process in which groups make multiple decisions as they analyze a problem and develop a plan for solving the problem or reducing its harmful effects.

Professional relationship   A relationship characterized by connections with people with whom you associate and work to accomplish a goal or perform a task.

Pronunciation   The process of putting all the correct sounds of a word in the correct order with the correct stress.

Proof   The arguments and evidence used to support and strengthen a persuasive claim.

Proxemics   The study of spatial relationships and how the distance between people communicates information about the nature of their relationship.

Proximity principle   A perception principle that explains why objects, events, or people that are physically closer to one another are more likely to be perceived as belonging together.

Psychoevolutionary emotion theory   A theory that explains the development and meaning of emotions.

Psychological reactance theory A theory that claims that when people perceive a threat to their freedom to believe or behave as they wishes, they may go out of their way to do the forbidden behaviour or rebel against the prohibiting authority.

Psychosocial context The psychological and cultural environment in which you live and communicate.

Public distance One of four spatial zones or distances, public distance is 12 plus feet.

Public group A group that discusses issues in front of or for the benefit of public audiences.

Purpose statement A specific, achievable, and relevant sentence that identifies the purpose and main ideas of your presentation.

Q

Questions of conjecture Questions that ask whether something will or will not happen in the future.

Questions of fact Questions that ask whether something is true or false.

Questions of policy Questions that ask whether and/or how a specific course of action should be taken.

Questions of value Questions that ask whether something is worthy—good or bad, right or wrong, ethical or unethical, best, average, or worst.

R

Race A socially constructed concept (not a scientific classification) that is the outcome of ancient population shifts which left their mark in our genes.

Racism The assumption that people with certain characteristics (usually superficial characteristics such as skin colour) have inherited negative traits that are inferior to those of other races; the culminating effect of ethnocentrism, stereotyping, prejudice, and discrimination.

Rate The number of words a person says each minute (wpm).

Rational decision maker A person who carefully weighs information and options before making a decision.

Receiver The person or group of people who interpret and evaluate messages.

Recency effect Our tendency to recall the last item in a sequence; the reason why audiences often recall a presentation's conclusion.

Reference groups Groups with whom you identify and who influence your self-concept.

Reflection Giving careful consideration or thought to events and experiences.

Reflective practice A tool used to learn through reflection and to act on this learning to create greater understanding.

Regulating nonverbal behaviour Nonverbal behaviour used to manage the flow of a conversation.

Relationship A continuing and meaningful attachment or connection to another person.

Relationship-motivated leader A leader who gets satisfaction from working well with other people even if the group's task or goal is neglected.

Religious literacy The ability to understand and use the religious terms, symbols, images, beliefs, practices, scripture, heroes, themes, and stories central to American public life.

Repetitive nonverbal behaviour Nonverbal behaviour that visually repeats a verbal message.

Rewards Recognitions received from others at home, at school, on the job, or in a community for good work (academic honour, employee-of-the-month award, job promotion, community service prize).

Rhetoric The ability to discover the available means of persuasion appropriate for a particular audience in a particular circumstance or setting.

Rhetorical devices Word strategies designed to enhance a presentation's impact and persuasiveness.

Rhetorical style A speaking style that features language designed to influence, persuade, and/or inspire.

Role Adopted patterns of behaviours associated with an expected function in a specific context or relationship.

Rumour An unverified story or statement about the facts of a situation.

S

Secondary emotion Subsequent emotional responses often caused by the beliefs we have about experiencing certain emotions. For example, feeling guilty for laughing at a funeral.

Secondary tension The frustrations and personality conflicts experienced by group members as they compete for social acceptance, status, and achievement.

Self-acceptance Recognizing, accepting, and "owning" your thoughts, feelings, and behaviour.

Self-appraisals Evaluations of your self-concept in terms of your abilities, attitudes, and behaviours.

Self-awareness An understanding of your core identity that requires a realistic assessment of your traits, thoughts, and feelings.

Self-centred role A role assumed by group members who put their own goals ahead of the group's goal; can adversely affect member relationships and prevent the group from achieving its goals.

Self-concept The sum total of beliefs you have about yourself.

Self-disclosure The process of sharing personal information, opinions, and emotions with others that would not otherwise be known to them.

Self-effacing humour Humour directed at yourself rather than at others.

Self-esteem Your positive and negative judgments about yourself.

Self-fulfilling prophecy An impression formation process in which an initial impression elicits behaviour that conforms to the impression.

Self-monitoring A sensitivity to your own behaviour and others' reactions as well as the ability to modify how you present yourself.

Self-promotion An impression management strategy for being seen as competent. The goal is to be respected by others.

Self-regulation The ability to control and regulate one's own behaviour—to monitor and respond appropriately to situations, people, events, and emotions.

Self-responsibility Taking responsibility and being accountable for your own happiness and fulfillment of your own goals without trying to control others.

Self-talk The silent statements you make to yourself about yourself.

Sexual harassment Unwanted sexual advances or inappropriate verbal or physical conduct of a sexual nature, which creates an intimidating, hostile, or offensive work environment.

Short-term memory The limited capacity to remember content immediately after listening to a series of numbers, words, sentences, or paragraphs.

Sign Something that stands for or represents a specific thing and often looks like the thing it represents.

Significant others People whose opinions you value, such as family members, friends, coworkers, and mentors.

Similarity principle A perception principle that explains why similar items or people are more likely to be perceived as a group.

Simplicity principle A perception principle that explains why we tend to organize information in a way that provides the simplest interpretation.

Situational leadership theory A theory that explains how leaders can become more effective by analyzing themselves, their group, and the context in order to find or create an ideal match between leaders and leadership roles.

Six-step model of conflict resolution A model which offers six steps (preparation, initiation, confrontation, consideration, resolution, and reevaluation) that help you move through a conflict toward successful resolution.

Skills Your acquired ability to accomplish communication goals when interacting with others.

Slang A short-lived, group-related, ever-changing, creative and innovative, often playful and metaphorical, colloquial language variety that is below the level of stylistically neutral language.

Social comparison The process of evaluating yourself in relation to others in your reference groups.

Social distance One of four spatial zones or distances, social distance is 4 to 12 feet.

Social empathy The ability to recognize feelings or circumstances faced by others in society

Social identity Your self-concept as derived from the social categories to which you see yourself belonging.

Social media Websites and other Internet programs that enable the creation, sharing, and exchange of ideas and knowledge.

Social networks Web-based communities that share a common interest or goal.

Social penetration theory A theory that describes the process of relationship bonding in which individuals move from superficial communication to deeper, more intimate communication.

Social skills Skills that assist interactions and communication between people.

Source A person or group of people who create a message intended to produce a particular response.

Speaker credibility The characteristics of a speaker that determine the extent to which an audience believes the speaker and the speaker's message.

Speaking style The manner in which you use vocabulary, sentence structure and length, grammar and syntax, and rhetorical devices to express a message.

Speech Framer A visual model for organizing presentation content that provides a place for every component of a presentation while encouraging experimentation and creativity.

Spontaneous decision maker A person who tends to be impulsive and make quick decisions on the spur of the moment.

Standard agenda A procedure that guides a group through problem solving by using the following steps: clarify the task, understand and analyze the problem, assess and choose solutions, and implement the decision or plan.

Statistics Supporting material that requires collecting, summarizing, analyzing, and interpreting numerical data.

Stereotypes Generalizations about a group of people that oversimplify the group's characteristics.

Stories Accounts or reports about something that happened.

Storming stage A group development stage in which members become more argumentative and emotional as they discuss important issues and vie for leadership.

Story fidelity The apparent truthfulness of a story and whether it accurately reflects audience values and knowledge.

Story probability The formal features of a story, such as the consistency of characters and actions, and whether the elements of a story "hang together" and make sense.

Storytelling A tool used to convey understanding and empathy for another person's experiences or circumstances.

Strategies Specific plans of action that help you achieve your communication goals.

Structure The organization of message content into a coherent and purposeful message.

Styles theory of leadership A theory which examines three distinct leadership styles: autocratic, democratic, and laissez-faire.

Subordinate terms The most concrete words that provide specific descriptions.

Substituting nonverbal behaviour Nonverbal behaviour that replaces verbal language; for example, waving hello instead of saying "hello."

Superior–subordinate relationships Professional relationships in which the superior (supervisor) has formal authority over the productivity and behaviour of subordinates (workers).

Superordinate terms Words that group objects and ideas together very generally.

Supplication An impression management strategy that often involves a humble request or appeal for help. The goal of supplication is compassion from others.

Supporting material Ideas and information that help explain and/or advance a presentation's purpose and key points.

Supportive behaviours Actions that create an encouraging and caring climate in which self-disclosure and responsiveness to feedback benefit both communicators.

Swearing Using words that are taboo or disapproved of in a culture, but that may not be meant literally and are used to express strong emotions and attitudes.

Symbol An arbitrary collection of sounds or letters that in certain combinations stands for a concept but does not have a direct relationship to the thing it represents.

Symposium   A public group in which group members present short, uninterrupted presentations on different aspects of a topic for the benefit of an audience.

Systematic desensitization   A relaxation and visualization technique that helps reduce communication apprehension.

T

Task-motivated leader   A leader who gains satisfaction from completing a task even at the expense of group relationships.

Task role   A group member role that positively affects the group's ability to manage a task and achieve its common goal.

Task structure   A situational leadership factor that assesses how a group organizes or plans a specific task.

Territoriality   The sense of personal ownership attached to a particular space.

Testimony   Supporting material that consists of statements or opinions that someone has spoken or written.

Texting   Brief, electronic messages sent between people on cellphones.

Theories   Statements that explain how the world works; they describe, explain, and predict events and behaviour.

Thought speed   The speed (words per minute) at which most people can think compared with the speed at which they can speak.

Touch approachers   People who are comfortable with touch and often initiate touch with others.

Touch avoiders   People who are not comfortable initiating touch or being touched.

Toulmin model of an argument   A model of an argument in which a complete argument requires three major components: a claim, evidence, and a warrant and, in some cases, backing, a reservation, and/or a qualifier.

Trait theory of leadership   A theory which identifies specific characteristics and behaviours associated with effective leadership.

Transactional communication model   A communication model that shows how we send and receive messages simultaneously within specific contexts.

Turn-requesting cue   Verbal and nonverbal messages that signal a desire to speak, such as leaning forward, providing direct eye contact, and lifting your hand as if beginning to gesture.

Turn-yielding cue   Verbal and nonverbal messages that signal that you are completing your comments and are prepared to listen; for example, you may slow down your speaking rate, relax your posture or gestures, or lean slightly away.

Two-thirds vote   A vote in which at least twice as many group members vote for a proposal as against it.

V

Valid   Well founded, justified, and accurate.

Value step   A step that captures audience attention by explaining how the message can enhance the success and personal well being of audience members.

Values   Beliefs held by individuals or cultures that influence behaviour—for example, right from wrong, just from unjust, and good from bad.

Verbal communication   The ways in which we use the words in a language to generate meaning.

Verbal expression   Communication through speech or written word, often associated with beliefs or opinion.

Virtual group   A group that relies on technology to communicate across time, distance, and organizational boundaries. A virtual group does not typically meet face-to-face.

Visualization   A method for reducing communication apprehension and for building confidence by imagining what it would be like to communicate successfully.

Volume   A measure of loudness in a person's voice.

W

Warrant   A component of the Toulmin model of an argument that explains how and why the evidence supports the claim.

Whorf hypothesis   A hypothesis that claims that language influences how we see, experience, and interpret the world around us.

Word stress   The degree of prominence given to a syllable within a word or words within a phrase or sentence.

Work group   Groups that are responsible for making decisions, solving problems, implementing projects, or performing routine duties in an organization.

Work team   A group given full responsibility and resources for its performance.

Working memory   The memory subsystem we use when trying to understand information, remember it, and use it to solve a problem or communicate with others; working memory allows us to shift message content from and into long-term memory.

Working memory theory   A theory that explains the dual-task system of working memory, which involves information processing and storage functions as well as creating new meanings.

Y

You language   Language that may be interpreted as expressing negative judgments about others.

Chapter 1

[1]Marilyn H. Buckley, "Focus on Research: We Listen to a Book a Day; Speak a Book a Week: Learning from Walter Loban," *Language Arts* 69 (1992): 101–9.

[2]In association with the National Communication Association, the Association for Communication Administration's 1995 Conference on Defining the Field of Communication produced the following definition: "The field of communication focuses on how people use verbal and nonverbal messages to generate meanings within and across various contexts, cultures, channels, and media. The field promotes the effective and ethical practice of human communication." See http://www.natcom.org.

[3]See Sherwyn P. Morreale, Michael M. Osborn, and Judy C. Pearson, "Why Communication Is Important: A Rationale for the Centrality of the Study of Communication," *Journal of the Association for Communication Administration* 29 (2000): 1–25. The authors of this article collected and annotated nearly 100 articles, commentaries, and publications that call attention to the importance of studying communication in contemporary society.

[4]Robert M. Diamond, "Designing and Assessing Courses and Curricula," *Chronicle of Higher Education*, August 1, 1997, p. B7.

[5]Jerry L. Winsor, Dan B. Curtis, and Ronald D. Stephens, "National Preferences in Business and Communication Education: A Survey Update," *Journal of the Association for Communication Administration* 3 (September 1997): 170–79. The authors conclude that a stronger emphasis should be given to training in listening and interpersonal communication in addition to developing competencies in group communication and presentation speaking.

[6]"Graduates Are Not Prepared to Work in Business," *Association Trends*, June 1997, p. 4.

[7]Business-Higher Education Forum in affiliation with the American Council on Education, *Spanning the Chasm: Corporate and Academic Cooperation to Improve Work-Force Preparation* (Washington, DC: American Council on Education, 1997).

[8]For a historical review of communication studies, see James A. Herrick, *The History and Theatre of Rhetoric: An Introduction*, 3rd ed. (Boston: Allyn and Bacon, 2005), and James L. Golden, Goodwin F. Berquist, and William E. Coleman, *The Rhetoric of Western Thought*, 4th ed. (Dubuque, IA: Kendall/Hunt, 1978).

[9]David Berlo, *The Process of Communication: An Introduction to Theory and Practice* (New York: Holt, Rinehart and Winston, 1960), p. 24.

[10]Myron W. Lustig and Jolene Koester, *Intercultural Competence: Interpersonal Communication Across Cultures*, 5th ed. (Boston: Pearson/Allyn and Bacon, 2010), p. 25.

[11]In this textbook, we prefer and use the broader term *presentational communication* rather than *public speaking* to describe the act of speaking before an audience. Public speaking is one type of presentational communication that occurs when a speaker addresses a public audience. See Isa N. Engleberg and John A. Daly, *Presentations in Everyday Life*, 3rd ed. (Boston: Pearson/Allyn and Bacon, 2009), p. 4.

[12]John McWhorter, *The Power of Babel: A Natural History of Language* (New York: A.W.H. Freeman, 2001), p. 5.

[13]See Richard L. Daft and Robert H. Lengel, "Information Richness: A New Approach to Managerial Behavior and Organizational Design," in *Research in Organizational Behavior*, ed. Barry M. Staw and Larry L. Cummings (Greenwich, CT: JAI Press, 1984), pp. 355–66; Richard L. Daft, Robert H. Lengel, and Linda K. Trevino, "Message Equivocality, Media Selection, and Manager Performance: Implications for Information Systems," *MIS Quarterly* 11 (1987): 355–66; and Linda K. Trevino, Robert H. Lengel, and Richard L. Daft, "Media Symbolism, Media Richness, and Media Choice in Organizations," *Communication Research* 14 (5, 1987): 553–74.

[14]Darren Rowse, "Twitter Is a Complete Waste of Time," http://www.problogger.net/archives/2008/06/06/twitter-is-a-waste-of-time.

[15]http://www.tumblr.com/about.

[16]Rob Anderson and Veronica Ross, *Questions of Communication: A Practical Introduction to Theory*, 3rd ed. (New York: St. Martin's Press, 2002), p. 69.

[17]Karl R. Popper, *The Logic of Scientific Discovery* (New York: Basic Books, 1959), p. 59.

[18]Excerpt from Stephen R. Covey, *The 7 Habits of Highly Effective People* (New York: Simon and Schuster, 1989), pp. 46–48.

[19]Rob Anderson and Veronica Ross, *Questions of Communication: A Practical Introduction to Theory*, 3rd ed. (New York: St. Martin's Press, 2002), p. 301.

[20]Richard L. Johannesen, *Ethics in Human Communication*, 5th ed. (Prospect Heights, IL: Waveland Press, 2002), p. 1.

[21]National Communication Association Credo for Ethical Communication, http://www.natcom.org/aboutNCA/Policies/Platform.html.

Chapter 2

[1]David Gates, "Finding Neverland," *Newsweek* (July 13, 2009), www.newsweek.com/id/204296.

[2]Hanish Babu, "How Did Michael Jackson's Skin Turn White?," http://skindisease.suite101.com/article.cfm/how_did_michael_jackson_skin_turn_white#ixzz0K6jQnBBy&D.

[3]hysperia, "On Michael Jackson," *mirabile dictu*, http://alterwords.wordpress.com/2009/06/26/on-michael-jackson. The blogger hysperia is a Canadian who was "once a lawyer, once a law professor, now a poet and a Feminist for forty years."

[4]Sharon S. Brehm, Saul M. Kassin, and Steven Fein, *Social Psychology*, 6th ed. (Boston: Houghton Mifflin, 2005), p. 57.

[5]"Self-Awareness," http://en.wikipedia.org/wiki/Self-awareness.

[6]Daniel Goleman, *Emotional Intelligence* (New York: Bantam, 1995), pp. 43, 47.

[7]Ibid., p. 43.

[8]"Self-Monitoring Behavior," http://changingminds.org/explanations/theories/self-monitoring.htm.

[9]Daniel Goleman, *Emotional Intelligence* (New York: Bantam, 1995), p. 43.

[10]Sharon S. Brehm, Saul M. Kassin, and Steven Fein, *Social Psychology*, 6th ed. (Boston: Houghton Mifflin, 2005), p. 65.

[11]Anthony G. Greenwald, "The Totalitarian Ego: Fabrication and Revision of Personal History," *American Psychologist* 35 (1980): 603–18.

[12]Min-Sun Kim, *Non-Western Perspectives on Human Communication* (Thousand Oaks, CA: Sage, 2002), p. 9.

[13]Richard E. Boyatzis, "Developing Emotional Intelligence Competencies," in *Applying Emotional Intelligence: A Practitioner's Guide*, ed. Joseph Ciarrochi and John D. Mayer (New York: Psychology Press, 2007), p. 42.

[14]Nathaniel Branden, www.nathanielbranden.com.

[15]David Nyberg, *The Varnished Truth: Truth Telling and Deceiving in Ordinary Life* (Chicago: University of Chicago Press, 1993), p. 81.

[16]Mark L. Knapp, *Lying and Deception in Human Interaction* (Boston: Pearson/Allyn and Bacon, 2008), p. 122.

[17]Albert Bandura, *Social Foundations of Thought and Action: A Social Cognitive Theory* (Englewood Cliffs, NJ: Prentice Hall, 1986), pp. 399–408. Quoted in William Crain, *Theories of Development: Concepts and Applications*, 4th ed. (Upper Saddle River, NJ: Prentice Hall, 2000), p. 203.

[18]Leon Festinger, "A Theory of Social Comparison Processes," *Human Relations*, 7 (1954): 117–140.

[19]Susan B. Barnes, *Online Connections: Internet Interpersonal Relationships* (Cresskill, NJ: Hampton Press, 2001), p. 234.

[20]Ibid., p. 91.

[21]Jeffrey Hall, Namkee Park, Ha Yeon Song, and Michael Cody, "Strategic Misrepresentation in Online Dating: The Effects of Gender, Self-Monitoring, Personality, and Demographics," paper presented at the National Communication Association Convention, 2008.

[22]Rebecca McCarthy, "Conviction Is Tossed Out in MySpace Suicide Case," *The New York Times*, July 3, 2009, p. A12.

[23]Several news outlet websites chronicle the events leading up to Clementi's suicide and the arrest and trial of Dharun Ravi. Jesse Solomon, "Roommate Indicted in Rutgers University Suicide Case," *CNN Justice*, April 21, 2011, www.cnn.com/2011/CRIME/04/20/new.jersey.rutgers.indictment/index.html; Brendan Davis, "The Glaad Daily: Dharun Ravi in Court," *glaad*, September 9, 2011, www.glaad.org/2011/09/09/the-glaad-daily-dharun-ravi-in-court-8-sentence-for-stonewall-attackers-and-more; Also see, http://abcnews.go.com/US/victim-secret-dorm-sex-tape-commits-suicide/story?id=11758716, www.nytimes.com/2010/09/30/nyregion/30suicide.html.

[24]www.tylerclementi.org

[25]Nathaniel Branden, www.nathanielbranden.com.

[26]Roy F. Baumeister, Jennifer D. Campbell, Joachim I. Krueger, and Kathleen D. Vohs, "Exploding the Self-Esteem Myth," *Scientific American.com* (January 2005), www.papillonsartpalace.com/exSplodin.htm; http://crane-psych.edublogs.org/files/2009/06/Self_esteem_myth.pdf.

[27]Nathaniel Branden, *The Art of Living Consciously: The Power of Awareness to Transform Everyday Life* (New York: Fireside Books/Simon and Schuster, 1999), pp. 168–69.

[28]"Women's Math Scores Affected by Suggestions," *Washington Post*, October 20, 2006, p. A11. This article summarizes a study published in the October 2006 issue of *Science*.

[29]http://plancanada.ca/page.aspx?pid=4440.

[30]Roy F. Baumeister, Jennifer D. Campbell, Joachim I. Krueger, and Kathleen D. Vohs, "Exploding the Self-Esteem Myth," *Scientific American.com* (January 2005) www.papillonsartpalace.com/exSplodin.htm; http://cranepsych.edublogs.org/files/2009/06/Self_esteem_myth.pdf.

[31]See Nathaniel Branden, *The Power of Self-Esteem* (Deerfield Beach, FL: Health Communications, 1992), pp. 168–69.

[32]Morris Rosenberg, *Society and the Adolescent Self-Image* (Princeton, NJ:Princeton University Press, 1965).

[33]Douglas A. Bernstein, Louis A. Penner, Alison Clarke-Stewart, and Edward Roy, *Psychology*, 7th ed. (Boston: Houghton Mifflin, 2006), p. 161.

[34]Ibid., p. 172.

[35]Lila Guterman, "Do You Smell What I Hear? Neuroscientists Crosstalk among the Senses," *Chronicle of Higher Education*, December 14, 2001, pp. 17–18.

[36]Holly St. Lifer, "Fear Factor: What We Touch Can Change How We Think," *AARP The Magazine* (November/December 2010), www.aarp.org/health/medical-research/info-09-2010/feel-factor.print.html.

[37]Douglas A. Bernstein, Louis A. Penner, Alison Clarke-Stewart, and Edward Roy, *Psychology*, 7th ed. (Boston: Houghton Mifflin, 2006), p. 162.

[38]Ibid.

[39]Richard E. Nisbett, *The Geography of Thought: How Asians and Westerners Think Differently . . . and Why* (New York: Free Press, 2003), p. 87.

[40]J. Richard Block and Harold Yuker, *Can You Believe Your Eyes?* (New York: Gardner Press, 1989), p. 239.

[41]Ronald B. Adler, Lawrence B. Rosenfeld, and Russell F. Proctor II, *Interplay: The Process of Interpersonal Communication*, 8th ed. (Fort Worth, TX: Harcourt Brace, 2001), p. 114.

[42]"The Golden Rule is found in the New Testament (Matthew 7:12, NIV) but is often confused with the related admonition to 'love your neighbor as yourself,' which appears repeatedly in both the Hebrew Bible and the New Testament . . . . The Golden Rule has also been attributed to other religious leaders, including Confucius, Muhammad, and the first-century rabbi Hillel." Stephen Prothero, *Religious Literacy: What Every American Needs*

to Know—And Doesn't (New York: HarperSanFrancisco, 2007), pp. 182–83.

⁴³George Bernard Shaw, *Maxims for a Revolutionist* (1903).

⁴⁴The discussion of communication apprehension is based on chapter 2 of Isa Engleberg and John Daly, *Presentations in Everyday Life*, 3rd ed. (Boston: Pearson/Allyn and Bacon, 2009), and chapter 3 of Isa Engleberg and Dianna Wynn, *Working in Groups: Communication Principles and Strategies*, 5th ed. (Boston: Pearson/Allyn and Bacon, 2010).

⁴⁵Virginia P. Richmond and James C. McCroskey, *Communication: Apprehension, Avoidance, and Effectiveness*, 4th ed. (Scottsdale, AZ: Gorsuch, Scarisbrick, 1995), p. 32.

⁴⁶Virginia P. Richmond and James C. McCroskey, *Communication: Apprehension, Avoidance, and Effectiveness*, 4th ed. (Scottsdale, AZ: Gorsuch, Scarisbrick, 1995), p. 41.

⁴⁷James C. McCroskey, "Oral Communication Apprehension: Summary of Recent Theory and Research," *Human Communication Research* 4 (1977): 80.

⁴⁸Michael J. Beatty and James McCroskey with Kristin M. Valencic, *The Biology of Communication: A Communibiological Perspective* (Cresskill, NJ:Hampton, 2001), p. 80.

⁴⁹Virginia P. Richmond and James C. McCroskey, *Communication: Apprehension, Avoidance, and Effectiveness*, 4th ed. (Scottsdale, AZ: Gorsuch, Scarisbrick, 1995), p. 108.

⁵⁰Sharon S. Brehm, Saul M. Kassin, and Steven Fein, *Social Psychology*, 6th ed. (Boston: Houghton Mifflin, 2005), p. 525.

⁵¹Anonymous quotation: www.cns.cornell.edu/documents/CAPESBerggren3-2-05.pdf.

⁵²Peter Desberg, *Speaking Scared, Sounding Good* (Garden City Park, NY: Square One Publishers, 2007), pp. 101–10. Desberg describes several effective relaxation exercises that readers can practice. Desberg notes that "Fortunately, it feels great to practice them" (p. 100).

⁵³See John A. Daly and James C. McCroskey, eds., *Avoiding Communication: Shyness, Reticence, and Communication Apprehension* (Thousand Oaks, CA: Sage, 1984); Virginia P. Richmond and James C. McCroskey, *Communication: Apprehension, Avoidance, and Effectiveness*, 4th ed. (Scottsdale, AZ: Gorsuch, Scarisbrick, 1995); Karen Kangas Dwyer, *Conquer Your Speechfright*, 2nd ed. (Belmont, CA: Thomson Wadsworth, 2005); and Michael T. Motley, *Overcoming Your Fear of Public Speaking: A Proven Method* (Boston: Houghton Mifflin, 1997).

⁵⁴Karen Kangas Dwyer, *Conquer Your Speechfright*, 2nd ed. (Belmont, CA: Thomson Wadsworth, 2005), p. 23.

⁵⁵Peter Desberg, *Speaking Scared, Sounding Good* (Garden City Park, NY: Square One Publishers, 2007), p. 60.

⁵⁶As cited in Virginia P. Richmond and James C. McCroskey, *Communication: Apprehension, Avoidance, and Effectiveness*, 4th ed. (Scottsdale, AZ: Gorsuch, Scarisbrick, 1995), pp. 97, 101. For more on systematic desensitization, see ibid., pp. 97–102; and Karen Kangas Dwyer, *Conquer Your Speechfright*, 2nd ed. (Belmont, CA: Thomson Wadsworth, 2005), pp. 95–103, 137–41.

⁵⁷Daniel Goleman, *Social Intelligence* (New York: Bantam, 2006), pp. 41–42.

⁵⁸From Virginia P. Richmond and James C. McCroskey, *Communication: Apprehension, Avoidance, and Effectiveness*, 5th ed. (Boston: Allyn and Bacon, 1998). Copyright © 1998 by Pearson Education. Reprinted by permission of the publisher.

⁵⁹Virginia P. Richmond and James C. McCroskey, *Communication: Apprehension, Avoidance, and Effectiveness*, 4th ed. (Scottsdale, AZ: Gorsuch, Scarisbrick, 1995), pp. 129–30. Reprinted by permission of the authors and publisher.

Chapter 3

¹http://blackhistorycanada.ca/timeline.php?id=1900.

²In 1967, the Supreme Court overturned the conviction of Richard and Mildred Loving, a young interracial couple from Caroline County, Virginia. "Richard Loving was white; his wife, Mildred, was black. In 1958, they went to Washington, D.C.—where interracial marriage was legal—to get married. But when they returned home, they were arrested, jailed and banished from the state for 25 years for violating the state's Racial Integrity Act." When they challenged the law in Virginia, "the original judge in the case upheld his decision [and wrote] 'Almighty God created the races white, black, yellow, Malay and red, and he placed them on separate continents. . . . The fact that he separated the races shows that he did not intend for the races to mix'" (National Public Radio, "Loving Decision: 40 Years of Legal Interracial Unions," *All Things Considered*, June 11, 2007, www.npr.org/templates/story/story.php?storyId=10889047).

³www.parl.gc.ca/About/Parliament/LegislativeSummaries/bills_ls.asp?ls=c38&Parl=38&Ses=1; www.census.gov/prod/cen2010/briefs/c2010br-02.pdf.

⁴www.statcan.gc.ca/pub/11-010-x/2011008/part-partie3-eng.htm; www.parl.gc.ca/About/Parliament/LegislativeSummaries/bills_ls.asp?ls=c38&Parl=38&Ses=1.

⁵Myron W. Lustig and Jolene Koester, *Intercultural Competence: Interpersonal Communication across Cultures*, 6th ed. (Boston: Pearson/Allyn and Bacon, 2010), p. 25.

⁶Intercultural authors use a variety of terms (*co-cultures*, *microcultures*) to describe the cultural groups that coexist within a larger culture. Using either of these terms is preferable to using the older, somewhat derogatory term *subcultures*.

⁷Adapted from www.salto-youth.net/diversity

⁸Based on Myron W. Lustig and Jolene Koester, *Instructor's Manual to Accompany Intercultural Competence*, 2nd ed. (New York: HarperCollins, 1996), pp. 72–74.

⁹Data from Patricia G. Devine and A. J. Elliot, "Are Racial Stereotypes Really Fading? The Princeton Trilogy Revisited," *Personality and Social Psychology Bulletin* 21 (1995), pp. 1139–50.

¹⁰Based on Lustig and Koester, *Instructor's Manual to Accompany Intercultural Competence*, p. 151.

¹¹Stella Ting-Toomey and Leeva C. Chung, *Understanding Intercultural Communication* (Los Angeles: Roxbury, 2005), pp. 236–39.

¹²Nicholas Wade, *Before the Dawn: Recovering the Lost History of Our Ancestors* (New York: Penguin, 2006), p. 183.

¹³Ibid.

¹⁴Ibid.

[15] National Communication Association, "National Communication Association Policy Platform," www .natcom.org/index.asp?bid=510.

[16] Shankar Vedantam, "For Allen and Webb, Implicit Biases Would Be Better Confronted," Washington Post, October 9, 2006, p. A2. See also www.washingtonpost.com/ science and http://implicit.harvard.edu.

[17] Allan Johnson, *Privilege, Power, and Difference* (Mountain View, CA: Mayfield Publishing, 2006), pp. 104–105.

[18] Ibid.

[19] www.cbc.ca/news/canada/nova-scotia/story/ 2010/02/22/ns-cross-burning-haunts-county.html

[20] www.washingtonpost.com/wp-dyn/content/ article/2009/06/10/AR2009061001768.html; Associated Press, "Guard Dies after Holocaust Museum Shooting," MSNBC.com, June 10, 2009, www.msnbc.msn.com/ id/31208188.

[21] Several websites describe the massacre and the online manifesto: See "Norway—Breivik Attacks, July 2011," *The New York Times*, Updated August 25, 2001, http://topics.nytimes.com/top/news/interna- tional/countriesandterritories/norway/index.html, as well as www.abacusnews.com/news/11/004-anders- breivik-latest-update.php; www.cbsnews.com/sto- ries/2011/08/04/501364/main20088232.shtml; www.tele- graph.co.uk/news/worldnews/europe/norway/8655175/ Norway-shooting-live.html.

[22] Judith Warner, "The Wages of Hate," Judith Warner Blog, *New York Times*, June 11, 2009, http://warner.blogs .nytimes.com/2009/06/11/the-wages-of-hate.

[23] www.crr.ca/divers-files/en/survey/ racismandprejudice-2010.pdf

[24] Brenda J. Allen, *Difference Matters: Communicating Social Identity* (Long Grove, IL: Waveland Press, 2004), p. 10.

[25] Stephen Prothero, *Religious Literacy: What Every American Needs to Know—And Doesn't* (New York: HarperSanFrancisco, 2007), p. 11. See also Prothero's religious literacy quiz, pp. 27–28, 235–39.

[26] Statements are based on three sources: Robert Pollock, *The Everything World's Religions Book* (Avon, MA: Adams Media, 2002); Leo Rosen, ed., *Religions of America: Fragment of Faith in an Age of Crisis* (New York: Touchstone, 1975); and *Encyclopedia Britannica Almanac 2004* (Chicago: Encyclopedia Britannica, 2003).

[27] According to Richard L. Evans, a former member of the Council of Twelve of the Church of Jesus Christ of Latter-day Saints, "Strictly speaking, 'Mormon' is merely a nickname for a member of the Church of Jesus Christ of Latter-day Saints." When asked whether Mormons are Christians, he answered, "Unequivocally yes." See "What Is a Mormon?" in Leo Rosen (Ed.), *Religions of America: Fragment of Faith in an Age of Crisis* (New York: Touchstone, 1975), p. 187; Robert Pollock describes Mormonism as a "prevalent Christian faith" in Robert Pollock, *The Everything World's Religions Book* (Avon, MA: Adams Media, 2002), pp. 49–51.

[28] Rita Hardiman, "White Racial Identity Develop- ment in the United States," in *Race, Ethnicity and Self:*

[29] *Identity in Multicultural Perspective*, ed. Elizabeth Pathy Salett and Dianne R. Koslow (Washington, DC: National MultiCultural Institute, 1994), pp. 130–31.

[29] William B. Gudykunst and Carmen M. Lee, "Cross- Cultural Communication Theories," in *Handbook of In- ternational and Intercultural Communication*, 2nd ed., ed. William B. Gudykunst and Bella Mody (Thousand Oaks, CA: Sage, 2002), p. 27.

[30] J. Richard Hoel. "Developing Intercultural Compe- tence," in *Intercultural Communication with Readings*, ed. Pamela J. Cooper, Carolyn Calloway-Thomas, and Cheri J. Simonds (Boston: Allyn and Bacon, 2007), p. 305.

[31] Geert Hofstede, *Cultures and Organizations: Software of the Mind* (New York: McGraw-Hill, 1997), p. 14. See also Geert Hofstede, *Culture's Consequences: Comparing Values, Behavior, Institutions and Organizations across Na- tions*, 2nd ed. (Thousand Oaks, CA: Sage, 2001), p. 29. In addition to the three intercultural dimensions included in this chapter, Hofstede identifies several other dimensions: long-term versus short-term time orientation, uncertainty avoidance, indulgence versus restraint, and monumental- ism versus self-effacement. For a summary of these ad- ditional dimensions, see Lustig and Koester, *Intercultural Competence*, pp. 113–24.

[32] Harry C. Triandis, "The Self and Social Behavior in Different Cultural Contexts," *Psychological Review* 96 (1989), pp. 506–20. See also Harry C. Triandis, *Individual- ism and Collectivism* (Boulder, CO: Westview, 1995), p. 29. Data from Geert Hofstede, *Cultural Consequences: Com- paring Values, Behavior, Institutions and Organizations across Nations*, 2nd ed. (Thousand Oaks, CA: Sage, 2001), p. 215.

[33] Data from Hofstede, *Cultural Consequences*, p. 215.

[34] Ibid., p. 53.

[35] Geert Hofstede, *Cultures and Organizations: Software of the Mind* (New York: McGraw-Hill, 1997), p. 28.

[36] Triandis, *Individualism and Collectivism*.

[37] Harry C. Triandis, "Cross-Cultural Studies of Indi- vidualism and Collectivism," in *Cross-Cultural Perspectives*, ed. J. J. Berman (Lincoln: University of Nebraska Press, 1990), p. 52.

[38] Data from Hofstede, *Culture's Consequences*, p. 87.

[39] Ibid., pp. 81–82, p. 96.

[40] Data from ibid., p. 286.

[41] Edward T. Hall, "Context and Meaning," in *Beyond Culture* (Garden City, NY: Anchor, 1997).

[42] Peter Andersen et al., "Nonverbal Communication across Cultures," in *Handbook of International and Intercul- tural Communication*, 2nd ed., ed. William B. Gudykunst and Bella Mody (Thousand Oaks, CA: Sage, 2002), p. 99.

[43] Shirley van der Veur, "Africa: Communication and Cultural Patterns," in *Intercultural Communication: A Reader*, 10th ed., ed. Larry A. Samovar and Richard E. Porter (Belmont, CA: Wadsworth, 2003), p. 84.

[44] Richard West and Lynn H. Turner, *Introducing Com- munication Theory*, 3rd ed. (Boston: McGraw-Hill, 2007), pp. 515–32. See Cheris Kramarae, *Women and Men Speaking: Framework for Analysis* (Rowley, MA: Newbury House, 1981). www.parl.gc.ca/ParlInfo/Compilations/ ProvinceTerritory/ProvincialWomenRightToVote.aspx

[45]Edward T. Hall, *The Silent Language* (Garden City, NY: Doubleday, 1959). See also Lustig and Koester, *Intercultural Competence*, p. 226.

[46]Edward T. Hall and M. R. Hall, *Understanding Cultural Differences: Germans, French and Americans* (Yarmouth, ME: Intercultural Press, 1990), p. 6.

[47]Dean Allen Foster, *Bargaining across Borders* (New York: McGraw-Hill, 1992), p. 280.

[48]Edward T. Hall, *The Dance of Life: Other Dimensions of Time* (New York: Anchor/Doubleday, 1983), p. 42.

[49]www.users.vioicenet.com/~howard/mindful.html. http://scholar.google.com/scholar?q=cultural+perspectives,+Banks,+2003&hl=en&as_sdt=0&as_vis=1&oi=scholart&sa=X&ei=zrPbT4qeOJS36QG2oaiOCw&ved=0CAcQgQMwAA or http://depts.washington.edu/centerme/Fs04banks.pdf.

[50]Ellen J. Langer, *Mindfulness* (Cambridge, MA: Da Capo, 1989), p. 11.

[51]Ibid.

[52]www.users.vioicenet.com/~howard/mindful.html.

[53]Langer, *Mindfulness*, p. 69.

[54]Richard Boyatzis and Annie McKee, *Resonant Leadership* (Boston: Harvard Business School Press, 2005), p. 112.

[55]www.integrativescience.ca/uploads/articles/2012Feb-Marshall-Two-Eyed-Seeing-Chapleau-First-Nation.pdf

[56]Richard Nisbett, *The Geography of Thought: How Asians and Westerners Think Differently . . . and Why* (New York: Free Press, 2003), p. xiii.

[57]Marvin Harris, *Cows, Pigs, Wars, and Witches: The Riddles of Culture* (New York: Vintage Books, 1975), pp. 11–34.

[58]Ibid., p. 30.

[59]Langer, *Mindfulness*, p. 69.

[60]See the following references: Howard Giles et al., "Speech Accommodation Theory: The First Decade and Beyond," in *Communication Yearbook*, ed. Margaret L. McLaughlin (Newbury Park, CA: Sage, 1987), pp. 13–48; Howard Giles et al., "Accommodation Theory: Communication, Context, and Consequence," in *Contexts of Accommodation: Developments in Applied Sociolinguistics*, ed. Howard Giles et al. (Cambridge: Cambridge University Press, 1991), pp. 1–68.

[61]Milton J. Bennett, "Becoming Interculturally Competent," in *Toward Multiculturalism: A Reader in Multicultural Education*, 2nd. ed., ed. J. Wurzel (Newton, MA: Intercultural Resources Corporation, 2004), pp. 62–77.

Chapter 4

[1]Don Gabor, *How to Start a Conversation and Make Friends* (New York: Fireside, 2001), pp. 66–68.

[2]Phillip Emmert, "A Definition of Listening," *Listening Post* 51 (1995), p. 6.

[3]Richard Emanuel et al., "How College Students Spend Their Time Communicating," *International Journal of Listening* 22 (2008), pp. 13–28.

[4]Lynn O. Cooper and Trey Buchanan, "Listening Competency on Campus: A Psychometric Analysis of Student Learning," *The International Journal of Listening*, 24 (2010), pp. 141–163.

[5]Andrew D. Wolvin and Carolyn G. Coakley, *Listening*, 5th ed. (Madison, WI: Brown and Benchmark, 1996), p. 15.

[6]Reported in Sandra D. Collins, *Listening and Responding Managerial Communication Series* (Mason, OH: Thomson, 2006), p. 21.

[7]Michael P. Nichols, *The Lost Art of Listening* (New York: Guildford, 1995), p. 11.

[8]Ralph G. Nichols, "Listening Is a 10-Part Skill," *Nation's Business* 75 (September 1987), p. 40.

[9]S. S. Benoit and J. W. Lee, "Listening: It Can Be Taught," *Journal of Education for Business* 63 (1986), pp. 229–32.

[10]The numerical ranges in Figure 4.1 summarize research on communication and listening time studies. See Andrew Wolvin and Carolyn Gwynn Coakley, *Listening* (Madison, WI: Brown & Benchmark, 1996), pp. 13–15; Laura A. Janusik and Andrew D. Wolvin, "24 Hours in a Day: A Listening Update to the Time studies," *The International Journal of Listening*, 23 (2009), pp. 104–120; Emanuel et al., "How College Students Spend Their Time Communicating."

[11]Florence I. Wolff and Nadine C. Marsnik, *Perceptive Listening*, 2nd ed. (Fort Worth, TX: Harcourt Brace Jovanovich, 1992), pp. 9–16.

[12]Nichols, M. P., *The Lost Art of Listening*, pp. 196, 221.

[13]Tony Alessandra and Phil Hunsaker, *Communicating at Work* (New York: Fireside, 1993), p. 55.

[14]Jim Collins, *Good to Great* (New York: HarperCollins, 2001), p. 14.

[15]Lynn O. Cooper and Trey Buchanan, "Listening Competency on Campus: A Psychometric Analysis of Students Listening," *International Journal of Listening* 24 (2010), p. 157.

[16]Many sources substantiate this list of poor listening habits including Judi Brownell, *Listening: Attitudes, Principles, and Skills*, 4th ed. (Boston: Pearson/Allyn and Bacon, 2010); Madelyn Burley-Allen, *Listening: The Forgotten Skill*, 2nd ed. (New York: Wiley, 1995); Ralph G. Nichols, "Do We Know How to Listen? Practical Helps in a Modern Age," *Speech Teacher* 10 (1961); Nichols, R. G., "Listening Is a 10-Part Skill"; and Wolvin and Coakley, *Listening*.

[17]Judi Brownell, *Listening: Attitudes, Principles, and Skills*, 4th ed. (Boston: Pearson/Allyn and Bacon, 2010), p. 14.

[18]Ibid., p. 16.

[19]Ibid., pp. 16–17.

[20]Ibid., p. 73.

[21]Statistics Canada, *Participation and Activity Limitation Survey*, 2006. Page 2, Table 1. www.statcan.gc.ca/pub/89-628-x/89-628-x2009012-eng.pdf.

[22]Ibid.

[23]Samuel E. Wood, Ellen Green Wood, and Denise Boyd, *The World of Psychology*, 6th ed. (Boston: Pearson/Allyn and Bacon, 2008), p. 199.

[24]Alan D. Baddeley and Robert H. Logie, "Working Memory: The Multiple-Component Model," in *Models of Working Memory*, ed. Akira Miyake and Priti Shah (Cambridge: Cambridge University Press, 1999), pp. 28–61; see also http://cogweb.ucla.edu/Abstracts/Miyake_Shah_99.html#intro.

[25]Laura Ann Janusik, "Building Listening Theory: The Validation of the Conversational Listening Span," *Communication Studies* 58 (2007), p. 142.

[26]Ibid.

[27]Peter Desberg, *Speaking Scared Sounding Good* (Garden City Park, NY: Square One, 2007), p. 127.

[28]Brownell, *Listening*, p. 168.

[29]Nichols, M. P., *The Lost Art of Listening*, pp. 36–37.

[30]Based on Wolff and Marsnik, *Perceptive Listening*, p. 100.

[31]Nichols, M. P., *The Lost Art of Listening*, p. 37.

[32]Isa Engleberg and Dianna Wynn, *Working in Groups: Communication Principles and Strategies*, 5th ed. (Boston: Pearson/Allyn and Bacon, 2010), p. 196.

[33]National Communication Association Credo for Ethical Communication, www.natcom.org/aboutNCA/Policies/Platform.html.

[34]Nichols, M. P., *The Lost Art of Listening*, pp. 42–43.

[35]Wolvin and Coakley, *Listening*, pp. 135–38.

[36]Based on Wolff and Marsnik, *Perceptive Listening*, pp. 94–95.

[37]Based on David W. Johnson's "Questionnaire on Listening and Response Alternatives," in *Reaching Out: Interpersonal Effectiveness and Self-Actualization*, 7th ed. (Boston: Allyn and Bacon, 2000), pp. 234–39.

[38]Nichols, M. P., *The Lost Art of Listening*, p. 126.

[39]Ibid.

[40]Nichols, R. G., "Listening Is a 10-Part Skill," p. 40.

[41]Mark Knapp and Judith A. Hall, *Nonverbal Communication in Human Interaction*, 6th ed. (Belmont, CA: Thomson/Wadsworth, 2006), p. 296.

[42]Sindya N. Bhanoo, "Ability Seen in Toddlers to Judge Others' Intent," *The New York Times*, November 16, 2010. www.nytimes.com/2010/11/16/science/16obchildren.html?_r=1&sq=toddlers%20intention&st=cse&scp=1&pagewanted=print.

[43]Kittie W. Watson, Larry L. Barker, and James B. Weaver, "The Listening Styles Profile (LSP-16): Development and Validation of an Instrument to Assess Four Listening Styles," *International Journal of Listening*, 9 (1995), pp. 1–13; Also see Kittie W. Watson, Larry L. Barker, and James B. Weaver, *Listening Styles Profile*, www.flipkart.com/listening-styles-profile-combo-package-book.

[44]Graham Bodie and Debra Worthington, "Revisiting the Listening Styles Profile (LSP-16): A Confirmatory Factor Analytic Approach to Scale Validation and Reliability Estimation," *International Journal of Listening*, 24 (2010), p. 84; Debra Worthington, Graham D. Bodie, Christopher Gearhart, "The Listening Styles Profile Revised (LSP-R): A Scale Revision and Validation," paper presented at the Eastern Communication Convention, April 15, 2011; personal email exchanges with Bodie and Worthington in April 2011.

[45]Nichols, R. G., "Do We Know How to Listen?," p. 121.

[46]Burley-Allen, *Listening*, pp. 68–70.

[47]Paul J. Kaufmann, *Sensible Listening: The Key to Responsive Interaction*, 5th ed. (Dubuque, IA: Kendall/Hunt, 2006), p. 115.

[48]Nichols, R. G., "Do We Know How to Listen?," p. 122.

[49]Deborah Tannen, *You Just Don't Understand: Women and Men in Conversation* (New York: Ballantine Books, 1990), pp. 141–42.

[50]Ibid., pp. 142–43.

[51]See ibid., pp. 123–48; see also Diana K. Ivy and Phil Backlund, *Exploring GenderSpeak* (New York: McGraw-Hill, 1994), pp. 224–25.

[52]See Tannen, *You Just Don't Understand*, pp. 149–151; Ivy and Backlund, *Exploring GenderSpeak*, pp. 206–8, 224–25; and Teri Kwal Gamble and Michael W. Gamble, *The Gender Communication Connection* (Boston: Houghton Mifflin, 2003), pp. 122–28.

[53]Elizabeth A. Tuleja, *Intercultural Communication for Business* (Mason, OH: Thomson Higher Education, 2005), p. 43.

[54]For other definitions and discussions of critical thinking, see Brooke Noel Moore and Richard Parker, *Critical Thinking*, 5th ed. (Mountain View, CA: Mayfield, 1998); John Chaffee, *Thinking Critically*, 6th ed. (Boston: Houghton Mifflin, 2000); Richard W. Paul, *Critical Thinking: How to Prepare Students for a Rapidly Changing World* (Santa Rosa, CA: Foundation for Critical Thinking, 1995); and Vincent Ryan Ruggero, *Becoming a Critical Thinker*, 4th ed. (Boston: Houghton Mifflin, 2002).

[55]Robert H. Ennis, "Critical Thinking Assessment," *Theory into Practice* 32 (1993), p. 180.

[56]Isa N. Engleberg and John A. Daly, *Presentations in Everyday Life*, 3rd ed. (Boston: Pearson/Allyn and Bacon, 2009), p. 59.

[57]www.slcc.edu/assessment/docs/CT_Appendices/Appendix%20D%20-%20Examples%20of%20Critical%20Thinking%20Question%20Stems.pdf.

[58]William V. Haney, *Communication and Interpersonal Relationships: Text and Cases* (Homewood, IL: Irwin, 1992), pp. 231–32, 241.

[59]Antonio R. Damasio, *Descartes' Error: Emotion, Reason, and the Human Brain* (New York: Penguin U.S.A., 1994), and *The Feeling of What Happens: Body and Emotion in the Making of Consciousness* (San Diego, CA: Harvest/Harcourt, 1999).

[60]Based on Andrew Wolvin and Laura Janusik, "Janusik/Wolvin Student Listening Inventory," in *Instructor's Manual for Communicating: A Social and Career Focus*, 9th ed., ed. Roy M. Berko, Andrew D. Wolvin, and Darlyn R. Wolvin (Boston: Houghton Mifflin, 2004), pp. 129–131.

[61]www.cyc-net.org/cyc-online/cycol-0404-reflective.html.

[62]www.brookes.ac.uk/services/upgrade/a-z/reflective_gibbs.html.

[63]Ibid.

[64]Paul J. Kaufman, *Sensible Listening: The Key to Responsive Interaction*, 5th ed. (Dubuque, IA: Kendall/Hunt, 2006), p. 115.

Chapter 5

[1]Isa N. Engleberg and John A. Daly, *Presentations in Everyday Life*, 3rd ed. (Pearson/Allyn and Bacon, 2009), p. 261. Survey responses were received from more than 600 students enrolled in a basic communication course at geographically dispersed institutions of higher education (community colleges, liberal arts colleges, and large universities).

[2]William O' Grady et al., *Contemporary Linguistics: An Introduction*, 4th ed. (Boston: Bedford/St. Martin's, 2001), p. 659.

[3]Mark Twain, Letter to George Bainton, October 15, 1888, www.twainquotes.com/Lightning.html.

[4]Nicholas Wade, *Before the Dawn: Recovering the Lost History of Our Ancestors* (New York: Penguin, 2006), pp. 36–37.

[5]John H. McWhorter, *The Power of Babel: A Natural History of Language* (New York: Times Books/Henry Holt, 2001), pp. 4–5.

[6]Nicholas Wade, *Before the Dawn: Recovering the Lost History of Our Ancestors* (New York: Penguin, 2006), p. 226.

[7]Geoffrey Finch, *Word of Mouth: A New Introduction to Language and Communication* (New York: Palgrave, 2003), pp. 5–10; William O'Grady, Michael Dobrovolsky, and Mark Aronoff, *Contemporary Linguistics*, 2nd ed. (New York: St. Martin's Press, 1993), p. 9.

[8]See Bart G. de Boer, "Modelling Vocal Anatomy's Significant Effect on Speech," *Journal of Evolutionary Psychology*, 2010, 8(4), pp. 351–366. http://uvafon.hum.uva.nl/bart/papers/deBoerJEP2010.pdf; www.babelsdawn.com/babels_dawn/2010/10/the-evolution-of-the-vocal-tract.html.

[9]Anne Donnellon, *Team Talk: The Power of Language in Team Dynamics* (Boston: Harvard Business School Press, 1996), p. 6.

[10]Victoria Fromkin and Robert Rodman, *An Introduction to Language*, 6th ed., (Fort Worth: Harcourt Brace, 1998), p. 3.

[11]Nelson W. Francis, *The English Language: An Introduction* (London: English University Press, 1967), p. 119.

[12]Geoffrey Finch, *Word of Mouth: A New Introduction to Language and Communication* (New York: Palgrave, 2003), p. 1.

[13]Ibid., p. 11.

[14]S. I. Hayakawa and Alan R. Hayakawa, *Language and Thought in Action*, 5th ed. (San Diego, CA: Harcourt Brace Jovanovich, 1990), p. 39.

[15]Ibid., p. 43.

[16]Adapted from Ogden and Richards, *The Meaning of Meaning* (New York: Harcourt Brace, 1936).

[17]Geoffrey Finch, *Word of Mouth: A New Introduction to Language and Communication* (New York: Palgrave, 2003), p. 28.

[18]Isa N. Engleberg and Dianna R. Wynn, *Working in Groups: Communication Principles and Strategies*, 5th ed. (Boston: Houghton Mifflin, 2010), p. 164.

[19]Vivian J. Cook, *Inside Language* (London: Arnold, 1997), p. 91.

[20]Geoffrey Finch, *Word of Mouth: A New Introduction to Language and Communication* (New York: Palgrave, 2003), p. 2.

[21]William O'Grady et al., *Contemporary Linguistics: An Introduction*, 5th ed. (Boston: Bedford/St. Martin's, 2005), p. 509.

[22]Myron W. Lustig and Jolene Koester, *Intercultural Competence: Interpersonal Communication across Cultures*, 6th ed. (Boston: Pearson/Allyn & Bacon, 2010), pp. 183–184.

[23]See Geoffrey Finch, *Word of Mouth: A New Introduction to Language and Communication* (New York: Palgrave, 2003); www.aber.ac.uk/media/Documents/short/whorf.html; www.users.globalnet.co.uk/~skolyles/swh.htm.

[24]Marcel Danesi and Paul Perron, *Analyzing Cultures: An Introduction and Handbook* (Bloomington, IN: Indiana University Press, 1999), p. 61.

[25]Ibid., p. 184.

[26]Larry A. Samovar and Richard Porter, *Communication between Cultures*, 5th ed. (Belmont, CA: Wadsworth, 2004), pp. 146–147.

[27]*The Washington Post*, April 6, 2002, p. A1, www.whitehouse.gov/news/release/2002/04/print/20020406-3.html.

[28]Geoffrey Finch, *Word of Mouth: A New Introduction to Language and Communication* (New York: Palgrave, 2003), p. 134.

[29]Ibid., p. 135.

[30]Ibid., p. 136.

[31]M. Schultz, "The Semantic Derogation of Woman," in *Language and Sex: Difference and Dominance*, ed. B. Thorne and N. Henley (Rowley, MA: Newbury House, 1975), as quoted in Geoffrey Finch, *Word of Mouth: A New Introduction to Language and Communication* (New York: Palgrave, 2003), p. 137.

[32]Robin Lakoff, *Language and Woman's Place* (New York: HarperCollins, 1975).

[33]Janet Holmes, "Myth 6: Women Talk Too Much," in *Language Myths*, ed. Lauri Bauer and Peter Trudgill (London: Penguin, 1998), p. 41.

[34]David Brown, "Stereotypes of Quiet Men, Chatty Women Not Sound Science," *The Washington Post*, July 6, 2007, p. A2. See also Donald G. McNeill, "Yada, Yada, Yada. Him? Or Her?" *The New York Times*, July 6, 2007, p. A13.

[35]Janet Holmes, "Myth 6: Women Talk Too Much," in *Language Myths*, ed. Lauri Bauer and Peter Trudgill (London: Penguin, 1998), pp. 42–47.

[36]Ibid., pp. 48–49.

[37]William V. Haney, *Communication and Interpersonal Relations: Text and Cases*, 6th ed. (Homewood, IL: Irwin, 1992), p. 269.

[38]Randy Cohen, "The Ethicist," *The New York Times Magazine*, July 26, 2009, p. 17.

[39]William O'Grady, Michael Dobrovolsky, and Mark Aronoff, *Contemporary Linguistics*, 2nd ed. (New York: St. Martin's Press, 1993), pp. 235–236.

[40]"The Leaked Memos: Did the White House Condone Torture?" *The Week*, June 25, 2004, p. 6.

[41]Anna-Britta Stenstrom, "Slang to Language: A Description Based on Teenage Talk," in *i love english language*, http://aggslanguage.wordpress.com/slang-to-slanguage/.

[42]Shirley Johnson, "What Is Slang?" Modern America, 1914-Present, www.uncp.edu/home/canada/work/allam/1914-/language/slang.htm.

[43]Brian Jones, Jr., "Sir John Harrington—Inventor of 'The John'," *Ezine*, http://ezinearticles.com/?Sir-John-Harrington—Inventor-of-The-John&id=3570402.

[44]Quoted in David Crystal, *The Cambridge Encyclopedia of the English Language* (New York: Cambridge University Press, 2003), p. 182.

[45]Kathryn Lindskoog, *Creative Writing: For People Who Can't Not Write* (Grand Rapids, MI: Zondervan Publishing, 1989), p. 66.

[46]William V. Haney, *Communication and Interpersonal Relations: Text and Cases*, 6th ed. (Homewood, IL: Irwin, 1992), p. 290.

[47]www.artbeyondsight.org/handbook/dat-accessibility-skills.shtml

[48]www.quillandquire.com/reviews/review.cfm?review_id=2150

[59]William Lutz, *Doublespeak* (New York: HarperPerennial, 1990), p. 3.

[50]Lyn Miller, "Quit Talking Like a Corporate Geek," *USA Today*, March 21, 2005, p. 7B.

[51]James V. O'Conner, *Cuss Control: The Complete Book on How to Curb Your Cursing* (New York: Three Rivers Press, 2000), p. 3.

[52]Natalie Angier, "Almost Before We Spoke, We Swore," *Science Times* in *The New York Times*, September 20, 2005, p. D6.

[53]Lars Andersson and Peter Trudgill, "Swearing," in *A Cultural Approach to Interpersonal Communication: Essential Readings*, ed. Leila Monaghan and Jane Goodman (Malden, MA: Wiley-Blackwell, 2007), p. 195.

[54]Natalie Angier, "Almost Before We Spoke, We Swore," *Science Times* in *The New York Times*, September 20, 2005, p. D6.

[55]James V. O'Conner, *Cuss Control: The Complete Book on How to Curb Your Cursing* (New York: Three Rivers Press, 2000), pp. 18–27; Timothy Jay, *Why We Curse: A Neuro-Psycho-Social Theory of Speech* (Amsterdam/Philadelphia: John Benjamins Publishing, 2000), p. 328.

[56]"Cleaning Up Potty-Mouths," *The Week*, August 18, 2006, p. 35.

[57]Natalie Angier, "Almost Before We Spoke, We Swore," p. D6.

[58]David Crystal, *Language and the Internet* (Cambridge: Cambridge University Press, 2001), pp. 238–39, cited in Crispin Thurlow, Laura Lengel, and Alice Tomic, *Computer Mediated Communication: Social Interaction and the Internet* (London: Sage, 2004), p. 123.

[59]Crispin Thurlow, Laura Lengel, and Alice Tomic, *Computer Mediated Communication: Social Interaction and the Internet* (London: Sage, 2004), pp. 124–125.

[60]"Leet," *Urban Dictionary*, www.urbandictionary.com/define.php?term=netspeak. Use "It's a variation of the word Elite" as a search string.

[61]Matt Richtel, "In Youthful World of Messaging, E-Mail Gets Instant Makeover," *The New York Times*, December 21, 2010, p. B4.

[62]For additional examples and warnings about overuse of symbols, see Deborah Jude-York, Lauren D. David, and Susan L. Wise, *Virtual Teams: Breaking the Boundaries of Time and Place* (Menlo Park, CA: Crisp Learning, 2000), pp. 91–92.

[63]www.idiomdictionary.com.

[64]R. L. Trask, *Language: The Basics*, 2nd ed. (London: Routledge, 1995), p. 170, 179.

[65]Based on Melinda G. Kramer, Glenn Leggett, and C. David Mead, *Prentice Hall Handbook for Writers*, 12th ed. (Englewood Cliffs, NJ: Prentice Hall, 1995), p. 272.

[66]Robert Mayer, *How to Win Any Argument* (Franklin Lakes, NJ: Career Press, 2006), p. 187.

[67]Stuart Chase, quoted in Richard Lederer, "Fowl Language: The Fine Art of the New Doublespeak," *AARP Bulletin* (March 2005), p. 27.

[68]Rudolf Flesch, *Say What You Mean* (New York: Harper and Row, 1972), p. 70.

[69]Joel Saltzman, *If You Can Talk, You Can Write* (New York: Time Warner, 1993), pp. 48–49.

[70]Virginia Richmond and James C. McCroskey, *Communication Apprehension, Avoidance and Effectiveness*, 5th ed. (Boston: Allyn and Bacon, 1998). © 1998 by Pearson Education. Reprinted by permission of the publisher. See also John Daly and Michael Miller, "The Empirical Development of an Instrument to Measure Writing Apprehension," *Research in the Teaching of English* 12 (1975), pp. 242–249.

Chapter 6

[1]Nina-Jo Moore, Mark Hickson, III, and Don W. Stacks, *Nonverbal Communication, Studies and Application*, 6th ed. (New York: Oxford, 2010), p. 4.

[2]Judee K. Burgoon and Aaron E. Bacue, "Nonverbal Communication Skills," in *Handbook of Communication and Social Interaction Skills*, ed. John O. Greene and Brant R. Burleson (Mahwah, NJ: Lawrence Erlbaum, 2003), pp. 208–209.

[3]From Sigmund Freud, *Fragment of Analysis of a Case of Hysteria*, Standard Edition, Volume 7, 1905, chapter 2: The First Dream. See Psychoanalytical Electronic Publishing, www.pep-web.org/document.php?id=se.007.0001a.

[4]Judee Burgoon, "Truth, Lies, and Virtual Worlds," The National Communication Association's Carroll C. Arnold Distinguished Lecture, 2005 annual convention of the National Communication Association, Boston, November 2005.

[5]Paul Ekman, *Telling Lies: Clues to Deceit in the Marketplace, Politics, and Marriage* (New York: W.W. Norton, 1992), p. 80.

[6]H. Dan O'Hair and Michael J. Cody, "Deception," in *The Dark Side of Interpersonal Communication*, ed. William R. Cupach and Brian H. Spitzberg (Hillsdale, NJ: Lawrence Erlbaum Associates, 1994), p. 190.

[7]Mark L. Knapp, *Lying and Deception in Human Interaction* (Boston: Pearson Education, 2008), pp. 217–218.

[8]Benedict Carey, "Judging Honesty By Words, Not Fidgets," *The New York Times*, May 12, 2009, p. D4.

[9]Judith Newman "Inside the Teenage Brain," *Parade Magazine*, November 28, 2010, www.parade.com/news/2010/11/28-inside-the-teenage-brain.html; See also National Institute of Mental Health, "Teenage Brain: A Work in Progress (Fact Sheet)," www.nimh.nih.gov/health/publications/teenage-brain-a-work-in-progress-fact-sheet/index.shtml.

[10]William D. S. Killgore and Deborah A. Yurgelun-Todd, "Neural Correlates of Emotional Intelligence in Adolescent Children," *Cognitive, Affective and Behavioral Neuroscience*, 2007, 7 (2), pp. 140–151; Deborah A. Yurgelun-Todd and William D. Killgore, "Fear-related Activity in the Prefrontal Cortex Increases with Age During Adolescence: A Preliminary MRI Study." *Neuroscience Letters*, 2006, 406, pp. 194–199.

[11]Interview: Deborah Yrgelun-Todd, Frontline, January 31, 2002, www.pbs.org/wgbh/pages/frontline/shows/teenbrain/interviews/todd.html.

[12]Ibid.

[13]Paul Ekman, "Communication through Nonverbal Behavior: A Source of Information about an Interpersonal Relationship," in *Affect, Cognition and Personality*, ed. Silvan S. Tompkins and C. E. Izard (New York: Springer, 1965), pp. 390–442.

[14]Judee K. Burgoon, David B. Buller, and W. Gill Woodall, *Nonverbal Communication: The Unspoken Dialog* (New York, McGraw-Hill, 1996), p. 286. See also Richard West and Lynn H. Turner, *Introducing Communication Theory* (Boston: McGraw Hill, 2007), pp. 152–153.

[15]www.cwhn.ca/node/40776.

[16]From the Federal Reserve Bank of St. Louis, *The Regional Economist* (April 2005), quoted in "Good Looks Can Mean Good Pay, Study Says," *The Sun*, April 28, 2005, p. D1.

[17]Angus Deaton, "Life at the Top: The Benefits of Height," www.princeton.edu/~deaton/downloads/life_at_the_top_benefits_of_height_final_june_2009.pdf.

[18]2011 Medicine Hat Police and Community Safety Survey, Sample Survey Results, page 92. http://medicinehatpolice.com/uploads/files/Med_Hat_Police_2011_Survey_Results_-May_2012.pdf.

[19]www.hrmonline.ca/article/tattoo-taboo-can-you-ask-workers-to-cover-up-123649.aspx.

[20]Son wants to gauge his ears? http://answers.yahoo.com/question/index?qid=20070913141142AAKPdRk.

[21]David Brooks, "Nonconformity Is Skin Deep," *The New York Times*, August 27, 2006, p. WK11.

[22]Moore, Hickson, and Stacks, *Nonverbal Communication: Studies and Applications*, p. 170.

[23]Thomas J. Stanley and William D. Danko, *The Millionaire Next Door: The Surprising Secrets of America's Wealthy* (Atlanta, GA: Longstreet Press, 1996), pp. 28, 31–35.

[24]Jo-Ellan Dimitrius and Mark Mazzarella, *Reading People: How to Understand People and Predict Their Behavior—Anytime, Anyplace* (New York: Ballantine, 1999), p. 52.

[25]Jeannette Catsoulis, "Look but Don't Touch: It's All About the Hair," *The New York Times*, October 8, 2009, http://movies.nytimes.com/2009/10/09/movies/09hair.html; Also see "Chris Rock, Official Trailer, Good Hair," YouTube, July 31, 2009, www.youtube.com/watch?v=1m-4qxz08So&noredirect=1.

[26]Mark L. Knapp and Judith A. Hall, *Nonverbal Communication in Human Interaction*, 4th ed. (Fort Worth, TX: Harcourt Brace, 1997), p. 229.

[27]Paul Ekman and Wallace V. Friesen, "Hand Movements," in *The Nonverbal Communication Reader: Classic and Contemporary Readings*, 2nd ed., ed. Laura K. Guerrero, Joseph A. DeVito, and Michael L. Hecht (Long Grove, IL: Waveland Press, 2008), 105–108. The original article, "Hand Movements," was published in the *Journal of Communication* 22 (1972), pp. 353–374.

[28]Roger E. Axtell, *Do's and Taboos Around the World*, 2nd ed. (New York: John Wiley and Sons, 1990), p. 47.

[29]Laura K. Guerrero, Joseph A. DeVito, and Michael L. Hecht, "Section D. Contact Codes: Proxemics and Haptics," in *The Nonverbal Communication Reader: Classic and Contemporary Readings*, 2nd ed., ed. Laura K. Guerrero, Joseph A. DeVito, and Michael L. Hecht (Long Grove, IL: Waveland Press, 2008), p. 174.

[30]Richmond, *Nonverbal Behavior in Interpersonal Relations*, p. 151.

[31]Larry Smeltzer, John Waltman, and Donald Leonard, "Proxemics and Haptics in Managerial Communication" in *The Nonverbal Communication Reader: Classic and Contemporary Readings*, 3rd ed., ed. Laura K. Guerrero and Michael L. Hecht (Long Grove, IL: Waveland Press, 2008), p. 190.

[32]Joseph B. Walther and Kyle P. D'Addario, "The Impacts of Emoticons on Message Interpretation in Computer-Mediated Communication" (paper presented at the meeting of the International Communication Association, Washington, DC, May 2001), p. 13.

[33]Richmond and McCroskey, *Nonverbal Behavior in Interpersonal Relationships*, pp. 75–77. Based on Paul Ekman and W. V. Frie, *Face*, 2nd ed., ed. Paul Ekman (Cambridge: Cambridge University Press, 1982), pp. 7–21.

[34]Summary of eye behavior research from Virginia P. Richmond, James C. McCroskey, and Mark L. Hickson, *Nonverbal Behavior in Interpersonal Relations* (Boston: Pearson/Allyn and Bacon, 2008), pp. 95–96.

[35]Gerald W. Grumet, "Eye Contact: The Core of Interpersonal Relatedness," in *The Nonverbal Communication Reader: Classic and Contemporary Readings*, 3rd ed., Laura K. Guerrero and Michael L. Hecht (Long Grove, IL: Waveland Press, 2008), pp. 125–126.

[36]Guo-Ming Chen and William J. Starosta, *Fundamentals of Intercultural Communication* (Boston: Allyn & Bacon, 1998), p. 91.

[37]Lyle V. Mayer, *Fundamentals of Voice and Diction*, 13th ed. (Boston: McGraw Hill, 2004), p. 229.

[38]Richmond and McCroskey, *Nonverbal Behavior in Interpersonal Relationships*, p. 103.

[39]www.hrsdc.gc.ca/eng/labour/labour_law; http://laws-lois.justice.gc.ca/eng/acts/C-46.

[40]Allan Pease and Barbara Pease, *The Definitive Book of Body Language* (New York: Bantam, 2004), pp. 193–194.

[41]Edward T. Hall, *The Hidden Dimension* (Garden City, NY: Doubleday, 1966).

[42]Moore, *Hickson, and Stacks, Nonverbal Communication: Studies and Applications*, p. 293.

[43]Richmond and McCroskey, *Nonverbal Behavior in Interpersonal Relationships*, pp. 199–212.

[44]Isa N. Engleberg and John A. Daly, *Presentations in Everyday Life*, 3rd ed. (Boston: Houghton Mifflin, 2009), p. 138.

[45]John A. Daly and Anita Vangelisti, "Skillfully Instructing Learners: How Communicators Effectively Convey Messages," in *Handbook of Communication and Social Interaction Skills*, ed. John O. Greene and Brant R. Burleson (Mahwah, NJ: Lawrence Erlbaum, 2003), pp. 892–894.

[46]Timothy G. Plax and Patricia Kearney, "Classroom Management: Contending with College Student Discipline," in *Teaching Communication: Theory, Research, and Methods*, 2nd ed., ed. Anita L. Vangelisti, John A. Daly, and Gustav W. Friedrich (Lea's Communication Series) (Mahwah, NJ: Lawrence Erlbaum, 1999), p. 276.

[47]Moore, Hickson, and Stacks, *Nonverbal Communication: Studies and Applications*, p. 375.

Chapter 7

[1]Jerry Lopper, "The Six Life Benefits of Happiness," November 19, 2007, http://personaldevelopment .suite101.com/article.cfm/the_six_life_benefits_of_ happiness#ixzz0JqwpOgDk&D.

[2]David W. Johnson, *Reaching Out: Interpersonal Effectiveness and Self-Actualization*, 7th ed. (Boston: Allyn & Bacon, 2000), p. 12.

[3]John M. Gottman with Joan De Claire, *The Relationship Cure* (New York: Three Rivers Press, 2001), p. 23.

[4]Daniel Goleman, "'Friends for Life': An Emerging Biology of Emotional Healing," *The New York Times*, October 10, 2006, p. D5. For a more detailed examination of this phenomenon, see Daniel Goleman, *Social Intelligence* (New York: Bantam, 2006), p. 10.

[5]William Schutz, *The Human Element: Productivity, Self-Esteem, and the Bottom Line* (San Francisco: Jossey-Bass, 1994).

[6]In his more recent works, Schutz refers to this need as openness. However, we find that students understand this concept better when we use Schutz's original term— *affection*.

[7]Based on material in Isa Engleberg and Dianna Wynn, *Working in Groups: Communication Principles and Strategies*, 5th ed. (Boston: Houghton Mifflin, 2010), pp. 82–85.

[8]Erving Goffman, *The Presentation of Self in Everyday Life* (New York: Doubleday, 1959).

[9]Based on Edward E. Jones and Thane S. Pittman, "Toward a General Theory of Strategic Self-Presentation,". in Jerry M. Suls (Ed.), *Psychological Perspectives on the Self*, Vol. 1 (Hillsdale, NJ: Erlbaum, 1982), pp. 231–262; see also

Sandra Metts and Erica Grohskopf, "Impression Management: Goals, Strategies, and Skills," in *Handbook of Communication and Social Interaction Skills*, ed. John O. Greene and Brant Burleson (Mahwah, NJ: Lawrence Erlbaum, 2003), pp. 358–359. Hans Grietens, *Attitudes Towards Social Limits, Undersocialized Behavior, and Self-Presentation in Young People* (Leuven, Belgium: Leuven University Press, 1999), p. 44.

[10]We have added the parenthetical cautions to the Jones and Pittman taxonomy of impression formation strategies.

[11]Daniel Menaker, *A Good Talk: The Story and Skill of Conversation* (NY: Hatchette Book Groups, 2010), p. 1.

[12]www.mindtools.com/pages/article/newTMC_88.htm.

[13]Daniel Menaker, *A Good Talk: The Story and Skill of Conversation*, p. 182.

[14]Maria J. O'Leary and Cynthia Gallois, "The Last Ten Turns in Conversations between Friends and Strangers," in *The Nonverbal Communication Reader: Classic and Contemporary Readings*, 2nd ed., ed. Laura K. Guerrero, Joseph A. DeVito, and Michael L. Hecht (Prospect Heights, IL: Waveland Press, 1999), pp. 415–421.

[15]Wendy Samter, "Friendship Interaction Skills across the Life Span," in *Handbook of Communication and Social Interaction Skills*, ed. John O. Greene and Brant R. Burleson (Mahwah, NJ: Lawrence Erlbaum, 2003), p. 641.

[16]Wendy Samter, "Friendship Interaction Skills across the Life Span," in *Handbook of Communication and Social Interaction Skills*, ed. John O. Greene and Brant R. Burleson (Mahwah, NJ: Lawrence Erlbaum, 2003), p. 662.

[17]William K. Rawlins, *Friendship Matters: Communication, Dialects, and the Life Course* (New York: Aldine De Gruyter, 1992), p. 181.

[18]Sandra Petronio, *Boundaries of Privacy: Dialectics of Disclosure* (Albany: State University of New York Press, 2003), pp. 5–6.

[19]Wendy Samter, "Friendship Interaction Skills across the Life Span," p. 661.

[20]William K. Rawlins, *Friendship Matters: Communication, Dialects, and the Life Course*, p. 105.

[21]www./virtue/87/-mindfulness/quotes.

[22]Malcolm R. Parks, "Ideology in Interpersonal Communication: Off the Couch and into the World," in *Communication Yearbook 5*, ed. Michael Burgoon (New Brunswick, NJ: Transaction Books, 1982), pp. 79–107.

[23]Joseph Luft, *Group Process: An Introduction to Group Dynamics*, 3rd ed. (Palo Alto, CA: Mayfield, 1984).

[24]Ibid.

[25]David W. Johnson, *Reaching Out: Interpersonal Effectiveness and Self-Actualization*, 7th ed. (Boston: Allyn & Bacon, 2000), p. 47.

[26]Luft, *Group Process: An Introduction to Group Dynamics*, 3rd ed.

[27]Ibid., pp. 58–59.

[28]David W. Johnson, *Reaching Out: Interpersonal Effectiveness and Self-Actualization*, 7th ed., p. 61.

[29]For more information on self-disclosure skills, see David W. Johnson, *Reaching Out: Interpersonal Effectiveness*

and *Self-Actualization*, 7th ed. (Boston: Allyn & Bacon, 2000), pp. 59–61.

[30]Jack R. Gibb, "Defensive Communication," *Journal of Communication* 2 (1961), pp. 141–148.

[31]Irvin Altman and Dalmas Taylor, *Social Penetration: The Development of Interpersonal Relationships* (New York: Holt, Rinehart, and Winston, 1973).

[32]Walid A. Afifi and Laura K. Guerrero, "Motivations Underlying Topic Avoidance in Close Relationships," in *Balancing the Secrets of Private Disclosure*, ed. Sandra Petronio (Mahwah, NJ: Lawrence Erlbaum, 2000), p. 168.

[33]*Shrek*, DreamWorks, 2003.

[34]Based on Jack R. Gibb, "Defensive Communication," pp. 141–148; also see http://lynn_meade.tripod.com/id61_m.htm.

[35]The original Gibb article was published in 1961 with no references or explanations of his research methodology. Although Gibb's climate categories are interesting, researchers have concluded that "the confidence placed in Gibb's theory of supportive and defensive communication as currently construed has been facile and empirically unwarranted." See Gordon Forward and Kathleen Czech, "Why (Most) Everything You Think You Know About Gibb's Supportive and Defensive Communication Climate May be Wrong and What To Do About It," Paper presented to the Small Group Communication Division at the National Communication Association Convention, San Diego, 2008, p. 16.

[36]Sharon Anthony Bower and Gordon H. Bower, *Asserting Yourself: A Practical Guide to Positive Change* (Cambridge, MA: Perseus Books, 1991), p. 9.

[37]Madelyn Burley-Allen, *Managing Assertively: How to Improve Your People Skills* (New York: John Wiley, 1983), p. 45.

[38]Bower and Bower, *Asserting Yourself: A Practical Guide to Positive Change*, p. 90. See also, "Assertiveness," athealth.com, January 6, 2010, www.athealth.com/Consumer/disorders/assertiveness.html.

[39]Bower and Bower, *Asserting Yourself: A Practical Guide to Positive Change*, pp. 4–5.

[40]Edmund J. Bourne, *The Anxiety and Phobia Workbook*, 5th ed. (Oakland, CA: Harbinger, 2010), p. 306.

[41]Ibid., p. 307. The example is adapted and written by the textbook authors.

[42]Ibid., p. 307.

Chapter 8

[1]Robert Plutchik, *Emotions: A Psychoevolutionary Synthesis* (New York: Harper and Row, 1980).

[2]www.infographicsarchive.com/interesting-facts/robert-plutchiks-psycho-evolutionary-theory-of-basic-emotions/#prettyPhoto/1.

[3]Sally Planalp, *Communicating Emotion: Social, Moral and Cultural Processes* (Cambridge: Cambridge University Press, 1999). www.ffri.uniri.hr/~ibrdar/komunikacija/seminari/Planalp,1999%20%20-%20Importance%20of%20emotions%20in%20interaction%20(Chapt.pdf.

[4]http://ontario.cmha.ca/mental-health/mental-health-conditions/mood-disorders.

[5]Moshe Zeidner, Gerald Matthews, and Richard D. Roberts. *What We Know About Emotional Intelligence: How It Affects Learning, Work, Relationships, and Our Mental Health* (Boston: MIT Press, 2012).

[6]Sally Planalp, *Communicating Emotion: Social, Moral and Cultural Processes*. www.ffri.uniri.hr/~ibrdar/komunikacija/seminari/Planalp,1999%20%20-%20Importance%20of%20emotions%20in%20interaction%20(Chapt.pdf.

[7]Steven Gordon, "The Sociology of Sentiments and Emotion," in *Social Psychology: Sociological Approaches*, ed. M. Rosenberg and R. Turner (New York: Basic Books, 1981).

[8]Kaplan, H. B., Stets, J. E., Turner, J. H., & Peterson, G. (2006). "Cultural Theory and Emotions," in *Handbook of the Sociology of Emotions*, p. 114.

[9]Daniel Goleman, *Working with Emotional Intelligence* (New York: Bantam Books, 1998), p. 317.

[10]Daniel Goleman, *Emotional Intelligence: Why It Can Matter More Than IQ* (New York: Bantam, 1995); Goleman, 1998; Hendrie Weisinger, *Emotional Intelligence at Work* (San Francisco: Jossey-Bass, 1998).

[11]Goleman, *Emotional Intelligence: Why It Can Matter More Than IQ*, pp. 27–28. See also Antonio R. Damasio, *Descartes' Error: Emotion, Reason, and the Human Brain* (New York: Quill, 2000).

[12]Ibid.

[13]Antonio R. Damasio, *Descartes' Error: Emotion, Reason, and the Human Brain* (New York: Quill, 2000).

[14]Laura E. Berk. *Child Development*, 9th edition (Upper Saddle River, NJ: Pearson) Ch. 10.

[15]John D. Mayer, Richard D. Roberts, and Sigal G. Barsade. "Human Abilities: Emotional Intelligence." *Annual Review of Psychology* 59: 507–536.

[16]Based on Daniel Goleman, *Emotional Intelligence*; Daniel Goleman, *Working with Emotional Intelligence*; Hendrie Weisinger, *Emotional Intelligence at Work* (San Francisco: Jossey-Bass, 1998).

[17]www.greatwestlife.com/web5/groups/corporate/@public/documents/web_content/s7_028872.pdf.

[18]Ibid.

[19]Moshe Zeidner, Gerald Matthews, and Richard D. Roberts. *What We Know About Emotional Intelligence*, p. 258.

[20]www.healthyworkplaces.info/wp-content/uploads/2012/10/emotional-intelligence.pdf

[21]Moshe Zeidner, Gerald Matthews, and Richard D. Roberts. *What We Know About Emotional Intelligence*, p. 258.

[22]National Communication Association Credo for Ethical Communication, www.natcom.org/aboutNCA/Policies/Platform.html.

[23]www.healthyworkplaces.info/wp-content/uploads/2012/10/emotional-intelligence.pdf.

[24]Brant R. Burleson, "Emotional Support Skills," in *Handbook of Communication and Social Interaction Skills*, ed. John O. Greene and Brant R. Burleson (Mahwah, NJ: Lawrence Erlbaum, 2003), pp. 589–681.

[25]www.healthyworkplaces.info/wp-content/uploads/2012/10/emotional-intelligence.pdf.

[26]Paula S. Tompkins, *Practicing Communication Ethics* (Boston: Allyn & Bacon, 2011), p. 83.

[27]Elaine E. Englehardt, "Introduction to Ethics in Interpersonal Communication," in *Ethical Issues in Interpersonal Communication*, ed. Elaine E. Englehardt (Fort Worth, TX: Harcourt, 2001), pp. 1–25; Carol Gilligan, "Images of Relationship," and Nel Noddings, "An Ethics of Care," in *Ethical Issues in Interpersonal Communication*, ed. Elaine E. Englehardt (Fort Worth, TX: Harcourt, 2001), pp. 88–96 and 96–103.

[28]Brant R. Burleson, Amanda J. Holmstrom, and Cristina M. Gilstrap, "Guys Can't Say *That* to Guys: Four Experiments Assessing the Normative Motivation Account for Deficiencies in the Emotional Support Provided by Men," *Communication Monographs* 72 (2005), p. 582.

[29]Susan M. Jones and John G. Wirtz, "How Does the Comforting Process Work? An Empirical Test of an Appraisal-Based Model of Comforting," *Human Communication Research* 32 (2006), p. 217.

[30]Cecilia Bosticco and Teresa L. Thompson. "Narratives and Story Telling in Coping with Grief and Bereavement," *Omega* 51 (2005), pp. 1–16.

[31]Ibid.

[32]Brant R. Burleson, "Emotional Support Skills," p. 553.

Chapter 9

[1]www.randstad.com/press-room/research-reports; www.backbonemag.com/Magazine/2012-06/canadian-workers-job-satisfaction-survey.aspx.

[2]Ibid.

[3]Daniel P. Modaff, Sue DeWine, and Jennifer A. Butler, *Organizational Communication: Foundations, Challenges, Misunderstandings* (Los Angeles, CA: Roxbury, 2008), p. 197.

[4]Ibid., p. 198.

[5]Ibid., p. 206.

[6]Ibid., p. 207.

[7]Robert Longley, "Labor Studies of Attitudes toward Work and Leisure: U.S. Workers Are Happy and Stress Is Over-stressed," August 1999, http://usgovinfo.about.com/od/censusandstatsitics/a/labordaystudy.htm.

[8]Modaff, DeWine, and Butler, *Organizational Communication: Foundations, Challenges, Misunderstandings*, pp. 236–236.

[9]Hal Plotkin, "Introduction," *Dealing with Difficult People* (Boston: Harvard Business School Press, 2005), p. 1.

[10]Hal Plotkin, "Feedback in the Future Tense," *Dealing with Difficult People* (Boston: Harvard Business School Press, 2005), pp. 132–137.

[11]Gilbert, *Communication Miracles at Work: Effective Tools and Tips for Getting the Most from Your Work Relationships*, p. 153.

[12]Ibid., p. 157.

[13]Based on Carley H. Dodd, *Managing Business and Professional Communication* (Boston: Allyn & Bacon, 2004), pp. 169–170.

[14]John Tschohl, Service Quality Institute, "Service, Not Servitude: Common Sense Is Critical Element of Customer Service," 2004, www.customer-service.com/articles/022502.cfm.

[15]Michael E. Pacanowsky and Nick O'Donnell-Trujillo, "Communication and Organizational Cultures," *Western Journal of Speech Communication*, 46 (1982), pp. 115–130; Michael E. Pacanowsky and Nick O'Donnell-Trujillo, *Communication Monographs* 50 (1983), pp. 127–130.

[16]Dodd, *Managing Business and Professional Communication*, p. 40.

[17]Devine, "Work and Career: Gossip Galore"; Carl Skooglund and Glenn Coleman, "Advice from the Ethics Office at Texas Instruments Corporation: Gossiping at Work" *Online Ethics Center for Engineering and Science* (2004), http://onlineethics.org/corp/gossip.html; Muriel Solomon, *Working with Difficult People* (New York: Prentice Hall, 2002), pp. 125–126.

[18]Joel Lovell, "Workplace Rumors Are True," *The New York Times*, December 10, 2006. www.nytimes.com/2006/12/10/magazine/10section4.t-9.html.

[19]Ibid.

[20]Ibid.

[21]Ibid.

[22]Rachel Devine, "Work and Career: Gossip Galore," *iVillage Work & Career*, www.ivillage.co.uk/workcareer/survive/opolotics/articles/#0,,156475_164246,00.html.

[23]Association of Corporate Counsel, "Workplace Challenges Associated with Employees' Social Media Use," *Legal Resources QuickCounsel*, www.acc.com/legalresources/quickcounsel/wcawesmu.cfm.

[24]Quoted in Samuel Greengard, "Gossip Poisons Business: HR Can Stop It," *Workforce* (July 2001), www.findarticles.com/p/articles/mi_m0FXS/is_7_80/ai_76938891.

[25]Samuel Greengard, "Gossip Poisons Business: HR Can Stop It," *Workforce* (July 2001), www.findarticles.com/p/articles/mi_m0FXS/is_7_80/ai_76938891. "Rumor Has It—Dealing with Misinformation in the Workplace," *Entrepreneur* (September 1, 1997), www.findarticles.com/p/articles/mi_m0DTI/is_n9_v25/ai_19892317.

[26]U.S. Equal Employment Opportunity Commission, "Facts about Sexual Harassment" (June 27, 2002), www.eeoc.gov/facts/fs-sex.html.

[27]Deborah Ware Balogh, "The Effects of Delayed Report and Motive for Reporting on Perceptions of Sexual Harassment," *Sex Roles: A Journal of Research* (April 2003), www.findarticles.com/p/articles/mi_m2294/is_2003_April/ai_101174064.

[28]www.chrc-ccdp.ca/publications/anti_harassment_toc-eng.aspx#; www.iapa.ca/Main/Articles/2009_workplace_violence.aspx.

[29]Ibid.

[30]Julie A. Woodzicka and Marianne LaFrance, "Real Versus Imagined Gender Harassment," *Journal of Social Issues* (Spring 2001), www.findarticles.com/p/articles/mi_m0341/is_1_57/ai_75140959.

[31]Modaff, DeWine, and Butler, *Organizational Communication: Foundations, Challenges, Misunderstandings*, p. 236.

[32]http://blogs.wsj.com/numbersguy/a-lifetime-of-career-changes-988

[33]Matt Villano, "What to Tell the Company as You Walk out the Door," *The New York Times*, November 27, 2005, p. BU8. Quoting Jim Atkinson, regional vice president, Right Management Consultants.

[34]Ibid.

[35]Dawn Rosenberg McKay, "Job Loss: How to Cope" (2009), http://careerplanning.about.com/od/jobloss/a/job_loss.htm.

[36]Based on Daniel P. Modaff and Sue DeWine, *Organizational Communication: Foundations, Challenges, Misunderstandings* (Los Angeles, CA: Roxbury, 2002), p. 202.

[37]Virginia Galt, "When Quitting a Job, Discretion Is the Better Part of Valor," http://globeandmail.workopolis.com/servlet/Content/fasttrack/2004041; Peggy Post, "Rules to Live By: Quitting Your Job," http://magazines.ivillage.com/goodhousekeeping/print/0,,636770,00.html.

[38]Based on "How to Cope with Job Loss," *eHow*, www.ehow.com/how_2084091_cope-job-loss.html.

[39]This definition is a composite of components found in most academic definitions of an interview. See, for example, Larry Powell and Jonathan Amsbary, *Interviewing: Situations and Contexts* (Boston: Pearson/Allyn & Bacon, 2006), p. 1; Charles Stewart and William B. Cash, *Interviewing: Principles and Practices*, 10th ed. (New York: McGraw-Hill, 2003), p. 4; Jeanne Tessier Barone and Jo Young Switzer, *Interviewing Art and Skill* (Boston: Allyn & Bacon, 1995), p. 8.

[40]Richard Nelson Bolles, *What Color Is Your Parachute? A Practical Manual for Job-Hunters and Career-Changers* (Berkeley: Ten Speed Press, 2007), p. 78.

[41]Accountemps study displayed in USA Today Snapshots, "Most Common Job Interview Mistakes Noticed by Employers," *USA Today*, October 17, 2006, p. B1.

[42]"Lying: How Can You Protect Your Company?" www.westaff.com/yourworkplace/ywissues37_full.html.

[43]Daryl Koehn, University of St. Thomas Center for Business Ethics, "Rewriting History: Resume Falsification More Than a Passing Fiction," www.stthom.edu/cbes/resume.html.

[44]Donna Hemmila, "Tired of Lying, Cheating Job Applicants, Employers Calling in Detectives," *San Francisco Business Times* 12, no. 29 (February 27–March 5, 1998), www.esrcheck.com/articles/Tired-of-lying-cheating-job-applicants-employers-calling-in-detectives.php.

[45]Barbara Mende, "Employers Crack down on Candidates Who Lie," *Wall Street Journal Career Journal*, www.careerjournal.com/jobhunting/resumes/20020606-mende.html.

[46]Wallace V. Schmidt and Conaway, *Results-Oriented Interviewing: Principles, Practices, and Procedures* (Boston: Allyn & Bacon, 1999), p. 84.

[47]Powell and Amsbary, *Interviewing: Situations and Contexts*, p. 47; Schmidt and Conaway, *Results-Oriented Interviewing: Principles, Practices, and Procedures*, p. 107; Stewart and Cash, *Interviewing: Principles and Practices*, p. 245; *Job Link USA*, "Interview," www.joblink-usa.com/interview.htm; *CollegeGrad.Com*, "Candidate Interview Questions," www.collegegrad.com/jobsearch/16-15.shtml.

[48]Schmidt and Conaway, *Results-Oriented Interviewing: Principles, Practices, and Procedures*, pp. 100–111.

[49]Bolles, *What Color Is Your Parachute? A Practical Manual for Job-Hunters and Career-Changers*, p. 82.

[50]Schmidt and Conaway, *Results-Oriented Interviewing: Principles, Practices, and Procedures*, pp. 34–37.

[51]Stewart and Cash, *Interviewing: Principles and Practices*, pp. 254–255; "Candidate Interview Questions," www.collegegrad.com/jobsearch/16-15.shtml.

[52]Schmidt and Conaway, *Results-Oriented Interviewing: Principles, Practices, and Procedures*, pp. 100–111.

[53]Mary Heiberger and Julia Miller Vick, "How to Handle Difficult Interview Questions," *Chronicle of Higher Education*, January 22, 1999, http://chronicle.com/jobs/v45/i21/4521career.htm; Allison Doyle, "Illegal Interview Questions: Illegal Interview Question Samples," http://jobsearch.about.com/library/weekly/aa0224032/htm.

Chapter 10

[1]http://en.wikipedia.org/wiki/Three_Days_Grace.

[2]Ibid.

[3]http://loudwire.com/singer-adam-gontier-explains-departure-from-three-days-grace.

[4]http://en.wikipedia.org/wiki/Three_Days_Grace.

[5]Steve W. J. Kozlowski and Daniel R. Ilgen (2006). "Enhancing the Effectiveness of Work Groups and Teams," *Psychological Science in the Public Interest*, 7 (3), p. 77.

[6]www.skills.edu.gov.on.ca.

[7]Peter D. Hart Research Associates, *How Should Colleges Prepare Students to Succeed in Today's Global Economy?* p. 7.

[8]www.canada.com/sports/2012-summer-games/events/rowing/index.html.

[9]Carl E. Larson and Frank M. J. LaFasto, *TeamWork: What Must Go Right/What Can Go Wrong* (Newbury Park, CA: Sage, 1989), p. 27.

[10]Jon R. Katzenbach and Douglas K. Smith, *The Wisdom of Teams: Creating the High-Performance Organization* (New York: HarperBusiness, 1999), p. 9.

[11]Robert B. Cialdini, "The Perils of Being the Best and the Brightest," *Becoming an Effective Leader* (Boston: Harvard Business School Press, 2005), pp. 174, 175.

[12]www.cbc.ca/news/canada/toronto/story/2012/04/25/toronto-ornge.html?cmp=rss

[13]3M Meeting Management Team with Jeannine Drew, *Mastering Meetings: Discovering the Hidden Potential of Effective Business Meetings* (New York: McGraw-Hill, 1994), p. 12.

[14]Deborah L. Duarte and Nancy Tennant Snyder, *Mastering Virtual Teams*, 3rd ed. (San Francisco: Jossey-Bass, 2007), pp. 21, 158.

[15]Engleberg and Wynn, *Working in Groups: Communication Principles and Strategies*, 5th ed., pp. 203–207.

[16]www.onlinecollege.org/2013/03/18/10-online-student-suggestions-surviving-group-assignments.

[17]Ibid.

[18]Ernest G. Bormann, *Small Group Communication: Theory and Practice*, 3rd ed. (Edina, MN: Burgess, 1996), pp. 132–135, 181–183.

[19]Pamela J. Hinds, Kathleen M. Carley, David Krackhardt, and Doug Wholey, "Choosing Work Group Members: Balancing Similarity, Competence, and Familiarity," *Organizational Behavior and Human Decision Process* 81.2 (March 2000): pp. 226–251.

[20]Ibid.

[21]Ibid.

[22]Ibid.

[23]Rodney W. Napier and Matti K. Gershenfeld, *Groups: Theory and Experience*, 7th ed. (Boston: Houghton Mifflin, 2004), p. 182.

[24]Bruce W. Tuckman, "Developmental Sequence in Small Groups," *Psychological Bulletin* 63 (1965), pp. 384–399. Tuckman's 1965 article is reprinted in *Group Facilitation: A Research and Applications Journal* 3 (Spring 2001), http://dennislearningcenter.osu.edu/references/Group%20DEV%20ARTICLE.doc. Note: Tuckman and Jensen identified a fifth stage—adjourning—in the 1970s. There is little research on the characteristics and behavior of members during this stage other than a decrease in interaction and, in some cases, separation anxiety. See Bruce Tuckman and Mary Ann Jensen, "Stages of Small-Group Development Revisited," *Group and Organization Studies* 2 (1977), pp. 419–427.

[25]Artemis Change, Julie Duck, and Prashant Bordia, "Understanding the Multidimensionality of Group Development," *Small Group Research* 37 (2006), p. 329.

[26]Ibid., pp. 331, 337–338.

[27]Susan Wheelan and Nancy Brewer Danganan, "The Relationship Between the Internal Dynamics of Student Affairs Leadership Teams and Campus Leaders' Perceptions of the Effectiveness of Student Affairs Divisions," *Journal of Student Affairs Research and Practice*, 40 (2002), p. 27

[28]Wheelan and Danganan, "The Relationship Between the Internal Dynamics of Student Affairs Leadership Teams and Campus Leaders' Perceptions of the Effectiveness of Student Affairs Divisions," p. 96.

[29]Ernest G. Bormann, *Small Group Communication Theory and Practice*, 6th ed. (Edina, MN: Burgess International, 1996), pp. 134–135.

[30]Donald G. Ellis and B. Aubrey Fisher, *Small Group Decision Making: Communication and the Group Process*, 4th ed. (New York: McGraw-Hill, 1994), pp. 43–44.

[31]Marvin E. Shaw, "Group Composition and Group Cohesiveness" in *Small Group Communication: A Reader*, 6th ed., ed. Robert S. Cathcart and Larry A. Samovar (Dubuque, IA: Wm. C. Brown, 1992), pp. 214–220.

[32]Patricia H. Andrews, "Group Conformity," in *Small Group Communication: Theory and Practice*, 7th ed., ed. Robert S. Cathcart, Larry A. Samovar, and Linda D. Henman (Madison, WI: Brown and Benchmark, 1996), p. 185.

[33]Nicky Hayes, *Managing Teams: A Strategy for Success* (London: Thomson, 2004), p. 31.

[34]Kenneth D. Benne and Paul Sheats, "Functional Roles of Group Members," *Journal of Social Issues* 4 (1948), pp. 41–49. We have modified the original Benne and Sheats list by adding or combining behaviors that we have observed, as well as roles identified by other writers and researchers.

[35]Ibid.

[36]Ibid.

[37]Based on Michael Doyle and David Straus, *How to Make Meetings Work* (New York: Jove, 1976), pp. 107–117. Several titles and behaviors are original contributions by the authors.

[38]James C. McCroskey and Virginia P. Richmond, "Correlates of Compulsive Communication: Quantitative and Qualitative Characteristics," *Communication Quarterly* 43 (1995), pp. 39–52.

[39]Eric Harper, David Cottrell, Al Lucia, and Mike Hourigan, *The Leadership Secrets of Santa Claus: How to Get Big Things Done in YOUR "Workshop" . . . All Year Long* (Dallas, TX: The Walk the Talk Company, 2003), pp. 78–79.

[40]Isa N. Engleberg and Dianna R. Wynn, *Working in Groups: Communication Principles and Strategies*, 3rd ed. (Boston: Houghton Mifflin, 2004), p. 207.

[41]Antony Bell, *Great Leadership: What It Is and What It Takes in a Complex World* (Mountain View, CA: Davies-Black, 2006), pp. 87, 91.

[42]Fred E. Feidler and Martin M. Chemers, *Improving Leadership Effectiveness: The Leader Match Concept*, 2nd ed. (New York: Wiley, 1984).

[43]Based on material in Engleberg and Wynn, *Working in Groups: Communication Principles and Strategies*, 5th ed., pp. 113–114.

[44]The 5-M Model of Effective Leadership© is based, in part, on Martin M. Chemers's integrative theory of leadership, which identifies three functional aspects of leadership: image management, relationship development, and resource utilization. We have added two more functions—decision making and mentoring—and have incorporated more of a communication perspective into Chemers's view of leadership as a multifaceted process. See Martin M. Chemers, *An Integrative Theory of Leadership* (Mahwah, NJ: Lawrence Erlbaum, 1997), pp. 151–173.

[45]Mike Krzyzewski, "Coach K on How to Connect," *The Wall Street Journal*, 16–17 July 2011, p. C12.

[46]Martin M. Chemers, *An Integrative Theory of Leadership* (Mahwah, NJ: Lawrence Erlbaum, 1997), p. 160.

[47]Harvey Robbins and Michael Finley, *The New Why Teams Don't Work: What Goes Wrong and How to Make It Right* (San Francisco: Berrett-Koehler, 2000), p. 107.

[48]Carol Tice, "Building the 21st Century Leader," *Entrepreneur* (February 2007), pp. 66, 67.

[49]Bell, *Great Leadership: What It Is and What It Takes in a Complex World*, p. 67.

[50]James M. Kouzes and Barry Z. Posner, *Credibility: How Leaders Gain and Lose It, Why People Demand It* (San Francisco: Jossey-Bass, 1993), pp. 230–231.

[51]Susan B. Shimanoff and Mercilee M. Jenkins, "Leadership and Gender: Challenging Assumptions and Recognizing Resources," in *Small Group Communication: Theory and Practice*, 7th ed., ed. Robert S. Cathcart, Larry A. Samovar, and Linda D. Henman (Madison, WI: Brown and Benchmark, 1996), p. 327.

[52]Chemers, *An Integrative Theory of Leadership*, p. 126.

Chapter 11

[1]Tim Dirks, *12 Angry Men* (1957), www.filmsite.org/twelve.html; *12 Angry Men* was remade for television in 1997. In this production, the judge is a woman and four of the jurors are African American. The producers decided against putting a woman in the jury because they didn't want to change the title. Still, most of the action and dialogue of the film is identical to the original. Modernizations include a prohibition on smoking in the jury room, the changing of references to income and pop culture figures, more dialogue relating to race, and profanity.

[2]Tim Dirks, *12 Angry Men*.

[3]Marshall Scott Poole and Randy Y. Hirokawa, "Introduction: Communication and Group Decision Making," in *Communication and Group Decision Making*, 2nd ed., ed. Randy Y. Hirokawa and Marshall Scott Poole (Thousand Oaks, CA: Sage, 1996), p. 1.

[4]Rodney W. Napier and Matti K. Gershenfeld, *Groups: Theory and Experience*, 7th ed. (Boston: Houghton Mifflin, 2004), p. 291.

[5]Peter R. Drucker, *The Effective Executive* (New York: HarperBusiness, 1967), p. 143.

[6]Marshall Scott Poole, "Procedures for Managing Meetings: Social and Technological Innovation," in *Innovative Meeting Management*, ed. Richard A. Swanson and Bonnie Ogram Knapp (Austin, TX: 3M Meeting Management Institute, 1990), pp. 54–55.

[7]Keith Sawyer, *Group Genius: The Creative Power of Collaboration* (New York: Basic Books, 2007), pp. 66–67. Sawyer attributes the story to Dale Carnegie.

[8]Irving L. Janis, *Groupthink*, 2nd ed. (Boston: Houghton Mifflin, 1982), p. 9.

[9]Ibid.

[10]John Gastil, *The Group in Society* (Los Angeles: Sage, 2010), p. 82.

[11]Ibid.

[12]Julia T. Wood, "Alternative Methods of Group Decision Making," in *Small Group Communication: A Reader*, 6th ed., ed. Robert S. Cathcart and Larry A. Samovar (Dubuque, IA: Wm. C. Brown, 1992), p. 159.

[13]Napier and Gershenfeld, *Groups: Theory and Experience*, 7th ed., p. 337.

[14]Donald G. Ellis and B. *Aubrey Fisher, Small Group Decision Making* (New York: McGraw-Hill, 1994), p. 142.

[15]John R. Katzenbach and Douglas K. Smith, *The Discipline of Teams* (New York: Wiley, 2001), p. 112.

[16]Ibid., p. 113.

[17]Randy Hirokawa and Roger Pace, "A Descriptive Investigation of the Possible Communication-Based Reasons for Effective and Ineffective Group Decision Making," *Communication Monographs* 50 (1983), p. 379.

[18]Scott and Bruce, "Decision Making Style: The Development of a New Measure." Reginald A. Bruce and Susanne G. Scott, "The Moderating Effective of Decision-Making Style on the Turnover Process: An Extension of Previous Research," http://cobweb2.louisville.edu/faculty/regbruce/bruce//research/japturn.htm; Decision Making Styles, UCD Career Development Center, 2006, http://www.ucd.ie/careers/cms/decision/student_skills_decision_styleex.html.

[19]Adapted from Karyn C. Rybacki and Donald J. Rybacki, *Advocacy and Opposition: An Introduction to Argumentation*, 4th ed. (Boston: Allyn & Bacon, 2000), pp. 11–15.

[20]Suzanne Scott and Reginald Bruce "Decision Making Style: The Development of a New Measure," *Educational and Psychological Measurements* 55 (1995): 818–831.

[21]Ronald T. Potter-Efron, *Work Rage: Preventing Anger and Resolving Conflict on the Job* (New York: Barnes and Noble Books, 2000), pp. 22–23.

[22]Isa N. Engleberg and Dianna R. Wynn, *Working in Groups: Communication Principles and Strategies*, 5th ed. (Boston: Pearson, Allyn and Bacon, 2010), pp. 214–215, by permission of the publisher and authors.

[23]Kenneth Cloke and Joan Goldsmith, *Resolving Conflicts at Work: A Complete Guide for Everyone on the Job* (San Francisco: Jossey-Bass, 2000), p. 23.

[24]See Kenneth W. Thomas and Ralph W. Kilmann, "Developing a Forced-Choice Measure of Conflict-Handling Behavior: The MODE Instrument," *Educational Psychological Measurement* 37 (1977), pp. 390–395; William W. Wilmot and Joyce L. Hocker, *Interpersonal Conflict*, 7th ed. (New York: McGraw-Hill, 2007), pp. 130–175.

[25]Isa N. Engleberg and Dianna R. Wynn, *Working in Groups: Communication Principles and Strategies*, p. 216. Based on Kenneth W. Thomas, *Intrinsic Motivation at Work: Building Energy and Commitment* (San Francisco: Berret-Koehler, 2000), p. 94.

[26]Jerry Wisinski, *Resolving Conflicts on the Job* (New York: American Management Association, 1993), pp. 27–31.

[27]Cloke and Goldsmith, *Resolving Conflicts at Work: A Complete Guide for Everyone on the Job*, pp. 109–110; *When and How to Apologize*, University of Nebraska Cooperative Extension and the Nebraska Health and Human Services System http://extension.unl.edu/welfare/apology.htm.

[28]Alex F. Osborn, *Applied Imagination*, rev. ed. (New York: Scribner, 1957).

[29]3M Meeting Management Team with Jeannine Drew, *Mastering Meetings: Discovering the Hidden Potential of Effective Business Meetings* (New York: McGraw-Hill, 1994), p. 59.

[30]Kelley with Littman, *The Art of Innovation: Lessons in Creativity from IDEO, America's Leading Design Firm*, p. 55.

[31]Ibid pp. 64–66.

[32]Based, in part, on Ibid., pp. 56–59. Also see Napier and Gershenfeld, *Groups: Theory and Experience*, 7th ed., p. 321.

[33]N. Engleberg and Dianna R. Wynn, *Working in Groups: Communication Principles and Strategies*, 5th ed. (Boston: Pearson/Allyn & Bacon, 2010), pp. 256–258.

[34]See Kenneth E. Andersen, "Developments in Communication Ethics: The Ethics Commission, Code of Professional Responsibilities, and Credo for Ethical Communication," *Journal of the Association for Communication Administration* 29 (2000): 131–144. The Credo for Ethical Communication is also posted on the NCA Website (www.natcom.org).

[35]John Dewey, *How We Think* (Boston: Heath, 1910).

[36]Based on Kathryn Sue Young, Julia T. Wood, Gerald M. Phillips, and Douglas J. Pedersen, *Group Discussion: A Practical Guide to Participation and Leadership*, 3rd ed. (Prospect Heights, IL: Waveland Press, 2001), pp. 8–9. The authors present six steps in their standard-agenda model by combining solution suggestions and solution selection into one step. We have divided this step into separate functions given that the solution suggestion step may require creative thinking and brainstorming. Given that the solution evaluation and selection step may be the most difficult and controversial, it deserves a separate focus as well as different strategies and skills.

[37]Edward De Bono, *New Thinking for the New Millennium* (New York: Viking, 1999) quoted in Darrell Man, "Analysis Paralysis: When Root Cause Analysis Isn't the Way," *The TRIZ-Journal*, 2006, www.triz-journal.com.

[38]"Avoid Analysis Paralysis," *Infusion Insight*, www.infusionsoft.com/articles/65-infusion-insight/615-avoid-analysis-paralysis.

[39]"Office Communication Toolkit: 7 Common Employee Gripes," *Special Report from Business Management Daily*, September 22, 2009.

[40]Tyler Cowen, "On My Mind: In Favor of Face Time," October 1, 2007, www.members.forbes.com/forbes/2007/1001/030.html.

[41]Sharon M. Lippincott, *Meetings: Do's, Don'ts, and Donuts* (Pittsburgh, PA: Lighthouse Point Press, 1994), p. 172.

[42]Karen Anderson, *Making Meetings Work: How to Plan and Conduct Effective Meetings* (West Des Moines, IA: American Media Publishing, 1997), p. 17.

[43]3M Meeting Management Team with Jeannine Drew, *Mastering Meetings: Discovering the Hidden Potential of Effective Business Meetings* (New York: McGraw-Hill, 1994), p. 78.

[44]Engleberg and Wynn, *Working in Groups: Communication Principles and Strategies*, 5th ed., pp. 299–300; Lippincott, *Meetings: Do's, Don'ts, and Donuts*, pp. 89–90.

Chapter 12

[1]http://cupwire.ca/articles/53955.

[2]http://news.gc.ca/web/article-eng.do?nid=670849.

[3]www.uncp.edu/home/acurtis/Courses/ResourcesForCourses/MarshallMcLuhan.html.

[4]Ibid.

[5]Ibid.

[6]www.huffingtonpost.ca/2012/11/20/generation-y-canada-millennials_n_2078000.html?utm_hp_ref=email_share.

[7]Dion Hinchcliffe, www.flickr.com/photos/dionh/373848076.

[8]www.merriam-webster.com/dictionary/social%20media.

[9]Ibid.

[10]Allison Stadd, "Guess What the World's Most Active Twitter City Is?" *All Twitter*, January 2, 2013. www.mediabistro.com/alltwitter/most-active-twitter-city_b33522

[11]Ibid.

[12]Kevin Duong and Stephanie Adamo, *Canada Digital Future in Focus, 2013*. www.comscore.com/Insights/Presentations_and_Whitepapers/2013/2013_ Canada_Digital_Future_in_Focus. page 23

[13]Marc Prensky "Digital Natives, Digital Immigrants," in *On the Horizon* 9.5 (October 2001) © 2001 www.marcprensky.com/writing/Prensky%20-%20Digital%20Natives,%20Digital%20Immigrants%20-%20Part1.pdf.

[14]Tim Lockette, "Future Doctors Share Too Much Information on Facebook," http://news.ufl.edu/2008/07/10/facebook.

[15]Reported in Laura M. Holson, "Tell-All Generation Learns to Keep Things Offline," May 8, 2010, www.nytimes.com/2010/05/09/fashion/09privacy.html.

[16]Kevin Duong, *Canada Digital Future in Focus, 2012*. www.comscore.com/Insights/Presentations_and_Whitepapers/2012/2012_Canada_Digital_Future_in_Focus.

[17]Mike Ribble, "Nine Themes of Digital Citizenship," *Digital Citizenship: Using Technology Appropriately*. www.digitalcitizenship.net/Nine_Elements

[18]"What Drives Co-Workers Crazy," *The Week*, February 23, 2007, p. 40.

[19]Ibid. See also "Proper Cell Phone Etiquette," www.cellphonecarriers.com/cell-phone-etiquette.html.

[20]http://education.alberta.ca/admin/technology/research.aspx.

[21]www.cbc.ca/news/technology/story/2012/02/15/technology-surveillance-bill-privacy.html.

[22]Richard Mason, "Four Ethical Issues of the Information Age," *MIS Quarterly*, 10.1 (March 1986): pp. 5–12.

[23]Mary Lind, "A Framework for Addressing Ethics in the Digital Age." *Proceedings of the Information Systems Educators Conference*, 2011, 28.1624. http://proc.isecon.org/2011/pdf/1624.pdf.

[24]Silvia Rosenthal/Tolisano "Are You Ready for Twitter? Checklist" http://langwitches.org/blog/wp-content/uploads/2012/08/Ready4TwitterChecklist1.pdf.

[25]Ibid.

[26]www.carlsonwagonlit.com/export/sites/cwt/en/global/insights/business-travel-in-2013/travel-management-priorities-2013/pdf/m-meetings-events.pdf.

[27]Silvia Rosenthal/Tolisano, "Are You Ready for Twitter? Checklist."

[28]Ibid.

[29]Adapted from Courtney F. Turnbull, "Mom Just Facebooked Me and Dad Knows How to Text: The Influences of Computer-Mediated Communication on Interpersonal Communication and Differences Through Generations," *Elon Journal of Undergraduate Research in Communication*, 1.1 (winter 2010). www.elon.edu/docs/e-web/academics/communications/research/01TurnbullEJSpring10.pdf.

Chapter 13

[1] http://en.wikipedia.org/wiki/Shad_(rapper).

[2] Ibid.

[3] Martin McDermott, *Speak with Courage: 50 Insider Strategies for Presenting with Ease and Confidence* (CreateSpace/Amazon: Martin McDermott, 2010), p. 52, 54. See www.martinmcdermott.com.

[4] The complete, 24-item survey is available in the *Instructor's Manual* that accompanies this textbook. Class results can be compared to those of both types of survey respondents: book buyers who speak professionally and students enrolled in a college public speaking course.

[5] We conducted the survey of book buyers in collaboration with the Market Research Department at Houghton Mifflin, a former publisher. Survey items included traditional topics usually covered in public speaking textbooks. Approximately two thousand copies of a two-page questionnaire were mailed to individuals who had recently purchased a commercially available public speaking book and who had used a business address to secure the purchase. We received 281 usable questionnaires, resulting a response rate of 11 percent. Respondents were geographically dispersed. Twenty-five percent worked in industry. Workers in government (10 percent), health (10 percent) and nonprofit organizations (10 percent) made up 30 percent of respondents. Nine percent came from the financial industry; another 9 percent worked in technology related industries. Approximately 25 percent of the respondents, including business owners and independent contractors, worked in "other" occupations. More recently, we administered a similar survey to 600 college students enrolled in a basic public speaking course. Respondents attended various types of geographically dispersed institutions of higher education (community colleges, liberal arts colleges, and large universities). We received more than six hundred usable questionnaires.

[6] Isa N. Engleberg and John A. Daly, *Presentations in Everyday Life*, 3rd ed.

[7] Gene Zelazny, *Say It with Presentations*, Revised (New York: McGraw-Hill, 2006), pp. 4–6.

[8] Engleberg and Daly, *Presentations in Everyday Life*, 3rd ed., p. 113.

[9] Malcolm Kushner, *Successful Presentations for Dummies* (Foster City, CA: IDG Books Worldwide, 1997), p. 21.

[10] Ibid.

[11] The earliest and most respected source describing the components of a speaker's credibility is Aristotle's *Rhetoric*, trans. Lane Cooper (New York: Appleton-Century-Crofts, 1932), p. 92. Aristotle identified "intelligence, character, and good will" as "three things that gain our belief." Aristotle's observations have been verified and expanded. In addition to those qualities identified by Aristotle, researchers have added variables such as objectivity, trustworthiness, co-orientation, dynamism, composure, likability, and extroversion. Research has consolidated these qualities into three well-accepted attributes: competence, character, and dynamism. We have used the term *charisma* in place of dynamism.

[12] Lane Cooper, *The Rhetoric of Aristotle* (New York: Appleton-Century-Crofts, 1932), p. 7.

[13] Ibid., p. 8, 9.

[14] Ibid.

[15] Julie J. C. H. Ryan, "Student Plagiarism in an Online World," *Prism*, December 1998, www.prism-magazine .org/december/html/student_plagiarism_in_an_onlin.htm.

[16] Michael M. Kepper with Robert E. Gunther, *I'd Rather Die Than Give a Speech* (Burr Ridge, IL: Irwin, 1994), p. 6.

[17] Daphne Duval Harrison, *Black Pearls: Blues Queens of the 1920s* (New Brunswick, NJ: Rutgers University Press, 1988).

[18] Stella Ting-Toomey and Leeva C. Chung, *Understanding Intercultural Communication* (Los Angeles: Roxbury, 2005), pp. 189–190.

[19] Some of the best research on the value of organizing a presentation was conducted in the 1960s and '70s. See Ernest C. Thompson, "An Experimental Investigation of the Relative Effectiveness of Organizational Structure in Oral Communication," *Southern Speech Journal* 26 (1960), pp. 59–69; Ernest C. Thompson, "Some Effects of Message Structure on Listeners' Comprehension," *Speech Monographs* 34 (1967), pp. 51–57; James C. McCroskey and R. Samuel Mehrley, "The Effects of Disorganization and Nonfluency on Attitude Change and Source Credibility," *Communication Monographs* 36 (1969), pp. 13–21; Arlee Johnson, "A Preliminary Investigation of the Relationship between Organization and Listener Comprehension," *Central States Speech Journal* 21 (1970), pp. 104–107; and Christopher Spicer and Ronald E. Bassett, "The Effect of Organization on Learning from an Informative Message," *Southern Speech Communication Journal* 41 (1976), pp. 290–299.

[20] Tony Buzon, *Use Both Sides of Your Brain*, 3rd ed. (New York: Plume, 1989).

[21] The Speech Framer was developed by Isa N. Engleberg as an alternative or supplement to outlining. See Engleberg and Daly, *Presentations in Everyday Life*, 3rd ed., pp. 217–218. © Isa N. Engleberg, 2003.

[22] Engleberg and Daly, *Presentations in Everyday Life*, 3rd ed., p. 216.

[23] Lee Towe, *Why Didn't I Think of That? Creativity in the Workplace* (West Des Moines, IA: American Media, 1966), p. 7.

[24] Samuel E. Wood, Ellen Green Wood, and Denise Boyd, *The World of Psychology*, 6th ed. (Boston: Pearson/Allyn & Bacon, 2008), p. 204.

[25] Ibid., 204–205.

[26] Engleberg and Daly, *Presentations in Everyday Life*, 3rd ed., pp. 251–256.

[27] Sections of Chapters 10 and 14 are based on Isa N. Engleberg and John A. Daly, *Presentations in Everyday Life*, 3rd ed. (Boston: Pearson/Allyn & Bacon, 2009); Isa N. Engleberg and Ann Raimes, *Pocket Keys for Speakers* (Boston: Houghton Mifflin, 2004); Isa N. Engleberg and John A. Daly, *Think Public Speaking* (Boston: Pearson/Allyn & Bacon, 2013), Chapter 15.

[28]This section is based on the research and theory-building of Katherine E. Rowan, professor of communication at George Mason University. See Katherine E. Rowan, "Informing and Explaining Skills: Theory and Research on Informative Communication," in *Handbook of Communication and Social Interaction Skills*, ed. John O. Greene and Brant R. Burleson (Mahwah, NJ: Lawrence Erlbaum Associates, 2003), pp. 403–438; Katherine E. Rowan, "A New Pedagogy for Explanatory Public Speaking: Why Arrangement Should Not Substitute for Invention," *Communication Education* 44 (1995), pp. 236–250.

[29]Rowan, "A New Pedagogy for Explanatory Public Speaking: Why Arrangement Should Not Substitute for Invention," p. 242; Rowan, "Informing and Explaining Skills: Theory and Research on Informative Communication," p. 411.

[30]Parts of this section are based on Isa N. Engleberg and John A. Daly, *Presentations in Everyday Life*, 3rd ed. (Boston: Pearson/Allyn & Bacon, 2009), Chapter 5; Isa N. Engleberg and Ann Raimes, *Pocket Keys for Speakers* (Boston: Houghton Mifflin, 2004), Part 8: Sections 25 and 26; Isa N. Engleberg and John A. Daly, *Think Public Speaking* (Boston: Pearson/Allyn & Bacon, 2013), Chapter 16.

[31]William J. McGuire, "Inducing Resistance to Persuasion: Some Contemporary Approaches," in *Advances in Experimental Psychology*, ed. Leonard Berkowitz (New York: Academic Press, 1964), pp. 192–229.

[32]Jack W. Brehm, *A Theory of Psychological Reactance* (New York: Academic Press, 1966). Also see Michael Burgoon et al., "Revisiting the Theory of Psychological Reactance," in *The Persuasion Handbook: Development in Theory and Practice*, ed. James Price Dillard and Michael Pfau (Thousand Oaks, CA: Sage, 2002), pp. 213–232; James Price Dillard and Linda J. Marshall, "Persuasion as a Social Skill," in *Handbook of Communication and Social Interaction Skills*, ed. John O. Greene and Brant R. Burleson (Mahwah, NJ: Lawrence Erlbaum, 2003), pp. 500–501.

[33]Stephen Toulmin, *The Uses of Argument* (London: Cambridge University Press, 1958). See also Stephen Toulmin, Richard Rieke, and Allan Janik, *An Introduction to Reasoning* (New York: Macmillan, 1979).

[34]Ibid.

[35]Thomas Sewell, "I Beg to Disagree: The Lost Art of Logical Arguments," *Naples Daily News*, January 14, 2005, p. 9D.

[36]Fred D. White and Simone J. Billings, *The Well-Crafted Argument: A Guide and Reader*, 2nd ed. (Boston: Houghton Mifflin, 2005), p. 93.

[37]Charles U. Larson, *Persuasion: Reception and Responsibility*, 11th ed. (Belmont, CA: Thomson/Wadsworth, 2007), p. 185.

[38]Ibid., p. 58.

[39]Richard M. Perloff, *The Dynamics of Persuasion: Communication and Attitudes in the 21st Century*, 4th ed. (New York: Routledge/Taylor & Francis, 2010), pp. 204–206.

[40]Ibid.

[41]Ibid., p. 376.

[42]See Alexander Todorov, Shelley Chaiken, and Marlone D. Henderson, "The Heuristic-Systematic Model of Social Information Processing," in *The Persuasion Handbook: Developments in Theory and Practice*, ed. James Price Dillard and Michael Pfau (Thousand Oaks, CA: Sage, 2002), pp. 195–211; Dillard and Marshall, pp. 494–495.

[43]Rives Collins and Pamela J. Cooper, *The Power of Story: Teaching through Storytelling*, 2nd ed. (Boston: Allyn & Bacon, 1997), p. 2.

[44]Walter R. Fisher, *Human Communication as Narration: Toward a Philosophy of Reason, Value, and Action* (Columbia, SC: University of South Carolina Press, 1987), p. 64, 65.

[45]Joanna Slan, *Using Stories and Humor: Grab Your Audience* (Boston: Allyn & Bacon, 1998), pp. 5–6.

[46]William Hendricks et al., *Secrets of Power Presentations* (Franklin Lakes, NJ: Career Press, 1996), p. 79.

[47]Malcolm Kushner, *Successful Presentations for Dummies* (Foster City, CA: IDG Books, 1997), p. 79.

[48]Fisher, *Human Communication as Narration: Toward a Philosophy of Reason, Value, and Action*, p. 24.

[49]Ibid., p. 68.

[50]Candace Spigelman, "Argument and Evidence in the Case of the Personal," *College English* 64.1 (2001), pp. 80–81.

[51]Based on Paul Galdone, *The Three Little Pigs* (New York: Houghton Mifflin, 1970).

[52]Walter Fisher, "Narrative as Human Communication Paradigm," in *Contemporary Rhetorical Theory*, ed. John Louis Lucaites, Celeste Michelle Condit, and Sally Caudill (New York: The Guilford Press, 1999), p. 272.

[53]Ibid.

[54]Summary of tips for using humour from Isa N. Engleberg and Dianna R. Wynn, *The Challenge of Communicating: Guiding Principles and Practices* (Pearson/Allyn & Bacon, 2008), p. 408; Slan, pp. 170–172.

Chapter 14

[1]www.shanekoyczan.com.

[2]http://tothisdayproject.com.

[3]Lani Arredondo, *The McGraw-Hill 36-Hour Course: Business Presentations* (New York: McGraw-Hill, 1994), p. 147.

[4]Jerry Della Femina, quoted in *Creative Strategy in Advertising*, 2nd ed., ed. A. Jerome Jewler (Belmont, CA: Wadsworth, 1985), p. 41.

[5]John W. Bowers, "Some Correlates of Language Intensity," *Quarterly Journal of Speech* 50 (1964), pp. 415–420.

[6]Max Atkinson, *Lend Me Your Ears* (New York: Oxford, 2005), p. 221.

[7]Marcel Danesi and Paul Perron, *Analyzing Cultures: An Introduction and Handbook* (Bloomington, IN: Indiana University Press, 1999), p. 174.

[8]Kathleen Hall Jamieson, *Eloquence in an Electronic Age: The Transformation of Political Speechmaking* (New York: Oxford University Press, 1988), p. 81, 84.

[9]www.fortmcmurraytoday.com/2009/03/03/founder-of-second-cup-shares-his-story.

[10]Lori J. Carrell and S. Clay Willmington, "The Relationship between Self-Report Measures of Communication Apprehension and Trained Observers' Ratings of Communication Competence," *Communication Reports* 11 (1998), pp. 87–95.

[11]Michael T. Motley and Jennifer L. Molloy, "An Efficacy Test of New Therapy ("Communication-Orientation Motivation") for Public Speaking Anxiety," *Journal of Applied Communication Research*, 22 (1994), pp. 44–58.

[12]Ty Ford, *Ty Ford's Audio Bootcamp Field Guide* (Baltimore: Technique, Inc., 2004), p. 19.

[13]Everett M. Rogers and Thomas M. Steinfatt, *Intercultural Communication* (Prospect Heights, IL: Waveland Press, 1999), p. 174.

[14]Rogers and Steinfatt, p. 172; Guo-Ming Chen and William J. Starosta, *Foundations of Intercultural Communication* (Boston: Allyn and Bacon, 1998), pp. 81–92.

[15]Arredondo, p. 238.

[16]Steven A. Beebe, "Eye Contact: A Nonverbal Determinant of Speaker Credibility," *The Speech Teacher* 23 (1974), pp. 21–25.

[17]Mark L. Knapp and Judith A. Hall, *Nonverbal Communication in Human Interaction*, 5th ed. (Belmont, CA: Wadsworth/Thomson Learning, 2006), p. 295.

[18]Cyndi Maxey and Kevin E. O'Connor, *Present Like a Pro* (New York: St. Martin's Griffin, 2006), p. 49.

[19]Peggy Noonan, *Simply Speaking: How to Communicate Your Ideas with Style, Substance, and Clarity* (New York: HarperCollins, 1998), p. 9.

[20]Thomas K. Mira, *Speak Smart: The Art of Public Speaking* (New York: Random House, 1997), p. 91.

credits

Chapter 1
p. 11: *Questions of Communication: A Practical Introduction to Theory* by Rob Anderson, Veronica Ross. Copyright © 2002 Bedford/St. Martin's Press.

p. 14: Courtesy of Karl Popper.

p. 15: *The 7 Habits of Highly Effective People: Powerful Lessons in Personal Change* by Stephen R. Covey, p. 47, Simon and Schuster, 2004.

Chapter 2
p. 22: Daniel Goleman, *Emotional Intelligence* (New York: Bantam, 1995), p. 43.

p. 24: Courtesy of Nathaniel Branden.

p. 26: Courtesy of Plan Canada.

p. 27: *Society and the Adolescent Self-Image* by M. Rosenberg. Copyright © 1965 Princeton University Press.

p. 29: Adapted from "Feel Factor: What We Touch Can Change How We Think" by Holly St. Lifer from *AARP The Magazine*, Nov./Dec. 2010.

p. 33: *Can You Believe Your Eyes?* by J. Richard Block, Harold Yuker. Copyright © 2013 Taylor & Francis.

p. 37: McCroskey, James, *Introduction to Rhetorical Communication*, 4th ed., © 1982. Reprinted and electronically reproduced by permission of Pearson Education, Inc., Upper Saddle River, NJ.

Chapter 3
p. 42: Courtesy of Canadian FAQ. Reprinted with permission.

p. 46: *Privilege, Power and Difference* by Allan Johnson. Copyright © 2001 McGraw-Hill.

p. 46: "The Wages of Hate" by Judith Warner from *The New York Times*. Copyright © 2009 The New York Times Company.

p. 47: Source: (pp. 130–131) Hardiman, R. (1994). White racial identity development in the United States. In E. P. Salett & D. R. Koslow (Eds.), *Race, ethnicity and self: Identity in multicultural perspective* (pp. 117–142). Washington, DC: National MultiCultural Institute/dg.

p. 53: Richard Nisbett, *The Geography of Thought: How Asians and Westerners Think Differently . . . and Why* (New York: Free Press, 2003), p. xiii.

p. 54: *Cows, Pigs, Wars and Witches: The Riddles of Culture* by Martin Harris. Copyright © 1989 Random House, Inc.

Chapter 4
p. 62: *The Lost Art of Listening* by Michael P. Nichols. Copyright © 1995 Guildford Press.

p. 63: Based on Lynn O. Cooper and Trey Buchanan, "Listening Competency on Campus: A Psychometric Analysis of Students Listening," *International Journal of Listening* 24 (2010), p. 157.

p. 64: Statistics Canada, Participation and Activity Limitation Survey.

p. 66: "Building Listening Theory: The Validation of the Conversational Listening Span" by Laura Ann Janusik from *Communication Studies* 58. Copyright © 2007 Taylor & Francis.

p. 67: Don Gabor, *How to Start a Conversation and Make Friends*, pp. 66–68.

p. 67: Michael P. Nichols, *The Lost Art of Listening* (New York: Guildford, 1995) pp. 36–37.

p. 68: Michael P. Nichols, *The Lost Art of Listening* (New York: Guilford, 1995), p. 11.

p. 70: From Knapp/Hall. *Nonverbal Communication in Human Interaction* (with InfoTrac®), 6E. © 2006 Wadsworth, a part of Cengage Learning, Inc. Reproduced by permission. www.cengage.com/permissions.

p. 71: Courtesy of US Chamber of Commerce.

p. 74: *Intercultural Communication for Business* by Elizabeth A. Tuleja. Copyright © 2005 Cengage Learning.

p. 75: Statistics Canada, Participation and Activity Limitation Survey. [http://www.statcan.gc.ca/pub/89-628-x/89-628-x2009012-eng.pdf].

p. 79: Berko, Roy M., Wolvin, Andrew D., and Wolvin, Darlyn R., *Communicating: A Social and Career Focus*, 9th ed., © 2004, pp. 129–131. Reprinted and electronically reproduced by permission of Pearson Education, Inc., Upper Saddle River, NJ.

Chapter 5
p. 86: Adapted from Ogden and Richards, *The Meaning of Meaning* (New York: Harcourt Brace, 1936).

p. 98: "Wordiness and Gobbleygook," Nipissing University.

p. 99: Richmond, Virginia P., and McCroskey, James C., *Communication: Apprehension, Avoidance, and Effectiveness*, 5th ed., © 1998, pp. 129–130. Reprinted and electronically reproduced by permission of Pearson Education, Inc., Upper Saddle River, NJ.

Chapter 6
p. 105: From Sigmund Freud, *Fragment of Analysis of a Case of Hysteria*, Standard Edition, Volume 7, 1905, Chapter 2: The First Dream. See Psychoanalytical Electronic Publishing, http://www.pep-web.org/document.php?id=se.007.0001a.

p. 111: Jo-Ellan Dimitrius and Mark Mazzarella, *Reading People: How to Understand People and Predict Their Behavior—Anytime, Anyplace* (New York: Ballantine, 1999).

p. 112: Richmond, Virginia Peck, McCroskey, James C., and Hickson, Mark L., *Nonverbal Behavior in Interpersonal Relations*, 6th ed., © 2008, pp. 75–77. Reprinted and electronically reproduced by permission of Pearson Education, Inc., Upper Saddle River, NJ.

Chapter 7
p. 124: Daniel Goleman, "'Friends for Life': An Emerging Biology of Emotional Healing," *The New York Times*, October 10, 2006, p. D5.

p. 127: *A Good Talk: The Story of Skill and Conversation* by Daniel Menaker. Copyright © 2010 Hatchette Book Group.

p. 128: *Friendship Matters: Communication, Dialectics, and the Life Course* by William K. Rawlins. Copyright © 1992 Aldine De Gruyter.

p. 129: Eckhart Tolle, *A New Earth: Create a Better Life* http://www.penguin.com.au/products/9780141042886/new-earth-create-better-life

p. 132: *Shrek*, DreamWorks Animation, 2003.

p. 133: Johnson, David H., *Reaching Out: Interpersonal Effectiveness and Self-Actualization*, 7th ed., © 2000. Reprinted and electronically reproduced by permission of Pearson Education, Inc., Upper Saddle River, NJ.

Chapter 8
p. 140: Based on the book *Emotion: A Psychoevolutionary Synthesis* by Robert Plutchik, Harper & Row, Publishers (1980). Visualization by Markus Drews, University of Applied Sciences, Potsdam, Germany, February 2007. Supervised by Prof. Matthias Krohn.

p. 143: "Cultural Theory and Emotions" by H. B. Kaplan, J. E. Stets, J. H. Turner, and G. Peterson in *Handbook of the Sociology of Emotions*. Copyright © 2006 Springer-Verlag Publishing.

p. 145: *Emotional Decisions* by Allison Barnes and Paul Thagard.

Chapter 9
p. 156: *Organizational Communication: Foundations, Challenges, Misunderstandings* by Daniel P. Modaff, Sue DeWine, and Jennifer A. Butler. Copyright © 2008 Pearson Education, Inc.

Chapter 10
p. 176: Steve W. J. Kozlowski and Daniel R. Ilgen (2006). "Enhancing the Effectiveness of Work Groups and Teams," *Psychological Science in the Public Interest*, 7(3), p. 77. Copyright © 2006 Sage Publications.

p. 177: Carl E. Larson and Frank M. J. LaFasto, *TeamWork: What Must Go Right/What Can Go Wrong*, p. 27. Copyright © 1999 Sage Publications.

p. 177: Jon R. Katzenbach and Douglas K. Smith, *The Wisdom of Teams: Creating the High-Performance Organization*, p. 9. Copyright © 1999 HarperCollins Publishers.

p. 179: Deborah L. Duarte and Nancy Tennant Snyder, *Mastering Virtual Teams*, 3rd ed., pp. 21, 158. Copyright © 2007 Jossey-Bass.

p. 179: Author: Melissa A. Venable, in "10 Suggestions for Surviving Online Group Assignments" March 18, 2013, Inside Online Learning Blog, OnlineCollege.org, http://www.onlinecollege.org/2013/03/18/10-online-student-suggestions-surviving-group-assignments

p. 182: Donald G. Ellis and B. Aubrey Fisher, *Small Group Decision Making: Communication and the Group Process*, 4th ed. pp. 43–44. Copyright © 1994 McGraw-Hill.

p. 183: Patricia H. Andrews, "Group Conformity," in *Small Group Communication: Theory and Practice*, 7th ed., Robert S. Cathcart, Larry A. Samovar, and Linda D. Henman, (Eds.), p. 185. Copyright © 2003 Oxford University Press.

p. 185: Based on Kenneth D. Benne and Paul Sheats, "Functional Roles of Group Members," *Journal of Social Issues* 4 (1948), pp. 41–49.

p. 186: Kenneth D. Benne and Paul Sheats, "Functional Roles of Group Members," *Journal of Social Issues* 4 (1948), pp. 41–49.

p. 190: Mike Krzyzewski, "Coach K on How to Connect," *The Wall Street Journal*, 16–17 July 2011, p. C12. Copyright © 2003 Dow Jones.

p. 191: Susan B. Shimanoff and Mercilee M. Jenkins, "Leadership and Gender: Challenging Assumptions and Recognizing Resources," in *Small Group Communication: Theory and Practice*, 7th ed., Robert S. Cathcart, Larry A. Samovar, and Linda D. Henman, (Eds.), p. 327. Copyright © 1996 Oxford University Press.

Chapter 11

p. 198: Based on John Gastil, *The Group in Society* (Los Angeles: Sage, 2010), p. 82.

p. 199: Rodney Napier and Matti Gershenfeld, *Groups: Theory and Experience*, 7th ed., p. 337. Copyright © 2004 Houghton Mifflin Harcourt.

p. 200: John R. Katzenbach and Douglas K. Smith, *The Discipline of Teams*. Copyright © 2001 John Wiley & Sons.

p. 200: Rybacki, Karyn Charles, and Rybacki, Donald Jay, *Advocacy and Opposition: An Introduction to Argumentation*, 4th ed., © 2000. Reprinted with permission of Pearson Education, Inc., Upper Saddle River, NJ.

p. 202: Isa N. Engleberg and Dianna R. Wynn, *Working in Groups: Communication Principles and Strategies*, 5th ed. (Boston: Pearson, Allyn and Bacon, 2010).

p. 202: Kenneth Cloke and Joan Goldsmith, *Resolving Conflicts at Work: A Complete Guide for Everyone on the Job*. Copyright © 2000 Jossey-Bass.

p. 206: From *Asserting Yourself: A Practical Guide to Positive Change* by Sharon Anthony Bower and Gordon H. Bower, copyright © 1991. Reprinted by permission of Da Capo Press, a member of The Perseus Books Group.

p. 211: M Meeting Management Team with Jeannine Drew, *Mastering Meetings: Discovering the Hidden Potential of Effective Business Meetings*. Copyright © 1994 The McGraw-Hill Companies.

Chapter 12

p. 218: March 4, 2013, 2013 Digital Future in Focus Series by Carmela Aquino. Reprinted by permission.

p. 220: Laura M. Holson, "Tell-All Generation Learns to Keep Things Offline," *The New York Times*, May 8, 2010. Copyright © 2010 The New York Times Company.

p. 221: Courtesy of Association of Information Technology Professionals.

Chapter 13

p. 232: Isa Engleberg.

p. 232: Martin McDermott, *Speak with Courage: 50 Insider Strategies for Presenting with Ease and Confidence*. Copyright © 2010 CreateSpace Books.

p. 234: Modified from Gene Zelazny, *Say It with Presentations*, Revised (New York: McGraw-Hill, 2006), pp. 4–6.

p. 236: Lane Cooper, *The Rhetoric of Aristotle*. Copyright © 1932 Appleton-Century-Crofts.

p. 236: Excerpted from "Student Plagiarism in an Online World" by Julie JCH Ryan, Prism, December, 1998 © American Society for Engineering Education (http://www.prismmagazine.org/december/html/student_plagiarism_in_an_onlin.htm).

p. 238: Michael M. Kepper and Robert E. Gunther, *I'd Rather Die Than Give a Speech*. Copyright © 1994 The McGraw-Hill Companies.

p. 241: Courtesy of Isa Engleberg.

p. 243: Samuel E. Wood, Ellen Green Wood, and Denise Boyd, *The World of Psychology*, 6th ed. Copyright © 2008 Pearson Education.

p. 250: Fred D. White and Simone J. Billings, *The Well-Crafted Argument: A Guide and Reader*, 2nd ed. Copyright © 2005 Houghton Mifflin Harcourt.

Chapter 14

p. 272: Mark Knapp and Judith A. Hall, *Nonverbal Communication in Human Interaction*, 6th ed. (Belmont, CA: Thomson/Wadsworth, 2006), p. 296.

index

ANSWERS TO TEST YOUR KNOWLEDGE QUESTIONS

Chapter 1
Answers: 1-e; 2-a; 3-a; 4-d; 5-c; 6-b; 7-e; 8-d; 9-d; 10-d

Chapter 2
Answers: 1-d; 2-d; 3-d; 4-e; 5-b; 6-d; 7-e; 8d; 9-c; 10-b

Chapter 3
Answers: 1e; 2-a; 3-d; 4-e; 5-b; 6-e; 7-a; 8-b; 9-b; 10-e

Chapter 4
Answers: 1-d; 2-d; 3-e; 4-b; 5-e; 6-c; 7-b; 8-a; 9-a; 10-a

Chapter 5
Answers: 1-b; 2-b; 3-a; 4-c; 5-a; 6-e; 7-e; 8-a; 9-d; 10-e

Chapter 6
Answers: 1-b; 2-a; 3-e; 4-c; 5-c; 6-b; 7-a; 8-e; 9-c; 10-b

Chapter 7
Answers: 1-b; 2-a; 3-c; 4-a; 5-b; 6-c; 7-c; 8-a; 9–d; 10-a

Chapter 8
Answers: 1-c; 2-d; 3-a; 4-d 5-a ; 6-e ; 7-e ; 8- c ; 9– a; 10-c

Chapter 9
Answers: 1-b ; 2-e; 3-c; 4-e; 5-a; 6-e; 7-b; 8-d; 9-e; 10-e

Chapter 10
Answers: 1-c; 2-c; 3-a; 4-b; 5-b; 6-e; 7-d; 8-a; 9-b; 10-e

Chapter 11
Answers: 1-e ; 2-b; 3-a; 4-c; 5-d; 6-e; 7-b; 8-c; 9-e; 10-c

Chapter 12
Answers: 1-b; 2-b; 3-b ; 4-d; 5-c ; 6-d; 7-b ; 8- e; 9-d ; 10-e

Chapter 13
Answers: 1-a; 2-c; 3-b; 4-d; 5-d; 6-b; 7-a; 8-e; 9-b; 10-a

Chapter 14
Answers: 1-d ; 2- a ; 3-b; 4-a; 5-c; 6-a; 7-e; 8-c; 9-c; 10-a

Notes

Notes

Notes

Notes

Notes

Notes

Notes

Notes

Notes

Notes

Notes